Follies & Grottoes

Sanderson Miller's folly at Radway Grange (see page 54).

BARBARA JONES

Follies & Grottoes

Constable London

Published by Constable & Co Ltd
10 Orange Street London WC2H 7EG
First published in 1953
Second edition heavily revised and enlarged 1974
Copyright © 1953, 1974 by Barbara Jones
Reprinted 1979

ISBN 0 09 459350 7

Set in Monophoto Garamond
Printed in Great Britain by
BAS Printers Limited, Over Wallop, Hampshire

To the Folly builders

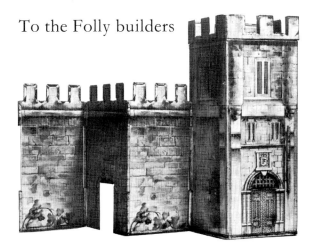

Some of the follies in this book are on common land or in public parks and are therefore easily visited, but many of them stand in private grounds, and their inclusion here should in no way be taken to mean that they are necessarily shown to the public. It would be sad if the great kindness of many owners in allowing me to make drawings and take photographs were to be repaid by unwelcome trespass; I beg that intending visitors should ask permission first.

Contents

Illustrations

The drawings, paintings and photographs not acknowledged here or in the text are by the author.

Foreword

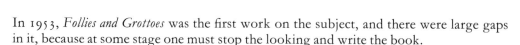

In 1953, *Follies and Grottoes* was the first work on the subject, and there were large gaps in it, because at some stage one must stop the looking and write the book.

In twenty-odd years a great deal of research has been done, by me and by many other people; it seemed time to add to the old book a large number of things I never found before, and also the many fine follies of Ireland and the few but startling follies of Scotland. Also, there is now room to include the enchanting exotics, the pagodas, pyramids and tea-houses, and there are a lot more pictures.

The plan of the book remains unchanged; first there are chapters on the setting and the styles of follies and on their strange and various forms. Then there is a topographical list by county. There must still be gaps, because again the looking had to stop, and I have in any case left out some dull little towers, and a lot of obelisks and columns. I would be grateful to be told of other omissions and of course of errors.

I have followed what I find to be the easiest way of dealing with *gothic*; *gothic* itself stands for architecture dating from the invention of the pointed arch to its last Tudor flattening under the weight of the Renaissance. *Gothick* stands for the revival of the style in the eighteenth and early nineteenth centuries, sometimes including a dash of romanesque and usually very freely interpreted. *Gothic revival* stands for the careful, scholarly approach that began in about 1830.

An apology: *England* is sometimes used for *Great Britain*. I think it is quite clear which it means where, and Great Britain does sit oddly in the world of Jardins Anglais-Chinois . . . .

Finally, it is pleasant to be able to say that in twenty years the attitude to follies has changed; once, it was common for a folly to be denied—no ancestor of mine ever did anything like *that*—or deprecated—we've never taken much notice of it. Today, many follies are loved and some have been restored; the work of the National Trust and the Landmark Trust and the Department of the Environment, and of many public and private owners calls for our most grateful thanks. But there are still vandals.

Acknowledgements

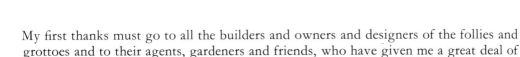

My first thanks must go to all the builders and owners and designers of the follies and grottoes and to their agents, gardeners and friends, who have given me a great deal of time-consuming help. Four people have refused me permission even to look; otherwise all has been kindness.

Many museums, public bodies and libraries have helped me with sometimes difficult research, and many people have talked and written to me during the last twenty years with new and most helpful information, discoveries, photographs and drawings. I have not listed them all, but I am not the less grateful.

I also want to thank Mary Adshead, the anonymous owner of the biscuit tin on page v, Oswell Blakeston, Clifford Barry, Messrs Braithwaite and Co, Ray Bryant and Peter Mason, Hugh Collinson, Maurice Craig, Jonathan Curling, Gordon Davies, Jonathan Delamont, the Department of the Environment, Eric de Maré, The Dole Pineapple Co. of Hawaii, Tim Fieldhouse, Desmond Fitzgerald, James Gardner, David Glover, Peter Goodliffe, Desmond Guinness, Eileen and John Harris, Jill and Bill Howell, Tom Ingram, Ronald Jessup, Horace Jones, A. F. Kersting, Edward Malins, Jean and John Morley, Peter Morter, The National Trust, Dorn and Richard Parkinson, Jeremy Portch, Peter Ray, Phoebe and Oliver Scott, Anthea and James Sutherland, Trocoll Industries Ltd., Muriel, Janet, Alison and Jonathan Venning, J. D. Waddell and Richard Young.

And finally my thanks to the Leverhulme Trust for a research award that made the travelling possible.

MEMORIAE SACRAM ESSE VOLUIT COBHAM

Introduction

A grotto is as easy to define as anything ever is—a pleasant rocky cave that may be natural, or nature improved, or entirely artificial, being made of rocks, and sometimes decorated with shells. *Grotesque* derived from it, and has now a meaning far from the noble rocks and pretty shells to which its early use refers.

A folly is a great deal more difficult; it might be defined as a useless building erected for ornament on a gentleman's estate, but that would apply equally well to garden temples, and there is a world of difference between temples and follies. Certainly, temples are generally in a classical style, and follies in gothick, but that is only part of the truth. There also is a difference of mood; a temple is an ornament, a folly is glass, and bones and a hank of weeds.

Follies are built for pleasure, and pleasure is personal, difficult to define. Follies are fashionable or frantic, built to keep up with the neighbours, or built from obsession. They are at once cheerful and morbid, both an ornament for a gentleman's grounds and a mirror for his mind.

Follies come from money and security and peace; poor men rarely build them. Leisure and a comfortable income are needed either to follow fashion or to promote the malaise and boredom that breed the more eccentric follies. So a folly is most likely to stand on a big estate. It may be a tower, a huge column, a pyramid, a sham castle or chapel (complete or deliberately ruinous); it may be the size of a summerhouse, or a false façade nearly 300 feet long. They are scattered all over England and Ireland, rarer in Scotland and Wales, most common where the climate is most temperate, although Yorkshire has dozens of beauties. Everywhere they are in great variety, some, as I have said, keeping up with fashion, some eccentric, some pure madness.

More mood and emotion are built into follies than into any other kind of architecture, so the good ones are not good in the manner of ordinary buildings. Normally emotion in architecture is expressed professionally in a distilled and controlled way, within a framework of mathematics and engineering and sometimes commonsense or a client's wishes; except when we have an innovating genius such as Paxton, or Gaudi (who was a rich man, able to go his own way or simply not build), architecture tends to evolve steadily on a basis of tradition. The motives behind folly-building are more naked, often evoking the spectator's emotions with uncivilized directness by stating those of the builder and nothing else.

Sometimes this simplicity came because there was not enough money to do anything else, sometimes because a folly gave a professional architect a chance to let himself go and have fun, and sometimes because a landowner was tired of letting his architect

The sixty-foot pyramid at Stowe, designed by Vanbrugh and demolished in the 1770s. There were more pyramids on the Boycott Pavilions, and others survive on the Temple of British Worthies and the Congreve Monument (see page 135).

prevail and wanted to do his own thing—had not '*Fait ce que voudra*' been carved clearly up at Medmenham by the fashionable Sir Francis Dashwood? What better chance than a folly, where even the Rule of Taste need not apply?

Follies are fragile. They are fragile for three reasons. First, money; most follies were built in the eighteenth century, a time of feverish rebuilding. A fortune had already been spent on pulling down the ridiculous Jacobean or Elizabethan house and putting up a baroque or Palladian one, another fortune on Spitalfields silks, specially woven carpets, and marbles and paintings from Italy, and a third fortune on landscaping the park in the new picturesque fashion to echo the paintings—we owe the preservation of some splendid seventeenth-century gardens solely to the fact that the money ran low before the park could be started. However much money there was, the big new house with all the smart embellishments cost more to maintain than the older smaller house, and more neighbours had to be entertained to show it all off, and there was rarely much money left over for the folly. So it was often built cheaply of local materials, or of wood, plastered or cemented over, or even of canvas on a wooden frame, painted to represent stone, making a great effect cheaply, and also quickly, before the fashion changed.

Second reason, luck. Even professional architects in the eighteenth century had no training in building castles, or hermitages, or Turkish tents, and much was often left to the estate builder or carpenter who had none either, and probably when the owner was his own architect, he left a very great deal indeed to the builder. With good luck, the builder might be a man of great taste and imagination and become a specialist; with bad luck, the thing fell down.

Third reason, distance. Vista-closers or eyecatchers might be some way from the house, hermitages were hidden in the rocks or woods, towers possibly on a distant hill; all were further from the protection of the gardeners than pavilions and temples, and without the added protection of their dignified names. Hooligans from the villages, hooligans out for the weekend from the cities, hooligans evacuated for the Second World War, and hooligans in the various home and allied armies have destroyed follies everywhere with venom and thoroughness. Even well built follies, flint towers, huge grottoes, whole walls of thick stone, have been demolished, fires have been lighted, no trouble spared. There's a folly, let's pull it down. But, as I have said, the vandal tide has now been offset a little by restoration.

Follies are personal in a way that great architecture never is. Their amateur quality makes them our own: never expect too much from other people's favourite follies. You will find that some of those that most appeal to me are dull when you visit them: others, that I have seen unsuitably—tired, or hungry, or cross, or at flat noon on a too-hot summer day—will give you a good hour of melancholy at three o'clock in the November dusk.

This uncertainty of pitch makes the recording of follies difficult. Enthusiastic letters have sent me miles to disappointment—but the next visitor may be delighted. One dreary Byeways-type guide to Yorkshire phrased a couple of sentences in the way that suggested that 50 years ago there might have been some form of garden ornament in a big park, so as it was on our way, we went, and found six fine follies in a setting of great picturesque splendour, all just on the edge of disintegration and apparently forgotten. But the next visitor may be disappointed.

Another and stranger aspect of folly hunting is the form of the final memory. After

The eyecatcher at Wroxton Abbey in Oxfordshire, a particularly fine one still standing on its hilltop in a landscaped park where most of the design distant from the house has been blurred by neglect.

six months the big exciting discovery has receded, while the forefront of the mind is occupied by a curious little brick job that was not even felt to be worth a photograph.

The setting of the follies is as remarkable as the architecture. The most isolated English cottage is set in civilization, with a bit of garden and a path, but follies can be jungly and embowered in brambles. Their most comfortable situation will be a hilltop, where even if the climb is exhausting the going is free, but many of them were built for a surprise at the turn of a path through the woods, and these are now often sunk deep in neglected undergrowth. They are cut off from worldly contacts, and lose all humanity, becoming more mineral than artifact, resolving into stones again. The undergrowth will be strong, coarse plants, bramble, bracken, elder, rosebay willowherb and ivy; the delicate rock plants and lichens will be forced up the folly walls by the spreading green tangle. Finally the elder and the ivy will climb the folly in their turn and ultimately destroy it.

The romantic temperament regarded certain trees as especially suited to follies and the top choice was certainly pines. There is even a dead one, surely deliberate, bleached dramatically white and overhanging one very sublime grotto. No other tree occurs nearly so often. Yew, which would seem so dark and gothic and with such melancholy graveyard associations is mostly found near grottoes. Ivy is everywhere; what was in the eighteenth century a cultivated and considered wildness has become, through neglect, more wild than nature itself. If the ground is clear, it may be sour and rough, for the best follies do not leap from lush meadows like mushrooms, but squat among the stones at the edge of the field like toads, with dead thistles and dry cowpats to adorn their curious beauty.

Follies are sometimes difficult to find without help, and the help is difficult to ask for. Some are known as 'X's Folly', but most things of that name turn out to be speculative houses, extravagant villas or over-ambitious farms. 'Folly' on the map may also mean a leafy lane ('feuillée') or a clump of trees on top of a hill (Berkshire) or a belt of trees round a barn (Wiltshire) or a footpath (Essex). There are a lot of Folly Farms in Southern England—'It's always been called that, there's nothing else.'

When we have to ask the way, whatever choice we make is wrong. If we ask for the Folly, endless synonyms must be used before someone exclaims that 'it must be Dobbin's Tower' and indeed perhaps it will be. If black experience in the last twenty villages has proved that the word 'Folly' is incomprehensible and we start asking for 'a curious building', the amazed inhabitant will cry 'You mean the Folly'.

Many of the most famous follies occur in magazine articles over and over again but some of them do not exist at all. For instance, my preliminary notes for the first book recorded 'Hamlet Seabrooke in Denbighshire, where Roger Seabrooke set out to build the greatest house on earth'. It was not in Denbighshire but in Buckinghamshire, it was not Hamlet Seabrooke, and Roger Seabrooke (though real enough) never set out to build the huge house. All that happened was that at about the middle of the seventeenth century the family built two farms and hadn't enough money to finish a third. Some of them went to Essex and some stayed where they were. A descendant was an inn-keeper at the King's Head in Ivinghoe. There was no 'great house', no gigantic ruins. The three small farms, Seabrook, Great Seabrook and Little Seabrook, stood on the quiet banks of the Grand Union Canal. One of them had antlers over the door.

Most follies were built during the eighteenth and early nineteenth centuries and were, with their landscapes, the subject of much theorizing by those interested in the picturesque. The theory and history of the movement are very well documented. From the early eighteenth century onwards there have been books establishing, expanding and confounding the various theories of landscape gardening, of ornamental architecture and of every possible application of taste to nature. More recently, excellent books have been written which examine all the earlier ones.

It is impossible to choose a date for the beginning of literary romanticism; the black horrors that engulfed the characters of Elizabethan tragedy merged imperceptibly into the black horrors that later engulfed, not so much the characters of eighteenth-century literature, as the prospects in which they moved. By 1700 the caverns are well estab-

The Chapel at Horace Walpole's Strawberry Hill.

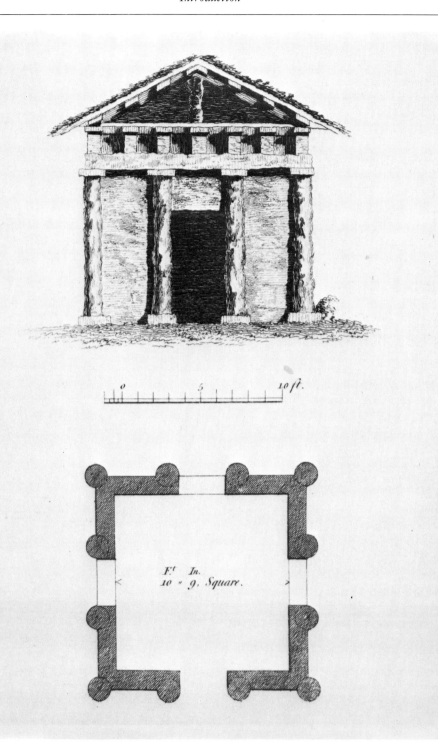

lished and have substituted for the importance of man the supremacy of the owl. Spenser, Milton, Young, Pope, Blair, Mallet, Shenstone, Gray, Walpole, Wharton, Peacock, Radcliffe, all lead imperceptibly on through the gloom for 250 years, and architectural dates have been correlated with the poets' dates, to show when the romantic movement in literature begat the romantic movement in the arts, but another set of dates could be made to show how the romantic movement made its first appearance in painting.

A great deal of work remains to be done on the history of the parks, the engravings of them, and the pattern books, sorting out fact from fancy, and artist copying from park or park from artist. Le Rouge's *Jardins Anglo-Chinois,* 1776–88 for instance, provides a splendid hotch-potch; the Halfpenny's Kiosks of 1752 are credited to them, William Wrighte's designs are weakly re-engraved, sometimes in part or in mirror image, and are not credited at all, Chambers was reprinted, but Thomas Wright not mentioned. Many engravings and paintings were not of finished buildings but of projects. Much writing was astonishingly angry.

'Influence' and 'taste' are words which constantly crop up in critical writing. They are always difficult to use, but especially so when discussing romanticism and classicism, which are themselves very dogmatic words that can be used to make artificial and annoying distinctions only too easily. Influence is a sufficiently difficult word to use of professionals, who, one can be reasonably certain, *do* see another's work. But with follies, everything is so unsure; Vanbrugh, Hawksmoor and Kent built some of the very earliest follies, and then the amateurs largely took over, and who knows what they saw and worked for, with whose aid and how; it is easy to oversimplify, and follies are by no means simple but the result of many fuddled 'influences'.

'Taste' is quite as risky. Consider our own involved taste; the cultivated mind today may specialize in A but still give much of its attention to Z; an abstract painter may pin up postcards of fluffy pussies in his studios—he likes a change, or they are perhaps his own paintings differently translated—and there is no reason to suppose that seventeenth- and eighteenth-century minds were any different, but the historian, to get his history done at all must keep the issues clear cut. All, again, difficult enough with ordinary architecture, but a thousand times more difficult with follies.

We may say with certainty that follies in general were inspired by romantic painting and poetry, and that their history, if we could trace it thoroughly enough, would probably be one of diffusion from a very few culture carriers, for they do fall into groups, certain counties—Surrey, Somerset, the Yorkshires—having more to the acre than others. But there is no point in getting involved in huge charts working out influences, since such unchartable things as *a nice change* must be responsible for a lot of follies. A gothick nonsense in the park is a change from a large Palladian house; everyone is logical, everyone is sentimental, there is no need to tie a folly to a poem—it is much better to enjoy them both as they are. This is not to say that the books about the literature and architecture of the period are not fascinating to read, simply that they are not absolutely essential to the enjoyment of follies; perhaps a book did influence a folly—probably it didn't; the inter-relationship is our pleasure at a distance.

A design for a Primitive Hut by William and John Halfpenny. Many designs for follies of all sorts were engraved, re-issued and even pirated.

The Beginnings

Voltaire was right to insist that we should cultivate the garden, and when we turn his advice to the plants inside the head, there is no doubt that we can cultivate them all our lives, for who shall stop us? But the garden round our feet, that enclosed piece of ground devoted to the improvement and arrangement of the natural scene and its products, then that garden, at any level from a row of lettuces to 2000 acres at Stourhead, demands not only a certain state of mind, but leisure, and leisure demands peace.

The extreme devotion of mediaeval Europe to Christianity found expression in war and in building. The largest and most elaborate buildings were all devoted to defence or to religion, in Britain and Ireland as elsewhere. The castles and the city walls built for defence had to take their chance of survival, but they were immensely solid, and at the end of the Wars of the Roses in 1485 a lot of embattled stonework was still intact, but unwanted. Sixty years later, after the Dissolution, the monasteries and abbeys were equally unloved and sometimes became, like the castles, useful quarries for new buildings. They were all to wait more than two centuries to become fashionable again as interesting relics of the Baron's Wars and desirable picturesque ruins to have on an estate.

The churches and cathedrals suffered less than the monasteries during the Reformation and most of them were prudently kept in use for the new religion. So when Britain was at peace at last and Protestant, there was an enormous legacy of superb stone architecture in the military and ecclesiastical gothic styles, standing among the wattle and daub and wood and plaster that made up most of domestic architecture.

By this same date in Italy, the Renaissance interest in classical literature had taken its century to influence architecture, and the new style was under way. It took another century to become a serious influence in Britain and still a third, until the first half of the eighteenth century, for the communication of visual ideas to speed up towards the dizzy pace of today, in one eye and out of the other.

Meanwhile, Britain and Ireland came out of the Middle Ages and began to move slowly into the modern world without any real change of style; Tudor architecture may be seen as more gothic than Renaissance, however much 'Italian' detail was added as the century went on. It was enough for the time being to have peace at home and be able to move out of the boring old castles and build unfortified houses with bricks, which had not been used since Roman times and so seemed new and modish, or with wood, or lath and plaster; local materials and builders remained the normal practice. And peace allowed glass; the panes were still small, but the area of window in a house like Little Moreton Hall in Cheshire must be near that of a modern tower block.

A design for a Grotto Ornament by Pierre Quentin Chedel.

The gardens also took a long time to change. Again, at first it was enough to take the fruit, vegetable and physick gardens out of the old constricting safety and spread them wider, adding flower gardens, replacing the moat with ornamental waters, and keeping merely such walls as were necessary to stop local pilfering. By the end of the sixteenth century there were ambitious gardens at many great houses and palaces, although the descriptions we have of them, with artificial mounts, arbours, trellis, trees, railed beds and hedges are, like Bacon's ideal garden, very mediaeval in concept. The European garden was, indeed, bound to develop from trees, shrubs, and water with architectural embellishments (and grass in the northern countries), because most of the native flowers were small and ended with early summer, and so did such exciting early introductions as the tulip from Turkey. All the big, later-flowering spectaculars like sunflowers and hollyhocks came into Europe much later, and made possible the horror of the herbaceous border; during the eighteenth century, the age of the landscape garden, most enthusiasts kept flowers to the walled garden or the glass-house; most flowers were grown for cutting.

Renaissance garden ornament started, like Renaissance architecture, in Italy. First, the study of classical literature made it clear that long before the gods of Greece and Rome were worshipped in temples, their shrines were made in natural caves, and also that the Romans built artificial caves in their gardens, perhaps for piety, perhaps also for shelter from the sun. Alberti was researching into the Roman grottoes by the middle of the fifteenth century, referring to the use of pumice, tufa, paint, shells and running water, and some Italian grottoes were made in his time, following the ancient descriptions.

A grotto by Giambologna in the garden of the Villa Pratolino near Florence. Giant dogs' heads like this one can be seen at Corby Castle (page 303).

None survive, but during the sixteenth century grottoes were fashionable in Italy and France and some very ambitious ones were built, with statues of giant water-gods and similar conceits, and some of these later works do survive. The English, so far as I can discover, were at first wary of grottoes in gardens, perhaps afraid of the effects of the colder and wetter weather on the expensive imported materials, and started (but not until the seventeenth century) with grotto rooms inside the house, but later on tufa was found here, and stalactites and stalagmites, and so some very fine grottoes were made in which coral and a few giant clams were the only exotics. Today we have stopped building artificial caves, but the natural ones keep their mysterious magic and every weekend, although they have been deserted by the gods, they are alive again with cavers and potholers.

Before we consider the first English grottoes, though, we should look at the first follies, the tentative beginnings of our architectural eccentricities. The earliest ones are doubtful and dull, more folly-story than folly building, like the tale of two sisters who were unable to decide between a tower or a spire for a church in Ormskirk and finally gave it both, a fat tower and a lean steeple. There are several of these marginal legends and then at last a building that might really be a folly.

Freston Tower

Freston Tower, on the banks of the Orwell, is an elegant brick tower, in no way unusual in its architecture, a church tower with lay detail one might say, about 10 feet by 12, six small rooms piled one above the other with increasingly large pedimented windows. At the corners are buttresses which rise above an arcaded balustrade at the top into four bed-post pinnacles. It may be a hunting stand, or a very early prospect tower, built by Edward Latymer in about 1549, or just possibly part of a demolished house, kept for such a purpose. An earlier date is suggested by the Reverend Richard Cobbold's novel of 1850, *Freston Tower; a Tale of the Early Years of Cardinal Wolsey*— Wolsey died in 1530. The most entertaining story is that Lord Latymer built it as a study for his daughter Ellen de Freston with one floor for each subject. First, a day was to be spent on the ground floor studying charity; then a day on the first floor at tapestry weaving; then up to music, then the ancient tongues, then the English writers, then painting, and at last to observation of the stars, presumably from the roof if fine. But why weren't the heavy looms on the ground floor? Another version takes the tapestries to the very top. . . . In any case the tower glowing in the sun has already the folly atmosphere, the isolation from its scene, separated from ordinary architecture by the eccentricity of the builder.

Two beautiful pale stone arches stand in a field at Holdenby, built with the curious Elizabethan inconsistency—the arches, if not refined, are at least graceful, and flanked by charming alcoves; then, above, everything goes to pieces. Each arch has three pinnacles of weak and wandering design, the central ones like hand mirrors supported upside down on the vaguest of scrolls. Labels bear the date 1583. They are all that remains of Sir Christopher Hatton's great house, and are probably the two arches that led into the Green Court. The house was bought by James I in 1607, and in 1651 by Captain Adam Baynes, who pulled it down. There is a much smaller house nearby in similar style incorporating other remnants and a new arch of 1659. It has been suggested that the two arches may have been moved at the time of the demolition, though it seems much more likely that they were simply left standing. They have become folly either way by their isolation on the grass.

Holdenby Arches

At the end of the sixteenth century comes an astounding folly, well preserved and wildly eccentric. Many of the later follies are but fashionable echoes, but this one is passionately individual, a stone bonnet for a very large bee. Sir Thomas Tresham lived at Rushton in Northamptonshire, and built a lodge there between 1593–5. He was of a Roman Catholic family which kept its faith through the Reformation, though Sir Thomas's father brought him up as a Protestant, presumably for safety's sake. However, in spite of the constant religious persecutions, prison, and endless restrictions even when out of it, Sir Thomas became a Catholic in 1580.

The late sixteenth-century mind was full of conceits, enigmas and curlicues, and these took such shapes as metaphysical poetry, but Thomas Tresham's conceits went on to paper as endless numerical calculations, chiefly built up on 3, 5, 7 and 9. Sir Thomas Browne's preoccupation with 5 became The Garden of Cyrus; the Tresham preoccupation with 3 became Rushton Triangular Lodge. It is said, of course, to represent the Trinity, but a broader concept would have suited that just as well; whether it began as the Trinity or as black magic so disguised (and Tresham's papers lend colour to either proposition), or just from interest, the translation of idea into architecture has lost all the subtleties of spiritual symbolism and produced instead a lovely essay in stone arithmetic, which stands in a corner of a thick wood, closely surrounded by trees and a rich green sea of breast-high nettles; the sharp angles rise like knives, the quite un-weathered stone retaining the emphasis of 60° corners. For it has three equal sides; each

Sir Thomas Tresham's Triangular Lodge; from a lithograph by Richard Beer.

one-third of a 100 feet long. Each elevation is square, and three sets of three three-by-three triangles stand along the tops of the walls. There are three floors, each with three windows on each side—at the bottom, small trefoil mouldings enclose triangular holes. On the next floor, the windows are cruciform arrow slits each terminated with a pierced trefoil (the trefoil was Tresham's emblem), and the top ones are larger trefoils enclosing 3, 7 or 9 triangular, diamond or circular holes, all nine different, above, are Latin inscriptions. The top triangles of the façades are crowned by triangular pinnacles, and, just as the mind reels, their sides are decorated with incongruous gothic flamboyant motifs and nice birds that lean back a little drunk up the triangle sides. All is crisp limestone, in narrow horizontal bands of white and yellow.

Inside, each floor has a hexagonal room; one of the three triangular corners thus cut off makes the stairs, and the other two are tiny three-sided rooms. These and the stair are lit by parts of the windows, and fine crazy patches of sunlight, distorted triangle, cross and circle, are thrown on to the walls. Plaques and shields on the outside are carved with symbols, and the lodge is finished with a central pinnacle more elaborate than the rest. Only nine gargoyles and some routine mouldings attach the building to the architecture of its period at all.

Tresham built three buildings. His Market House at Rothwell, now a public library, has no characteristics of folly, but Lyveden New Building (or New Build, or New Bield), ten miles away across the flat countryside is another lovely eccentricity, a house so folly in intent that we must break our rule and look at it.

Lyveden was never finished. It was probably designed by a professional, Robert Stickels, or his relative Robert Stickells, just before Tresham's death in 1605, and its superbly built stone shell stands in a rough field, displaying the mathematics of 3, 5, 7 and 9, this time chiefly 5. The plan is cruciform, symbolic of the Passion, or, again, of black magic. Each arm of the cross is square with a bay window on the end wall; this starts 5 feet from the corners, and each of its 5 sides is also 5 feet long. With the main walls added in, each wing has 81 feet of wall, 9 times 9, and the wings and the central space enclosed by them make 5 squares. The frieze above the windows of the main floor carries 7 carved panels of the emblems of the Passion, repeating on and on round the building. The top frieze has quotations from the Latin Bible carved all round, one letter to one foot, exactly worked out and, height of ingenuity, 'Jesus' and 'Maria' open and close the words on each end face. Over the main door, even each word has five letters. Inside, floors and staircase are gone; a few panels remain carved with the Tresham trefoil, which may well have started the whole thing. Beside the house are the remains of an arrangement of canals and artificial mounts known as the Water Orchard.

After Tresham's magnificent and sustained folly building (nothing later will surpass the Lodge for pure conceit, though other builders will be much more neurotic) very nearly a whole century passed, apparently enlivened only by such curiosities as carved balustrades round the tops of houses and a number of hunting lodges, useful little buildings which are always masquerading as follies without deserving the name at all. One or two houses are also well established as follies because they were too ambitious, or built too far from water, and that seems to be all. But then there are the tombs; John Donne shivering in St Paul's, precarious on an urn, trying to get warmth from his shroud, and a hundred lesser mementoes mori, marble tombs carved with alabaster skulls and scythes, and fading white wooden boards, with black skulls painted in the corners, or hourglasses with bats' wings. And there are the poems, the eye looking through Vaughan's large dusky glasse at life, as later one looked out from the drawing room at Hafod through mauve tinted panes so that the landscape was always stormy. It was impossible that these people felt at home in the gardens of straight walks and open parterres; the black melancholy of the tombs and the poems must have been echoed in black melancholy gardens somewhere, for the hard folly shapes of a topiary maze by no means balance the more subtly involved conceits of their thoughts on mortality and death. And indeed though the great landscaped parks with ample space for every kind of folly, grotto and hermitage did not develop until the eighteenth century, nevertheless there were earlier, smaller, gardens that carried out all the conceits we might expect.

Thomas Bushell was one of Francis Bacon's gentlemen in waiting. After Bacon's death in 1626 he went to live in Oxfordshire

where having some land lyeing on the hanging of a hill faceing the south, at the foot whereof runnes a fine cleare stream which petrifies, and where is a pleasant solitude, he spake to his servant Jack Sydenham to gett a labourer to cleare some boscage which grew on the side of the hill, and also to dig a cavity in the hill to sitt, and read or contemplate. . . . The workman had not workt an hower before he discovers not only a rock, but a rock of an unusuall figure with pendants like icecles as at Wokey hole (Somerset), which was the occasion of making that delicate grotto and those fine walkes.

Here in fine weather he would walke all night. Jack Sydenham sang rarely: so did his other servant, Mr. Batty. They went very gent. in cloathes, and he loved them as his children. He did not encumber himself with his wife, but here enjoyed himself thus in this paradise. . . . In the time of the civill warres his hermitage over the rocks at Enston were hung with black-bayes.[1] . . . When the queen-mother came to Oxon to the king, she either brought (as I thinke) or somebody gave her an entire mummie from Egypt, a great raritie, which her majestie gave to Mr. Bushell, but I beleeve long ere this time the dampnesse of the place has spoyled it with mouldinesse. The grotto below looks just south; so that when it artificially raineth, upon the turning of a cock, you are entertained with a rainebowe. In a very little pond (no bigger than a basin) opposite to the rock, and hard by, stood a Neptune, neatly cutt in wood, holding his trident in his hand, and ayming with it at a duck which perpetually turned round with him, and a spaniel swimming after her which was very pretty, but long since spoyled.

(Aubrey—who almost alone in his day was always ready to admire an 'extraordinary rich and noble Gothique building.')

In 1635 and 1665 Hammond and Celia Fiennes recorded a grotto at Wilton; its façade has been moved on to a house, and the grotto has gone, but here probably was the start, just as the start of sham castles may have been at Ballymount on the outskirts of Dublin where there is a seventeenth-century castellated gate-house and a mount, which looks artificial, crowned by the remains of a small brick tower 10 or 12 feet square with

---

[1] Black baize.

chamfered corners, on a round stone bastion with a few steps of an external spiral stone staircase. Doors and windows are now indistinguishable, and only three corners stand, to the spring of the arches. Dublin will surely soon engulf it.

Tunnelling also began in the seventeenth century. William Harvey, who died in 1657, had caves in his garden at Combe in Surrey where he meditated in summer, and two brothers of the Howard family began digging tunnels on their estates, also in Surrey. Henry Howard, later sixth Duke of Norfolk, owned Albury Park; the grounds were laid out for him by John Evelyn who owned Wotton nearby, where he very ingeniously turned his moat into a terrace by throwing earth from a hill into the feeding stream, which carried it down into the moat to fill it up. At Albury he planted a Yew Walk, made a quarter of a mile of terraces, an equally long canal, and a 'crypta', or subterranean passage, 160 yards long, tunnelled through the bottom of a hill north of the house. Most of this remains. It was a notable work for the time, and Evelyn was probably right to state that 'such a Pausilippe is nowhere in England besides'—Posilippo was a grotto near Naples; the English have always loved an exotic name. Hollar made an engraving of the tunnel entrance with grot-work in the 1650s, so it may have been built in the 1630s or 40s. A younger brother, Charles Howard, who also owned Greystoke Castle in Cumbria where later there will be more follies, made another tunnel at Deepdene near Dorking, but, alas, there are now no recognizable remains of the tunnel and grottoes here, so we must rely on Aubrey:

The honourable Charles Howard of Norfolk hath very ingeniously contrived a long Hope—i.e. according to Virgil, Deductus Vallis—in the most pleasant and delightful solitude for his house, gardens, orchards, boscages, etc. that I have seen in England. It deserves a poem and was a subject worthy of Mr. Cowley's Muse. The true name of this Hope is Dibden quassi Deep Dene.

Mr Howard hath cast this Hope into the form of a theatre in the sides whereof he hath made several narrow walks, like the seats of a theatre one above another, above six in number, done with a plough, which are bordered with thyme, and some cherry trees, myrtles etc. There was a great many orange trees and syringas, which were then in flower. In this garden 21 sorts of thyme. The pit as I may call it is stored full of rare flowers, and choice plants. He hath there two pretty lads, his gardeners, who wonderfully delight in their occupation, and this lovely solitude, and do enjoy themselves so innocently in that pleasant corner, as if they were out of this troublesome world, and seem to live as in the state of innocency.

In the hill on the left hand, being sandy ground is a cave digged thirty six paces long, four broad, and five yards high; and at about two thirds of the hill (where the crook, or bowing, is) he hath dug another subterranean walk or passage, to be pierced through the hill; through which as through a tube you have the vista over all the south part of Surrey and Sussex to the sea. The south side of this hill is converted into a vineyard of many acres of ground which faceth the south and south west. The vaulting or upper part of those caves are not made semicircular, but parabolical, which is the strongest figure for bearing and which sandy ground naturally falls into then stands. And thus we may see that the conies (by instinct of nature) make their holes so. Here are caves for beer etc.

On the West side of the garden is a little building which is (as I remember) divided into a laboratory and a neat oratory, by Mr. Howard. Above the hill on this west side, is a thicket of black cherry-trees, with those walks, and the ground abounds with strawberries. The house was not made for grandeur, but retirement,—a noble Hermitage—neat, elegant, and suitable to the modesty and solitude of the proprietor, a Christian philosopher, who in this iron age, lives up to that of the primitive times. Here Mr. Newman (his steward) gave me a very civil entertainment, according to his master's order; where the pleasure of the garden etc, were so ravishing that I can never expect any enjoyment beyond it but the kingdom of heaven. It is an agreeable surprise here to the stranger that neither house nor garden can be discovered till you come just to it, as if it squatted down to hide itself.

Here are no ornaments of statuary or carver; but the beauty of the design and topiary speaks for itself and needs no addition out of the quarries. In short, it is an epitome of Paradise, and the Garden of Eden seems well imitated here. . . .

Chemistry was above all Charles Howard's favourite occupation, 'for the more commodious prosecution of which he erected laboratoires; and in subterraneous grots, formed for that purpose, had furnaces of different kinds, the flues of which in some places are yet to be seen.'

One can but hope that Aubrey's memory of his visit was accurate, for the walk from the north side of the hill through the telescope of the tunnel to the golden view must have been an amazing experience. There is, though, the nagging doubt aroused by Prosser who, when he visited the house in 1828 to compile his book on *Picturesque Surrey,* stated that the tunnel was only started, and fell in one morning while the workmen were at breakfast.

Two Howards in Surrey, later Howards at Greystoke, more Howards in Yorkshire, mark the awful beginnings of the network of aristocratic and gentry relationships that ties almost every folly builder to all the others (the *nouveaux riches* are quickly absorbed). Any family tree will lead on to a dozen more, a daughter will marry another folly in the north, or a son marry an heiress and inherit her father's eyecatcher. There is no end to it and I leave it to readers who enjoy genealogy. Another interest which can feed endlessly on follies is of course psychoanalysis; some follies owe very little to the romantic movement—the impulse to build a high tower for the sake of the prospect certainly shows admiration for the picturesque, but some of the towers are such eyesores, so dully pedestrian, with such small windows and enclosed summits, that the prospect theory must be discarded. Towers of this sort are hardly romantic; they enhance no view and commemorate nothing, they are merely the result of a desire to build a tower, a pleasingly simple opposite to the equally Freudian desire to dig a very long tunnel. So the tunnellers wished to return to the womb, the pyramid and obelisk builders were really making linguses and enormous columns which are beyond the size of ornaments may be claimed for virility symbols. It is a fine wide field and, again, there could be no end to it. Each folly can be examined in this way; it is clear at once where fashion suggested one folly, and where neuroses urged up another. But these speculations can be added by the reader, for I shall pursue them no further.

Survival is capricious. The heaviest monument to memory may be destroyed—the Pyramids will become sand—or the monument may remain though none recollects the subject of it, while the words printed on a cinema ticket thrown at the back of a drawer may last for centuries. Scraps of paper, indeed, have the most tenacious lives and so perhaps have all the predecessors of paper, for a folly made of bark has survived from the end of the seventeenth century in Exton Park, Leicestershire. We must in passing regret the loss of another at Halswell in Somerset, where the Kemys Tynte family built Robin Hood's temple, described as 'a Druid's Temple in a just style of Bark etc., the view quite gloomy and confined, nearby is a gushing fall which hurts not the moods raised by so sequestered a scene'. But nothing could be more gloomy than the temple of bark and nails in the woods at Exton. I found it by chance, looking for something else, which seems the best way to find things until someone inevitably tells you that Horace Walpole had a word for it, and that word, serendipity.

Exton Park is very beautiful, mostly farmed now, with open cart roads between the fields of corn. Almost two miles from the burnt-out ruins of the house is a valley with a stretch of ornamental water. On the far side of it the corn curves on again, but on the near side is a wood. A path goes into it, out of the wind, and the first thing is a game-keeper's larder, plump furry corpses newly dead and twisted shreds of old ones, to colour the rest of the wood, appearing suddenly in stray twigs and leaves. The path leads to a green clearing on the water's edge, facing east and shaded by high trees. Here stands Fort Henry, a stucco pleasure-house of the most refined and elegant late eigh-teenth-century gothick, and still exquisite, with the thinnest of ogival arches and feathery pinnacles outlined in white on dark green. Its elation and assurance still overcome the fallen plaster and bare laths, (though time is always on the side of decay), and now res-toration is intended. No gothick decoration anywhere at any time was better than this. Other lovely pavilions are in equal danger, and have as little chance of official aid and comfort, for they combine two unforgivable sins—they are late in date and much too frivolous. Solid Elizabethan is still any building's best passport to preservation.

Exton Park. Fort Henry, from an old picture postcard.

At the edge of the clearing gapes the remarkable hollow of a bark boat house (the shed is nothing, it is the space it encloses which is odd), and up a ride in the devastated woods is the bark temple, perhaps built as a band-stand for dances by the lake, but an innocent purpose for it seems unthinkable. It is round, domed, 25 feet across, top-heavy, with a top-heavy arcade 60 feet long running right and left from the back half of it. A massive, shallow conical roof and the heavy eaves plainly faced with wood underneath it are supported on a circle of arches and round columns, much diminished by the roof; the arcades have thick roofs of shingle with enormous overhang, supported by square pillars, dwarfed again. The grey unfluted columns run up into blocks of wood which have Oxford frames of bark underneath for capitals. Above, the arches and the curving surface over them are faced with strips of bark, but the columns are shedding patches leprously all over, and everywhere there are nails. Asked to design horror, to create an architecture of blood and crucifixions, one might perhaps start with wood, with wild excesses of rustic rococo, but the most tortured agonies of branches could not rival the oppressive atmosphere of this neat Roman Doric architecture. It is not even neces-

Exton Park. The Bark Temple.

sary to see the black nails from which the bark has fallen, or the torn skin of the bark before it falls, for even at a distance the air under the dome and through the arcades is not the air of the beech woods.

There is one much later folly so completely in the heavy melancholic taste of the late seventeenth century that we must look at it here, years out of its context. Jonathan Tyers bought Vauxhall Gardens in 1733 and by the next year was driven by the constant gaiety and merrymaking to create its contrast. He bought Denbighs in Surrey—many of the early follies were in Surrey, for during the seventeenth and eighteenth centuries the whole county (south of London which feels sunnier, already a landscape with lovely open downs and wooded valleys, and easily accessible from Town) became an almost continuous stretch of parks, first the hermitages of a solitary few and later the urbane and graceful estates of the fashionable.

Denbighs is wonderfully situated on the crest of the North Downs above Dorking, looking past Leith Hill towards the sea. It was originally a farm, but Mr Tyers transformed it; the 'principal scene was a wood of about eight acres, which he denominated Il Penseroso. It was intersected with many pleasing walks, and in the centre was a small temple loaded with inscriptions of the most grave and solemn kind; while a clock, concealed from the view, struck at the end of every minute, and forcibly proclaimed the rapid flight of time'.[1] Other accounts take us past Il Penseroso to the end of the grounds where an iron gate led into the Valley of the Shadow of Death. The gate piers were coffins, with the skull of a famous highwayman on one and of a famous harlot on the other. Beyond were terrible tableaux of warning and despair. This is still the black melancholy of the seventeenth century, of the skulls and the black-bayes, oddly surviving; indeed when the Hon. Peter King later bought the estate, his lighter, more eighteenth-century gloom disapproved of Il Penseroso, and he swept the conceits away, no doubt preferring the later melancholy that aimed at a delicious frisson rather than at the guilty leaden sinking of the lazy heart caused by the minute clock sounding in the wood.

[1] Shoberl's *Surrey*, 1813.

A grotesque detail.

The Landscaped Parks

———————◆———————

The gloom of Denbighs was probably the most complete expression of black-bayes melancholia produced in any garden, but it was made altogether out of its time and must not stay in the mind as in any way typical, for most of the great landscapes and gardens of the first half of the eighteenth century seem to shine on the wettest day with the morning sunlight of innovation, of the beginning of the picturesque landscape, of all the excitement of its pioneers.

The design of the English garden in the seventeenth and early eighteenth centuries derived first from the gardens of Italy and France, and later from the Dutch influence of William of Orange. Its history is deeply interesting and very well researched; here it must be enough to simplify it all to the general statement that the garden extended the rectangular plan of the house, running as far out as means or inclination allowed, still with canals, formal lakes, bowling-greens, long avenues, vistas, pleached alleys, statues, knot gardens, neat orange trees brought out for the summer, and a great many trees, bushes and hedges. Natural trees were planted or encouraged in the park beyond, but almost everything near the house was trained and trimmed into rigid geometry; a curve was an exact curve, a bush best clipped into a cone, at most a peacock. It was the golden age of topiary, and we are lucky that when taste swung far away from the formal garden there were always people so stubborn or so poor or so sure of their own taste that they kept their alleys and topiary, so that one can still see such gardens as Levens, and smell the great yew and box hedges baking in the sun.

Apart from the topiary, though, which was probably finer and more frenzied in England and Ireland than anywhere else, the formal garden never reached here the magnificence of some of the great gardens of the continent; climate and temperament and the lie of the land were not quite right for it, and the painters and poets began to criticize. 'Began' is hardly the right word, for English poetry from Chaucer on has always drawn more from the beauty of nature than from any other single source. Possibly we shall never establish exactly how the revolution really started, if the changes were foreshadowed by the sight of open country far down the great vista at Versailles, if the classical ruins and the paintings of Salvator Rosa, Claude and Poussin were as influential as some say, or if *pittoresco* ('like a painting') turned into picturesque was merely a useful jargon word. Certainly Addison and Pope, in 1712 and 1713, attacked the formal garden with rigour and with wit, but a lot of landowners must have been ready for the change, and some, possessing great tracts of wild and varied country, must have seen its beauty for themselves. Certainly, too, such accepted pioneers of the romantic landscape as Stephen Switzer, Charles Bridgeman and William Kent often designed more formally

Follies and grottoes were carefully set in the landscape to give the visitor an interesting objective, or a restful pause or a thrill of alarm; it was also important for the return to the house to be well composed. This is the cascade at Attingham Park, Salop (see page 380).

than later workings over their parks would let us immediately see. But somehow it all happened, and it happened here because here the climate could sustain in reality the landscapes so freely composed by the artists, from whom green demanded only paint, while from a gardener it demanded water. So England and northern France (but earlier and chiefly England) became the workshop for the translation of the picturesque from poem to reality, from two dimensions on canvas to three dimensions in the park.

Soon after the liberation of the trees the desire for picturesque architecture began. First came the discovery by those fortunate enough to have (or quickly to buy) an estate with a genuine gothic ruin on it, that an eyecatcher, or *pointe-de-vue*, or object, was already *there*, beautifully placed in a valley (the monks of old knew how to site an abbey), or dominating a lofty hill (the barons chose carefully too). One of the earliest and best of the great landscapes of this type is Duncombe Park in North Yorkshire, where the ready-made object is nothing less than the ruins of Rievaulx Abbey. The estate was bought in 1689 by Sir Charles Duncombe, a banker, whose niece inherited it in 1711, when her husband took the Duncombe name. Much of the work must have been at least continued by them, but as the new house was illustrated in Vitruvius Brittanicus in 1713, the initiative probably came from Sir Charles, though we are now unlikely to find out if the inclusion of Rievaulx was chance or intention. Certainly the existing great terrace high above the Abbey was not started until 1758; it is a superb half-mile sweep of wide mown grass backed with beech-trees. Once there were twelve viewpoints towards the ruins through the trees that grow below the terrace on the hillside, though these are now much overgrown and the view over-farmed. The pleasure of the terrace now is all its own, high and light, a curve running from an Ionic Banqueting Hall attributed to Vanbrugh (1730, with Kent furniture) at the north end to a round Tuscan temple at the south, invisible from each other and both most beautiful.

Rievaulx Abbey.

Claremont

The earliest big castle-works, unless there are surprising discoveries to come, were all the work of Vanbrugh. The first were for himself, at Claremont in Surrey. He bought the site in 1708 and built a castellated house which he sold in 1715 to the Earl of Clare, later Duke of Newcastle, who commissioned him to enlarge it and to build the Belvedere, the first gothick folly. It is, of course, always possible that Vanbrugh had planned it when he owned the house, but it was actually built in 1717, a typical and very splendid piece, the early gothick style completely realized and assured. The tower is massive (no false façades yet) built of brick on an artificial wooded mount near the house. The plan is H-shaped, the crossbar making the main two-storey rectangular structure, and the uprights four taller square towers with castellated tops. A spiral stair goes up one of them and round-headed windows and doors go all round. And so do the flat horizontal bands that Vanbrugh seems to have invented, and that were widely copied for follies every-where, either projecting as here or perhaps set flush, dressed stone in rough-hewn; a sensible steal, for they were cheap to build and almost always look good.

Vanbrugh meanwhile built some nice castle-houses for himself and speculation in Blackheath and in about 1719 he built at Castle Howard, about a dozen miles from Duncombe Park, the first really large sham castles in England, the models for many succeeding fortified farms, castles, cottages and screens. The drive from the south is over undulating wooded ground; at the bottom of the last valley before the house, the road goes under a low, narrow, pedimented arch, the Carrmire Gate, almost certainly designed by Hawksmoor, but Vanbrugh in style. Up the other side, the road passes through a cutting whose sides get lower as the road reaches the top of the hill, and then under another much bigger arch supporting a massive pyramid. The cutting and an obelisk seen through the arch draw the eye irresistibly onwards, so that it is difficult to pause and see the wall running away on either side, but it is a very heavy wall, and along it eleven fortified towers, round or square, buttressed, machicolated and em-battled, protect the castle's southern approaches. On either side of the central arch three towers are repeated in reverse order making a large, almost invisible symmetry, only discernible to a retentive eye going along the wall itself; from the drive the effect is lost as the distance is too great. To the right of the arch, between the eighth and ninth towers, is a farm with a semicircular tower tacked on to one wall, the first castle farm, ancestor of Greystoke and Gilling. The last tower on this side is the best of the series, it is circular with eight castellations, and, below the gaps between them, eight gothick windows filled in with stone set back from the wall and pierced with cruciform arrow slits. Below them are eight more slits identical to those above but cut in the wall itself, a simple subtlety.

Letters from Vanbrugh discuss the finish for the towers; should they have caps or spires? 'I have seen one upon a round tower in the walls of Chester, that I thought did extremely well'; two drawings of alternatives went with that letter, and another letter again disapproves of an obviously reiterated suggestion: 'The spires upon steeples are not meant for coverings, but as ornaments, to be seen a great way off. But towers upon walls are unsuited to them and are suppos'd to be lodgings, or storehouses, and as such only require a covering which may however be in a degree ornamental but should not look too light or trifling.' Whatever was settled upon has gone.

Returning to this wall from the north, it is hidden from the drive by trees, but beyond the arch, at the bottom of the valley, the pedimented arch that we came through on the way up, unnoticing, drawn by the obelisk, is found to be another fortification which

Castle Howard. Vanbrugh's Pyramid Gate in the middle of his castellated wall, and the Carrmire Gate, probably by Hawksmore, in the outer wall. There is another pyramid in the grounds.

was hidden from the south by trees. The result of this camouflage is that the journeys to and from the house are enlivened by monuments to catch the eye, but they are different buildings each way, so that here are two surprises where many architects would have been satisfied with one.

The smaller fortification is magnificent; from the central arch a castellated wall goes out on each side to a round turret, and the junction of the wall with the arch is masked by square pyramids. The turrets are more exciting than those on the other wall, castellated with tall narrow cruciform arrow slits below, then a plain round moulding and on the ground a door with round stone loopholes either side, set in the bastions which slope down at an angle to the ground. The flanking towers are like parts of Vanbrugh's house at Maze Hill and indeed this whole work, more than the larger wall, displays in miniature all Vanbrugh's genius; each pyramid and castellation is stone designed in space, never a professional cliché, or a detail remembered from someone else's work. Vanbrugh was as great an artist in the gothick as in the classical manner; indeed, since his own house is in the gothick taste, and as not one of his buildings is free of a gothick air, he may be considered to have preferred it, and though most clients were all for columns and pediments, Vanbrugh built enough gothick to show what superb houses he would have designed had he lived until the middle of the century—the whole character of the style would have been different.

Here then are the first great gothick works[1] but they are set symmetrically and firmly across an enormous piece of axial and parallel planning which was intended to continue with equal symmetry towards the Temple of the Four Winds and the Mausoleum that were built a little later; the basic layout at Castle Howard is predominantly formal. Here also is the first and most magnificent pyramid, built by Hawksmoor to enshrine a colossal bust of Lord William Howard, a large echo of the pyramids on the Carrmire Gate and the Gate House.

Meanwhile, at Studley Royal, some 25 miles to the west, work was beginning on a remarkable piece of transitional landscaping, both free and formal, on a very large scale indeed. Its creator was John Aislabie, who was Chancellor of the Exchequer when the South Sea Bubble collapsed. He had to retire, obviously with plenty of money, to Yorkshire—much landscaping and folly-building was both initiated and continued in Yorkshire throughout the eighteenth century—the warmer and more suitable south here followed the northern lead.

John Aislabie's gardener was William Fisher, and work began in about 1720. The walk today starts through wrought-iron gates with a big lake on the left, across a weir flanked by two square fishing houses with water-rustication and attendant sphinxes. After the square stepping stones of the weir a broad mown walk runs to the right under fine beeches beside a long straight canal, and then the trees open out to the exactly right boundary of the roving eye into a wide amphitheatre with the Halfmoon Pool and the Moon Pool set in mown and sloping banks. The Temple of Piety lies beside the Moon, but before the broad curve reaches it, a narrow path turns back unobtrusively

[1]But see Hurstbourne Priors, page 336.

Castle Howard. Four of the eleven towers in Vanbrugh's wall.

to the left and runs up through the trees to a tufa arch into a dark curved passage cut through on to the top of the steep bank. There are several alcoves along its undecorated length, perhaps once for statues. Only trees can be seen as the passage ends in another arch, but to the right, set over the quadrant of the passage is an octagon temple in neat stone gothick with both pointed and round arches, a central room, and pinnacles. It is now being restored—perhaps the busts of famous ladies, some crowned and some with wreaths of laurel, may be found and replaced in their niches (was this octagon the Temple of Fame, and not the open rotunda on Roman Doric columns called so, to which the ride along the cliff-top now leads?). In any case, at the rotunda, the path turns left, and runs down a ridge of beech and yew in the woods and comes out at the back of a stark wooden hut, painted emerald green.

Through the plain door is the Surprise; the hut becomes three slender gothick arches in a little pavilion, elegant enough to frame but not to distract from the view of Fountains Abbey far below at the end of its lawns. The trees are now too high on the right, and perhaps the water too tidied, but even in a downpour it is a brilliant composition, with low dark yews in the foreground to keep the line of sight returning always on the ruins. In the middle distance is a perfectly placed group of big trees with a copper beech before it for emphasis, and further to the left again, the darkness of a single yew. Other landscapes change artfully as we walk but here is the most perfect of the static compositions, by Poussin, Claude, Gainsborough or Girtin, endlessly changing for us with the weather and the seasons, while a painting changes only with our mood and the light in the room.

Studley Royal. The octagon at the top of the grotto tunnel, in course of repair.

By now, clear patterns are emerging for all but the most eccentric and individual follies. Sham castles have started, the tunnels continue, Studley has added a little grot-work and an octagon folly to the concept of a view with a real ruin; we shall see every variety of sham church or castle, with false façades, eyecatchers, screens and prospect towers, pyramids rather later, labyrinths, grottoes and hermitages. Lord Bathurst built a sham castle at Cirencester House in Gloucester in 1721, with the assistance of his friend Pope who had already started the first grotto, at Twickenham. The castle was quite small, a tentative essay, but so successful that they enlarged it in 1732. The next year Mrs Delany wrote to Swift that Lord Bathurst had 'greatly improved the house in the wood, which you may remember but a cottage. It is now a venerable castle and has been taken by an antiquarian as one of King Arthur's!!' Most later folly builders were content with 'the true rust of the Barons' Wars'.

Mrs Delany (first Mrs Pandarves or Pendarves—and Delany is sometimes Delaney) was one of the most energetic and skilful of the amateurs, best known for her superb paper mosaics of flowers—the ten volumes of *Flora Delanica* are now in the British Museum. But she also designed and made or advised on a number of grottoes, notably a famous one at Bulstrode, now demolished, and her amusing letters often refer to follies; all the early folly and grotto builders knew one another, and constantly visited and assessed one another's works—the references are innumerable. She worked with Dr Delany on their garden at Delville near Dublin, also gone, a 'shallow valley with a stream'—a meadow with one hayrick, an old castle with a cave to make a grotto under-neath, a portico, a beggar's hut, and 'several prettinesses I can't explain to you'. And in 1752 she gave a ball with one room decorated as a wood with a grotto, and a gothick chapel as sideboard.

Alfred's Hall is the work of the first Earl Bathurst, who lived to be 91 in an age when 50 was a long life. He is often referred to in eighteenth-century correspondences as the vivacious Earl Bathurst; with good reason, for he went for long walks in the park at Cirencester right up to the end of his life, and at 85 sat up with his friends when his son went to bed early. 'Let us have another bottle,' he said.

The park is thickly planted with timber, and an avenue, not centred on the house, runs from the Lodge gates through Oakley Wood to Sapperton, a distance of more than four miles. Lord Bathurst achieved a wonderful balance between the formality of the grand avenue and the picturesque eighteenth-century garden. The avenue is about 75 yards across, and the sides are not closely defined by planting particular trees as at Badminton, the general impression being of an enormous ride cut through natural woods.

Past the lodge gates the drive rises slightly, and about two hundred yards up on the right is the Hexagon, a temple built of rusticated stone of a very massive order, beauti-fully lichened purple and yellow on the Cotswold stone. Architecturally this is not a very exciting building, for its like is in every eighteenth-century pattern book, but in winter thinly seen through the mist, and with brown leaves and the yellow earth, it is very pleasing. It is a building which adapts perfectly to every seasonal change of light and colour.

The drive continues up the hill to the crest. Then a path leads to a little rusticated stone pavilion inscribed POPE'S SEAT. The trees are thinner here, and the muddy track winds on, past the Horse Guards, two sentry boxes which stand on either side of the

avenue, to the Round House. This is a round tower joined to a low brick cottage. The
tower has the usual arrow slits and castellations. The path goes on through the mist
and trees, emerging suddenly into open land where the main avenue becomes a wide
grassy space surrounding the Square House. This is a little square cottage, the walls
rising in castellations in front of the roof, and at the west end is a small square tower
which just rises above the level of the main roof. The drive continues across the open
park to Ivy Lodge, a folly built by the first Earl which has been converted into a house
for the farm manager. In the centre of a long façade of yellow Cotswold stone is a
square tower, and at either end is a crowstepped gable. The right-hand gable and the
tower have mullioned windows with leaded glass. The left-hand gable also has mullioned
windows, but the lead for the glass is scored on the cement which fills them in, for this
end of the building is merely a wind-break for the orchard behind.

At this point a valley crosses the park, and the drive goes in a north-westerly direction through Oakley Wood to Alfred's Hall, one of the first and best sham ruins. The
wood immediately around it is made forbidding by evergreens, yew and fir, so that
light is filtered through a green gloom. Rhododendrons and laurels crowd up to the
mouldering walls, and the clearing of grass in front of the building is bordered with
black trees.

Alfred's Hall itself is a long room screened on all sides with castellated walls. The
main front of the building faces the clearing, and is a most impressive mixture of sham
ruin and real structure. To the right of the two entrance doors as one faces the building,
the wall comes forward in a semicircle, turns back in a wall pierced with a gothick
window, and then fades down to the ground. To the left the curtain walls are more

Opposite, *Alfred's Hall*. Below, *details*.

elaborate, pierced with broken doorways and windows, and interrupted with small buttresses. Behind this wall is a small courtyard with steps down to a cellar and up to a room above. Here is the shell of a semicircular tower. Behind the Hall is a lawn and the remains of a low wall which ran on in an ellipse from the front of the building right round to the other side again. Like the clearing in front this lawn is bordered with ever-green shrubs. From the back, Alfred's Hall could not be taken for a ruin, there are very odd stained glass windows and the walls are not broken in any way, but the mediaeval feeling and true baronial rust are very successfully achieved.

Lord Bathurst and Pope made of Alfred's Hall a building which it is difficult to equal as a convincing sham. In an age of symmetry they abandoned regularity, to give their work the real horrid feeling of conglomeration, as opposed to architecture, which characterizes so much mediaeval building in this country. The later builders of sham castles tended much more to symmetry; Sanderson Miller's classicism is barely dis-guised by the gothick skins that cover his buildings. They show the mediaevalism of an unscholarly mind, charming but inaccurate, having neither the conglomeration, nor any feeling of discomfort, cold or smell; it is as much an idealization of a mood as the Lyrical Ballads. But Bathurst and Pope really achieved the amorphous squalor of the Middle Ages; eighteenth-century neatness is only seen in the lettering of 'Alfred's Hall' over the main entrance.

Sham castles like Alfred's Hall sometimes had rooms, and often looked quite con-vincing from several angles, but a real sham castle must have been expensive to build and an economical substitute was quickly devised; anyone who had no real hankering after the Middle Ages and who merely wished to keep up with a smart neighbour could, at a fraction of the cost, have a fake sham castle by putting a one-brick-thick face (per-haps bigger than the building behind) on to a convenient cottage or farm. Then from the house, or from such walks as visitors were taken, it looked as good as the sham castle on the next estate.

The castles were the first follies to appear in the parks, but others quickly followed, and an eager improver could add an eyecatcher, a prospect tower, a grotto, a tunnel, a hermitage, or a pagoda; or have them all; or invent something for himself. Any of these might be designed in the gothick, Roman, Chinese, Moorish, Greek or Druidical styles— they came into fashion roughly in that order, but gothick and classical outlasted the others into this century. The styles, like the types of building, could be happily used all at once or something new invented. What was chosen for what site in what style, depended on taste, place, money, materials and fashion; success was as capricious as survival.

We have now seen an early tower at Freston, the early grottoes (still inside the house), the first tunnels, and the first piece of pure fantasy at the Triangular Lodge, as well as the first fortifications and castles, so this is the place to look at a few of the other things most favoured by the folly builders, and at some of the particular folly materials.

The eyecatcher at Rousham, Creech Arch, and designs for a hermitage, a building in the Chinese taste and a tower.

Screens, eyecatchers and false façades are all very much alike, flat elevations of castellated buildings or temples with no depth, arranged to complete a landscape. Eyecatchers, though, to justify their dramatic name, the suggestion that the building is an unpleasant little animal that lives by snaring the eyes of visitors in a net as they look about them, must be far from the houses they embellish, perhaps a mile or more away on the top of a hill, and of finely fantastic shape. An eyecatcher can be a very startling folly; even from a distance it is of course clear that the building is not 'real', but we presume that if not ancient it is at least solid, its brittleness merely characteristic of all eighteenth-century gothick. In fact it is a piece of flat scenery standing like a sheet of cardboard on its hill. The façade itself is an amusing surprise, but to walk as one sometimes can through a front door to find nothing, into the space and air and grass we have just left is a violation of all the principles that have surrounded us from the cradle, and, indeed, of that cradle itself, and it never ceases to stir our emotions. Here and there in England is a parish church that once had a rood loft and, this being destroyed, the little spiral staircase hidden in the wall that led to it remains unblocked. Suddenly at the top we are out high on the church wall. The stairs have ended at nothing and only the drop to the chancel floor is at our feet. The strongest sensation of stairs that lead to nothing is felt at the great Indian observatories where tall stone flights climb up to end at the last step in the sky. No mountain could compare. Meanwhile the folly screens do very well.

Mr Dennis Bond of Creech Grange in Dorset built in 1740 a particularly good eyecatcher. The white Portland stone and ashlar arches and pinnacles on the bare crest of the chalk downs between the Grange and the sea are massive in an earlier, Vanbrugh manner. The place is very high and open, with an enormous sky, short chalky turf and gorse. We so often see Portland stone in a city, blackened with the handsome stains of soot and ending on a pavement, that it is a great surprise here, with grass at the foot of the arches and through them, and the sky all round; we can walk to and fro from grass and sky to grass and sky. Its heavy solitude is magnificent, bleaching in the sun and salt air on the top of the cliffs.

Hermitages were sometimes homes for tame anchorites, but sometimes the name was used for a building so distant from the house that it might be considered a retreat; from what, depended on the builder.

Pagodas should be just that, towers with a multitude of upswept roofs, and dragons and bells on the eaves, but some of them are pavilions, and the influence of China on them is very faint.

Prospect Towers give shelter to the sightseer, perhaps improve the view from the house, add another county or so to the five or seven visible from the simple hill and have, if they are very good, a little of the staircase to space feeling. At Leith Hill the tower adds enough to the height of the hill to top a thousand feet.

By the eighteenth century, Pyramids, Arches, Obelisks, had quite ceased to be the wilde enormities of ancient magnanimity, and though Obelisks still commemorated vainglory, Pyramids had become embellishments. Their simple geometric shapes and the similar but more subtle cones stand oddly here and there in the landscape, but are surely an obvious choice; what is really surprising is that only at Swanage is there a globe—one would expect a nation of folly builders, given to scattering their parks with stone curiosities of every sort, to have realized that nothing could make a better contrast with trees, and cause more surprise in the woods, than the satisfying bulk of a great globe.

A Building in the Chinese Taste.

An amateur, untrained in the visual subtleties of the golden section, sometimes turned to the beautiful shapes of solid geometry and built a cone, a cube or a cylinder—an eye-catcher like Wroxton for instance is first seen not as a mock-up of the turreted structure of a real castle but as two golden cylinders. Castellations tended to be square with square spaces between, mouldings to have flat rectangular sections, and wall surfaces to be broken with protruding bricks or stones rather than elaborate bonding and coursing; follies were built with the directness and complexity of a doodle on the blotting pad.

But there is in fact less solid geometry than one might hope; alas, it was left to the French Revolutionary architects like Boullée and Ledoux to plan for 'real' architecture so based on geometry, though Joseph Gandy at least designed a pretty pair of cone-lodges.

At first the materials used for follies were the brick, stone, wood, glass and slate of ordinary architecture, while grottoes added by their very nature rock, shells, minerals, pebbles, mirror-glass—everything to provide glitter and a rich texture. Other materials came into use as folly-building spread; flint, if available, was one of the best materials, for its complex texture and subtle colour made a good contrast to the usually simple and unsubtle designs—it was evidently considered undignified for big houses—Goodwood is a rare exception.

'Tufa' is constantly referred to in eighteenth-century accounts of grottoes and one tends to accept it as vaguely volcanic. Investigation, however, shows that some of this curious exotic was in fact obtained near Bath. Clearly, then, one feels, it is limestone, with the soft parts worn away by water into these holes and spikes. But the process is much more complicated. When the water of an underground spring in limestone country contains carbon dioxide, it can act on the calcium carbonate of the stone to form a bicarbonate. The water reaches the surface under reduced pressure, and this, with evaporation, turns the soluble bicarbonate back to the insoluble carbonate, which then forms a deposit on the limestone round the spring, and this is tufa. Presumably the water does in fact mould it into its aqueous shapes, though not in the obvious way. It was sometimes called *Pierre Antidiluvienne*.

A hermitage had to look as if the hermit himself had made it, so here the favourite materials were treetrunks, branches, twigs, cones and bark, all most ingeniously used, with moss infill, and pebbles for the floor; the best of them, though, were very carefully designed, like Thomas Wright's Root House at Badminton. Roman cement was another favourite material, a cheap maquillage to transform a brick tower into a stone one. It mellows and cracks very well, but must have been startlingly stark when new.

And, for a quick cheap castle, there was always canvas; as so many real shams looked like scenery, many builders went further and actually made them so, of canvas on wooden frames, painted. It probably looked very well. One thinks of it at once as tatty, as the standard sets for the Yeomen of the Guard out on hire cheap to a provincial Light Opera and Dramatic Club for one last spell before they are repainted; the colour is thin and grey, the cloth sags, no illusion is left. But in fact it would be fairer to suppose something more like the sets for a new musical, fresh and crisp and taut, well built and painted to deceive.

Tufa. Part of the façade of the ice-house at Buckland House (see page 376).

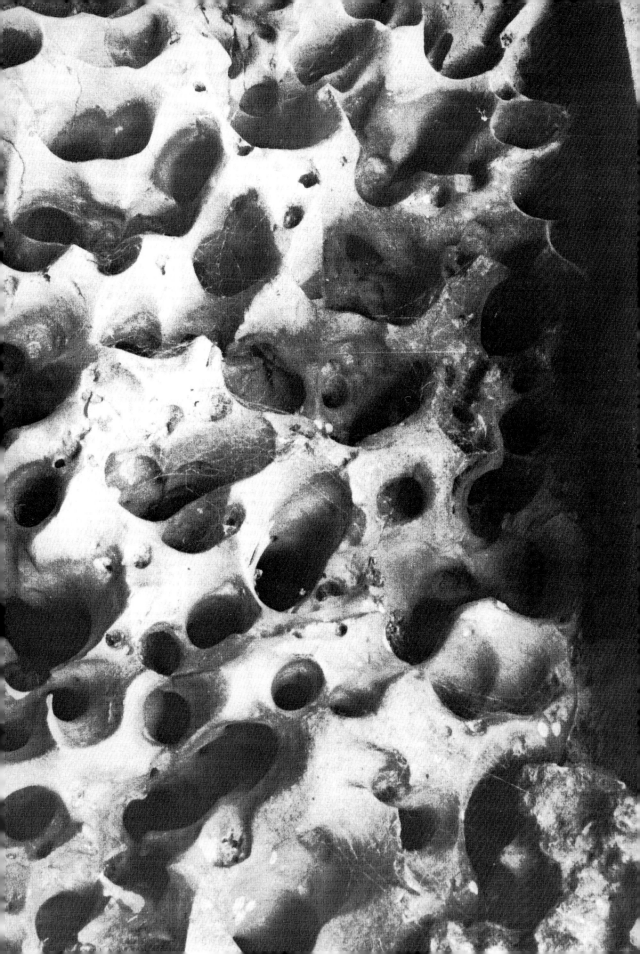

However, neither the ornamental purpose of follies, nor their usual gothick style, nor their materials, could, severally or together, give them such constant similarity in their diversity, and at the same time separate them so far from ordinary architecture, and one other factor does indeed unite them: most follies were designed by amateurs. Some amateurs know by instinct all that art can demand, but generally the compulsion under which an amateur builds, whether it is fashion or obsession, fails to instruct him in the principles of architecture and his mind leaps back to building-blocks, forgetting every piece of architecture he has seen since he played with them, just as we always leap back to childhood experience, even if only for a second or so, when we start something new. So we shall often miss the refinement and urbanity of professional architecture, and often gain a fine bold simplicity; neither the impulse to build, nor the naked geometry of the first idea passes through the filter of taste and rules, but remains alien to the trained eye; designs of squares, equilateral triangles and diamonds are not the common currency of sophisticated architecture, and the folly builders used them all, for it is easier to make a window double square than π. Or they used detail oddly; a very slender gothick column will appear to support a great mass of flint, or a large console will support nothing, or arrow-slits and big square castellations may outweigh the whole structure, so that the folly, already a mere shell or screen, will fade further under its load of giant ornaments.

Some of the amateur follies are magnificently beautiful, some are small and foolish and very touching, some of them are terrifying, few are negligible.

If importance was ever in doubt, if the little folly when built was felt to be inferior to the dream, or to the folly in the next park, a foreign name could be supposed to help, although the picturesque landscape was so well done here that it became known throughout Europe as *le jardin anglais* ... A wooden, tin or canvas umbrella erected over a circular seat for shade at a viewpoint sounded better as an *ombrello* (*parasol* had been in use for more than a century; old fashioned). *Rocaille* was preferred to rococo, a

An ombrello.

simple covered arcade at Rousham was called *praeneste,* and franglitalio words were widely invented, generally enjoyed a short life of various spellings, and died, existing only in accounts of visits and in early guide-books. Certain phrases, though, persist, like *ferme ornée* (first applied at Wooburn, where Philip Southcote is believed to have invented 'the belt', a perimeter walk through trees which also prevented the eye from straying on to a neighbour's composition) and *cottage orné,* usually rustic and thatched. All through the century *genius loci* was felt superior to 'the spirit of the place', and to say that an improver had caught it was the highest praise that could be given.

Duncombe and Studley Royal show some of the earliest moves away from formality, but the full development of the *jardins anglais* began in the south. Two of the earliest and best were both designed by amateurs—Stourhead, in Wiltshire, and Pain's Hill, in Surrey. Stourhead has more beauty, Pain's Hill more charm. Stourhead has been lucky, it belongs to the National Trust; Pain's Hill is being cut and replanted by a timber company, its grotto has been destroyed, and it is, I think, now beyond help. Two hundred years ago, before the timber was grown, the rather open park that we see in the engravings was one of the five-star visits for the man of taste, and also, Shoberl tells us, 'Mr. Hamilton indulged the public with a sight of the beauties of this place; and even allowed the use of small chairs drawn by ponies, which were provided by the inns at Cobham'. Today, though the trees are mature as their creator never saw them, the park is declining under our very eyes, the trees numbered and the undergrowth unchecked. There will be in this book more complaints of this sort, that dull, routine Cotswold manor houses should be protected while one of our two best gardens goes to ruin. I make no apology for complaining—if we complained more, we should lose less.

The Hon. Charles Hamilton, 1704–86, fourth son of the sixth Lord Abercorn, was a noted amateur of the picturesque and gave excellent advice on improvements to his friends, including Lord Lansdowne at Bowood. At Pain's Hill, on a very beautiful and well-watered natural site of about 400 acres, Charles Hamilton worked on his estate, creating, with real and artificial hills, a large lake, an intricate system of canals, and some fine ornaments, a living image of the paintings of Poussin. Poussin, however, no matter how closely studied, could not have inspired Pain's Hill without genius in Mr Hamilton, and genius of a very rare sort—it is difficult enough for painters and writers to put what is in their heads down, undistorted, into paint or words. How infinitely more difficult it must be, then, to work with 400 acres, at first naturally pretty, and then, and at one's own command, suddenly all raw earth, puddles, planks and naked little trees with labels hanging down. I am one of those people who can neither arrange any kind of flowers except large, foolproof bunches of primroses, nor cheerfully undertake even the improvement of a window-box full of weeds; it is certain, I feel, to look worse afterwards. The pleasure of such gardens as Pain's Hill is thus always heightened for me by the most profound awe that here someone stood in the mud more than 200 years ago at four o'clock on a winter afternoon—or, perhaps worse, on a summer morning when the old undisturbed gardens of timid neighbours were glowing smugly in the sun—stood and calmly *knew* that it was going to be all right.

Past the house, the garden runs down in a wide straight avenue of shrubs and high grass to the bottom of a valley, and then the shrubs become trees continuing on over the next hill. At the top, a cross ride to the right leads to the Gothick Temple, but the main avenue goes on with a nice new conceit, its whole width filled by a nineteenth-century Japanese garden, heavily overgrown. At the bottom is the lake, now surrounded by trees but once more open. To the left, the path runs round the lake, but all the best of the landscaping is the other way, along a green path with the tree-covered slope rising on the right and the lake almost screened by trees and bushes on the left.

The atmosphere is one of pleasure; Charles Hamilton's delight in his work remains, and pleasure still colours everything. We easily forget that he finally went bankrupt doing it all.

Along the pleasant path by the lake is the Gothick Ruin, so enclosed by trees and the shadows of the trees that it is almost invisible in the wood, even though it is 50 feet long, and was at least two storeys high. There are the front halves, three sides each, of two hexagonal gothick towers that have what appear to be pinnacles at the corners, but these are the remains of higher building. The tower-fronts are joined by a curtain wall with three tall arches and everything is brick with clinging patches of roman cement and ivy. There are holes for floor joists and stretches of ruined wall running back from the path; once there may have been little rooms in the towers, with a corridor along the wall over the arches. Certainly there used to be more of it.

Further on, the lake narrows and then opens to the right round the hill, and we, keeping ahead, cross a charming wooden bridge of an early oriental pattern[1]—the wooden bridges here may have been the prototypes—on to an island, shady and brown with bracken. One moves instinctively towards its slight summit which is covered with laurels and ivy among the trees, and there, suddenly, is a startling thin jagged tufa arch like a torn and petrified crown of thorns. It is quite invisible among the leaves of the laurel and ivy until one is on top of it, and then the grey is not shadow but stone.

The island is cut in two by water at its highest point, and a wonderfully elaborate and haphazard tufa bridge crosses the cleft, very broad so that it does not appear to be a bridge at all, and the eye is not allowed to fall to the water but runs ahead down a slope of shaded grass with toadstools growing under the most magnificent cedars of Lebanon, whose flat branches sweep the water of the lake; the beauty of the place is beyond words. Another wooden bridge can be seen to the left crossing to the far side of the old narrow part of the lake, and there are pieces of stone carved with wreaths to lure us over, but a stronger compulsion turns one to circle the grass under the great cedars instead, looking at the main expanse of the lake, and turning back to the bridge to look at the scattered twists of tufa beside it, and at an alcove, less sharp and needly than the arch, full of holes like a sponge, or a pile of skulls. Behind the alcove, one can climb down the cleft beside the bridge and reach the edge of the water underneath it. Once the whole span was covered with the artificial stalactities of thousands of pieces of felspar.[2] At the

---

[1] An engraving of Pain's Hill in Le Rouge shows the bridge with a gentleman nearby hand-cranking a little Chinese paddle-boat.

[2] The Swedish artist Piper, visiting in 1779, described the 'transparent spars, stalactites, crystallization and the like, some descending from the vault in the form of hanging pyramids, chandeliers, and baldachinos, some rising like pillars from the floor. . . . These catch the sunbeams which are reflected from the surface of the water outside and break into the grotto.'

Pain's Hill. The gothick octagon.

far end the overgrowth on the bank suggests some kind of ruin under it, and opposite us is a little rocky entrance in the bank. Across the bridge and down the other side, the entrance, almost at water level, leads into a winding passage lined with spar, gleaming much more softly here in fainter light, from grilled openings in the roof and walls and a tiny side chamber looking out under the vault of the bridge. Through the passage are the heartbreaking ruins of a large and very splendid grotto. The roofs are down and all is desolation. It was almost intact at the beginning of the war but soldiers quartered here destroyed it.

Back under the cedars and over the bridge we saw before, Mr Hamilton's gaiety re-asserts itself; there is a lot of the park still left to see. The path beyond the bridge is on a narrow strip of trees and grass, lake on the right and the River Mole which bounds the park on the left. The river and some stretches of artificial canal begin to wind, elaborately so that the paths seem to go for miles, and yet openly so that there is a complete change of atmosphere from the elegant artifice of the Grotto Island, and in 200 yards the watery greenness has set a rural mood. On an end of land is the Roman Mausoleum, hidden in the trees. The brick and stone are very ruined indeed, but the proportions and the round arches suggest the classic taste. It is in the form of an arch, and in each side is a door opening in a little room lined with small niches, perhaps for urns, but Horace Walpole says not: 'The Ruin . . . has great faults. It represents a triumphant Arch, and yet could never have had a column which would certainly have accompanied so rich a soffit. Then this Arch is made to have been a Columbarium. You may as well suppose an Alderman's family buried in Temple Bar.'

Further on still, the river leaves the canals and runs into the open fields, with a huge iron waterwheel made by Bramah,[1] but we turn back to go round the main sweep of the lake. At the end of it we are back at the foot of the hill below the cross ride and look up a most beautifully flowing grassy slope to the Gothick Temple or Tent (attributed to Batty Langley, but I doubt this). Now we can walk up to it, past the round foundations of the Roman Bath —several buildings are gone; I could not find the Turkish Tent, the Hermitage of gnarled roots has been long destroyed and the Temple of Bacchus we know to have been part papier-mâché, so its disappearance is not surprising. The Temple is, of course, pure garden architecture, and we have no excuse but its remarkable grace for looking at it, but what more excuse is needed? Horace Walpole did not like it:

> . . . made worse by pendent ornaments in the arches, and by being closed in on two sides at the bottom with cheeks that have no relation to Gothic. The whole is an unmeaning edifice. In all Gothic designs, they should be made something that was of that time, a part of a church, a castle, a convent or a mansion. The Goths never built summer-houses or temples in a garden. This of Mr. Hamilton's stands on the brow of a hill—there an imitation of a fort or watch-tower would have been proper.

[1] Derek Clifford in his *History of Garden Design* says that this is the first recorded use of cast iron in gardening.

Pain's Hill. Two details of the gothick octagon, the grotto entrance and the prospect tower.

There is in fact a watch-tower as well, on rising ground further from the house, a square castellated one with a round turret rising above it crowned with just such a cap as Vanbrugh contemplated for the fortifications at Castle Howard, all very correct, so Walpole might have forgiven the Temple, to which we will return: a stone platform 3 feet high stands on the top of the slope, on which is a ten-sided fantasy of wood and plaster, most amazingly preserved, restored once, but cracking badly. Each side contains a large ogival arch, a quatrefoil over it, and fretwork castellations at the top. Up each angle runs a slender buttressed pinnacle, rising, crocketed, above the walls. All is lightness and elegance. Inside, the angles take half-pillars from which springs fan-vaulting, meeting over the quatrefoil windows and joining, via some fine free ribbing joined with ogives, at a pendent in the centre. More pendents (the ones Mr Walpole disliked) are in the arches, unsupported, and certainly at the back there are two pairs of arches, separated by a pair of open ones, where half screens rise halfway towards them, echoing their shape. They are very skilfully contrived to suggest that the back is closed without in any way spoiling the open appearance from the other side. This makes one stand with one's back to the screens looking at the view down the hill to the lake.

It would be now quite reasonable for the reader to cry 'we have been here too long, still at Pain's Hill and only 1740; if we visit every estate in this fashion, we shall never be done and the book never be back at the library'. But here there is a sham ruin, and a prospect tower, and the ghost of a grotto, and tufa, and a Roman Mausoleum, and once there was a Hermitage, and it was the first improvement in this manner, on this scale, and of this beauty; here is what the later amateurs of the picturesque were aiming at, and even if few of them achieved it, this sets the note—the hilly site, the winding enclosed river, the open lake, the romantic island with great cedars and an almost hidden grotto, and the calm view through the swinging arches of the temple. This was the setting once, perhaps now sold and built over, perhaps cut off from the house and forlorn, perhaps so altered that we shall hardly recognize it again, of hundreds of sham castles, screens and towers. Today they have acquired their own notable beauty of decay, of thistles, stones, brambles and falling ceilings; but this was, once, the folly scene.

At Stourhead in the early 1740s, the banker Henry Hoare made the most beautiful garden of its kind remaining in England, a remarkable early romantic landscape, now surely at its best, with the great trees in their prime.

No landscape gardener was employed here until Capability Brown came in 1750; for nearly ten years Mr Hoare planned and excavated and planted by his own judgment and the result is a garden so perfect that one cannot quite believe it; the early summer mists lift from it like gauzes from a transformation scene, and there are the lake and the prospects, now enclosed, now distant, but always in focus. It sacrifices the long vista of Versailles which leaves the imagination troubled and uncomforted, and achieves instead, as does no other garden, a balance between intimacy and space so just that one wonders if serenity may have a mathematical constant. At Stourhead the changing prospects add up and subtract in such a way that the mind moves out across the waters just to the limit of release and never to disquiet. Nothing could be more difficult to achieve than this—it is one of the things that painting seems to me quite unable to achieve, for the third dimension is necessary to it, and it is elusive enough in sculpture and architecture, though when once it has been achieved, even a photograph will show it. Marini's 'Horse and Rider' in the Tate Gallery has it, and so have Vezelay and Vierzehnheiligen and Mereworth Castle. This emotion, an elated calm, a serene bliss, is so rare, in fact, that the word for it eludes one; it is too peaceful for ecstasy, too alive for sublimity; at Stourhead where it has been captured on so large a scale, there is the added poignancy of the mortality of the trees. The creator cannot have seen what we see now, nor can it long survive, for the gardens are now mellow and perfect, with the romance of a little neglect; restoration and replanting must soon follow, and perfection fail.

Most improvers added to their gardens their own conceptions of the gothick dream, perhaps a sham church or a folly castle, and Mr Hoare did indeed build a picturesque cottage, but one of his best views, across the lake from the grotto, includes the genuine village church in a composition which must have been the despair of half England. The colonnaded temples, the rotunda, the charm of a grass-paved stone bridge, and the perfectly composed swans are not within our province, but we may allow anticipation to be roused by a wonderful construction of stone and tufa, a foretaste of the grotto. There is a dark water-entry, so involved and romantic that we are swept through it and over a huge complexity of rocky arch without realizing that it has taken us over a quite invisible road that cuts the park. The brio of this arch has its purpose, to defeat the road; the entrance to the grotto (which we have seen across the water, just visible enough for curiosity) is much more sombre and dignified, and the grotto itself is restrained, moving always within the sensible limits of rock, flint and pebbles. There are no shells at all. The entrance is down a path by the water, curving under a rock arch, and later on into a grot of jagged rocks which twists round to a bigger and more architectural arch. On the three sides of the stone pediment is inscribed

Intus aquae dulces, vivoque sedilia saxo
Nympharum domus

and it leads into a severe little square anteroom, walled with flints, floored with pebbles, and roofed with vermiculated rock.

The shock-tactics of a later grotto like Goldney's would be unthinkable here. The water and rocks of the bridge across the road suggested the gothic beauties of wild nature, and preliminary gentle rock work has led us into the grotto unalarmed. Now the anteroom suggests the elaborate work beyond and collects the sound of water. Ahead the long vista leads straight across the grotto, through another similar flint room, on to the River God leaden in his cave beyond. But the circular main chamber of the grotto checks the axial plunge in its round rocky vault. It is calm, echoing gently with water, just that dim cool refreshment from a hot day that a large park demands: grottoes are for the south; northern England is cold enough. The floor is again pebbles (a discomfort to the foot common in grottoes), but now arranged in concentric circles of different colours. On the left is the curb of a fountain, whose waters run from the back of a cave which arches over a white-painted lead statue of a nymph asleep on a mossy rock. A verse is at our feet:

Nymph of the grot, these sacred springs I keep
And to the murmur of these waters sleep.
Ah spare my slumbers, gently tread the cave,
And drink in silence or in silence lave.

From the darkness behind her pours one of the sources of the Stour.

The light comes, filtered and green from the water, through a low arch opposite where one may sit and look out at the lake, and in the four segments of the grotto wall between the entrances, the nymph, and the arch are four little niches each of which will seat one person. Conversation is impossible; the hard discomfort of all grotto seats, either sharp with rocks or bumpy with pebbles (there must once have been cushions) discourages it, and in any case grottoes are not for gossip, but for melancholy. It comes quickly here, a calm melancholy, that induces one to walk slowly on to the wilder but smaller cave of the River God, lit by an eye of daylight from above, and then back to sit in the dark grotto. The charm of Cheere's statues, a verse approved by Pope, and the magnificence of enclosing as fountain the headwaters of a river are contemplated, and then the last thought fades, and melancholy's quiet enchantment holds the mind, to change the aspect of the park outside and colour the rest of the walk.

The filtered light alone has not this effect, there must also be the chill of water, and the dampness of the earth that creeps into the most closely shelled-over grottoes, and above all there is the strange texture; nothing is soft or even smooth, but everywhere rock and flint and stone, synonyms for hardness, surround us in fact instead of in simile, and the body shrinks away from the walls, disliking contact even with the pebbles of the floor. This aloofness from one's surroundings produces a lovely range of sensations, from melancholy here to a taut alertness in some of the later grottoes where darkness and earth induce not melancholy but fear.

Stourhead. Opposite, *the grotto.* Above, top left, *the Rustic Cottage and* top right, *the Rustic Convent.* Above,
Alfred's Tower on Kingsettle Hill, from an old postcard.

Stourhead is not only beautiful, but accessible, maintained, and very fully researched. Ever since Henry Hoare's day, the grounds have been so often visited, admired and described, and so many of Hoare's own records remain, that we probably know more about it than about any other garden. It is therefore, though it lacks the magic of Pain's Hill, probably the best place in which to see what the original setting of many follies must have been at least trying to achieve 200 years ago.

Avoid rhododendron time. Loudon tells us that 'the first rhododendrons and azaleas were introduced into England by Mr. Thorburn who was gardener to Mr. Hamilton', but this is not to say that they were lavished about in the nineteenth-century manner. For one thing there can't have been enough of them, and for another both Hamilton and Hoare would have realized how damaging to their subtle green landscapes would be the great clusters of at least the pink and magenta varieties. Also it seems that the Stourhead rhododendrons (or their forebears) were planted by Sir Richard Colt Hoare in the 1790s; he visited Fonthill in 1806 and Beckford said that 'Sir Richard had no taste'. He certainly put up the dull Rustic Cottage and pulled down some pretty follies.

The obelisk and the serious classical temples built at Stourhead by Henry Flitcroft—the Pantheon, the Temple of Apollo and the Temple of Flora—are all still there, and a number of the follies, as well as the grotto and the tufa arch are also still safe; the Cross and St Peter's Pump, both brought from Bristol, Alfred's Tower, the Rustic Cottage and the Rustic Convent. A grotto boathouse, the Gothick Greenhouse, the Hermitage, Turkish Tent, Chinese temple and Chinese umbrello were demolished by Sir Richard. The umbrello was drawn by Piper in 1779, a true umbrella crowned by a pineapple, supported on a Roman Doric column with a seat round the bottom. (See page 38.)

Mrs Lybbe Powys described the Turkish Tent in 1776, 'very pretty; 'tis of painted canvas, so remains up the whole year; the inside painted blue and white in mosaic.' Incredibly, one tent of this sort, Chinese instead of Turkish, still survives (probably because it is always taken down in the winter) on a lawn in Northamptonshire, but that is for later; having looked at the folly setting at Pain's Hill and Stourhead, we must go back to its chief ingredient, the gothick style.

But not before looking for contrast at one site that was left almost untouched, for though they were designed in good natural settings, both Pain's Hill and Stourhead cost a lot of work and money. They both demonstrate of course that desire and time and money were not enough; great taste was needed too, and the eighteenth-century books on landscaping continually stress this; the first requirement for the improver was that feeling for the *genius loci*. Given the right site and sensitivity, much could be accomplished with a ruin or two and carefully planted trees; it was not always necessary to dam a river or to move a hill. Crowcombe Court in Somerset has one of the best landscapes of this almost natural sort, a rich combe running southwest off the Quantocks, with its stream brought down through a series of pools and quiet cascades; we are sure that the awful roar of water and the terrible clash of giant rocks were never wanted here, the mood was for the sublime picturesque of Claude Lorraine, and the mood remains today. By its angle in the hills Crowcombe must be very lovely early in the day, walking up the combe with the trees black against the low morning sun, but the new day has its briskness, and the low sun in the evening has a more golden light.

The planting is superb, with a variety of fine but simple trees so that interest in exotics does not distract the eye. There are beech, sycamore, ash, fir and yew, in constantly changing patterns of green, set in great ferns and thick mosses; this is the warm south of Somerset. High on the west bank with evergreen trees behind, and dark while the visitor is still in sunshine, is a sandstone and ironstone castle, part real gothic from the demolition of Hallsway Manor, part sham, a complication of arches and shadows, heavily overgrown. It is reached from the sunshine over a fine red sandstone and tufa bridge, and afterwards there are two paths running a long way up the levels of water, or a route back by a higher brighter path with another bit of ruin, not seen before, this time all sham, and down through the beeches in the last of daylight, one of the most beautiful landscapes in the world.

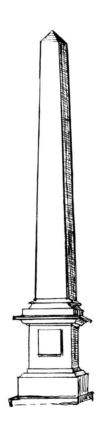

The Gothick Style:
Ruinous and Full of Owls

Most follies are in the gothick taste, which soon after Vanbrugh's monumental (and expensive) fortifications developed a second manner for follies, very thin and elegant, a descendant of the Neville screen at Durham rather than of the border castles. The two continued side by side.

The follies that could be taken for mediaeval work could be counted on the fingers of one hand; both the details and the proportion are different, in spite sometimes of a pretension to accuracy—clearly the creative urge in this style still persisted in follies, as in such churches as Tetbury, so that the builders, aiming for scholarship, made something new; the style is generally considered to have died out in hangover parish churches, and the follies, if considered at all, are classed as revival. It is equally arguable that all through the eighteenth century gothic architecture still had considerable vitality, creative force and validity, and the true revival did not begin until the 1830s, the gothicisms of the previous 150 years being more really the survival of a still lively tradition.

At Shotover in Oxfordshire stands the earliest gothick false façade I know of, closing the vista down the lake from the front of the house. It is very assured, and has been ascribed to both Hawksmoor and Vanbrugh, with a date of about 1720, soon after James Tyrrel's new house was built between 1715 and 1718. But lately the original drawings and plan by William Kent have been found; they were auctioned in 1971 and went to America, safe but far from Shotover.

Vanbrugh paid a visit in 1725 and is thought to have designed the gardens, which are finely wooded, and superbly laid out, though now overgrown.

There is an obelisk and a garden house that might be Vanbrugh's standing among pines on a knoll. It is a little like the Boycott Pavilions at Stowe, or Archer's larger one at Wrest.

Going from the house, down the east side of the lake a yew hedge hides an enchanting conceit, a castellated stucco potting shed. On the garden side it is painted to look like stone, the paint is very faded but it is still possible to see the ghosts of a row of painted doors, counterfeits of French windows with semicircular fanlights. At the end of the lake is the lichen-patched limestone of the Kent façade, standing in a tangle of rushes, ground-elder and ivy, with peppermint underfoot.

There are three arches below a castellated pediment and they open on to a vaulted shelter. Elaborate towers stand at either end, their detail very finely carved, and hidden behind the screen is a large barn.

A view of Old Sarum from an engraving of 1798. Old Sarum was a hill fort which became a Romano-British village, a Saxon town and finally a Norman town which although it had a castle and a cathedral can never have looked like this splendidly imaginative picture, a folly wedding cake of portcullises.

Shotover

Early façades and sham castles, like the walls at Castle Howard usually stand on rising ground. The trees around them are grouped to great advantage, and they promote mediaeval thoughts for a walk in the park. Early sham castles are almost always fashionable and calm.

The desire to use real ruins or parts of them in sham ones was very persistent, and the growing interest in mediaeval history by no means prevented some landowners from pulling down what they did not want, however old and splendid, to put up what they did. Shobdon in Hereford and Worcester is the tightrope example; it is impossible to make up one's mind if Lord Bateman's destruction of the Norman church and the building of a new one in the 1750s was crime or creation. The old church was very like Kilpeck and therefore a great rarity (but we do still have Kilpeck), and the new one is easily the finest gothick rococo church in the country. Lost, it really would be irreplaceable. Standing inside its dazzling, heart-stopping, blue and white, one can only say that this was worth any vandalism at all. But then, up on the hill, for the view from the vanished house, stands Shobdon Arches. In the distance it is an amateur-folly design, a five-fold screen symmetrically unfolded, with three gables, cross, trefoil and pinnacle. Arrived, the heart sinks, for it has been built up from the Norman chancel arch of the old church and the arches of the two Norman doorways (cut down) as the forward centre and the set-back ends of the screen, while the tympana of the doors are used to decorate the linking folds. The weather on the hilltop has erased all it can reach, though some wonderful stretches of shaft remain, decorated with people, Viking dragons, birds and lions in swirls, zig-zags, variety and zest. Old church or new? A difficult choice.

Shobdon Arches.

Left, *Shobdon Arches, a detail of the Romanesque carving.* Opposite, *the sham ruin at Hagley.*

At about the same time, not far away in Warwickshire, Sanderson Miller was at work at Edge Hill. Some trick of fame and the size of his castles together preserve his memory while the names of more inventive designers are lost. He was also, at least at the beginning, an amateur; the English love amateurs, employ them whenever possible, and seem less unwilling to pay them. Sanderson Miller (1717–80) inherited Radway Grange from his father when he was twenty, and began to improve the grounds with fountains and cascades. In 1744 he built the Thatched Cottage, his first building, and was putting gothick fronts on the sixteenth-century house. Between 1747 and 1750 he built Radway Tower, or Castle, to mark the spot where Charles was supposed to have raised the standard before the battle of Edge Hill. The tower is illustrated on the title page.

All the work is in yellow freestone. On one side of the main road is the sham ruin of a large arch, and opposite, on the other side is the entrance to the Tower. This must once have had two fat square castellated towers flanking the gate, but now the right-hand one is sawn off at an angle and has a roof and chimney. Through the gate an immovable stone drawbridge crosses to the 'lofty octagonal tower', castellated and machicolated. It is now a pub, but the picnic room, with pretty plasterwork and elegant windows and niches, remains empty. The Bishop of Ossory visited the Castle in 1756; 'in one of these niches is to be placed Caractacus in chains, modelled, under Mr. Miller's directions, by a countryman of great genius now established in London'. But Caractacus when finished was too big for the niche and had to go in the garden which was once reached by a second, wooden, drawbridge across the moat. There is still some old stained glass in the windows which may have been sent to Miller by Lord Coventry, when he was still Lord Deerhurst and had not yet inherited Croome to improve. On 3 September 1750, a party was given to open the Castle, but some guests seem to have disliked it, for George Lyttelton wrote, on receiving another invitation, 'Mrs. Lyttelton will like to dine at the house better than at the Castle, and my stomach prefers hott meat to cold, though not my taste; so, if you please, we will dine at the foot of the hill. . . .'

However George Lyttelton inherited, and started his fine house and grounds at Hagley, and as well as employing Miller to design the house (against the powerful advice of Horace Walpole who was championing Chute, the architect of Strawberry Hill), he ordered, though clearly not for picnics, a sham castle which was built of sandstone on rising ground in the park and when finished forced even Walpole's reluctant admiration. This castle is built round a court, four walls about 75 feet long, with towers at the corners, enclosing a yard with a keeper's hut and chickens. A contemporary account describes how,

> to keep the whole design in its purity, to wipe away any suspicion of its being any otherwise than a real ruin, the large and mossy stones which have seemingly tumbled from the tottering and ruinous walls, are suffered to lie about the different parts of the building in the utmost confusion. This greatly preserves its intent and confirms the common opinion of every stranger of its early date; while, to carry a stronger face of antiquity, ivy is encouraged to climb about the walls and turrets, and it now so closely embraces those parts with its glossy arms that it is impossible to look upon it without a suggestion of its being as ancient as it really appears.

The ivy is still there, glossy as ever, and there are some big beeches, but the utmost confusion of stones seems diminished, and rooms much larger than the existing cottage must have been pulled down, for Sir George wrote in 1749: 'I forget now how many chairs are wanting for the Castle, but how can I bespeak them without the model you drew for them? You know they are not to be common chairs but of a Gothick form. . . . Have you ordered a Proper Table to be made for it? . . .'

There seem to have been a lot of trouble and changed plans at Hagley, but we may get this impression because so much correspondence about it has been preserved; when every landowner was an amateur of taste, it is unlikely that any of them left his architect alone for long. One letter is very sad—'Do you reflect, my good Friend,' says Sir George, 'how much the Beauty of Hagley might have been improved by two Hundred Pounds? It would have built an elegant Temple in the place of the old decayed wooden Arches at the top of the Forest Lawn, or it would have raised another Tower to make the Castle less like a Church. . . .' However, he had managed to find £25,823 3s. 4¼d., he had his castle, some lovely garden ornaments and urns, Athenian Stuart's first Doric Temple, and the praise of Walpole:

> There is extreme taste in the park. The seats are not of the best, but there is not one absurdity. There is a ruined castle built by Miller that would get him his freedom even of Strawberry, it has the true rust of the Barons' Wars . . . And there is a Hermitage so exactly like those of Sadeler's prints, on the brow of a shady mountain, stealing peeps into the glorious world below. And there is such a pretty well. . . . And there is such a pretty wood. . . . And there is such a mountain. . . . Miller has built a gothic house at Hagley for a relation of Sir George: but there he is not more than Miller; in his castle he is almost Bentley.[1]

Lord Chancellor Hardwicke wanted a castle at Wimpole, but at the beginning dealt with it entirely through Sir George, who wrote to Miller:

> . . . I found it would be better for him not to copy mine, but have something like the same idea, but differing in many respects, particularly in this, that he wants no house not even room in it, but merely the walls and semblance of an old castle to make an object from his house. At most he only desires to have a staircase carried up one of the towers, and a leaded gallery half round it to stand on and view the prospect. It will have a fine wood of firrs for a backing behind it and will stand on an eminence at a proper distance from the house. . . . with regard to the dimensions of my Ld. Chancellor's castle, you are not confined, but may make it of just what height and breadth you think fitt.

Miller evidently sent suggestions off by return for Sir George thanks him a few days later:

[1] Bentley, Chute and Walpole himself formed the Strawberry Hill Committee to make decisions on the alterations and decorations of Walpole's house at Twickenham. Walpole never did much folly work at Strawberry Hill, perhaps because the grounds were small, but spent many happy hours and letters praising and condemning the castles and eyecatchers of others.

The view of Wimpole which you have seen will give you a pretty just idea. . . . It is a hill about half a mile from the house to which the ground rises gently all the way. My Ld. agrees with your notion of having some firrs before part of the walls. As the back view will be immediately closed by the wood there is no regard to be had to it, nor to the left side, but only to the front and right side as you look from the house. As my Lord designs it merely as an object he would have no staircase nor leads in any of the towers, but merely the walls so built as to have the appearance of a ruined castle. For materials he has freestone, or a mixture of flint pebbles and other stone, of which an old church in the parish is built, and also bricks in his neighbourhood.

The sham ruin at Wimpole.

The next year, Lord Hardwicke himself wrote to Miller saying that there was no hurry, and the fair prospect of unlimited height and breadth must have receded, especially as the Lord Chancellor was notoriously mean (Judge Gripus, they called him), though very rich—he had paid Lord Oxford £100,000 for the Wimpole estate in 1740, and given about £24,000 in 1725 for Hardwicke. However, the castle was built and the height and breadth are indeed portentous: there are more than 200 feet of wall 2 feet thick and three towers 20 feet across; it is built of brick faced with ashlar, on rising ground with trees behind, just as the intention was, and equally no regard was given to the back. There are two main stretches of wall, at right angles, joined by one tower and terminated by the other two. The west face is slightly bowed, with a large door in the jagged wall and a pointed window above. The south face is more fragmentary still and the tower at the far end a mere stump: as far as silhouette goes, against the dark trees, the ruin is well conceived and most suitably overgrown, heavy with ivy, elder and haw-thorn, encased on the west with brambles and seeded thistles. The towers are curious, though; most eighteenth-century buildings were made sharp and new, and have mellowed, the houses have lovely stains and lights, the garden temples have lichens and moss, the mouldings are softened but still clear. Some of the sham ruins, however, built crumbled and broken with considerable skill, planted deliberately with ivy and small trees, dedicated to decay, have oddly reversed normality and now appear crude and new. The towers of Wimpole are scarred, certainly, but the effect is not that of the passage of two hundred years—still less of six hundred—but rather that of bomb splinters on a concrete air-raid shelter. So today the enormous ruin has a curiously modern air and to get back to what Lord Hardwicke imagined, we must read the verse under a pretty 1780 engraving which shows the ruin more complete than it is now and so more ruinous—

> When Henry stemmed Ierne's stormy flood,
> And bowed to Britain's yoke her stormy brood,
> When by true courage and false zeal impelled
> Richard encamp'd on Salem's palmy field,
> On towers like these Earl, Baron, Vavasor
> Hung high their floating banners on the air.

Other castles, projected if not completed, are mentioned in Sanderson Miller's letters, a grotto at Wotton, a summerhouse at Enville; Belhus, Lacock, a castle for Lord Chet-wynd; a letter from Lord North rejoices that 'our tower can be built cheaper than was imagined'. Lord North also had a Miller 'gothic open rotondo' with screens raised or lowered by screws—'if you think we shall escape a wet day tomorrow, I hope we shall have the pleasure of your company to cold meat and Iced cream at the Chinese House'. But the tower was so cheap that it fell down.

Although so many of Miller's letters have been preserved, the best of his follies, the large conspicuous castle façade built above Bath for Ralph Allen seems to have only Miller's name, and the date, 1762. It is a fine eyecatcher, a black sharp outline against the sky, utterly unreal, a cardboard fort in a toyshop; and it is safe, given with its land to the city in 1921. There is a central open arch flanked by the front halves of two round towers, and on either side two low walls end in square towers. The tops are castellated; it is about 40 feet high, all made of roughly-dressed stone with smooth-dressed frames

Ralph Allen's sham castle

to the rows of blind windows and arrowslits. This is one of the best, and best known, sham castles in the country.

Besides Sanderson Miller's, there is an extraordinary number of other sham castles; sometimes it seems as if every estate in England must have had its counterfeit fortification, complete or artfully ruined, a little bit of Olde England among the pheasant preserves. The memory calls up a few of them very clearly, and then a host of lesser ones pop anonymously into the mind, like chess rooks, dull big stone castles, pretty little brick ones, well preserved shams near the house, crumbling stumps in the woods, round, square or triangular.

Sometimes the memory calls up the trees that choke them more clearly than the follies themselves, as at Hackfall Woods near Grewelthorpe, landscaped on a natural site as fine as Hawkstone's, but entirely different in atmosphere, the follies built with a less sure hand, a little weak for the magnificent setting. It is now almost entirely overgrown, and we must see it first through other eyes.

Twentieth-century guide books do not mention Hackfall, nineteenth-century ones praise the woods; only the eighteenth-century ones have glowing descriptions of artificial ruins, so it seemed unlikely that much could be left of Mr Casmey's Gala Day. I asked a woman the way, and it was through that gate into the dullest of flat fields with a straggle of copse running beside them on the left, and a few cows, rough grazing. If not ducal planting with its five-mile avenues and distant pavilions, Hackfall must once have had at least what our notebooks call gents' relish, but here there is no trace of any landscaping at all. Beside the third field, however, the wood gets thicker and suddenly there is a sham castle on the edge of it, an irregular stone one with a tufa doorway, . dilapidated castellations and the usual arrow-slits, windows and buttresses. Inside the corners half-columns of Roman cement are neatly scored with rustications. It is, one feels, a regulation bad folly, oak-tree background, curious details, rank grass foreground, all the standard equipment of the ill-considered sham, carelessly placed and roughly finished, making or offering no view. From the inside, though, a path goes into the wood, and suddenly it is obvious that we have come in the back way. The castle was to be seen from this side, not from the fields; here the woods are in John Martin's style, the flat pasture has become the steep gorge of the Ure with another valley joining it, and the ruin though still dull is wonderfully set on a bluff above their junction. The path slants slowly down the side of the gorge and 20 feet from the top of the cliff Yorkshire has vanished; the sheltered semi-tropical coves of south Cornwall are the nearest thing to Hackfall. The woods fall sheer, hot and damp; there are ferns six feet high, and black earth, sundews and rushes, the whole hillside is quivering with water. Further on, as we look back, we see that the main part of the woods is behind us, that the path is zig-zagging to lose height and will turn back on itself along the bottom of the valley; a short cut down a treeless gap will save a lot, for here the descent is easier than the undergrowth of the path, steep, but with trees at the bottom to catch one's fall. Here the one who suggests the short cut should be sent ahead. He will plunge down at a great rate and clutch at the branches of the nearest oak, which is now, too late, seen to be covered with suspicious long beards of moss. The dead wood cracks, and a tourbillion of branches, arms, legs and cameras goes on to the bottom. When the clouds of pale green dust have settled, the rest of the party can descend on all fours: everywhere the trees are dead, and break under the hand. At river level everything is a waste of giant burdock, but some of the trees are alive. Just up from the bottom is Fisher's Hall, a stone octagonal pavilion with a damaged hipped roof and a beautifully cut gothic door over which is carved W.A. 1750. The domed ceiling is made of local tufa and other water-accretions. At the bottom of the valley, there are fewer trees and the path is easier to follow, across stepping stones and past a grotto of tufa and jagged rocks at the edge of a clearing, with a pool under the trees, and all the ground thick mint and thyme instead of grass. The open beauties of the poem are lost in dead trees and their parasites, a whole valley of decay and rotting grass round an oasis of thyme. A path goes up the side of the valley opposite the castle. On one side is a stone half-octagon block house—Sand Bed

A VOICE FROM HACKFALL.

Welcome thrice welcome, strangers all,
That visit me the famed Hackfall—
Yea, welcome as the bloom of May
To celebrate our Gala Day !
Welcome art thou O aged sire
Whose silvery locks all must admire,
And thou fair matron by his side,
His helpmate on life's stormy tide !
And manly youth and blooming maid,
Thrice welcome to our woodland shade,
Where stands the veteran the oak,
That long has stood old tempest's stroke;
Also the stately ash you'll see
With arms out-stretched to welcome ye
To view Dame Nature's works of art,
Which you'll find here in every part,
Mix't with the handy work of man
Upon a grand romantic plan.
You'll find not far down in the glade
The Alum Spring, a grand cascade,
Whose silvery stream appears to sing
An anthem to the bloom of spring,
And on its rippling harp to play
A welcome to our Gala Day.
Now turn thy steps towards the right,
And view that grand imposing sight--
Tis Mowbray Castle, in decay,
The relics of a by-gone day;
Whilst shelving rocks on which it stands
Look awful, yet majestic grand ;
If that old Castle could unfold
The deeds it witnessed of old
No doubt to what it would give vent,
Would fill us with astonishment
But as it can' t, we' ll pass along
Whilst songsters welcome you with song—
And squirrels on the branches play,
Their frolics on our Gala Day !
Let Sand Bed Hut attention call,
From thence pass on to Fisher's Hall,
And Lime House Hill you'll find a treat,
Then rest awhile on the green seat --
Where River Ure comes rolling by
In silver vested majesty.
Next at the splendid grotto call,
In front of the great Water Fall--
Whose crystal stream with brilliant crest,
Flows gleeful from Dame Nature's breast,
And sings its little child-like song
As joyfully it rolls along.

Now here we must stop once again
To view the pretty Fountain Plain,
Where if you had the mind and will
And music, might dance a quadrille,
And when you're weary of the dance,
Behold now what a charming chance
To rest, the rustic temple neat
Is here, where you can have a seat,
And when recruited, once again
We'll pass along unto Tent Plain—
Lo here the Weeping Rock appears,
Showering forth her crystal tears;
Let not her tears your sports annoy,
Perhaps she weeps but tears of joy
To help to wash dull care away
From Hackfall on our Gala Day.
But here's Mount Pleasant just in view,
A place more pleasing far to you,
But at a proper distance keep,
Nor try to jump the Lover's Leap.
To Mowbray Point at last we've got,
A very interesting spot,
As here you stand for miles you see
A very charming scenery,
Of miles of rich and fertile land,
All variegated and most grand:--
Hambleton's Hills from here you view,
And famed Roseberry Topin too,
Tanfield and Kirklington you'll see,
With Pickhill, also Baldersby;
York Minster too, tho' far away,
Is seen from here on a clear day.
Now friends look round you till you tire,
And then there's one thing I desire,
That's if you'll be advised by me
To go and take a cup of tea,
And with some friendly neighbour talk,
About each spring and zig zag walk ;
Of castle bold and grotto neat,
And thank LORD RIPON for the treat,
Pray that his Lordship may have health
To live and taste the sweets of wealth,
And that his LADY long may be,
Sharer of his felicity—
Whilst their dear children try to bless
The noble pair with happiness.
Now in conclusion, let me say,
I hope you've past a happy day,
So now good-bye, yea, one and all,
Whilst I am truly yours, HACKFALL.

MAY, 1859.

BY JAMES CASMEY, NAIL MAKER, GRUELTHORPE

J. H. Taylor, Printer, 28a, Market Place, Ripon.

Hut, perhaps—a folly in the palaeolithic taste, made of huge lumps of stone, raftered with whole trees and roofed with more slabs, these thickly grown with grass. Indeed from this point on the vegetation is indomitable all the way up the cliff—there are even too many hart's-tongues, and the rosebay willowherb, unlike the pretty pink spikes on open sites in London, meets overhead, and its untidy downy seeds cover everything; they fill the mouth, the eyes, the ears, veil the blackberries and hide the follies. But the top of the hill is clear at last and a beautiful folly is on the summit, placed just like the sham castle opposite, gorge in front and pasture behind, though here the Janus landscape is echoed in a two-faced folly, which was probably the refreshment room in Mr Casmey's day.

In the woods is a stone alcove set between two arches, the alcove taller and broken away so that it remains itself only a tall arch of rough stones. Out in the fields it is a demure classical façade with gothick windows and doors above which can be seen the tree-grown arches. This part has three little rooms with lovely ogee alcoves, black and white on dark green walls, and, black on every light surface, white on every dark, all the regular folly graffiti, tiny pencilled rhymes and huge chalk drawings, like a railway waiting room. One ceiling has fallen in.

A hundred years after its creation, as we know, Hackfall was in its prime, the trees full grown, the paths and green seats trimmed, but a second century has destroyed it. The buildings except for Mowbray Castle and the double folly at Mowbray Point are small and dull (a last little dullard is also at Mowbray Point, only stone walls with gothick windows left, pretty with sunset on its golden stone, but nothing in any other light), and the patch of warm climate that made the woods so rich has now destroyed them; from above, their green crowns still billow finely up and down the two steep valleys,

The double folly at Mowbray Point, Hackfall

but underneath moss chokes everything. The death of the trees, and the overwhelming life of ferns, rushes, grasses, dock, mullein, moss, foxgloves, peppermint, thyme, willow-herb, everything larger and thicker and greener than normal, and the hidden situation below the level of the ordinary Pennine-foothill landscape, all give Hackfall an extraordinary atmosphere, as if the river-bed had sunk with the woods and everyone forgotten where they were.

A very firm and positive folly, hard purplish-black like an aubergine or a round box of pills from the chemist, the absolute antithesis of Hackfall, was built at about the same time, 1750, just outside Bristol. William Reeve was a copper-smelter, a Quaker like Thomas Goldney, and he built for himself a beautiful gothick house at Brislington during the 1740s, very elegant and restrained—it would be nice to know the name of the architect. A castle air is lightly achieved by castellating the top of the house and the porch, which also has a gothick door and ogival niches on each side, while the pediment and icicle-rusticated pilasters remain classical, as do the windows and the smooth rustication of the ground floor. Then back to gothick for the glazing bars and pretty ogees above the first floor windows—an enchanting blend, which, however, did not satisfy Mr Reeve for long, because in 1750 he got a vast quantity of copper slag in blocks from the smelting works at Crew's Hole just over the Avon, and built a black castle for stables on the other side of the Bath-Bristol road. All semblance of connection between the two, of a well-run estate, has gone. The main road tears through, there is a tram depot on another corner, and the stables, Arnos Castle, belong to Bristol Corporation Tramways; club rooms, canteen, and bowling green.

This is set back from the road, a sham castle on something approaching a true castle plan—a rectangle of castellated wall enclosing a courtyard, with a tall round tower at

Arnos Castle

Arnos Castle and, right*, its bath-house*

each corner, a square one over the entrance and, across the court, a rectangular keep. It is big, absolutely crisp and new, made of the black sheeny blocks and trimmed with white, mortar courses, pinnacles, castellations, windows and great white crosses like the Swiss flag. The detail of doors, windows and crockets is very delicate, but the stone is still sharp and all seems very solid. On the south side, enclosed by a high wall, are the smooth rinks of the bowling green, the gentle calls of skip, the click of the woods and their occasional trundle into the pebble verges. In front of the barbaric façade, the slow angular dance of the players continues all afternoon, the weaving to and fro on one leg to speed the true run of a wood, and the mimic pats and exhortations of a partner who, at the far end, knows that *he* could have done better, got closer to the jack, scattered the opponents, but is still willing to influence the end of the run with ritual gestures and to calm, with an almost papal benediction of his upraised palm, the bowler who is now following the curved path of his wood in a slow motion run usually only seen in experimental films.

The bowlers have decorated the interior of Arnos Castle very nicely. They love it, and it is clearly in safe hands. At first they may have regretted so unusual a club house but now they are proud of it, and recount tales of the days when Mr Reeve's house became a convent and the nuns of old came under the road by a secret passage to bathe. 'The Devil's Cathedral, this place is called, the Devil's Cathedral.' But its strangeness is friendly, almost cosy: there could be no more unsuitable name; it has a note of peevishness, even. Perhaps . . . yes. Horace Walpole came in 1766: 'I was struck with a large Gothic building, coal black and striped with white, I took it for the Devil's Cathedral. I found it was a uniform castle lately built and serving for stables, and offices to a smart false Gothic house on the other side of the road.' Walpole's lightest word, like Johnson's, lasts a long time.

The Bath House was added in 1760 and stood at the end of the bowling green and a little netted vegetable garden, between Arnos and the road, from which it looked very delicate and pretty; road-widening threatened it, and it has now fortunately been re-erected at Portmeirion by Clough Williams-Ellis. There is a colonnade with a curved centre and two wings which end in little square pavilions, orientally domed. The columns arc in slender groups of four with foliated, almost feathered, capitals, and the pavilions have elaborate gothick doors. These pleasingly prove to be false, carved in the solid stone. In front, on the grass, stands a stone coat-of-arms, lion, unicorn, crown and wreaths of flowers. Inside were several once pretty rooms and a most beautiful bathroom with an open arcade of cusped ogival arches and a coved ceiling over the sunk bath. The plaster-work of this ceiling, by Thomas Patey the Bristol plasterer, was of the greatest elegance, a wreathing of waves and masks, shells and dolphins, which, like all good rococo, had some details in lower relief to give the third dimension, creating here and there a complete world seen through the framing flourishes. Below the ceiling a pro-jecting moulding ran round supported on alternating corbels and acanthus leaves; each corbel was resting on a little caryatid head, a series of different faces round the wall. All, alas, in the past tense for the plaster-work fell before the removal.

Outside on the road stands a huge gate in Mr Reeve's most oriental-classical-gothick manner. As this is held to be one of the old city gates, error may preserve it, but its only link with true antiquity was four mediaeval statues (perhaps from a real town gate) which were put up in some of the niches in 1769 and taken away again in 1898.

The gate is tall and flat, a triumphal arch that has been under a steam roller, set in a negligible wire fence; behind it is the elaborate coat-of-arms, equally flat, and then the delicate screen of the Bath House and, last, beyond the green, the bold Castle; one, two, three, four like the paper figures that stand up inside a valentine, though here the four figures are in jumbled styles and sizes, a valentine from a chic little interior decorator's shop that sells pretty trifles for Christmas presents, mended and cannibalized, but this one has been stuck up wrong. It is disoriented, too, among the tram lines and waste grassland, grown with ragwort and old iron, that lies beside and behind it instead of a fine park. Other follies throw down welcoming bits of flint and rubble to the advancing weeds, thus leaving gaps in their walls as flowerpots for more weeds; the ironwork of their staircases and railings bends to meet the brambles and slowly the whole folly will fall into the landscape. But Arnos Castle regrets the tidy days, and sits tightly drawn in on itself, having nothing to do with the waste. Only on the neat bowling green side does the vigilant black and white surface permit an ornamental pyrus japonica or two.

I think we may presume William Reeve to have been a self-made man—he was a copper-smelter, not merely the son of one, and cannot have had much time for touring Europe and collecting culture. Yet he achieved a very pretty house, he employed Thomas Patey very successfully, evidently giving him, the little corbel heads might be argued to show, a rather freer hand than most patrons, and in Arnos Castle he used a new medium magnificently, taking, which few did, a plan that looks completely medi-aeval on paper and building on it the most startlingly bold and assured walls. Probably he had an architect, for the details of the stonework are very accomplished (though a good mason in those days could do wonders by himself), but the slag idea was all his own, and the result is a work of art that travels in Italy could not have bettered.

Croome Court, Hereford and Worcester, has every kind of estate embellishment, Grotto, Bridge, Temple and Panorama, all by Robert Adam, a Prospect Tower, a Sham Castle and one of those inaccessible, boxy little temples whose names on the estate maps,

in this case 'The Owl's House', draw one for a mile or two across the hot fields for almost nothing.

George William, 6th Earl of Coventry, was responsible for all this. He also married the most beautiful of the Gunning sisters, who died of consumption at Croome eight years later. His second Countess was a woman of great common sense, who, when Broadway Tower was suggested as an improvement for the view from Croome, caused a beacon to be lighted on the top of Broadway Hill fifteen miles away to make sure that a tower would indeed be visible, thus breaking the pleasant folly tradition that at least a hundred feet of solid hilltop must intercept the line of vision between any tower and either its object or its builder. This tower also has a rather excessive list of counties visible from the summit, thirteen instead of the usual modest seven. It was built in 1797, a castellated and machicolated hexagon with three taller round towers at alternate angles. The design is remarkably ugly, and the stonework, efficient consistently with the Countess and the county-list, is starkly well preserved.

Closer to Croome is Dunstall, a sham castle, the exact antithesis of the tower, with no date, no story, no view, no picture postcards, very beautiful and solitary, standing by the road over Defford Common among black stooks of beans. It is the perfect example of one of the best kinds of folly, that created a new kind of architecture instead of trying to copy the Middle Ages—Dunstall pays only the vaguest tribute to gothic themes.

Three enormously tall towers of rough-hewn pale stone, two round and one square, one ruined and two almost complete, stand joined in an obtuse angle by two hollow walls, each pierced with a soaring arch almost as high as the towers, one round-headed, the other with five lights.

At some time two cottages seem to have been built against the folly, but these are gone now, and so has the plaster that may have finished the arches, unless they were designed to appear hollow as they do now, so that one can look up the great cavities to the top. The central tower has the remains of a spiral staircase and of an extra turret-storey. The castellations are almost rotted away with weather and weeds, there are cracks and fallen stones but the castle has the certainty and calm of all beautiful buildings, which is increased in the best follies by the fact that no utilitarian purpose need dilute them; often architects are unable to use this freedom, and the folly looks meaningless and forlorn, but a few, like Dunstall and Slindon, stir a singing elation on a fine day, the quality of summer warmth and the smell of poppies.

Another mood for a sham castle is summer twilight in the cooler air of Wales; Clytha Castle in Gwent is the perfect castle for this hour, for it faces to the north in front of high dark trees, pale without sunshine, an almost moonlit folly on a low hill. The façade consists of two huge fat towers, round on the left, square on the right, joined by a low wall that sweeps up between them to a point in what can only be called an inverted pendentive. Behind the square tower is a tall slim round one, and behind that again a low tower like a drum. All the tops are castellated, and the central point of the wall ends in a tiny square turret. Big quatrefoils and arrow-slits like gigantic key-holes alternate with the windows.

Even the obvious decay of the round tower does not prepare us for the open, nettle-grown court behind it where the sun catches the back of the tower and the thin wall; we

The sham castle at Dunstall

expect the fabric of follies to be ruinous and preservation is always a surprise, but the façade of Clytha is neat, and the neglected court is unbelievably sad. The square tower has an entrance here, to two rooms about 20 feet square, the upper one, which is reached by a spiral stair, being of the greatest elegance, with pretty plasterwork and faded colour. The shutters of the gothick windows open with the faint tearing of hundreds of webs on to the view down towards the house. In the field below a bull appears and shows far too much interest in the neglected camera, but the sadness of the place is unbroken, sticky and resilient as the spiders' webs.

A tablet on the wall explains:

> This building was erected in 1790 by William Jones of Clytha House, fourth son of John Jones of Lanarth Court, the last surviving child of Sir Wm. Morgan of Tredegar. It was undertaken to relieve a mind sincerely afflicted by the loss of a most excellent wife whose remains were deposited in Lanarth churchyard A.D. 1787 and to the memory of whose virtues this tablet is dedicated.

(June 1974. Changes; the cobwebs and the fallen plaster have gone, and a big notice declares that Clytha Castle Folly is being restored by the Landmark Trust.)

Clytha and Ralph Allen's façades are examples of the eyecatcher type of sham castle put up for private or public pleasure on a hilltop, and they show well the normal style and size. But some people were much more ambitious.

At Bladon in Derbyshire is a very large red brick castle of 1790, as impressive a house as most would wish. It is in fact a folly, Hoskins' Folly, a sham castle built on the hilltop to be seen from a smaller Georgian house, now gone. In 1801 or 1802 Mr Hoskins tried to turn it into a house, but could not find water. He was another of the folly builders who really did go bankrupt.

Here is Bladon in 1854:

> Finely situate on the crest of an extended eminence, overlooking an almost boundless prospect towards the west, as well as the east, and distinguished by an aspect of striking picturesqueness, stands the well-wooded mansion, whose castellated fabric has received the designation prefixed . . . This stately-looking and agreeable residence was originally erected, about the year 1801, in the form of a mere prospect-building, and consisted of vacant walls, and of external representations of towers, and of other characteristic features of a genuine pile of Gothic architecture; but it was afterwards, at very considerable expense, converted into a commodious and elegant habitation by the tasteful owner, Abraham Hoskins, Esq., whose spacious and handsome abode, with its ample shrubberies and park like grounds, added an ornamental character to the valley beneath, while it presented also a conspicuous object, as seen from the far extended level country bordering the Trent. The late Mr. Hoskins . . . was celebrated for his fine breed of greyhounds, and for the unusual magnitude and superior arrangement of his agricultural premises; while his extensive and skilfully constructed hothouses were equally the subject of admiration throughout the neighbourhood. Few gentlemen have been more justly noted for the maintenance of a liberal style of hospitality, or for the exercise of a quiet, unobtentious course of benevolence.[1]

[1] R. Bigsby, *History of Repton,* 1854.

Clytha Castle

Bladon

Here is Bladon in 1971: the drive runs up to a gatehouse with two octagon towers, set in a wall that ends with two big three-storey castellated square towers, enough sham castle for most builders all by itself, but inside, the work runs round three sides of a rectangle well over 200 feet long, with the main front of the folly to the left, a noble pile of castellated keeps, an arcade and turrets, and more wall and a nice round cobby tower ahead. The view from the front would have been towards the house across park and country, but from the back, dropping sharply from a terrace, is a finer view over superb beeches towards Burton-on-Trent. This face, long and simple between the big square towers, made up with the gatehouse the original folly. The tall octagon towers, the central block of rooms, the arcade of Tudor windows, the rest of the walls and the round tower were the work of 1801. A small wing on the gatehouse side and a bay window in the middle of the Stoke front were added in the 1890s in another attempt towards habitation and the wing is now a house and very snug, though Mr Hoskins' main attempt at a house is roofless, mostly floorless, and derelict, probably the result of fire. But it is a very noble pile, precluded by brick as its material from the true rust of the Barons' Wars, but certainly one of the finest follies in England.

For contrast in scale, a small castle to be seen from a very large house, there is a pretty stone gothick folly at Milton Abbey in Dorset. The ruins of the original Abbey, with their little town of Milton Abbas, were much admired in the eighteenth century, and Joseph Damer must have been envied when he bought them in 1752. But after he was made Lord Milton in 1754 he amazingly pulled down most of the ruins to take the fine site for his new house (by Sir William Chambers), and also took down the village, which was far too encroaching, though he had to break the dam of his half-finished lake and wash away the resistant villagers to do it. He built a new village running up the hill, with chestnut trees set between the cottages (until these were taken down it was the prettiest model village in England). But there was still some stone left over after all this, and in about 1790 he put up a new ruin, suitably ecclesiastical in style across the lawns from the house at the edge of a wood, beautifully built from dressed stone with no damned scholarship, but with every folly trimming including a yew on each side and a dead tree. It is particularly interesting because it is one of the very few follies for which the original design exists; many of them look as if they were built from verbal instructions or at most a scribble and it is of course part of their charm. But here there is a pen and wash drawing in the RIBA collection and, stranger still, the actual folly even after 180 years, is more elaborate than the design (Chambers again?). This shows only a stretch of ruined wall, with one pointed door and window, ending on the right in an octagon turret with the stump of a conical spire, decorated with neat projecting stones. The actual building has no window, but two spires which were once finished and given finial crosses, a much taller arch and a castellated gable-end over it with a big trefoil. Moreover, behind are long side walls with doors and windows and a chapel to the west. A pretty folly with an odd history.

The design for the folly at Milton Abbey

Rockingham. The castle on the lake.

Two of the best sham castles are at Rockingham in Roscommon.

This was one of John Nash's finest houses, built for the King family in 1810. It has had two fires, but remains triumphantly beautiful with some lovely details. The demesne now belongs jointly to the Forestry Commission and the Tourist Board, and is a quarter-hearted public park. So far, though some magnificent planting has been cut down and whole wildernesses of saplings allowed their freedom, the beauty of the level landscaping early on a spring morning still triumphs.

There is a wide serene lake and an island in it, and on the island trees and a sham castle with a tall turret reflecting in the water, a Ludwig dream.

On the island are yews, pines, ivy and some later laburnums and the two-storey castle, built of rendered brick trimmed with stone. Some plasterwork remains inside and there are fireplaces—there will have been moonlight processions by boat to dine; it is easy to dismiss accounts of the special quality of moonlight in Ireland, caused by the damp air, and of how the great yew gardens were planted to be seen in just this light, a few times each summer, but the accounts are true; the moonlight here *is* different, a little warmer and the shadows richer.

The front of the castle has a central bow with the door and three pointed windows for the grand room upstairs, and a semicircle of castellated wall enclosing a raised garden. At the back are turrets, one square low and one square tall.

On the shore of the lake, within easy reach of the house is a round castellated pavilion set out in the lake, for fishing and for a fine view of the castle. The interior was probably decorated; it is now very plain with ridiculous rough-cast, and slat seats, but the roof has been beautifully restored with planks tapering to a circular centre.

The park is very large and has several lodges; one is a colonnade curved backwards, with pediment to match, like its name, Tiara. And there is a good rustic bridge of amusing rockwork.

The best thing, though, is to catch sight from the castle island of a turret across the lake and far in the woods, and track down the second castle, quite lost even among bare trees; probably even the turret top is invisible in summer, for it is a mile from a road,

Rockingham. Above, *the castle in the woods;* Below, *details from it.* Bottom left, *the castle on the island;* Right, *a grotto bridge.*

and two miles from the house. It faces full south, a big castellated fort 75 feet square, with a square lightly battered tower at each corner, all different, all different heights. An arch in the front wall with sliding portcullis gates with the date 1839 leads into the overgrown courtyard and opposite, across the full width of the yard is a series of ruined rooms behind a fine wall with blind rectangular windows, the upper ones painted sham, and a central round one over the door (on the outside of the east wall are four more painted windows, white on black). This wall is so well detailed that it probably fronted finely decorated rooms, but the inside was turned into a keeper's cottage long ago and was lived in until the mid 1960s.

The back towers are the biggest, one castellated in crowsteps; the other, tallest, takes a spiral stone stair for the view, and probably also—for there is a door—on to a walk above the rooms, there and back again.

In seven years the woods have begun to take over, and there are saplings everywhere, in the courtyard, and springing on the towers, and there is a fine frosting of white lichen on the castellations. So far, all is well, but the little trees must go soon or they will win.

Just as gothick began when gothic was still a surviving style, so the gothic revival, when scholarship replaced fantasy, began before gothick had run its course. There is a late castle by the sea at Donaghadee in County Down which seems to point the change, a half-way castle built by the squire in 1818. Scholarship may have recommended the site, a mound said to have been the motte of a late Norman castle (and certainly suitably placed for one), and also the little keep with its central circular tower looks much closer to Windsor Castle than to Vanbrugh's work at Castle Howard a century earlier. There are two little square towers of one storey each with round-headed windows, the larger with its castellated drum and four octagon turrets linked to the smaller, which received only one turret, so that the most picturesque view was from the sea. Below, extending the composition down the steep mound, is a piece of castellated walling with the remains of a bastion, and there is a brick bastion-lookout on the shore below. It is absurd that anything so tiny should recall Penrhyn, but the flavour is there.

Meanwhile, as gothick followed its tough or elegant, amateur or professional, solid or gimcrack course through the eighteenth century, wilder styles for follies were being both proposed and executed.

The sham castle at Donaghadee

The Folly Style:
Flints and Irregular Stones

GROTESQUE ARCHITECTURE or RURAL AMUSEMENT

consisting of plans, elevations and sections for

Huts	Cascades
Retreats	Baths
Summer and Winter Hermitages	Mosques
Terminaries	Moresque Pavilions
Chinese, Gothic and Natural	Grotesque and Rustic Seats
Grottoes	Green Houses, etc.

Many of which may be executed with
Flints, Irregular Stones, Rude Branches, and Roots of Trees

was written by William Wrighte and published in 1767. It was by no means the first folly pattern book (Batty Langley's *Gothic Architecture improved by Rules and Proportions In many Grand Designs* had come out in 1742 and there are dozens of others), but it is certainly one of the most charming, a small book of 28 engraved plates of conceits and a frontispiece showing a park (with grotto, ruin and Moorish temple) where a gentleman and his architect, hermits and workmen are all busy about the grotesque. Underneath is a typical piece of easy Verse, incomprehensible but Grand:

> Where Severn, Trent or Thames's Ouzy side
> Pours the Smooth Current of their easy Tide,
> Each will require a sameness to the Spot,
> For this a Cell, a Cascade or a Grot;
> The Moss, or gliding Streams productive Store,
> To grace the Building on the Verdant Shore,
> There the rough Tuscan, or the Rustic fix
> Or Pebbles, Shells or calcin'd Matter mix,
> The frozen Isicles resembled form
> Or Sea-green Weed your Grotto must adorn.

Plate I shows the smallest and cheapest Hut, 10 foot 9 inches square, made of trees and lined with moss, 'intended to represent the primitive state of the Dorick Order'. A Hermitic Retreat, also made of trees but twined with ivy is little different, but the Hermit's Cell has seating alcoves on either side and a skull over the door, while an

A design for a Rural Bath from Grotesque Architecture.

Oriental Hermitage is getting quite complicated; it is built round a central tree which comes out at the top like a chimney brush, has a tablet in Arabic, a roof in the Chinese taste, a couch, and seats of retirement. The Winter Hermitage should be 'lined with wool or other warm substance intermixed with moss' but the Summer one only needs an owl placed on the top and a floor 'paved with sheeps' marrowbones placed upright, or any other pretty device'. The Augustine Hermitage (classical) and the Rural Hermitage made of trees with a gazebo above are still moderately economical, but a Modern Grotto requires a bath, tufa and a shell ceiling, while a Gothic Grotto has no less than six rooms lined with shells. The Chinese Grotto on Plate XI is already beyond the gentry estate, 75 feet long, 'to be placed at the head of a grand canal, with a bath (A), and a Chinese temple (B) attached'; a second Gothic Grotto with Cascade and wings is entirely ducal, covered with shells, gems, coral and statues. A Rural Grotto of rough rude stone to be set 'in a morass, near some water' is certainly less ambitious, but a Triumphal Cascade has four walls, a Romantic one three and 'two sea gods lying on their oozy couch', all clearly considerable undertakings. Then, before all but the richest clients have taken fright, we are shown a simple Rustic Seat and a Grotesque or Rural Bath, a sort of wig-wam with dishmops sticking up on top, containing merely three seats and a central water. These, however, are but sops, for huge Rural, Circular, and Turkish Mosques follow, with minarets, cabinets, little domes, and a 'fountain for sabateons'.

The Moresque Temple has 'Moors heads with crescents, roses and stars . . . on top is a pine, which should be double gilt . . . style of architecture is a medium between the Chinese and Gothic, having neither the levity of the former nor the gravity of the latter'. The design is acknowledged to the Alhambra, 'the old cassavee'.

Plate XXVII is the most endearing nonsense of all, a Moresque Pavilion of the great-est gaiety, rising lightly round an open spiral staircase, a gothic fretwork floor between two classical ones, just touching the fringe of the orient with a few plaster moors' heads and a pennant on the top. The book ends with a greenhouse, zigzag arcades of rough stonework absolutely smothered with plants in pots.

Grotesque Architecture has that absolute conviction which is as rare in fantasy as it is common in causes. Almost anyone seems able to throw assurance into his voice up-raised on religion, race, politics, or the superiority of handicraft over the machine, and the plain mediaevalism of a routine sham castle sometimes gets a share of conviction, too, but writing, painting, filming or building a credible fairy-tale is probably the most difficult thing that a sophisticated artist can undertake. Brighton Pavilion has this quality, a certainty that makes all the surrounding bowfronted houses and cast iron piers become themselves the unreality while the folly Pavilion sits shining in the middle of them all, a serene fact.

Charles Hamilton achieved it at Pain's Hill, which has this same effect on Surrey, and Hawkstone in Salop is another estate which shakes the reality of its surroundings, a landscaped park more completely in the spirit of *Grotesque Architecture* than any of the more rugged landscapings of the later eighteenth century; by now the aim of the pic-turesque was wildness.

To begin with it was probably done very rapidly, workmen and architects and churned-up earth and new hills all over the place just like the frontispiece of the book, for Sir Richard Hill only inherited the estate from his father Sir Rowland, first baronet, in 1783, and the present Lord Hill has a beautiful black book of most exquisite watercolour drawings, a Survey and Particulars of the Manor, which shows that most of the existing conceits, as well as the destroyed heather-hermitage and moss temple, were all there in 1787, though of course it is always possible that the painter ran a little ahead of perform-ance.

The map shows that the natural site was perfect, with water, a complex arrangement of hills, a lot of red sandstone and a real castle. This and the work done to it are probably as fine now as they have ever been, a piece of picturesque landscaping in the naturalistic style that uses even its conversion into a golf course to advantage, for the great green sweeps are thus well cared for, and from the heights of Grotto Hill the little figures of the golfers with their tiny cries and red flags animate the scene without annoyance—and the park has neither the abandoned solitude nor the municipal over-population, necessi-tating railings, notices and asphalt paths, that make, one or other of them, the atmo-sphere of most parks today. Naturally one will not abandon decay, never admit for a moment a failure of sensibility towards desolation (and rotten leaves do indeed best frame the folly), but the liveliness of Hawkstone on a sparkling summer morning is all enchantment; this is what the creators of the parks were aiming at, a sunny green peace with the macabre well hidden, a shock round the corner devised chiefly to point up the gaiety and calm of the landscape. Today, seeing only that abandoned or municipal melancholy in almost every park we visit, it is easy to accept melancholy as the intended mood; many of the great estates have now become so sombre that the effect of the follies is reversed, and an Awful Ruin, discovered suddenly, gives no delicious thrill of fear but a moment's cheerful release in curiosity from the heavy sadness of the rides and woods.

Hawkstone has four diverse hills and a series of valleys and open glades between them. 'The Walks', says the Survey, 'are continually assuming new forms and varying their outlines so as to appear as different parts of the country from what you have passed, constantly exhibiting something new and shifting between the grand, the magnificent, the soft and the sublime.' On the way from the Hotel and Clubhouse (the Hills' original house is now separated from the park) the landscape is open and flowing, with a little lake. The wooded Elysian Hill, which has no conceits, rises on the right and Red Castle further on to the left. Here there is a big outcrop of rocks piled up through some very picturesque oaks, and the quite genuine red sandstone ruins of a mediaeval castle, bolstered up with bogus fortifications and half a dozen little look-out towers on rocky eminences. There is a deep ravine in the rock with a dark semi-circular opening at one end, an ice-house perhaps, called the Dungeon. Once down, it is practically impossible to climb up the sides of the ravine and at the other end the way is blocked by a stone wall, but the trap is counterfeit, and a little cleft in the rock leads to a tunnel, and out to the hillside again. The ruin was once extensive and there is a good view of the cliffs and pine trees of Grotto Hill beyond.

From the lower slopes of this, however, a rock bridge with wooden handrails takes one first across the Gulph 'calculated to inspire solemnity', and on to the Terrace Hill. Here the path rises, over thick dead leaves under beech trees, and swings to the right under a wall of rock covered with bright green moss. Rhododendrons close in, the level of the rocks rises and the path becomes a little ravine, all moss and splashes of sunlight, and out on to a clearing. Suddenly a gorge 30 feet deep cuts up into the hillside, imposing a cathedral hush which cannot be kept, for the dead leaves rustle deafeningly. The ravine

View of the Grotto Rock.

Citadel.

flattens out, and the cliff-top path sweeps on through the rhododendrons up to a column of solid unfluted doric in red sandstone on a huge square pedestal. A staircase spirals darkly to the top and straight out on to the flat undefended abacus of the capital. Above, on top of the staircase lantern, are the feet and toga-tails of a statue, but these are not visible from the ground. The views are superb. The house is still invisible but the Red Castle dower house, 'The Citadel', shows to the south-west. The abacus is swarming with ants; do they climb the staircase for the view? Or, if they live here, what do they eat? Perhaps ants are less dreary than one had thought?

A little red tower among the trees can be marked for general direction; there may be a path, but the rhododendrons are thick everywhere. This is the White Tower shown in a painting on vellum in the Survey, but today the tower is red—red brick on a red sandstone plinth. From a distance it is a crude romanticism, the most simple castellated octagon, but the details, the slight recession of alternate walls, the cornice, and above all the very elegant classical door with a gothick frieze in the entablature, are all most delicate, and so is the plasterwork inside, soft dark faded red on pale green walls, where the mixture of styles continues most satisfactorily, key-pattern frieze and classical cornice, then ogees over windows and a gothick central feature in the coved octagonal ceiling.

From the tower, the paths continue; one has steps cut in the sandstone, along a naturally worn balcony and round a steep ravine. It is a foot wide, with a sheer cliff on one side and a 60 foot drop on the other. Only the tops of the oak trees below provide a false sense of security (there is a safer path through the shrubs), and it is clear that drama is ahead.

Hawkstone. Two early nineteenth century views and, right, *the White Tower.*

Back across the Gulph, a very trifling and unobtrusive path winds steeply up the back of Grotto Hill, pausing among the heavy rhododendrons at a semicircular stone seat, and then on through a cleft in the rock, thick with moss and ferns, floored with skeleton leaves, getting steadily darker and narrower. A great carved gothic stone lies across the path, which is then closed by the rock. The path cuts through it, opens again for a mo-

The LABYRINTH at HAWKSTONE
sketch plan

The Labyrinth

ment to the sky, and then runs straight into the rock face, into absolute darkness. The narrow tunnel is over 6 feet high, but the silence and blackness are so complete that it is difficult to walk upright under the intangible pressure of the rock. The tunnel winds on for nearly two hundred feet, but at last patches of mere darkness show in the black, and the tunnel turns into a round chamber lit faintly from a distant eye in the roof. The gloom and earthy terror are complete. At last the eye begins to pick out an enormous, clumsy, hewn arch; through it, the way divides and returns on each side. The rustications of the arch and the recess have been picked out with black paint lest sombreness somehow fail. Further on is another room, larger, with two exits and three false ones, lit again by dim eyes from the sky, hewn into vaults that arch straight down into four great piers of rock. The most hidden dark hole, squeezed behind the heaviest pier, opens at last to the green subterranean light of a gallery 80 feet long, still all in the rock, and supported by pillars cunningly cut to emphasise the natural strata, so that they spiral and twist uneasily away from us. Once the whole gallery was painted bright emerald green; much of the paint has gone—it is stronger at the far end, increasing the perspective—but even today it is the Palace of King Neptune from the pantomime.[1] Everywhere, round openings and lepers' slits give vistas into darker or brighter parts of the cave, through into the ruined grotto or up through sunbleached grass to the sky. One crevice in the roof leads to darkness filled with the rustling and squeaking of innumerable bats. At the far end of the gallery is an exit on to a series of rock galleries in the sun, but opposite the entrance from the labyrinth is another exit through the grotto, still cut in the rock but now well lit, a ruin; destroyed, says the proprietor of the hotel, by some cyclists who were refused tea. It is about 20 feet square with little caves at the sides. Once the rock pillars were covered with shells and stalactites and crystals, there was a dome of coloured glass, glass in the gothick fenestration of the door, and the 'wax effigy of the ancestor of a neighbour'. Now only a handful of shells remains, and the fossils of shells in the plaster. The empty door opens on to a terrace looking out over the sunny park, up the Elysian Hill. The drop is absolutely sheer. The Survey says:

> Through a part of this rock the present owner has with great exertions and much taste made an extensive cavern and grotto, supported within by several rude pillars which were left of the stone in forming it and curiously ornamented with spar petrifactions, stained and painted glass and other suitable appendages, and at the west end is a door opening to a gallery in the rock so immediate on the precipice as to strike the visitor with terror in looking down, and yet so far is it beneath the summit, that Ravens build their nests in the spontaneous growing wood on the Knob above, thence denominated the Ravens' Shelf.

Today, the Survey seems to have understated the cavern and overstated the gallery; perhaps the author suffered from vertigo—I am certainly afraid of the dark.

The outside of the grotto is partly natural rock and partly built up with blocks of stone to a craggy sky line. Above it is an arch, a fake ruin of red sandstone crowned with a weathered, sinister carving of a winged sphinx. On the terrace is a dead pine-tree, so perfect in this setting that one is convinced that it was deliberately killed.

There is also a Lion's Den in the park, though no account of lions. The Watch Tower, an arcaded Peacock House like an orangery, the Gothick Boathouse, a moss temple, the heather hermitage and Neptune's Whim, 'built at the foot of a windmill to look like Holland' are all gone. The menagerie had birds and monkeys, while black, white and golden rabbits ran about the park.

Most of these were done before 1784 by Sir Rowland. Another Sir Richard Hill who succeeded him landscaped a Swiss scene, a scene in Otaheite, an obelisk, the Tuscan column with the remains of Sir Rowland's feet (1785), a gothick sandstone summerhouse and several small towers and fortified walls, which remain only in fragments.

It must have been delightful to see the follies set off by animals which if not specially designed were at least chosen in special colours for them, though few gentlemen took

---

[1] The present owner of the Citadel suggests that the labyrinth was ready-made, a Roman copper mine, in which case the green colour could be natural. The Survey however expressly states, as we shall see, that the then owner made the excavations. The colour, though, is a very coppery green, and the labyrinth may have been painted with a preparation of some copper salt which would turn green after exposure to air, much as one of the hills in the Imperial City was coloured green in the time of Marco Polo.

such trouble to surround their fantasies with appropriate fauna; peacocks were common, there were zebras at the Jungle, and more recently Lord Berners dyed white pigeons pink and blue and green, but most follies seem to have been left to take their chance, and have attracted, along with the sere and prickly weeds they affect—teazles, briony and the rusty umbrellas of dead cow parsley—chiefly snails and moths. Not the big ones, the hard striped Hawkmoths or the great soft brown Lappet, Goat and Old Lady moths, not even the Gothic Moth, but hundreds of tiny dim moths, whose presence seems unsuitable till, remembering one a little richer in colour than the others, we attempt to look it up and find the names of the moths; Lunar Thorn, Isle of Wight Wave, Barrett's Marbled Coronet, Chinese Character, Iron Prominent, Lesser Lutestring, Mouse, Muslin, and Neglected; Dark Arches, Rosy Footman, Stranger, and Pale Shining Brown, Oblique Carpet; The Glaucous Shears, the False Mocha, the Satyr Pug, the Heart and Club, Clay, and the Lead-coloured Drab; the Confused, the Conformist, the Concolourous; the folly names—The Whim, White Nancy—are pedestrian beside them.

The Needle's Eye, though, is a good name, and a very beautiful folly. It is at Wentworth Woodhouse in South Yorkshire, a long way from the house, at the top of an

NEEDLE'S EYE

avenue of beeches and it is impossible to find out anything definite about it except the story, for once at least possible, that it was built when a crack whip claimed at a party that he could drive a coach and horses through the eye of a needle. This challenge was taken up and the rest of the night clearly spent in defining the eye of a needle. Agreement must have been reached, for here is the eye, a tall stone pyramid, black with soot, pierced from north to south by an ogival arch, faintly like part of a needle's eye and certainly terrifyingly narrow, for the apparent width has been further diminished with blocks of stone; it occurs to me that as well as a special eye there may well have been a special coach. Certainly, even without the blocks, the arch is too narrow to have been designed as a normal entrance gate, though it is most beautifully built of finely dressed stone and on top is a good flamboyant, but not flaming, urn, twined with flowers.

The Needle's Eye is part of a spectacular group of large and very well built follies that run across the estates of Wentworth Woodhouse and Wentworth Castle, with a Marker Obelisk between them, by A61 (the main Barnsley–Sheffield road), enclosed in a tiny garden of marigolds on the edge of a yard full of giant tip-up trucks. The earlier follies are at Wentworth Castle, erected by Thomas Wentworth, first Earl of Strafford of the second creation. At the entrance to the estate is Steeple Lodge, castellated and charming; its three-storey square tower has an ogival door and windows on the ground floor, quatrefoil windows on the second and pointed ones on the third. At each corner on top is a black pinnacle; Steeple Lodge is very like the church, which is near the house.

Up a fine lime avenue from the house is an obelisk, once crowned by a gilded sun,

TO THE MEMORY
OF THE RT. HON. LADY MARY WORTLEY MONTAGU
WHO IN THE YEAR 1720
INTRODUCED INOCULATION OF THE SMALL POX INTO ENGLAND FROM TURKEY.

From the obelisk a castellated wall runs by a wide grass ride towards the hilltop, to Stainborough Castle, one of the earliest and most elaborate gothick follies. Yew trees lead to a big oval enclosure, walled inside a dry moat. At intervals of about 100 feet are higher castellated square towers. Inside is a grass rampart with trees round a beautiful central lawn with daisies and a headless statue by Rysbrack of Lord Strafford standing in classical robes on a plinth up three wide steps. The inscription states that he was Viscount Wentworth de Wentworth Et de Stainborough, and Wentworth Castle was once called Stainborough, and the mound is the site of an ancient Danish camp, so a castle was clearly a necessity. In the *Leeds Art Calendar No. 66,* Mr T. F. Friedman attributes it to Gibbs, who was at Wentworth Castle in about 1725; this early date agrees with the

Wentworth Castle. Opposite, *Steeple Lodge beside the main road.* Below left, *Lord Strafford's headless statue, and* right, *Stainborough Castle.*

round-headed windows, and the very complicated design is obviously professional.

Stainborough had grown in stature by 1768 when it was referred to in 'The Rule of Taste' as the 'Ruins of a large imaginary City on an opposite hill, well placed . . . Nobody has a better taste than this lord.' By 1853 (*Stainborough and Rockley,* by the author of *Village Rambles*) it had diminished again and was regarded as a model, though an inscription read 'rebuilt in 1730', but admiration continued. Lord Strafford still had 'the expression of his features open and dignified', but the ivy was beating the castle, which had four big round towers. Now the back two are a pile of rubble; probably they were built less carefully than the two fine front ones, which are in stylish and massive gothick with the round-headed windows. Between them, the wall is pierced by a heavy boldly detailed arch—if not Gibbs, possibly Vanbrugh? The lawn runs up a ramp to the castle, and steps lead on to the arch. On the left is a room with the remains of plaster-work, on the right a spiral stair with thinning treads goes up to the roofless top and the splendid views, and another down in darkness to the ground floor of the other tower. There was once a rampart walk above the arch, and from the lower level of the lawn a bigger arch ran at right angles to the other under the whole castle; this, now part of the rubble, must have been the entrance from the moat, probably over a wooden draw-bridge, now gone; even in new ruins this remains one of the most beautiful ruined castles, with the secluded peace of the lawn and its melancholy statue enclosed by the rampart-walk and the low walls.

Stainborough of course relates much more to the early gothick of Castle Howard than to the period of Hawkstone, but the other Wentworth follies are all later and it is pointless to separate them. Still early, in the first Earl's time, there are ornaments, another obelisk of 1734 to Queen Anne, and also a rotunda and a temple. In 1756, the second Earl built a very elegant gothick summer-house called the Umbrello in Menagerie Wood, to the specifications of the Strawberry Hill Committee, but in 1949 all the pinnacles had gone and the roof was a shell; now it is only rubble.

At Wentworth Woodhouse, the follies again fall into two groups. First is the bear pit. The entrance is near the camelia house, with a cast iron inscription over the door

> There is healing in a garden
> When one longs for peace and pardon
> Once past the gate no need to wait
> For God is in the garden.

Inside a stair spirals down into the pit which is about 20 feet across with two small dens for the bears. There is a red brick vaulted ceiling, and where it meets the walls, are carvings on the ledges—two gryphon-like monsters, a lion, and another lion with a human head. Between the dens, a rough rock tunnel curves out into the lower level of a pretty Japanese garden through a remarkable arch of early seventeenth-century work, possibly reassembled a century later. There is massive carving, with an armorial beast and shield above the entry; toothy mouths holding great clover-heads turned outwards; and clover-heads turned in below a central lump of tufa. At the far end of the garden is a grotto to match, built up of early fragments into a small temple-shaped arrangement with life-size Roman soldiers on guard. One has weathered almost to the elegance of a skeleton, noseless, one arm gone; the other is soot-black, mouth a hole, pot-bellied.

Beyond the park to the east is Hoober Stand built by Flitcroft, one of the finest follies anywhere, about 100 feet high, of golden-brown and sooty stone, tapering, three-sided, like the prow of some triangular ship, it soars against the sky. A beautifully constructed spiral staircase goes to the top, where there is a small hexagonal lantern with a domed roof of stone surrounded by a stout iron railing. In the spaces between the lantern and the corners of the pyramid are stone sundials. The inscription reads:

1748. This Pyramidal Building was Erected by his MAJESTY's most Dutiful Subject, THOMAS, Marquess of ROCKINGHAM In Grateful Respect to the Preserver of our Religion, Laws and Libertys, KING GEORGE The Second. Who by the Blessing of God having subdued a most Unnatural Rebellion In Britain, Anno 1746 Maintains the Balance of Power, and Settles A Just, and Honourable Peace on Europe. 1748.

Wentworth Woodhouse. Above, *one of the Roman soldiers and* right, *the splendid bulk of Hoober Stand.*

Above, *Wentworth Woodhouse. Kepple's Column and a souvenir of it in crest china, maker unknown; this is the only crest folly I have seen.* Opposite, *Tollymore Park. Two of Lord Limerick's follies.*

The Needle's Eye is in a wood nearer the house, and to the north is Keppel's Column, built in 1782 by John Carr, who built the magnificent mausoleum and, I feel sure, the Needle's Eye of 1780 as well, though there is no evidence for this.

Admiral Keppel commanded the Channel Fleet at the battle of Ushant in 1778. Due to the corruption of Lord Sandwich the ships were in a bad state of repair, and because many of them were dismasted through weather and battle, they were unable to manoeuvre sufficiently to win the battle decisively. For his apparent failure Keppel was courtmartialled, but was acquitted. His friend Charles, 2nd Marquess of Rockingham, before his death in 1782 started to build this immense Doric column; it was completed by his successor, the 2nd Earl Fitzwilliam, and bears an inscription saying that the pillar commemorates the 'naval glory of England and their common friendship with Admiral Keppel'. One hundred and fifteen feet high with the entasis rather more pronounced on one side than the other, it completely dominates the tall trees beside it.

The 2nd Marquess of Rockingham also started the manufacture of Rockingham china, commissioned Stubbs to paint his Whistlejacket, and while at Westminster dressed up as a girl and was shown over the school by the headmaster. His column is so notable a landmark that a crest souvenir was made of it.

There is a slight but charming folly near the Mausoleum gates, the Round House, which looks like three storeys of a red brick windmill. It is castellated with a little castellated porch, and inside is the cosiest house that can be imagined.

Tankersley used to be part of the estate, and had Lady's Folly, a dull routine bit of square stone classicism, much damaged, and surrounded by open-cast workings. It has now wisely been demolished.

The importance of the lie of the land and its fertility in folly building are never as important as the character, tastes and money of the builder. Hawkstone's follies are enhanced by the trees, and half of the works at Tollymore in County Down are submerged in them, though the other half are in the clear round the edge of the park, but a great deal of charm in the designer emerges through his bumbling and badly landscaped follies. Thomas Wright probably worked here,[1] as at Belvedere, but these follies look different from the Jealous Wall; perhaps here he only made sketches and local men worked them out a little differently, perhaps he designed only the castle follies; certainly their special feature is a local material, big stones worn towards spheres in the River Shimna. Sir Richard Colt Hoare, successor at Stourhead, visited Tollymore in 1806 and felt that the plantations wanted 'the judicious application of the axe; particularly to the fir tribe, which rather preponderate too much'; a just view, especially as it is now a Forest Park with the house gone and the trees multiplying. One entrance is through the Barbican Gate, a charming squat rough stone castle with an arch between two round towers with trefoils and arrow-slits. These are outlined with broad bands of dressed stone flush with the surface and look very like Wright's work. An obelisk to the death of the second son of the second Earl Roden stands in the open in Monument Field, but the earliest work is all of the time of Lord Limerick, who became first Earl of Clanbrassil of the second creation in 1756. He built the house (now gone) in about 1730, and the Barbican and the Horn Bridge (we begin to descend into the woods) at about the same time. The very picturesque gorge alternates dashing water and worn rocks and still pools, but there are now far too many firs and rhododendrons. To the right lies the Hermitage,

[1]See pages 180 and 222.

where the path winds through a central rock grotto about 12 feet long built out over the river under a small dome. Once there was a seat and a bust; a plaque remains inscribed in Greek by the 2nd Earl *Clanbrassil to his very dear friend MONTHERMER 1770.* Lord Monthermer died aged 35, the widely travelled heir to Boughton, a man of great taste of whom too little is known. Above the grotto the cascades of the Pinkwell join the river, and there is a waterfall further up the Shimna; below, is the Old Bridge, 1726, Foley Bridge, 1787 and Ivy Bridge, 1780. These two were built by the second Earl and here for the first time we see the big round stones set into Foley Bridge. There is also a large and startling rock carved in large black capitals by the third Earl.

STOP

LOOK AROUND AND PRAISE

THE NAME OF HIM WHO MADE IT ALL

SEE 1st CH^P JOHN 3 VERSE

Back at the top is the Clanbrassil Barn (and we are back to Lord Limerick, again in about 1730), a delightful sham church with an octagon tower, very thin pinnacles and a steeple. The arch beside it has the round stones for crockets, for quatrefoils in relief and for acorns on its top and octagon pinnacles. Out through the second Earl's imitation of the style, the Bryansford Gate of 1786, and on the road to Hilltown are Lord Limerick's Follies. All were there in 1744. The tallest is a hexagonal tower, castellated with large oval stones split lengthways and set up on end, curved side out; so far as I know a decoration unique to Tollymore; Wright was not in Ireland until 1745–6, but even though they cannot have been his idea, the stones would have pleased him. The other ornaments are like those of the Barbican, pointed arches and arrow-slits. On top is a slender conical spire circled by half-spheres of stones in three rings. There are circular towerlets each side of a field gate, similar but simpler, their cones plain.

Lord Limerick or Thomas Wright or the stonemason worked most beautifully in this style. There is a less successful cottage façade with flying buttresses (possibly altered or by another hand), and a return to mastery with a stout arch through the park wall, rectangular in plan, with the cone now a pyramid flared at the base, flying buttresses to the wall, boulders and flat bandings. A group of small but very beautiful follies.

And two more small but enchanting follies in Galway at Lawrencetown, on the old demesne of Belview. One is to take the eye from far down the road, a small screen in three bays with flying buttresses and the flat folly dressing to arches, slits and circles. There are only three castellations, each over a circle and with a small octagonal pinnacle on top. Old photographs show one remaining cross pattée, but that has gone now, and so has the cross from the other folly, a cottage of 1792 with an eyecatcher façade. A few years ago it had a castellated pediment, four pinnacles, a stout cross on top and twelve panes of glass in the big pointed window. Repairs have left the pediment plain but there are still two pinnacles and magnificent flying buttresses. At the far end of the drive is the Volunteer Arch, a good classical piece with a sphinx couchant over each side gate

Opposite, above, *Tollymore Park. The Barbican Gate.* Below, *the eyecatcher at Lawrencetown.*

and an urn on top, to commemorate the Irish Volunteers of 1782. The stone from the burnt house has mostly been taken, and everything is desolate with the three follies left standing on the flat land among skinny trees and ivy and moss, but the people in the cottage love it, and the eyecatcher is one of the prettiest anywhere.

The style occurs again at Bardsea in Cumbria on the peninsular opposite Barrow-in-Furness, isolated even in summer from the inferno of the Lakes. On the map, it all looks flat, so near sea level, but on its small scale, the country is rolling, with beech woods. The Bradyll Mausoleum stands overlooking Conishead Priory (where the family lived) from a higher hill north of the village in the wind and sun, above a beech and haw-thorns blown almost horizontal by the southwest wind. The grass is brilliantly green under pale dead heads blown across like the trees. The hilltop is terraced flatly on lime-stone outcrops, with weathered forms that have been used for walls in the villages. To the west is a golf course, and the thin cries come up just as they do at Hawkstone, but to a far wilder folly. It stands on a circular plinth 3 or 4 feet high and about 40 feet across that once had railings and a gate, a folly triangular in plan, built of coursed and random limestone, picked out here and there with lines of dark stone and a corbel or two of red sandstone; the texture is very rich.

Each corner is blunted by a buttress and above is a plain corbelled entablature follow-ing the line of the buttresses, then a short demonstration of the triangle plan, then another band of stone; on top a dome, with a pinnacle-pyramid at each corner. There is a dull lantern on top, but the urn that crowned it is lying in the grass. On each face about 6 feet up is a stone niche with coral brick voussoirs, inside an arch of brick to the ground, inside an arch of dressed limestone. In the niche to the south is a solitary urn with inscriptions. A lovely, lonely folly in a beautiful place.

The folly at Rubane in Co. Down is set in a rookery in a flat landscape, and survives remarkably well in the grounds of a boys' school. It is about 25 feet high, 12 square, plain stone back and sides, to be seen from the front, where its elaborations are faced with water-worn tufa-like pebbles, even on the square-ogival dome. Slender pinnacles at the corners and the top have all gone, and so has the coloured glass from the lantern. Inside are the remains of fine rococo plasterwork. This is one of the obstinate little follies that stay in mind by their strangeness. It is, though, the strangeness of amateur variation on normal themes—Rubane had plasterwork, castellations, pinnacles, an arcade, a dome —the designer mixed classical and gothick, certainly, but no more than any gentleman might have done, and to enchanting effect; it is referred to in *Ireland Observed* as 'splendid' and so it is, no mean feat for a building 12 feet square.

Opposite, *the Bradyll mausoleum at Bardsea*. Below, *the folly at Rubane*.

Scotland has two follies of a different sort of strangeness. Both are botanical. One is a stone pineapple that rises high above a terrace in the grounds of Dunmore Castle in Stirlingshire. The terrace stands behind an old orchard, full of apple trees and the pale fluffy seeds of willow-herb, and a narrow path leads through to the building under the terrace, stone and vermilion brick with blind windows and a central portico with a pedimented Venetian arch turned pink with lichen. On the keystone is the date 1761, and in the pediment a heart with a flower and the motto '*Fideamus in Adversis*', looking later and clumsier. Through the portico, the vanished glasshouses to right and left could be reached. The walls have cavities and there are the remains of furnaces whose chimneys sit on top of the walls disguised as urns. Above, the astounding pineapple rises almost 40 feet. First, 10 feet of circular drum with seven ogival windows matching a door to the terrace and pretty but routine fenestration, with curved panes. Then there is a crown of grey-green stone leaves, curving out four feet and more, crisp and unsupported; the window mouldings run up through foliations to make the central ribs of the largest leaves, everywhere is ingenuity and elegance—even the window-mouldings end in a complex zig-zag base that is wholly pineapple. The fruit is constructed in eight elaborate courses diminishing to a second crown of smaller leaves, as carefully carved as those below. Inside for contrast is total simplicity, no plasterwork, no ornament at all except stark flat rectangular stone mouldings round the windows and door, as if to cancel out the ogee curves. There is a high plain dome and a stone floor. All is crisp and beautifully preserved and the pineapple sits above the orchard with the assurance of superiority, the exotic above the common fruit, the folly above architecture.

The pineapple, large and beautiful, expensive to grow and delicious to eat, was a symbol of luxury and pride from its first introduction, and Charles II was painted receiving one. Gentlemen had them carved on gateposts, and they were the correct centre-pieces for grand dinner parties until at least the end of the nineteenth century, when a pine could be hired for a guinea a night, two guineas more if eaten.

Pineapples were grown in Scotland at least as early as 1732, and it is reasonable to suppose that they were a speciality at Dunmore, but there is no account of them, and we do not know even the architect.

Below left, *Dunmore Pineapple from the terrace, and* opposite, *from the orchard. Lithograph by Barbara Jones.* Below right, *the Dole watertank, Honolulu.*

A stolid little brick shadow of Dunmore sits on the Wiltshire Downs put up for Wexcombe Waterworks in 1899, a round tower in smooth brick with headers protruding on the dome and a tuft of headers on the top. The only other large one I know of is the 100,000 gallon watertank for the fire control system of Dole Company in Honolulu, its crown 195 feet from the ground above the main office. It was made of metal, painted, in 1928, to the design of Sydney D. Walker, a water-systems engineer, and makes a nice parallel in the worship of the pine.

The other Scottish botanical folly is at Lanrick Castle in Perthshire, a 60-foot stone tree among trees in a wood, stained and mossy like them, only visible at first for its greater girth. For 30 feet it is a carefully built tree, with branches and branch-scars. Then instead of leaves there is a crown of tall flat stone triangles, inclining outwards. Here all likeness to a tree ends; three 15-foot Tuscan columns support a circular platform. A central column has now fallen and lies at the foot of the tree, but another column still stands in the centre of the platform. It once supported an acorn which is now on the ground with the column and three points of the crown. Over each column of the first tier is a square ornament on ball feet capped with flames and carved with anthemion ornaments which suggest the earlier half of the wide range of dates: it was probably put up by Sir Evan John Murray Macgregor in the first half of the nineteenth century. Local legends say that it is the family tree of the Macgregors, each branch a sept of the clan, each scar a death . . . Whatever intention lay behind it, or none, the result is a most startling and sinister folly.

'The Whim' at Blair Atholl (Perthshire is rich in follies) returns to the simple rectangle-and-pyramid style. It was built in 1762 and an unsigned sketch for it is in Blair Castle; it is thought that the Duke designed it himself and this seems probable. Certainly the family owned both Blair and Dunkeld and one Duke put up a number of follies and Chinoiseries on both estates and another took most of them down, leaving a dull hermitage at Dunkeld and this nice toy fort up behind the castle. Ninety feet of wall about 9 feet high support a terrace, now grassed over, with the remains of a privet hedge along the front. At each end is a square tower with large round-headed arches and pyramid roofs with large crosses on top. At the back of the terrace rises a simple screen of arches and castellations, three feet thick.

Below, *the Whim at Blair Atholl*. Opposite, *the tree at Lanrick*.

The results of travel, money, leisure and taste are interestingly displayed at West Wycombe where considerable effort has produced a most entertaining whole, consistent, but with no single really good building. The atmosphere is good, the flint work excellent, the stories most exciting, but each individual object is weak, one starts to criticize at once, only St Crispin's Cottages disarm one utterly; nevertheless the quantity of follies, the very sinister atmosphere and the sheer weight of legend and personality make West Wycombe one of the most important folly sites in the country.

In 1752 or 1753 Sir Francis Dashwood leased Medmenham Abbey, by the Thames near Henley, and prepared it for the use of the Order of Saint Francis of Medmenham. It is round this Order that the vicious legends of West Wycombe centre, but the name is nearly forgotten, replaced by 'Hell-Fire Club', although the real Hell Fire Club was dissolved in 1736; the poetic English will always cherish a fine name and forget a dowdy one, so 'Hell-Fire Francis' continues to lead the mild revels, celebrating the black mass on desecrated altars, eating strange foods served a 100 feet above or below the earth, drinking wine poured by naked girls and looking at the portraits of the Kings of England which hung above the long drinking sofas in the Chapter House.

The Abbey was beautifully converted, with a sumptuous cell for each Friar, a Temple to Cloacina and a Trophonius' Cave in the grounds, and the stories of debauches began. Some of the stories are undoubtedly true, and all of them have affected the rest of the English follies—this small group of men has acted as a large stained-glass window, casting lurid patches of colour on the harmless pavilions and belvederes of hundreds of small estates. They were rich, and childish men; they were bored. Earlier in the eighteenth century it had been possible to relieve tedium by slipping out at night to gouge out an eye or to extend a citizen's mouth with a razor, but this became dangerous after a time, even illegal, and it was necessary for 'a person of flighty imagination and who possessed a fortune that enabled him to pursue that flight, cloyed with common pleasures, and ambitious of distinguishing himself among his companions' to resolve 'to try if he could not strike out something new, that should at the same time please his own taste and do honour to his genius. The mere gratifications of sense, in their utmost extent, not answering his design, he had recourse to the assistance of imagination to enhance them'.[1] So what more natural than Medmenham and West Wycombe? At Medmenham, Wilkes is said to have dressed a baboon in scarlet, with horns, and hidden it in a chest in the chapel. Just as the usual evening service invoking the Devil was at its climax, he pulled a concealed string, opened the box and out hopped the ape, on to the shoulder of Lord Sandwich, who in the general terror and confusion and cries of repentance, kept his head admirably, apologizing for his half-measure sins—would do better if given time. . . . It was Lord Sandwich who preached lewd sermons to a congregation of cats and, tiring of it, later bribed a printer for proof sheets of the *Essay on Woman* so that he could get Wilkes impeached for obscenity; there is no doubt that the assistance of imagination does help one to spend money more intelligently.

The Medmenham meetings were only held twice a year, but still they all got bored, and when Walpole visited the place in 1763 he found the Abbey 'very ruinous and bad', empty of everything but a few bits of broken furniture. The Order was broken up and Sir Francis, still with some of the more imaginative brethren, had turned his attention

---

[1] *Chrysal* by Charles Johnston, 1768; a great repository of legends about Sir Francis Dashwood. Another account is in *Nocturnal Revels* by a Monk of the Order of St Francis. Two vols. 1779. Anonymous.

to his house at West Wycombe, six miles away across the Chilterns. Medmenham only emerges into the light once more, when on 24 May 1771, the Chevalier d'Eon de Beaumont was examined there by a jury of aristocratic ladies who could only arrive at a verdict of Doubtful on his sex, which was very awkward as over a hundred thousand pounds' worth of bets were involved. In 1777 a case about this money was brought, and the new jury settled for female, after which the Chevalier spent the rest of his life dressed as a woman, only to be pronounced definitely male at his death.

There is a lot to see at West Wycombe; house and park on one side of the road, village in the middle, and church and mausoleum on the other side, only an hour from London by train and most of it belonging to the National Trust—though perhaps it has never been in such grave danger as most folly sites, for Sir Francis' reputation has endeared it to every one and there have always been visitors.

The house was designed by Nicholas Revett and John Donowell, and decorated by Borgnis, an old-fashioned baroque painter brought to England by Sir Francis for his house and church. He died here, and is buried with the Friars.

For miles along the railway or the road, the golden ball on top of the church is visible to the traveller. The usual approach is from the prosperous and spreading town of High Wycombe, along almost three miles of houses, a long straight road made by Sir Francis. For the last part of it, the church is visible immediately in front on top of a steep hill. At the foot, High Wycombe really falls back, the road forks round the hill and a fat 'collom' (built at a cost of £27 7s. 8d. to commemorate the finishing of the road) announces the distances,

> From the University Miles XXII
> From the City Miles XXX
> From the County Town Miles XV
> Sir F. Dashwood derae Christianae MDCCLII

It is a very meek collom, with a stone pudding on top to echo the ball on the church; alleviation of boredom by public works.

West Wycombe. The golden ball on the church and the view from it.

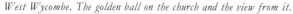

On the left, though, is a gate into the park between two square lodges, at first glance alike. The left-hand lodge, Kitty's Lodge, is inhabited and cheerfully faces west, a stone cube with a pyramidal roof; on the top of this, and at each corner, is a stone ball bisected by a projecting square equator. The other lodge, Daphne's Temple, sunless among trees, faces it with an identical front, but is a sham, a wall only, with a false door, and at the back the lodge becomes an open temple with the roof supported on eight Ionic columns whose plaster caps are dissolving fast. On the inside of the entablature is inscribed

Nympha precor
Penela mane
Nympha mane
Daphne dicatum.

There are some very exciting accounts of the layout of the park. Wilkes' 'I must own the noble lord's gardens gave me no stronger idea of his vertue or patriotism than the situation of the new built church did of his piety' raises all sorts of speculations—what eighteenth-century gardens, now lost, could Wilkes have seen that made him consider patriotism indispensable as a theme for landscaping? And how was it symbolized? Parterres of geranium, lobelia and white alyssum in the shape of a Union Jack were not yet invented, nor were royal portraits in fireworks. One can imagine a clockwork device concealed in a Temple of British Kings to play Rule Britannia every hour, but would that have appealed to Wilkes? Little effort is needed, however, to find out how the gardens lacked at least virtue—they are said to have been laid out in the shape of a naked woman, every walk and wood and clump of trees dedicated to a joke that could not have been truly enjoyed till the invention of the aeroplane; four engravings of the of the gardens by William Woollett after Hannen are claimed by the *Dictionary of National Biography* to show this gigantic graffito, but I could detect no trace of her on any of them, and the park was later done over by Repton so that Nature, as a contemporary *History and Antiquities* points out, 'being stripped of the gaudy trappings of art, will assume her wonted loveliness . . . the gardens are contracted, some useless and unmeaning buildings removed, and cattle will be allowed to graze on the banks of the lake'. So we must abandon the lady, with many regrets for a style of gardening which might have produced wonderful results today; guests would be shown the new landscaping by helicopter—no muddy paths, no damp grass.

We may be sure that Woollett's engravings would have shown her if they could, for they have certainly embellished the cascade at the end of the lake. This is a stone ramp sewn with triangular teeth to throw the water up into grotesques, and flanked at the bottom with two piers made of flint and tufa, their niches full of ivy and rushes. In the engraving it appears as a magnificent semicircular treble cascade with a tufa arch over a reclining Neptune at the top. Certainly a lot has gone, for a painting in the estate office shows a round temple on a small hill beyond winding water with a rustic bridge. Inside the temple and all round it are ghostly white statues, and a double rank of them with gesticulating arms goes down the hill to the water's edge where a scarlet gondola rows past them.

The gondola could go round the lake and the Music Temple by Revett, and through a beautifully shaded ornamental canal, one lovely vista closed by the distant church, and others showing the open park, the farm, and Repton's cows. All the farm houses and a number of other buildings are flint, superbly handled; very dignified and rather French in design. The walls are flint, too, with the pyramid-capped piers so usual to folly builders, and at one point a farm lane goes through a flint gate straight from the park into a suburban road. The change of atmosphere is so intense that one walks to and fro, enjoying it, equally pleasant on both sides, here the eighteenth-century countryside and garden, lying in the sun barely changed, there the pink and brown twentieth century, still too new, with no yard of transition between them; impossible not to feel that a vacuum hangs between park and traffic, the gears on the road and the shunting on the railway are so quiet.

Round the perimeter of the park are the follies, all for the view from the house, and to be admired on the boundary walk or ride.

One is that rarity, a folly in the classical taste, a cottage like a skyscraper with a pediment at the top, craning up to be seen. The second one has almost gone—a cottage with a sham ruin clapped on to one end of it, a big flint pointed arch; the chimney has flint arches to match. Once I think they must have been open, but now a red brick lining shows; all crumbling rapidly.

Nearby, St Crispin's survives in wonderful condition. The flint cottage, named for the local shoemaker, lies along the road to Sands with a higher wing across the middle of it, which has been given a steep pitched roof. The end of this extension, which makes the cottage drawing room, faces the big house a mile away, and against it is the prettiest sham church tower I have ever seen, three storeys high, with buttresses and flanking piers and four white pinnacles. It is all flint with courses and facings of vermilion brick and elaborate white wooden tracery in the windows of the top floor, which is dummy— the ground floor, though, is a nice bay window for the drawing room. Chickens, and a kitchen garden in front, the main cottage, and others near it, all disappear from the house, and the tower is almost convincing, but across the cabbages it is small and intimate, a toy church, with a lovely model quality as if it had been printed on a large sheet of cardboard, coloured appropriately flint, scarlet and white, and carefully cut out with nail scissors, taking special pains with the pinnacles.

There are several other survivors of what must have been one of the largest groups of follies and ornaments in the country; Robert Adams' Cockpit of 1767–8, a large flint screen to the stables *'Libertati amicitiaeque sacrum'*, with coupled columns and a pediment; through the arch can be seen a copy of the Apollo Belvedere in a niche; a routine temple with a Tuscan portico; a pedimented lodge grandly called the Temple of Flora; the Temple of the Winds (presumably by Revett), in flint and stone, with a flint screen of arches and obelisks standing in front.[1]

In the village there is a very good flint rectory, an echo of Mereworth (which the Dashwoods also owned), as it has one central round chimney, but here there is no dome to take the flues and they curve bulkily through the attics. They say that a previous

[1] Gervase Jackson-Stops tells me that the date is now known to be 1759, which makes it, as he says, 'the second earliest strictly neo-classical building in Europe, just beaten by the Doric Temple at Hagley', which was built in 1758, based on the Hephaestaeon. It seems likely that Donowell built Kitty, Daphne and the Cascade before 1752, and had done at least some work on the Church, while Revett more and more took charge (Donowell went in 1764), and, ten years or more after the Temple of the Winds, built the Round, Music and Flora Temples, St Crispin and the Pepperpot Bridge.

vicar, Timothy Shaw, was a Friar, and drowned himself at Medmenham in 1761 in remorse for his wicked life, but the list of vicars and rectors (unless rigged) does not include his name, and he will have to go with the garden plan.

Gone for certain are a Druid's Hut, which is now an ordinary cottage and a 'lewd temple' mentioned by Wilkes, dedicated to Tristram Shandy's 'Tetragrammaton', but Repton probably demolished many more.

Bubb Dodington, Baron Melcombe when he died in 1762, left £500 to Sir Francis Dashwood for 'building an arch, temple, column, or additional room' for his ashes. Sir Francis decided on a splendid mausoleum at the east end of his church. This occupied for some years both him and his architect Nicholas Revett.

Wilkes, and later a lot of other people, made witty cracks about a noble lord building a church at the top of a hill for the convenience of the town at the bottom and said that he believed it to be the first church which had been built for the prospect. As it is undoubtedly one of the most delightful of prospects, it is sad to take the credit for it from Sir Francis, but a church was built up there in Norman times for the village of Haveringdon, now gone, and the bottom half of the existing tower is twelfth-century work.

The church is wonderful inside; its elevation washes it with a particularly clear light, and the ceiling is painted to imitate elaborate plaster work. There are real plaster wreaths and cupids on the lovely dilapidated colour of the walls.

An Italian font stands in the centre of the nave, with a serpent winding up its pedestal after a dove which is trying to join three companions on the rim. Magnificent Chippendale reading-desks, on platforms with drawers for vestments, stand on either side.

The chancel is abruptly dark and narrow, with Spanish leather on the altar and a black-avised Judas by Borgnis on the ceiling, so it is just possible on a lowering day to find something sinister in the air, though I was once, by accident, locked in alone at dusk, and barely alarmed, more interested in the choice between breaking glass and ringing the bells. For back in the open nave, in the chalky crumbling light, everything is clarity and peace. However a hundred years ago the atmosphere, or the sensibility of the beholder, must have been stronger, for in 1845 someone piled prayer books round the alien font and tried to burn the church and its legends of black magic to the ground.

The tower may be climbed; as far up as the top of the nave roof it remains routine parish church, and the stairs go pleasantly up through the ringing chamber, written over with records of tremendous peals and with so many scribbled names that they have become a texture on the walls. The stairs continue up past the bells into a great clear room open on all sides to the sky through four huge arches. Then higher, up an even smaller stair out on to the flat square roof. Above, on a cloudy day, the golden ball falls down towards you. A narrow iron ladder climbs its thin stem, handrailed with loose, swaying chains; a trap-door is cut in the lower half of the globe and swings curving down from its equator. The inside is full of beams, and there are three narrow wooden seats. Wilkes wrote that it was 'so very convenient on the inside for the celebration not of devotional but of convivial rites, that it is the best Globe Tavern I was ever in': even if the inside has been altered since (and it doesn't look it), it must have been remarkably cramped and uncomfortable for an orgy; we must admire the fortitude of the eighteenth century.

The outside of the fantastic crow's-nest is covered with gilded lead, and four round windows look down over Buckinghamshire swimming beneath, miles of ploughed

West Wycombe. St. Crispin's.

sweeps and dark woods. It is immeasurably isolated.

To the east the view is towards London, down the hill and along the dead straight road. In the foreground is the Mausoleum, dedicated to Bubb Dodington as it should be, though a much larger inscription inside is to Francis Baron le Despencer. 1763 was a busy year; the mausoleum was begun, the church finished and consecrated, and Sir Francis became Lord le Despencer, the abeyance of the barony of his maternal grandfather being terminated in his favour; he at once ordered a new japanned coach with the motto Pro Magna Charta in gothic lettering on the panels.

The mausoleum is open to the sky, a slightly flattened hexagon of knapped flint walls broken on the three sides towards the view by enormous arches outlined with rough flint. It encloses long grass, wild strawberries and a profound melancholy. A beautifully detailed entablature runs along the top of the walls, supported by Doric half-columns between the arches. Everything looks quite solid, flint and grey stone, at first glance, but the columns are Roman cement on brick, and the entablature, breaking open at the corners, shows ragged laths framing holes full of jackdaws.

We can look through the iron grilles in the arches at the interior where ivy fingers into the alcoves and considers the annihilation of the few remaining urns and monuments. They seem to have been mostly portrait busts of members of the family or the Order: only the headless pedestals of Borgnis and Lord le Despencer remain, but the latter's wall monument in the next niche is intact. Then there is another headless, nameless bust. Then a yellow marble urn to the poet, Paul Whitehead:

> Unhallowed hands this urn forbear
>   No Gems nor Orient Spoil
> Lie here conceal'd—but what's more rare,
>   A HEART, that knew no guile.

This unsophisticated organ was left by Mr. Whitehead to Lord le Despencer, who put the urn on a pillar in his garden until he had prepared a terrific funeral; he was Colonel of the Bucks Militia, and had a whole company of them to march with the heart for two complicated hours about the house and grounds, up to the church and round the mausoleum. For years the dried and shrivelled heart was shown to visitors, but in 1839 someone stole it. What with arson and theft, the whole place would seem to have been enormously appreciated in the 1830s and 1840s.

After the unavailing poetry of Paul Whitehead come two niches with indecipherable pedestals, and then in the centre of the back wall a large monument, taken from the old church, to Mary Fane, Lord le Despencer's mother, and also to Mary King, his father's third wife. Their eyes turn to heaven and they are surrounded by weeping cupids, but most oddly for their time, the inscriptions make no record of their virtues. Then a modern memorial and then the pedestal which once upheld the likeness of Thomas Thompson, local doctor and member of the Order. Then three more niches; a heap of terra-cotta pieces of face and toga, the stem of another portrait and some fragments of marble. Somewhere once was Bubb Dodington; his head has been seen this century in the grass.

A flat roof supported above a pedestal by four columns protects a well-preserved and absolutely nauseating urn to the memory of Sarah Baroness le Despencer who finished a most Exemplary Life January the 19th MDCCLXIX. It has weakly waving handles, four repellent masks and stands on four lions' feet bunched together. A worse piece of artwork has never been designed.

Under the hill are chalk caves that may be explained either as excavated for the Friars when Medmenham became untenable for orgies, or as caves left when chalk was taken between 1748 and 1752 for the new road; certainly the excavations followed a plan that is now very useful for the son-et-lumière entertainment in 'The Hell-Fire Caves', complete with waxworks and refreshments. A quarter of a mile of tunnel winds down to the Robing Room (the names are local legend if not Friar), the Catacombs of Rome, a dry stream bed, once the River Styx, the big Banquet Hall with four Monk's Cells, and finally the Inner Temple. On the way were a Buttery and a Cursing Well. The entrance to the caves is built on a platform levelled into the steep hillside and backed by a cliff grown over with yews. It is made of flint triangles and pyramids; thin and flat, it stands in two dimensions before the black entrance to the third. It is more like a child's model fortress than anything else, but even with the gay café in front it is a terribly unpleasant toy.

West Wycombe. Below left, *a folly cottage and,* right, *the Mausoleum*. Bottom, *the entrance to the Hell-Fire Caves*.

The Exotic Styles

—◆—

The British Isles are rather cold, rather damp, sometimes rather warm; there are no extremes of temperature or weather, no siroccos or tornadoes—the very words are foreign. All the excitement of violent weather, love of deserts, high mountains, rain forests, black skins and slanting eyes has to be in the head, or copied, and copied it is. We take most lovingly to the exotic, to tea, to coffee, to kangaroo-tail soup, to anything hot, cold, high, deep, extreme, that will take us away from that dangerous edge of things, the temperate. The Emperor of China had only one château; the British Isles had dozens of pagodas and hundreds of obelisks, and Sweden, with its even dimmer climate, had essays in the Chinese taste beyond anything attempted here.

The histories of the China trade and the Indies trade are as deeply absorbing as the history of garden design, but here again we can only look at the briefest outline. The Chinese never liked foreigners, but never missed the advantages of foreign trade, and more than a thousand years ago Canton was a powerful international market, with foreign traders allowed in settlements—not always to China's advantage, for in 758 A.D. the Moslem colony sacked the city and this must have been one of the reasons for the deep distrust later shown to traders from the West. Most of the first Europeans were Portuguese, early in the sixteenth century, but (through such misunderstandings as a salute of guns which was taken for hostility) the Chinese soon closed Canton to all foreign shipping, and trade was unofficial and furtive. It is easy to see how expensive the porcelains and silks were by the time they reached Europe, with rarity and the danger of the long voyages added to their alien beauty. In 1557, the Portuguese were allowed to settle at Macao, and they held the trade till the end of the century. In 1600, the Dutch began to seize Portuguese ships and, based on Formosa, established sole trading rights with Japan, so Amsterdam was the European centre for the seventeenth century. In 1699 the *Macclesfield* collected the first 'full and rich' cargo for England, and in 1715 set up a permanent factory. London took over from Amsterdam, and tea brought the biggest profit.

Some of the scrolls and porcelain showed a new and enchanting architecture. By the 1730s the time had come for a change from Palladianism, and gothick was not to every-one's taste. Cathay could provide a different answer. But the traders could provide no information, for they saw no more of China than Macao. The only Europeans who reached the interior of China were the Jesuit missionaries, accepted as men of taste and learning. The Emperors in their turn were fascinated by Western painting and perspec-tive, and employed the Fathers not only as councillors but as court painters and archi-tects. In 1737 the Emperor K'ang Hsi asked the most famous of the painters, Fra Castiglione, to design him a European palace, and Yüan Ming Yüan, that unique rever-

The Pagoda at Alton Towers (see pages 119 and 235).

sal of Chinoiserie, was built on the Western Hills near Peking. Only fragments of it remained in the 1930s (today I think nothing), but there are hints of its richness and beauty, its strange linking of Orient and Occident not by an architect but by a priest, in the surviving engravings (and there is an east-west self-portrait of Castiglione with a startling waist-high Pekinese dog in a collar with bells). Later the Emperor's grandson Ch'ien Lung saw a French engraving of a big fountain and asked for one. Fra Benoit was found to have some knowledge of mechanics, so he bravely made a fountain and finally there was a group of white marble buildings round it, Hsieh Ch'i Ch'ü. The largest had Louis Quinze windows and a curved roof, and Fra Benoit probably exceeded his French original, for there was a clock with twelve marble animals that spouted water from their mouths at two-hour intervals to fall through cascades into a marble aqueduct. All was destroyed in 1860 by English and French troops.

Meanwhile the Fathers sent back to Europe accounts of China. They started with the philosophy; they saw absolutely clearly that the minds of their Chinese friends were as good as their own, and that any religious changes could only be brought about very slowly, by the influence of equals on equals, possibly in both directions. Certainly they were prepared to match the traditional Chinese tolerance of alien religions, but the Vatican was not, and stopped it all. Chinese philosophy, though, became fashionable; Fra Couplet's *Confucius Sinarum Philosophus* published in Paris in 1687 was the standard work, soon translated into French, English and Swedish, and followed by many other works. Leibnitz wrote in 1697 that the Chinese should send missionaries to Europe to teach natural philosophy in return for our teachings on revealed religion, and later Voltaire wanted to abandon revealed religion altogether. The arguments went on for more than half a century and every educated European had at least a garbled idea of Chinese philosophy, with interest in the people, the country, and the history kept alive by the publication between 1702 and 1776 of 34 volumes of *Lettres édifiantes et curieuses écrites des Missions Etrangères*. Much of the literature was published in France, so *Chinoiserie* became the accepted word for Chinese decoration and design, though most of its influence on French garden design was finally via England. . . .

Written information about the gardens had come early in the seventeenth century and fallen flat—the gardens of Italy and Holland still had their time to run, and in England the gardens were still small, all knots, topiary, and straight alleys. The artificial hills of Chinese gardens, and the deep grottoes for the summer, and the labyrinthine paths, and the desirability of rare animals and birds were all described with love by the Fathers. One Father said that it was sad that there were so few flowers (Europe was still growing them in neat beds and pots and the tulip was king) but he admired the rivers winding through the green landscape. Accounts came of enormous hollow rockeries with cascades, and of hills covered with marble 'interwoven with Plats of Grass', of brass trees, and walks mazing along for several miles.

Athanasius Kircher's *China monumentis qua sacris qua profanis, illustrata* was published in Amsterdam in 1672, and in 1687 Kneller painted the portrait of an early Chinese visitor, Shên Fu-tsung, holding a crucifix (a painting that changes one's ideas of Kneller as the Indian portraits at Osborne change opinions of Winterhalter). It is impossible to tell just how the influence of the descriptions and engravings, and the Chinese porcelains and silks themselves, began to influence the gardeners. Certainly the writers and philosophers like Shaftesbury, Addison, Steele and Pope wrote in praise of Chinese or at least of 'natural' gardens, and Sir William Temple produced that vital thing, the word, sharawadgi. Its derivation has been carefully investigated[1] and is uncertain (Temple may have invented it), but it was used in the eighteenth century to convey surprise, something impressive or elegant produced with careless grace. Temple wrote in his mysteriously famous essay *Upon the Gardens of Epicurus* published in 1690,

> There may be other Forms wholly irregular, that may, for ought I know, have more Beauty than any of the others; . . . the *Chineses* . . . have a particular word to express it; and where they find it hit their Eye at first sight, they say the *sharawadgi* is fine or is admirable. . . . But I should hardly advise any of these Attempts in the Figure of Gardens among us; they are Adventures of too hard atchievement for any common Hands; and tho there may be more Honour if they succeed well, yet there is more Dishonour if they fail, and 'tis twenty to one they will.

My own feeling is that the influence of Claude and Poussin has been exaggerated and too little attention paid to the imported fans, screens, and above all the scrolls, paintings in a form much better suited to the unfolding of a landscape than the European rectangle. Surely these visual things had more influence on the landscape designers than any written descriptions even if the best possible source, the Fathers' beautiful measured drawings, were never seen in England.[2]

In any case, Temple was wrong; twenty to one they succeeded. Even on the landscapes that remain after nearly two and a half centuries we can award Honour, and certainly the contemporaries of the designers thought so; Paris remained the centre for Chinese studies, but the gardening style was accepted as *le jardin anglais* or *anglais-chinois*; France and the rest of Europe adopted it from England.

Different people of course took different examples and inspirations, used different architects and sometimes had vigorously different ideas of their own. Stourhead and Pain's Hill, for instance are very different; Stourhead was probably influenced by European paintings, while Pain's Hill looks definitely and most successfully Chinese, even if Mr Hamilton may have thought he was chasing Salvator Rosa.

The fact is that between what people wrote and said and what they did, between the theorists and the visual people, between the architects and the amateurs, between the creators and the fashionable, between legends and scrappy records, we know even less about the eighteenth century than we do about our own, and less still about its architecture, and less still about its follies, and least of all about Chinoiserie.

What did the early pagoda-builders really know? Osvald Siren's extensive researches suggest that their most reliable source was the illustrated report, published in Dutch, German and English, (1669) by Johan Neuhof, describing the Embassy of the East India Company of the United Provinces, which travelled in China between 1653 and 1657.

The first known building in England referred to as a Tea House or China House was built in the 1640s at Beckett in Oxfordshire. It is a simple square building with a big flat pyramidal roof, one storey, all four sides alike, with a central door and two windows,

---

[1] *Architectural Review*, Dec. 1949.

[2] There is a collection of their gouaches in the Bibliothèque Nationale.

all quite European in style, oddly recalling St Paul's, Covent Garden, and indeed just possibly by Inigo Jones. There is no visual trace of China here; the idea of a tea house and its setting by water is all. James Lee-Milne suggests it was once a brew-house, and that as the wide overhanging eaves are built on more modern rafters, the Chinese effect may have been attempted when the Chinese bridge nearby was made.[1]

Batty Langley by 1728 had the labyrinthine idea, but only at second-hand; the first builder of a surviving Chinoiserie to go to China himself and come back and work on it was Lord Anson, who not only reached Canton and saved it from destruction by fire, so that the Emperor was well disposed, but also captured the annual Acapulco-Manila galleon.[2] This was said to be the Navy's largest single prize, so Anson on his return in 1744 had plenty of money as well as porcelain and other treasures. Also, his elder brother Thomas (who had succeeded to Shugborough in 1720) was a founder member of the Society of Dilettanti, and had travelled much farther than Italy and Greece.

The Ansons and Lady Anson and brother officers set about Shugborough with the naval riches, and the Chinese House was probably the first thing built, in 1747, even before the new wings were finished on the house. As the work of one who had seen so much, it is very meek, a rectangular building about 20 feet by 16 with the up-flung eaves too clumsy, but with a pretty double Chinese hat on top, and fretted windows. Inside, to our astonishment, a scarlet screen and bells cannot disguise the fact that the lively decoration is more rococo than Chinese.[3] Nothing could be prettier than the monkeys and ribbon-held birds, but they are unexpected—and then it is clear that the theme is cormorant-fishing, something Anson must have seen and translated into *singerie*.

[1] *The Age of Inigo Jones,* Batsford, 1953.

[2] *A Voyage round the World in the years 1740–44,* by Lord Anson. Various editions.

[3] Though Thomas Pennant, writing in 1782, says that it is 'a true pattern of the Architecture of that Nation, taken in the country by the skilful pencil of Sir Percy Brett'.

Below, *Shugborough Park; the Chinese house and a detail of the interior.* Opposite, above, *a Termany Seat in the Chinese Taste.* Below, *engravings of elevation and section of the pagoda at Kew Gardens, 1763, and the pagoda today.*

Then William and John Halfpenny published their books of Chinese designs, and so did Edward, and Darby, and C. Over, and Sir William Chambers, all in the 1750s, all claiming to be new, but all very alike and mostly relying on the application of dragons, bells, lattices, circular doors and curved roofs to Western shapes for their evocation of Cathay. Sir William Chambers' *Designs of Chinese Buildings, Furniture, Dresses, Machines and Utensils,* London, 1757, is the most famous, because he designed the big 1761 Pagoda in Kew Gardens which is 163 feet high, a stolid octagon tower of stock bricks with round-headed windows. The charming railings and the whingding on top lend it a little grace but even when all its finial dragons were in place on the eaves of the ten roofs it must have failed in fantasy.

But poverty in the books of designs and stolidity at Kew are a poor indication of the lovely extravagances that were built, first in Britain and then all over Europe, in the Chinese taste to match the gardens.

Only a dozen or so pagodas and tea houses remain to us; the delicate trellises and bells, dragons and upcurved roofs were mostly made of wood and, unloved, have decayed, like the tragic ruin of a pretty tea house that is rotting in the woods at Enville. The superb Fishing Temple built at Virginia Water for George IV can only be seen in drawings, and his Pagoda by John Nash in St James' Park burnt down before the victory celebrations that were its purpose had even started. Only in Sweden were the royal Chinoiseries so carefully built and carefully maintained that they are intact to this day.

Still, there are some pretty things and some very unlikely survivals—what could be more startling than an eighteenth-century Chinese tent made of oil cloth, standing on a lawn in Northamptonshire? This is at Boughton House, where it is re-erected every summer. Records often refer to Chinese, Moorish or Turkish tents, and they were presumably portable like this one, but I have heard of no other surviving. It was made

Below, *Boughton House; detail of the interior decoration of the Chinese tent.* Right, *Brighton Pavilion.*

by Smith Baber whose Patent Floor Cloth Manufactory was opposite the Barracks in Knightsbridge, and was originally itself in London, in the garden at Montagu House, Whitehall. At Boughton, topiary walls descend from the terrace to a broad and beautiful tree-lined vista mown in flawless stripes. Instead of an eyecatcher away on the horizon, the twelve-sided tent stands on the left, with a wooden base and frame. The Chinese roof, painted in faded red and white stripes, is crowned by a lovely dragon with an open pink mouth and under each curving rib a wooden bell hangs at the eaves. The floor is wooden with raffia matting, and the walls between the pillars, all painted black, are divided horizontally, like stable doors, but the upper parts are hinged at the top so that they can be flapped up to provide extra shade or kept down against the wind. Against the back four walls are padded seats on fretted frames. The ceiling panels are painted on a Chinese yellow ground with fine lively dragons, some answering to our notions of real dragons, some pure fantasy. They are very like the gay dragons of Brighton Pavilion; as the tent is late eighteenth century and the Pavilion was finished in 1820, is it possible that there is any connection? I have seen no other dragons so similar. And this is where it should be said that the Chinese decorations at Brighton are the zenith of the style here, just as the exterior is the zenith of the Indian style, so that the Pavilion must be seen even though it is a palace and not a folly.

Another Chinoiserie that has been moved is the tea house in the woods above the Liffey at Harristown House, Kildare, a simple building with elaborate painted decoration both inside and out that was recently moved from Wootton House near Aylesbury. Between the lattice windows outside are panels, painted with Chinese ladies dancing, holding a fan, a musical instrument, a fishing-rod, a yo-yo. Above are seated Buddha-like figures, grotesques. They look as if they were retouched by a less loving hand last century, but they are marvellously preserved. The interior painting, though, is professional work of great quality, done by someone with both delight in the Chinese style and real mastery of decorative painting. The lower panels are pale lime green framed in pink wood and decorated with light baroque designs imitating gilded carving and touched with real gold. Between the lattice windows are delightful panels; an elaborately dressed mandarin rides a pussy-tiger, a lady holds an upturned flask, there is an old man with a whisk and a servant with a lantern.

Below, *Harristown House. The Chinese tea-house and details of the exterior decoration.* Opposite, *the pagoda at Cliveden.*

Yet a third transplant is the cast-iron pagoda in the water-garden at Cliveden. It was made for the 1851 exhibition and is now on a mown island in the lake, with water-lilies, wistaria, goldfish, stone bridge, and stepping stones. It is a gay little open hexagon with scale-painted roof in orange on emerald, then a circular latticed lantern under an orange roof with a ball and spike finial impaling a green and gold dragon with a scarlet multi-forked tongue. The upturned eaves leap into curlicues; such light-heartedness was rare at the Great Exhibition—even the stuffed frog-barber and parasol-frog from Wurtemburg must have seemed heavy beside it.

Alton Towers in Staffordshire has our best pagoda which is very like Chinnery's 1840 painting of the one at Chusan—perhaps someone else had brought back an earlier sketch. It was called the Duck Tower and was built in the late 1820s, and was planned to reach 88 feet in six storeys. Forty illuminated Chinese lamps were intended, to be supplied by a small gasholder, dragons were to spout water from eyes, nostrils, fins and tails, and a column of water 70 feet high was to spring from the summit.

Only three storeys were built, and there is no sign of the gasholder but the jet of water rises and it is ravishingly pretty among the trees.[1] Nine rings are suspended from a pole on top, and the green roofs are delicately ribbed, and ornamented with bells under the eaves. The walls are elegantly detailed in cast iron, a skeletal scale-pattern painted cream, and each has a large open ogee arch (which may be considered gothick), painted dark green, while the eight ribbed structural pillars are striped. We shall see it again with the other follies at Alton.

Most of our Anglo-Chinese gardens have either been re-landscaped into something simpler or become overgrown, and the intention lost, but a very good one glows with life at Biddulph Grange in Staffordshire, which is now a hospital; nothing could have been more admirably preserved and lovingly tended—it was wonderful to hear 'It's difficult, but we do our best' instead of 'Oh, I believe there *is* something of the sort in the woods; bit overgrown I expect, haven't seen it for some years . . .' or 'That fell down a *long* time ago.' The Chinese garden was designed by James Bateman of Knypersley Hall in about 1840 on a rocky site above the Trent valley (like Alton but much smaller). Nowhere has so little land been designed to give such a sensation of size.

The walk starts along a terrace, with the house on the left hand, towards tall trees that occupy the eye. At the end the path turns to the right, through ferns, rocks, and rare conifers, with twisted pieces of dead trees lining the stepped and winding descent.

Ahead are two rock archways, and more paths with magnificent ferns, and to the left via a rockery, steps divert up to a Chinese pavilion with a view back to the house across a deep dell with a pagoda-pavilion and a complicated willow-pattern bridge. The main path continues to the dell, divides round a big clump of foliage, rejoins through boulders—by now the rocks are huge—the oriental plants begin, and we reach the bridge, rebuilt, and kept painted. It crosses an irregular pond on to a little mown lawn with a scarlet, white and green temple built above a wall from which a huge brown cow looks down, with an ochre moon between her horns. On either side of the lawn is a massive Chinese gate, and lead dragons are let into the grass. On to a little court with a glazed earthenware lion and a large dragon pot on the walls, a turn past a stone toad and into the pavilion, which has a bamboo seat and alcoves and grotesques. At the far side is an absolutely black grotto passage which leads into a superb rock garden in pure Chinese taste with earth, water, narrow and broad flat stones and huge boulders, chosen with great discrimination and set among ferns and foliage without a flower in sight. Then escape from the involuted garden and the grotto is complete, and we are out on to a lawn before the house with a big lily pond set in the curves of sloping mown banks.

To the right a bridge is now visible which must lead back to the garden, but instead it is at a higher level and there are sphinxes and clipped yews and a gate into a passage between high banks and all is Egypt with a rustic lining.

[1] Photograph on page 108.

The Chinese garden at Biddulph Grange.

This is one of the most extraordinary buildings ever designed. The anteroom to the inner shrine is square with four entrances all lined with wood and the roof worked in dark concentric squares of branchwork. To the left is a rustic alcove and ahead a large and sinister stone carving of the utmost grotesquerie, top lit; a baboon in a belt with a large buckle. There is a seated Egyptian figure too, quite normal. When the baboon has been sufficiently admired one may leave him by steps to his left that lead up to a sham timbered summerhouse on top, another shock that has been well concealed by step-pyramids of yew that from the other side seemed the influence of Saqqara. Or the ante-room before the god may be left through the fourth entrance which is under another, different, summerhouse two storeys high with a lattice window; 1856. From here a long grass walk stretches down an avenue of trees to calm the surprised spirit and there is a side path back to the Chinoiserie.

So far as I know there are no written theories, no volumes of justification, no word at all, but James Bateman must have been one of the greatest romantic gardeners, an artist able to use his site to the utmost in a composition all his own while understanding with a clarity remarkable for his time the underlying principles of his two inspirations, both the sinuous and graceful surprises of Chinoiserie (and we have forgotten a gothick prospect tower surprise on the way) with a touch or two of horror and a black grotto, and the sombre axial planning of Egypt, moving steadily into the darkness.

The pagoda had a remarkably long run; there is a most mad and pitiful little nine-teenth century one in galvanized iron like several collapsing umbrellas one on top of the other at Tenbury Wells in Hereford and Worcester. It stands at the entrance of a failed pump room and brine bath, an attempt at spa-status so tenuous that William Addison never listed it in *English Spas*. There is an octagon belfry under one frill and three frills drooping to a two-storey base with white gothic windows. It is on a brick plinth perhaps 8 feet across and a tiny passage leads into the derelict pump room with tin wings to an arched brick central façade. The brickwork here and on two chimneys is stylish, a com-plication of black, red and white, but the pagoda is quite overshadowed by the splendid central market building, and no one could tell us anything of the spa, the waters, the date or the builders.

Throughout the nineteenth century China, and later Japan, held their influence in other fields, particularly graphics; tea packets and tins were often Chinese in design wherever their tea came from, and at least one notable matchbox still exists labelled with a mandarin, views and Chinese characters, bogus or real; the wood engravings are charming and the design was entered at Stationer's Hall. It was bought early this cen-tury as a curio when an ironmonger's shop in Middleham was selling up and now keeps its exotic pride of place in a china cabinet.

Egypt appeared early among the follies when the entire mummy decayed in the hermitage at Enston before the Civil War. After that, until the interest aroused by the publication of the researches by Napoleon's expedition, and their beautiful illustrations, the Egyptian style was influential only via Rome with the sphinx and the obelisk, and the pyramids which the Romans adopted as funerary monuments.

There are dozens of obelisks to be seen in all sizes, and very few are of special interest, though many look well as vista-closers or at the intersections of grass rides in woods. For example, there is one at Moreton House in Dorset. It was described lovingly and at length in a contemporary newspaper so we know that the pedestal is 16 feet high and

10 feet square, the obelisk 51 feet 4 inches, made of Portland stone. It weighs four tons, and the 9-foot urn is nailed to the top with a bar of copper 20 feet long, and it was designed by James Hamilton of Weymouth. How dull it sounds! But it was put up in 1785–6 by Captain John Houlton to the memory of James Frampton, who died in 1784, in the centre of one of his first plantations of trees, and is a charming and melancholy obelisk, still among the trees.

The two most splendid obelisks are in Ireland. One was built by Mrs Conolly of Castletown to relieve famine in the winter of 1739–40. It was probably designed by Richard Castle who had been assistant to Sir Edward Pearce, the designer of the house, who was working at Carton only four miles away. The 140-foot obelisk was set two miles northwest of the house on the highest point of land at the end of the main vista— the land in fact belonged to Carton, but in 1968 it was bought for Castletown, and the obelisk has been restored by the Irish Georgian Society. Ordinary obelisks being two-a-penny, this one is surprising because it crowns an elaborate and lovely structure, in pale grey stone yellowed with lichen. It starts with five arches, increasing in height toward the centre, with the largest one and the smallest two set forward. These small ones support square cupolas with acorns on top; each of the recessed ones carries another arch its own height and, above, square pillars echoing the obelisk and crowned with pinnacled urns and eagles. Over the big centre arch stands a pedimented room with smaller arches for the views, and two more tiny ones at the side. Above soars the obelisk. More arches are cut in the sides of the centre bay at first-floor level—there are fourteen altogether, a very complicated composition leaping alive in the landscape. But Mrs Conolly's sister wrote in March 1740 'My sister is building an Obleix to answer a Vistoe from the Bake of Castletown. It will cost her 3 or 4 hundred pounds at least, and I believe more. I don't know how she can dow so much and live as she duse.'

The obelisk at Castletown. On the following page, *a lithograph of it by Richard Beer.*

The other fine Irish obelisk is at Stillorgan on the outskirts of Dublin. Stillorgan was a great house with formal gardens and an extensive park. It is now difficult to guess where the rest of it was, but the huge obelisk informs us precisely how grand. It rises nobly, as no other obelisk rises, in the garden of the nineteenth-century Hospice, serene and overwhelming, probably built in 1727 for the second Viscount Allen, and attributed both to Edward Peale and to Richard Castle. The obelisk is more than 100 feet high, and finely cut in granite on crossed grotto arches made of huge lumps of uncut rock. These lead into a large vaulted chamber, and over them climb double staircases to a platform from which there are four more rusticated entrances into a mausoleum in the base of the obelisk.

It is well looked after and has been given a palm tree or two, but Pearce's grotto is in sad and straightened condition, cut right away even from the obelisk, in the grounds of a house in Park Avenue. Through the modern garden is a small piece of the sunk central walk of Stillorgan's formal garden, leading straight to the very large brick grotto, impressive and chilling, a stark and extraordinary work. There are seven chambers, above ground but banked over and top lit, entered through a panelled wall. The anteroom has become a lean-to shed; then come the seven, cross-vaulted and domed alternately, with the central dome of the line larger and lanterned. Perhaps the usual decoration of shells and minerals, spar and coral was to be added later? But the brick work is precise and beautiful, even the Friday mosque at Isphahan flicks into mind; an excessive thought, but something brings it. What was this grotto for? A place to walk on a wet day, exercising a spare and cultivated mind? To be decorated with mosaics? Did Lord Allen go to Ravenna on his Tour? 'No one has a better taste than this lord'; he would surely repay research.

The obelisk at Stillorgan.

The obelisk on a cross-vaulted arch which looks like the Bernini fountain in the Piazza Navona in Rome, was a particularly Irish fashion, and others survive. One at Belan, Kildare, is very pitiful and pretty, lost in the fields, its arches falling and a crowning eagle now without head or outstretched wings, altogether not long for this world but beautiful enough for there to be talk of restoration. (Belan's other folly will probably decay—it is an experiment like the crown of Lanrick but a failure, two stone stages with four columns atop holding up a roof with a single central column, now without a capital. Even if it had an eagle, which I doubt, it was a poor folly.)

Most of the early pyramids are tall and Roman in proportion, like the tomb of Cestius that the Grand Tourists saw, and many eighteenth-century tombs both inside the churches and out, were based on this sort of pyramid. When they are large enough one hears about them; there is a famous one for Mad Jack Fuller, and a beauty at Castlerickard in Meath, the monument to Swift, ingeniously built with the stone courses set, not horizontal, but at right angles to the steep sides, centreing in a lozenge inscribed SWIFTE.

But there are larger and finer pyramids outside the churchyards; we have seen the Needle's Eye at Wentworth Woodhouse, pure folly, but most eighteenth-century pyramids are likely to be memorials or mausoleums, even when they are part of a landscape scheme like that first one at Castle Howard or like the Stanway pyramid in Gloucestershire. This was built in 1750 by Robert Tracy in memory of his father, across the 'cascade glade', on the main axis, once crossed by a high level canal. The cascade has gone, but the pyramid is a beauty, about 70 feet high standing on a cubed base of golden stone with four open arches about 20 feet square. It is canted off inside to an octagon with a shell-headed niche in each wall. A fine plaster ceiling with shells and cupids fell in the Second World War, and the conical structure of the pyramid is revealed. A painting in the house shows the view from it, across the canal with a boat, and on the banks strollers, and a plump gentleman with a telescope. Behind the house the Cotswolds are unchanged.

The obelisk at Belan.

Obelisk-pyramids reach their crazy peak at Tong in Salop. Tong was the Vernons' castle—their tombs are in the Church—and although later associations with Lady Mary Wortley Montagu and Mrs Fitzherbert could hardly have been romantic in the middle of the eighteenth century, there was enough genuine mediaeval glamour at Tong to satisfy almost anyone. The house was bought from the second Duke of Kingston by the rare exception in about 1758. He was George Durant, who came of a Worcestershire family and was just back from Havana, twenty-five years old with a large fortune. The traditions that Hengist of Hengist and Horsa had built the beginnings of the Vernons' castle meant nothing to a determined builder, and in about 1764 he pulled down almost the whole of the old late gothic house and put up a new gothick house, a splendid essay in the mediaeval taste by Capability Brown. Calvert's 1830 *Picturesque Views of Staffordshire and Shropshire* describes it: 'fancifully composed, partly of Moorish, and partly of Gothic architecture, and produces a grand effect from the numerous and widely extended minarets and pinnacles, and the stately crown given to the whole by two lofty and magnificent Turkish domes'. In spite of such domes and minarets as remained twenty years ago, it did not look as if any oriental effect was intended at all; on one of the surrounding walls of the park is a bas-relief of the house as it was in its heyday, and it was much more like the engravings of Nonsuch than the East. A few details looked faintly Indian, certain windows on the side turrets for instance, but they occurred again over the central door in a more elaborate form and were then indisputably gothick. The beautiful remaining façade was demolished in 1954.

George Durant died in 1780 and was succeeded by his son, another George, who was then only four. When he grew up there was no excuse for him to pull down the still modish house and he set himself to embellish the park and the outbuildings. 'His eccentric character,' says Griffiths,[1] 'is indicated by the quaint buildings, monuments with hieroglyphics, and inscriptions alike to deceased friends, eternity, and favourite animals, which were then to be found on every part of the demesne.' Only Convent Lodge and the Egyptian Aviary remain, but Mr Griffiths records some more: a real hermit lived in a cave in the rocks of the gorge, a gentleman called 'Carolus' who had seen better days and lived happily in the Tong hermitage until his death, recorded in the *Gentleman's Magazine,* in 1822. There was a Dropping Well inscribed 'Adam's Ale licensed to be drunk on the premises 1838'; a stone pedestal with a ball on top, inscribed AB HOC MOMENTO PENDET ÆTERNITAS. GEO. DURANT AN. 1821; and the jaw bones of a whale, that favourite piece of nature's gothic, arched over one of the paths with MORS JANUA VITAE and POST TOT NAUFRAGIA PORTUM on the jaws. The coal house had MAUSOLEUM over each of its three doors and a pyramid at Belle Isle Cottage, PARVA SED APT. His father was commemorated by a pedestal bearing an urn and the words of Wren's epitaph in St Paul's SI MONUMENTUM REQUIRIS, CIRCUMSPICE. Here and there, where a convenient stone face offered itself, BEATI QUI DURANT appeared, which was surely true.

Convent Lodge remains in excellent repair. A gate and a stretch of ornamental wall would seem outside the scope of this book, for odd or beautiful entrances are common enough, but this is a gate too crazy and too curious to leave out. The gates themselves are cast iron, just lattice-work set in a rich ecclesiastical border, but the piers that support them are covered with the most extraordinary symbolical carvings, and so is a stretch of wall to their left as one looks in. The piers are square, about six feet high, surmounted by tall pyramids as high again. Up each edge of the pyramids climbs a rich

[1] G. Griffiths. *A History of Tong, Shropshire.*

swag of fruit and leaves and flowers, artichokes and grapes, all joining at the top in a cluster of pointed leaves on which sits a pineapple with, of course, another cluster of pointed leaves on top again. On the sides of the pyramids are carved a hand, a serpent biting a foot, kneeling feet, interlaced triangles, a halo. On the inner sides of the piers, carved Tudor roses act as bosses for the gate hinges and the other faces carry Maltese crosses, a rose, a setting and a rising sun, and fire. Two pieces of thick rope, one long and one short, are carved in the pinkish stone bracing the top of each pier. They start joined in single knots from which their huge tasselled ends hang down on each side of the hinge, run round the pier and loop together again on the opposite sides, where the short lengths end in tassels and the long ones run on, up and down along the castellations of two walls that curve out for about 25 feet on each side of the gate to two more piers with similar ropes, and ships, a sheaf of corn, a skip of bees, a cornucopia, a pierced heart, a Roman lamp and book, a Staffordshire knot, a basket of fruit, a tree, a book again, a snail, a butterfly, a snake swallowing its own tail, a bat, a coil of rope, a flower, anchors, arrows, crosses and lyres. They are all carved with some skill in technique but much crudity of drawing, and this is even more noticeable in a series of plaques that decorate the walls and also a further stretch of wall that runs on to the left. The central panels of the curved walls are bas-reliefs that show the house as it used to be, front and back, with all the minarets and domes, and the other panels, all about a yard square and a yard apart, have rococo shields bearing arms, a cross in a circle, an imperial crown, a mitre, a fleur-de-lys and a huge butterfly. Between them are cut Christian and St Andrew's crosses right through the thickness of the wall, and there are also seats, two sets of three niches, inscribed SISTE VIATOR and RESTEZ ICI, invite the educated traveller to pause, and, perched between them on top of the wall, is the Pulpit from which Mr Durant and his wife could watch them sit, and perhaps talk to them. The Pulpit is octagonal, made of open gothick arches with their spandrels carved with cross-keys, stars, an hour-glass, serpents, lamps and a wreath. On top of its shallow dome is a thick green head of weed hair and a stone globe of the world supported by a serpent. George Durant's seat inside the Pulpit, commanding the road, is formed by the front ends of two lions with crossed paws, backed up against one another to leave a smooth saddle between them. There are more animals outside, for where the wall runs into the sides of the Pulpit are two hideous stone snakes holding rings in their teeth through which are looped the tassels of the rope-ends.

The animals, ropes, knots, artichokes and grapes suggest very forcibly indeed Manueline gothic transmitted through Durant's eye to an English stone-carver; perhaps the elder Durant had engravings of architecture seen on his travels, or perhaps his descriptions inspired his son. Or the similarity may be chance. The presence across the park of the Egyptian Aviary at Vauxhall Farm, however, seems proof of influence on the building styles of the younger Durant. The Egyptian Aviary is a pyramidal hen-house about 20 feet high, no mere conversion of a folly to a farmer's convenience but consecrated from the first brick to its purpose: it is dedicated AB OVO. The pyramid is built up on a stone base in four stages of yellow brick trimmed with vitrified brick quoins, and separated by three projecting courses of stone. At the top is a stone cap pierced by egg-shaped holes. The house stands on a base of pink sandstone, which has a little door for the hens and another door for a very small egg-collector.

Tong. The gates at Convent Lodge.

Tong. The Egyptian Aviary at Vauxhall Farm.

At the top on the stone cap is carved 'Egyptian Aviary 1842' (or 1812, the figures are vague) and on the other side AB OVO. A little way down is an enchanting carving of a swan and rushes like a butter mould, set among the bricks on a piece of sandstone brick size. Another side has TRIAL BY JURY, and two inscriptions that are indecipherable. On the next stage down is a carving of a cat carrying a kitten in her mouth, TRANSPORTA-TION. Down again to SCRATCH BEFORE YOU PECK, BETTER COME OUT OF THE WAY LOVE and LIVE AND LET LIVE. There is also a carving of a cock, and TEACH YOUR GRANNY has been recorded, but must be one of the illegible pieces. To aerate the hens, the sides of the pyramid have bricks removed in various diamond and cross patterns, all outlined with dark blue vitrified bricks. A very fine folly.

Blickling Hall in Norfolk has a beautiful and sober pyramid by Bonomi erected in memory of the Earl of Buckingham who died in 1793, raised on a base 45 feet square in taut grey stone blocks 2 feet deep, seen down a wide avenue of yews. The door, win-dows and heraldic cow, hound and bull are all most finely detailed and very English, and the proportions of the pyramid are Egyptian, not Roman.

The rarer step pyramids like the one at Saqqara were also imitated, but on an even smaller scale, at Halswell, Mount Mapas, and The Neale, but I have not been able to find out what inspired them; certainly the Halswell pyramid was built before the books that followed Napoleon's 1798 campaign, after which Egyptian motifs other than obelisk, pyramid and sphinx begin to appear on follies—the pylon entrance was liked, and there were gardens like Biddulph and Stancombe. But in spite of a fashion for 'Egyptian' furniture early in the nineteenth century, a few isolated buildings, an instructive Egyptian Court in the Crystal Palace and later some epic films, Egypt never seriously caught the imagination of the English until the discovery of the tomb of Tutankhamun in 1922. Before that, the Egyptians were either mummies and a specialized taste, or hieratic figures with eyes in the sides of their heads walking stiffly sideways on flat feet or sitting, hands on knees, gazing beyond one, shadowy behind the overpowering stones of the Great Pyramid and the Sphinx (the garden sphinxes were small and sexy). They were improbable and remote, while the Chinese, though far away, were alive and had been seen to be human, smoking pipes and playing musical instruments, making porcelain and building pagodas. They were emperors, nobles, traders and peasants, just like Europeans, and so offered a fine inspiration, at once comfortable and exotic. Now that one young Pharaoh is Tut to us all, any future fashion for folly building may be expected to include a hypostyle hall or two.

India influenced wallpapers and fabrics (and literature a little) but had far less influence on architecture and on follies in particular than China or even than Egypt, in spite of Sezincote and the Brighton Pavilion. Only at the end of the nineteenth century shall we see a large folly with some Indian detail, though there is some similarity between a 1789 Daniell drawing[1] of a conical milestone on the Grand Trunk Road and both Mount Mapas at Killiney and the conical folly at Barwick. But this is a passing thought, and the likeness is probably coincidence, though certainly painting, drawings and books of Indian architecture were popular. There seems no reason for it; as inspiration India just never caught on.

In many eighteenth-century topographical drawings, tour books and estate records, we find references to Moorish Kiosks and Turkish Tents. Most of them have gone, some were designed and never built. In the engravings they are very like the Chinese pavilions with curved roofs, but can sometimes be distinguished from them by the crescent on top. One lovely Moorish Temple survives at Elvaston Castle in Derbyshire (no crescent). The grounds were beautifully landscaped by William Barron of Edinburgh in the early 1830s for the fourth Earl of Harrington, with a big serpentine lake and an extensive series of random grot-works, very Chinese, some of the best rocaille we have. The largest piece is about 150 feet long, with arches, holes, sandstone, marble, tufa and minerals. One small piece intrudes into the formal garden across the lake in front of the house, a great stretch of lawn with topiary, very fat and sassy with new plants coming on in beds, little tufts of box like feather dusters.

Once this lawn had a unique folly, a sham ruin in topiary. An engraving shows a great serpentine wall of tope, with what appear to be porters' chairs and suspended swaggy bits scattered. The text explains how 'l'ancien *pleasure-ground* d'Elvaston-Castle ... offrait, dans une enceinte de palissades de verdure faisant office de rempart, quantité d'arbres et d'arbustes taillés de manière à figurer les ruines épasés d'un temple.'[2]

At the end of this and to the right is an enclosed lawn and the Moorish Temple, with its remarkable silhouette which is echoed in one of the lodges; the sides swing in with concave curves at the top and the roof joins them with two more, au Chinois, but edged

---

1 RIBA Drawings Collection.

2 *L'Art des Jardins*. Baron Ernouf. Paris 1890.

Above, *the Moorish Temple at Elvaston.*
Left, *ornament in the Japanese garden at Batsford.*
Opposite, *the pagoda at Peasholm Park.*

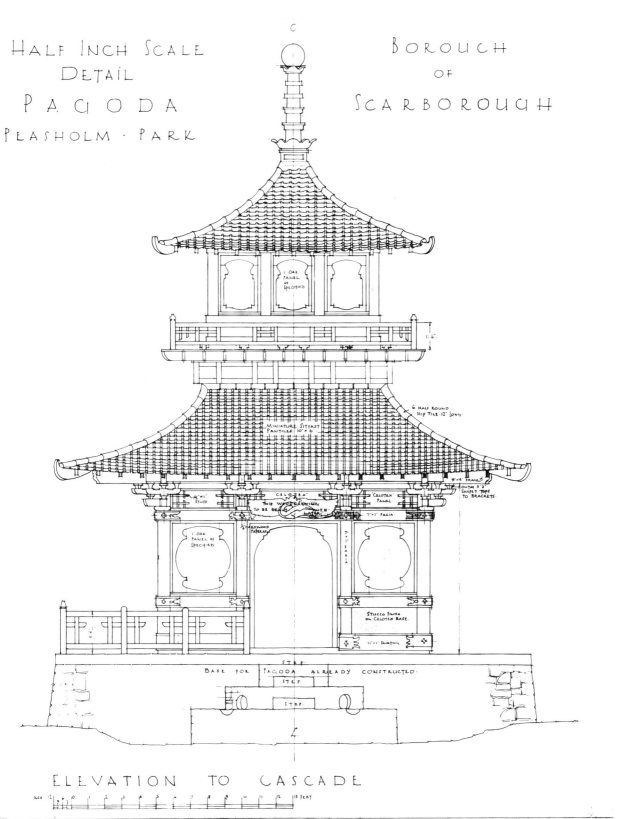

HALF INCH SCALE DETAIL PAGODA — PEASHOLM · PARK

BOROUGH OF SCARBOROUGH

ELEVATION TO CASCADE

with delicate villa bargeboarding. The entrance is by a coffered door from a raised terrace at the back into a fine room about 25 feet square painted with Moorish-gothick paired twisted columns. The side windows are oval, with lattice tracery filled with lattice glass, and the big window on to the garden is very large and vaguely Alhambra-ish with the same tracery and an iron balcony in the purest debased baroque. The entrance hall of the house (Elvaston is a public park) should not be missed. It is fan-vaulted gothic with elaborate carving and gilding in the highest Victorian romantic style, with the important carving painted in transparent colour over metal—the 'done metallic' of the fairground. Above the fireplace is a huge blazonry of fleurs-de-lys and leopards, with Gallantry on the left and Courtesy on the right.

The last of the exotic influences was that of Japan, coming long after that of China because Japan did not admit foreigners even for trade until 1868. Japonaiserie has been almost wholly disastrous, being generally confined to miniaturizing; small rockeries, small stone lanterns of repellent ugliness, bronze storks and a glut of azaleas, double pink cherries and coloured acers. The Japanese tea house at Batsford, set in Lord Redesdale's gardens, and the 'pagoda' at Peasholme Park in Scarborough are the prettiest Japanese buildings I have found. The Peasholme pagoda, which cost about £700, and its cascade £2,500, was designed in 1929 by George Alderson to complete a Japanese theme started for the new public park in 1912 by an earlier borough surveyor, Harry W. Smith. It stands on high wooded ground with the magnificent rocky cascade falling from it into a lake, an open, two-storeyed building with wide-swinging eaves, a low pavilion on the shore, and a floating band-stand for concerts on the lake which cleverly has a flat roof with fretted supports and upturned corners, so that the Japanese theme is continued, but the pagoda dominates. Lanterns hang from slanting poles on the shores; if it were a work of the eighteenth century, secluded and aristocratic, it would receive much admiration, for the whole composition is charming, a notable end to a short-lived style.

TEMPLE MORESQUE

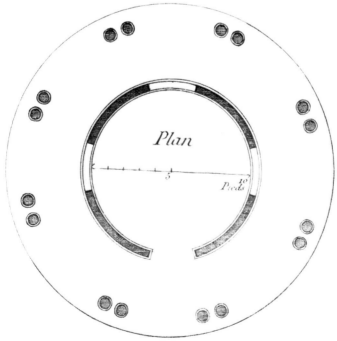

Plan

5   10
             Pieds

Follies in the Classical Style

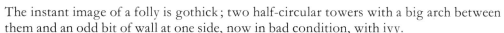

The instant image of a folly is gothick; two half-circular towers with a big arch between them and an odd bit of wall at one side, now in bad condition, with ivy.

The secondary image may be beyond style, an eyecatcher like Rousham, or a grotesque like Jack the Treacle-eater.

The third image will probably be that of a pagoda or a Chinese tea house.

The classical folly image comes last, but in fact there were many such follies, and some are on a very grand scale: they have lost their place because columns and pediments disguise them as the rotundas and tempiettos of routine garden architecture.

This disguise conceals sham ruins, eyecatchers, vista-closers, prospect towers—every form of folly except those inescapably gothick thoughts, the sham castle and the ruined abbey.

One of the earliest classical sham façades was added to the Whitehouse at Chillington in Staffordshire in about 1725, possibly by Francis Smith of Warwick, the architect of the house, from which the farm was then no doubt shockingly visible. But there is also a possibility that it was designed by James Paine. It is a very simple and elegant design, subject at the time of writing both to offers of official help with restoration and to the threat of a new motorway.

Another early classical folly, and easily the largest, is at Chatelherault on the outskirts of Glasgow, forlorn on the very edge of a gravel pit, but to be saved. It was designed by William Adam for the Duke of Hamilton, appearing as *The Dogg Kennel* in Vitruvius Scoticus, *The Wham* to the Reverend William Patrick (presumably the same name as the Blair Atholl *Whim*?), and said to be designed 'after the model of the Citadel of Chatelherault in Poitou about 1732.' The date is unconfirmed but likely.

None of the names prepare one for its grandeur, a long and very elegant screen once beautifully ornamented with urns, about 280 feet long, a mile south of the Hamilton's palace, pinning into Palladian order a banqueting hall-summerhouse-hunting lodge at one end, simpler rooms at the other for staff, the kennels (which have gone) and a formal walled garden, for these were still fashionable in Scotland, where the design of the landscape did not change as fast as the design of the house.

The fine plasterwork of the lower rooms in the west pavilion was destroyed by fire in 1944 but one even more elaborate upper room survives; all was probably the work of Clayton, and what remains is superb.

One place, Stowe in Buckinghamshire, has almost everything possible to the classical style including a small sham ruin. It also has a sham castle, a gothick pavilion, and a tower. An Egyptian pyramid, a Chinese house, a Witch's House and the only known Saxon Tower have all gone, with at least ten other conceits. Stowe is a great problem

The National Memorial on Calton Hill, Edinburgh (see page 422).

Glasgow. The classical façade at Chatelherault.

for folly definition, for 37 things still survive and some of them are very borderline.

If we dismiss at once as garden ornament the Doric and Corinthian arches, four lodges, three bridges (Kent's shell one of *c.* 1740 seems never to have had more than a scattering of shells), the menagerie, the rotondo, five Classical temples, a lion fountain, two shelters (one gothick) and five pavilions (even the lovely Boycott ones), and at last dismiss as marginal five monuments, then seven assorted follies are left, only three of which are in the gothick taste. Let us look at these first. There is the Gothick Temple designed by Gibbs, and begun in 1741—one of the best buildings on the estate. It is triangular in plan with pentagonal turrets at the corners; one carries a tall tower with the stairs and the others very elegant gothick lanterns. The walls between the turrets have castellated gables which shield the roof. Inside is a hall which rises the height of the building and has a domed ceiling bearing the arms of the Temple family, and the first floor has a gallery with tall windows looking out on to the park. This is one of the few buildings at Stowe which does not play tricks with scale when photographed: Kent's Temple of British Worthies, for instance, can be photographed so that it appears about 50 feet high, when in fact it is very much smaller. The Gothick Temple is built of a rich ginger ironstone so hot in tone that on a fine day it looks as if it has just come out of the oven.

The Bourbon Tower is by Vanbrugh, a circular stone building with a band of round-headed arches for decoration and round-headed windows; a rare Norman excursion—it would be nice to have a date closer than 1713–26. There is a narrower octagon tower to crown it, possibly later. The earthwork was added in 1845, and the name was given in honour of a visit in 1808 from the future Louis XVIII when in exile. Sir Henry Williams Wynn was there:

> The dinner, *entre nous,* was the worst I ever saw upon a Table, and worse served than anything I ever saw before. Lord Buckingham took care of the King and the rest of the Blood were obliged to take care of themselves, without a servant *literally* to take away their plates, or a glass of wine within their reach. The table was covered with dishes, which were so cold that they were not eatable, with the exception of a *cold* Pye which from its proximity to an immense fire, was warmed up again.

There is also Stowe Castle, a mile to the east, a massive wall articulated on five square towers and forming the back of a farmhouse with two pretty ogival doors. This was one of Lord Cobham's last works, in the late 1740s, and nothing is yet known of its designer but it is a fine convincing folly.

On at last to the classical follies, all by Kent. The largest and most famous is the Temple of British Worthies, 1735. This is a semi-circle of niches with a stepped pyramid in the centre and a horse-shoe hole that once held a Mercury. Eight portrait busts were made by Rysbrack in 1732 for the Saxon Tower and eight more added by Rysbrack or Scheemakers the next year to complete this more ambitious commemoration. The first Worthies are Queen Elizabeth, Shakespeare, Bacon, Milton, Hampden, Newton, Locke and William III. The second ones are King Alfred, the Black Prince, Gresham, Sir John Barnard, Drake, Raleigh, Jones and Pope.

One of the most charming of the conceits at Stowe is the Congreve Monument designed by Kent in 1736. This is a small tall pyramid with a half-urn on the front carved with masks, panpipes, bow and arrows, sword and leaves. On top sits a beautifully carved monkey, admiring into a looking-glass.

Nearby is Kent's Pebble Alcove, a classical façade to a rustic TEMPLA QUAM DILECTA, restored by Benjamin Gibbon in 1967. Lord Cobham's coat-of-arms dominates the composition, in the middle under a shell-design cove. But all is pebbles, black, white, red, yellow and grey set in cream plaster, with the signs of the zodiac, a robin, stars, a butterfly, a bunch of cherries and a whale.

The Hermitage, Kent again, is not at all what one expects, a little stone pavilion, carefully slightly ruined, with a wreath and pipes.

The grotto must have been beautiful. It was made in 1741 and its sad remains, undecorated and unsafe, stand smothered in trees above the Shell Bridge at the head of the water once known as the Styx. Passages of rock and tufa curve from both sides into a square cross-vaulted room with a niche and a big opening on to the water and the view.

Two fine exotics are completely lost. The Chinese House can still be seen on an engraving made in 1750. It was said to have been decorated by Mr Slauter, painted on canvas outside, and 'India Japann'd Work' in, with a picture of a sleeping lady. It had a curved roof and dragons. Vanbrugh's big Pyramid was probably more in the Roman than Egyptian mode, being so early, but Scheemaker's carvings in the pediment of the Temple of Peace and Concord also have an African note that should not be missed, a fallen Egyptian statue, some squat stout palms and a cadaverous lioness.

Vanbrugh and Kent, at Stowe and everywhere else they worked, used classical and gothick architecture alike exactly as they pleased, entirely for their own aesthetic ends.

But other architects and men of taste were not all of this temper. In 1732, the Society of Dilettanti was formed; *dilettante* today means dabbling, then it meant serious study. Two hundred and fifty years ago it was still a commonplace for an amateur in any art or science to become, like Vanbrugh himself, a most thorough professional without a raised eyebrow anywhere; as *dilettante* derives only from *delectare,* any professional should still find it an important thing to be.

The Society was founded to encourage the study and enjoyment of Greek classical art and had great influence, I am inclined to think a bad one, delightful though many of the buildings it produced were. Rome had been accepted gladly and from any source, and was bashed and bandied about at will. Greece became a matter of earnest scholarship and many architects were afraid to put a foot wrong. I have never been able to understand why 'scholarly' should be a word of positive praise when applied to a derivative style.

The first influence in the landscaped parks came from the architects James Stuart and Nicholas Revett who went to Greece and spent several careful years measuring and drawing classical buildings. The first volume of *Antiquities of Athens* was not published until 1762, seven years after their return, but meanwhile they had designed a number of copies and essays which were widely copied in their turn. The first one known anywhere is at Hagley, 'Athenian' Stuart's Doric Temple of 1758, with a portico of six columns prostyle, based on the Hephaestion; it might be a measured drawing. Next, the Temple of the Winds at West Wycombe in 1759; (the freer translation of the Athenian original suggests that the work was done by Donowell working to Stuart's instructions rather than by the master himself). Soon there was a Doric temple at Shugborough, probably by Stuart, and also another Temple of the Winds by him, and a Hadrian's Arch and a Choragic Monument of Lysicrates called The Lanthorn of Demosthenes; the Ansons had a fairly full set, and had also been among the first with the Chinese style.[1] The most beautiful Tower of the Winds is the one Stuart did for Lord Londonderry at Mount Stewart in County Down, much later, about 1780, superbly and elegantly decorated, a wonderful bog fir floor almost mirroring a ceiling of top Irish-standard plasterwork.

From Hagley on, Greek revival spread all over Europe and America; it lasted for about two centuries. The Adam Roman and Pompeiian styles ousted it for a little, but after that scholarly principles began to attack Rome too and of course the gothick. The influence of China waned, and only amateur grotesque kept the follies fanciful. But this lies in the future; back to the eighteenth century.

Horton Hall in Northamptonshire has two classical follies, an eyecatcher called the Tripartite Arch, a good Ionic span of three open arches, put up in the eighteenth century across the drive from Horton to Castle Ashby and based like most eighteenth-century arches on the lower part of the Arch of Constantine. Later, the two smaller arches and the circular openings above them were filled in and rooms added at the back. Still later, more rooms were added behind these, and little kitchens yet further back. The big centre arch remains open.

[1] See pages 112 and 389.

Stowe. Above, *the Gothick Temple; from a lithograph by Leonard Rosoman.* Below, *the Temple of British Worthies.*

Horton Hall. The rustication on the Menagerie.

Across the river, a tributary of the Nene, and now very isolated across the fields, a long walk along the edge of the wheat, is the Menagerie, a fine building by Thomas Wright,[1] superbly finished in every detail, and now to be preserved. The shutters are closed but the magnificent damaged interior with carved columns and fireplaces can be seen through cracks. The centre room has a flat plaster ceiling coved down to the walls, with a winged Father Time in the centre, and a sun over the bay window. A guilloche moulding runs round and there is some plasterwork of corn, ribbons and medallions unusually freely running along the cove. There is a scroll pediment over the mantelpiece, where there was probably once a painting.

But the outside is even better than the inside with heavy rustication round the doors and windows of the big rooms and the side screens, rustication not in the usual diamond, vermiculated or cyclopean styles but in curls, long six-inch curls carved on keystones and cills, and flatter curls on the voussoirs and frames, as though the owner's great wigs had been stuck to the stones and petrified there.

There are two other arches for special mention; one is Heaven's Gate on Siddown Hill above Highclere Castle, an eyecatcher from the house and a frame for the view down the beeches from the hill. The road passes a circular Grotto Lodge, exceptionally well built in knapped flint with stone trim and an octagonal castellated chimney on top. It is entered via a smaller tower with a conical roof, joined on by castellations and an arrow-slit but has no grotto at all. The little road dwindles past woods and fields up

[1]See pages 91 and 222.

into the tall beeches on the hill, and becomes sodden and almost lost but reaches Heaven's Gate at last

ROB^T HERBERT
Hunc Arcum
Posuit An° D
1731

It is a very thin red brick span of three arches about 60 feet high and a 100 feet long with a pediment over the central arch and urns at the ends. It is very beautiful and very neglected, heavily grown with nettles and brambles and ash saplings, and the beeches lower down are too high, but the Gate is quite cut off in style and atmosphere from the Barry house of 1837 and the visitor is happy with it hidden.

The Triumphant Arch at Parlington Park[1] in West Yorkshire is much more prosperous; it was indeed built while the house it was to ornament was not. Today, there is no house at all; the pre-Georgian one was demolished in 1950. The Gascoigne family, Roman Catholic and Tory, went to Parlington in 1721, but Sir Thomas stayed mostly abroad, in Paris or on the Grand Tour. He married in 1772 and decided to improve the estate. He, and his son and son-in-law commissioned designs from John Carr in 1772, and later from three other architects. One of the first two designs was commissioned, stone delivered, abandoned for no known reason. Also in 1772 John Carr produced a pretty design for a chapel and chaplain's house disguised as a castle, with two-storey buildings at each end of an enclosed garden. It looks very like the earlier deer-folds at Sudbury and Bishop Auckland. Again, it was not built, though a circular gothick cow-shed was built and the ruin survives. In 1780, though, newly a Protestant and Member of Parliament, and firmly on the neo-classical wave, Sir Thomas decided on an arch; there is a sketch, probably his own, on the usual Arch of Constantine lines. In 1781 Thomas Leverton exhibited a drawing in the Royal Academy and a working drawing is inscribed 'To that Virtue which for a series of Years resisted Oppression & by a glorious Peace rescued its Country & Millions from Slavery. T.G. Dedicates this Arch. 1782.' At last it went up, beautifully built of now richly and variously weathering stone with excellent lettering on both faces, now bluntly

LIBERTY. IN. N. AMERICA. TRIUMPHANT. MDCCLXXXIII.

In 1806 the Prince of Wales set out for Parlington on a tour of Yorkshire, drove through the park as far as the arch, and turned back.

The estate was inherited in 1810 by Richard Oliver Gascoigne, whose taste reverted to the mediaeval. Near the arch is a square six-storey red brick castellated water-tower with white stone dressings, awkwardly placed and toy-like, and on the other side of the estate is The Old Chapel, tastefully sited on rough ground in a plantation in the bend of a stream, two pillars of an arch and two odd bits of wall; if any documents for these later works exist, no one has recorded them yet. And in any case the Triumphant Arch is the thing.

Disgust with Republican sentiments fortunately did not prejudice the Prince of Wales

---

[1] Information from an article by T. F. Friedman in the Leeds Arts Calendar, No. 66, 1970.

against classical architecture, for later he provided us with our only big classical sham
ruin, by the lake at Virginia Water in Surrey.

The water, almost two miles long, is one of the largest artificial lakes in England,
cunningly designed by Thomas Sandby some time soon after 1746 for William Duke
of Cumberland to drain the surrounding moorland while appearing ornamental. Later
a cascade was added and a cavern, the Robber's Cave, made of huge stones dug up on
Bagshot Heath and 'supposed to have belonged to a Druids' Temple'. At one point a
wide avenue of lawn leads up through magnificent cedars, and the more usual Surrey
birch and beech, away from the side of the lake. In pairs, lines and groups, standing
singly or joined by pieces of entablature, dozens of pretty Roman columns follow the
ride up, under the brick and concrete of a modern viaduct, to a little group round a
Greek altar stone. A great number of columns, caps and bases lie in front of them,
scattered on the ground. They were all brought to England by 'a wealthy traveller' in
1821, mostly from Leptis Magna, and are said to have lain in the courtyard of the British
Museum for some time till George IV had them brought here, where they were arranged
for him by Sir Jeffrey Wyattville. The composition might have been more effective, for
though individual groups are picturesque enough, it is always more pleasing to look
across rather than down the rows, until the last stretch of scattered fragments by the
water's edge, which is very charming indeed; it is hard to see why so many columns
ruined in the grass and set by water and fine trees should not make an almost endless
series of superb compositions, but there it is: they don't. Nevertheless, Virginia Water
is still an excellent object for an expedition from London.

There are two huge temples in the North, though, that make up for Virginia Water,
the National Memorial in Edinburgh and the Penshaw Memorial. Both are Doric. The
Edinburgh temple, a reproduction of the Parthenon, was begun as a memorial to the
Peninsular and Waterloo campaigns in 1822, but the money subscribed ran out and no
more came in, so it stands bleakly dark on Calton Hill, half a temple, bisected longways.

The Penshaw Monument at Houghton-le-Spring, Tyne and Wear, is black and visible
for miles. First it is like a big comb stuck into its distant hill top, then a change in the
direction of the sad colliery roads masses the end columns together and it looks almost
as it should, until another turn gives us a huge hollow tunnel. Then it disappears completely among slag-heaps, open-cast, cement works, chimneys, pit-wheels and drifts of
black, white, and grey smoke. At last it stands clear and sudden on its hill, a Doric
peripteral temple, 100 feet long, 53 feet wide and 70 feet high, with eighteen unfluted
columns, roofless and built from coarse local sandstone. The base is invisible until the
last few yards of the hill, and conversely when you climb upon it, you walk across the
banded shadows and see nothing but sky. One column appears to have held a spiral
staircase, but the entrance is now blocked.

The monument, a fairly close copy of the Temple of Theseus at Athens, was built in
1844 to the memory of the first Earl of Durham, Governor-General of Canada. The
laying of the foundation stone was a tremendous ceremony, led by the Earl of Zetland,
who was Grand Master of the Freemasons of England, and attended by large numbers
of Masons from the northern lodges. It is a most impressive place; the Greeks can never
have anticipated how beautiful their white painted temples, designed for a blue sky,
would look when transplanted to industrial England, placed against smoke, baked
black with soot, and used for absolutely nothing.

The sham ruins at Virginia Water.

The Grottoes

We left the beginning of the fashions for grottoes on page 15, with Aubrey's description of Thomas Bushell's grotto at Enston, with the mouldy mummy and the wooden Neptune. One senses a criticism in the description; possibly Aubrey did not feel that outdoor grottoes were suitable to the English climate and the other grotto-makers of the seventeenth century seem to have agreed with him—the only ones I know are built inside the house, rooms in the architecture of the time decorated with fantastic materials, rather than the fantastic architecture of later grottoes. They both, though, set the slow grotto pace; however fashionable grottoes later became they can rarely have been built solely for fashion; no labour can require more love than the excavation of a cave, or the erection of an artificial one and then the careful covering of its every surface with shells, spar, pebbles and bones, though some of the experts and professionals must have worked fast. A few grottoes remain as labyrinths, cut with little or no decoration, deeper and deeper into the rock like the Surrey tunnels, sometimes with an impulse that had little to do with the romantic movement, sometimes perhaps abandoned before the shells were stuck on, from despair or change of heart; in 1788 the extravagant Lord Donegal had '£10,000 of shells not yet unpacked'. Despair certainly inhibits restoration today; several owners have sad sacks of fallen shells, to be put back one day, but few do it.

The early grotto rooms, though, are wonderfully preserved. One is at Skipton Castle, North Yorkshire. In the gatehouse of the castle, and attributed to Lady Anne Clifford, is a heavy seventeenth-century room lined all through with grey foggy stone, volcanic and pitted, with the architectural details picked out with ear shells. The windows and door, which were altered in about 1800, and two niches are enclosed in heavy arches. In the tympanum over the door is a winged cherub face made of shells and lustreless mother of pearl. There is a tiny font with another head above, and a nice podge-faced sun rising from the sea against a sky of brown pebbles over the window. Everything is very massive. The most elaborate part of the decoration, in the fourth niche, is a figure known as Neptune, a reclining hermaphrodite covered with pieces of the mother of pearl. The little figure is beautifully modelled and surmounted by a big head with cat's ears and heavy jowl. A good grotto. A much larger room, a startling and impressive work most wonderfully preserved, is at Woburn Abbey, Bedfordshire. This is a room c. 1630, about 20 feet square with one side opening through three arches on to the garden and the other three most elaborately decorated. It was probably designed by Isaac de Caus. The roof is a simple, shallow, cross vault, the bays filled with four indentical strap-work patterns worked in ear-shells on a varied background of smaller shells. It is as precise as plaster. Up to the spring of the vaults the walls are rusticated with alternate bands of icicles and ear-shells running horizontally round, and the lunettes above are filled with

The central grotto at Ascot House, looking towards the lake (see page 160).

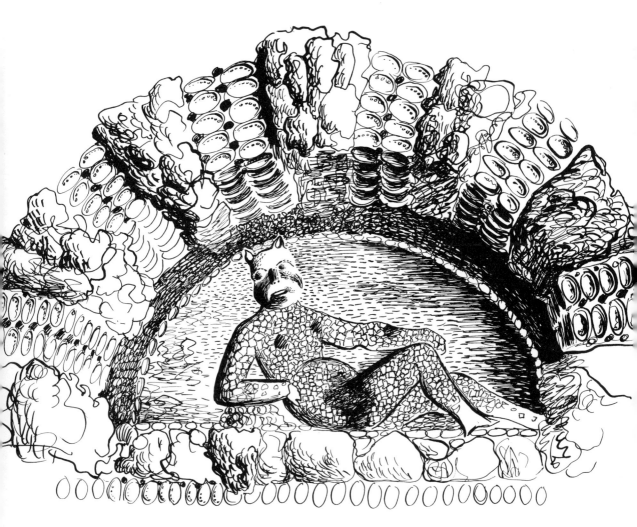

the most elaborate shell mosaic in bas-relief, a different Neptune mask in each, flanked by mermaids, boys on dolphins and, on the wall opposite the arches, male and female figures reclining on scallops pulled by dolphins over wonderfully managed waves whose glittering facets catch the light and seem to move. This main wall has a fountain, which alas does not play now, in a niche filled with curiously formed rock and tufa, and the other walls have heavily pedimented doors with reclining cupids in full relief in stone, for earthy contrast with the watery nymphs above. Once this room, which is in the early part of the house, must have opened freely on to the garden at least in summer, for the French windows filling the arches are later; beside one of them a date, 1660, is carved in the stone, but the strap-work ceiling is earlier; the shell-mosaic is wonderfully done, tight and precise, and may well have taken so long to do that by the time the roof was finished architectural taste had changed a little—the masks in the lunettes certainly look later, and the icicles later still; but the whole room has an air of being a design by Inigo Jones for some water-masque[1]—about 90 years will pass before anything else so fine is attempted, and then everything will be different.

[1] Walpole does in fact refer to a Jones grotto at Woburn, but I can find no other references.

The complicated and slightly inaccurate geometry of shells never ceases to amaze. Sometimes our collective eye may ignore them for years; they are, indeed, unfashionable today, but still to be seen in an occasional cottage or in the homes of architects and painters as inspiration on the mantelpiece, though a subtle difference may yet be observed between the shells in these two situations, for in the cottage they will be real shells of the larger and more bumbly kinds, while in the intellectual home they will probably be the tight engravings from old natural history books. It is impossible for the most sensitive and observant of artists to really see everything all the time; many things, even for him, are merged, for years or for ever, in the general blur of his surroundings, however much less cloudy that blur may be than the thick fog of imperception at which so many eyes would seem to stare. Every now and then, however, something swims suddenly into focus for him, and colours, for weeks or for ever, all his thought and work. The influence of some natural or manufactured form, of fern fronds in the Middle Ages or of nuts and bolts in the twentieth century, may consequently spread to other artists and become temporarily universal: the thing shines clear in every eye for a time and then sinks back out of focus while everyone observes something else.

Opposite, *the grotto room at Skipton Castle, late seventeenth century (see page 145)*. Above, *the grotto room at Woburn Abbey*.

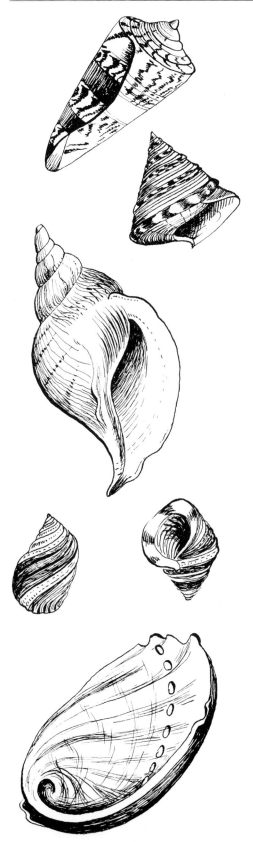

So shells. Eighteenth-century Europe really saw them. Scallops and conches and Spanish purples, giant clams from the tropics and ear shells from the Channel Islands were collected and loved, their subtlety much admired by an age with an eye for line. They were found to be bold and almost simple, like mussels, strong dark blue on the thin ridges outside and shining but chalky white inside, stained sometimes with the blue. Or like the Dolphin shell, infinitely twisted and frilled, although still built up on an almost simple substructure. Or reproducing, like certain clams, the undulating surfaces of the sea itself. Nothing about a shell is quite as it appears to be at first glance; tiger shells look sharply black and white, but the stripes and spots are never truly regular, ultimately unresolvable, and never quite black or quite clear, but swimming slightly as in the tides of some solid sea. There is no edge to, and no possibility of matching, the soft or rosy pinks that flush within so many shells; the colour retreats to the heart of the spiral as we look or sinks below the indefinite surface, soft and warm to the eye, hard and cool beneath the finger, matt and gleaming, at once chalk and china.

The larger shells are also exotic; they add to their own peculiar beauty the glamour of foreign parts and even simple grottoes usually have at least one big conch or clam in the middle of the most important piece of decoration. Probably the native shells were little thought of before the huge Pacific beauties came over, but these were expensive, and even well-to-do ladies like Mrs Delany made expeditions to the local seaside when shells were needed in quantity.

For the pleasure of examining individual shells and collecting single exquisite specimens soon palled, though when the British seaside holiday became a national institution in the nineteenth century, shells enjoyed their predestined popularity (de-

layed by a hundred years but universal), and
they decorated souvenirs and bimbelo-
teries until the end of the century. A specimen souvenir which I have is made of a
scallop shell, on to which is stuck a little
heap of small shining shells and fragments
of shingle, crowned by a larger scallop
standing up like a fan, acting as alcove for a
terra-cotta bust, the head and shoulders of
a rather unattractive old man in a night-cap.
He is the descendant of a life-size marble
nymph, and his scallops are a last echo of
the fantastic use which was suddenly found
for shells in the 1730s and 1740s.

For about twenty years (and sporadically
after that) duchesses, bankers, poets, Mrs
Delany, and Mr Pope gathered shells on the
shore, begged them from travellers, scram-
bled for them at sales and bought whole
shipments when they had to. Specimens of
minerals, felspar and fossils joined the
shells, and the lovely glittering collections,
fresh from the sea, not dusty and brown
as we see them now, were turned into
grottoes. Rooms, caves and whole suites of
underground apartments, furnished with
baths and marble seats, carpeted with moss
for special occasions and tinkling perpetually with cascades, were entirely encrusted with shells and spar in half the great
houses in England. The grottoes were cold,
damp, hard, spiky and utterly impractical,
and they cost a tremendous amount of time
and money, but nothing in all architecture
can have been more beautiful than one of
the great grottoes in its hey-day, pink and
white with shells, glittering with spar and
heightened with quartz and corals.

No one was bored with natural history;
it had not long existed, and all was fresh to
the eye, and knowledge was simple and
limited. Some grottoes were started as huge
show-cases for collections of fossils and
strange petrifactions, but even the most
fashionable and frivolous ones aimed at
variety, and had lists of the specimens to

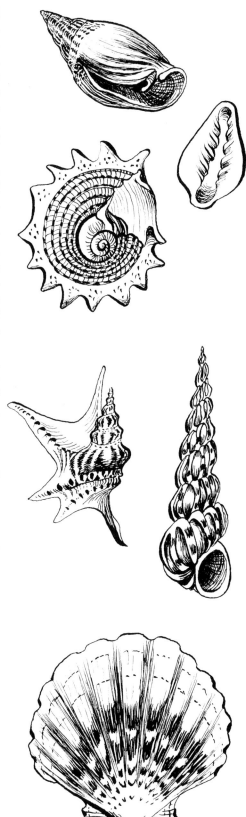

guide the visitor. Sometimes today a guide book or a gardener may retain the tradition of the wonders, and will point out a huge brain coral from the Pacific with an awe as amazingly crystallized as the walls of the cave itself. But in general no one cares about the curiosities today; they are all in the school books and the museums, and our surprise is over by the time we are ten, if we ever had it. The shells and spar are invisible. Grottoes are invisible, too. They have petered out with a few shell-decorated gardens and the children's architecture of dust and orange-peel in the streets, begging a 'Penny for the grotto'.

When a house was put up for sale in the eighteenth century, a grotto was a good selling feature, as a swimming-pool is today, and in 1755 one advertisement adds to its catalogue of amenities 'Merlin's Cave, in shellwork, composed of over a thousand beautiful shells with a cascade of looking glass playing in the middle'. For contrast, a few years ago the present owners of one of the best grottoes bought a charming house and garden for all the usual reasons, and then found to their amazement that they also owned an enchanting and complicated grotto of considerable size which had never been mentioned at all. Undoubtedly the agent regarded it as 'odd', if not positively detrimental to the property. Generally, though, one may say that a grotto will be better regarded than a folly; such of them as have escaped destruction are quite kindly spoken of.

'First' is always important, and special acclaim must go to the first grotto-builder. If we discount Woburn and Skipton, which are isolated in every way, in time, place, style and feeling, from all the later ones, then Alexander Pope's grotto at Twickenham is probably the first, since he was working on his picturesque garden as early as 1718. The grotto is internationally famous and heavily preserved. It is on the simple plan of a trident-head with a very long centre tine. The side aisles do not connect with the main one in any cunning way; there is not even the surprise of a window opening between them. There are no traces of those stalactites from Wookey Hole (one is shown the stumps) which Mr Pope's friends shot down like sitting pheasants and presented to him for his grot. There are no shells, only petrifactions and rock, a few pieces of mediaeval carving and a little quartz. All is dark and dim, even the two mirrors in which Pope is said to have watched the world go by on the river, sitting with his back to the door. It has suffered more than one would expect the work of so great a poet to be allowed to suffer; it simply cannot be recognized from the contemporary descriptions; it has been kept, and that is all. The main road ran between Pope's house on the river and his garden, so the grotto tunnel not only linked the two but was a great object in its own right. 'From the river you see through my Arch up a walk of the wilderness to a kind of open temple, wholly composed of shells in the rustic manner.' Kent's drawing in the British Museum shows an octagonal dome on eight rusticated square columns that curve outwards at the feet, as if sagging under the dome; the charming drawing includes a large kind Kent with his arm encouragingly round the shoulder of a small Pope, and Pope's dog Bounce. (A Kent drawing for a gate at Holkham has a nice zany donkey standing in the main arch, and there is a drawing of Chiswick with two Men of Taste arguing away while a little dog lifts a leg and pees on one of them. Architectural drawings have got duller.)

Pope said that from the Shell Temple 'you look through a sloping arcade of trees, and see the sails on the river passing suddenly and vanishing, as through a perspective glass'. There were doors at each end and when these were closed, wrote the Swedish minister Gyllenborg in 1725, the grotto became 'on the instant a *camera obscura,* on the walls of which all the objects of the river, hills, woods, and boats are forming a moving picture in their visible radiations'. Some part must have been smooth and white to achieve this; Pope does not say. He describes the sparkle of luminous minerals, ores, 'Cornish diamonds', 'Brazilian pebbles', crystal, amethyst, quartz, and the angular pieces of looking-glass, now so dead. In the roof was a mirror star with a single lamp hanging, 'an orbicular figure of thin alabaster'. And there was a little spring for the sound of water.

Pope and Kent looking at the Shell House.

The next grotto, much more ambitious, was made by Thomas Goldney of Bristol, 1696–1768. His father, a merchant and shipper, had bought land at Clifton at the end of the seventeenth century, and Thomas Goldney, who inherited in 1731, improved the house and grounds, leaving a memorandum book with a number of dates and details of the work. He was a partner in the Coalbrookdale Iron Company and founder of a Bristol bank, but perhaps retained enough connection with shipping to get his collection of exotic shells easily—the fossils and minerals he used are chiefly local and all British.

The memorandum book does not say when excavations began, but in 1737 he 'finished the Subterraneous Passage to the Grotto and began upon the Grotto the same year'. In 1753 he began a Great Terras, and in 1757 finished the Rotunda—for things above ground with plants go faster than below with shells—and at last at the end of 1764, after about 27 years of effort, he finished the grotto. During that summer he had made a Tower, a pretty castellated one with a fine view, for the fire engine that supplied water to the grotto and a lily pond. The grotto waters still run (but now by electricity), and the noise of the cascade does not murmur but fills the whole place, echoing over the pool and singing in the great shells. The entrance is through a yew hedge from the lawn into a tunnel, silent and dark till we turn a corner to hear the roar of water for the first time. Four pillars encrusted with minerals support the roof whose vaults are hacked in rough grotesques from limestone.[1] On one side The Lion's Den is formed of curious rocks, to shelter a marble lion and lioness who glare whitely at the visitor with blind eighteenth-century eyes. Past them, the grotto ends abruptly at a pool and, halted, we look on up a narrow cleft. Apparently far away, greenly lit past the jagged teeth of wonderfully eroded rock which mask the opening, a marble Neptune reclines in an elaborate cave. His right arm rests on an urn from which the water spouts, to leap and tumble over the rocks, ending with a cascade from the flutes of two giant clams into the pool at our feet. The rest of the grotto is no better than many others, but the cascade is theatrical and fine, a masterpiece of shifting light and water, sound and shadow.

It is possible to climb up a dark passage parallel to the cascade and see Neptune in profile, even more dramatically lit, through an opening among the rocks. The bright stillness of the figure is a long way from Bristol, and this surely is what a grotto is for, the invocation of a new world. The pleasant cool house and its sunny garden are superbly set above the city, but as we walk down the lawn our pleasure in it is of our daily world; then before the expected green terrace can display the tremendous view, the path descends into darkness and opens, not on to the hot landscape but on to tortuous rocks in a cold gloom, and the enclosed echoes of the cascade. The life of the city is petrified, and half a million people and their domestic cats have become Neptune with his lions. Ultimately Goldney is terrifying; however fine the shellwork, however cunning the scale of the cascade, the water dominates everything; at last the damp air chills the spine and the crash of the waters turns every meek little shell into a tiger's mouth.

After Goldney, the real splendour of the shells begins, and soon the great period of grotto-building, with the shadowy genius of Josiah Lane.

[1] Round a roof light, the date and initials 17 TG 39 are set in shells. The craftsman was Mr Warwell.

Thomas Goldney's grotto in Bristol. It now belongs to the University, and is very well cared for – probably the only grotto that keeps all the roaring torrents and drama of the eighteenth century. It makes a remarkable contrast to the grotto at Stourhead.

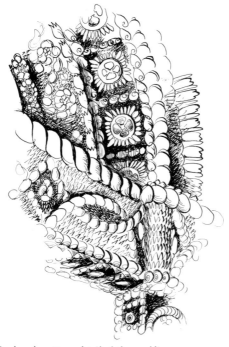

Goodwood grotto; a detail of the moulding.

Goodwood Park in West Sussex has a brilliant grotto, a small pavilion on a hill, its strangeness of a different flavour; instead of creating a new architecture with its unfamiliar materials, it creates the old architecture with them, lining every moulding, arch and wall of standard Georgian with shells used just as most people were using wood or stone or plaster. The grotto is 12 feet square with an alcove opposite the door and a vaulted roof. There are niches for seats in the alcove and for urns in the walls. It is a very pretty ordinary room, lit by the sun, with no trace of romantic gloom or frowning rocks; all that surprises the first glance is the shining colour, white and pink and mauve, picked out elegantly with black. There are rococo panels, swags round mirrors and slightly clumsy urns, and a rich dado, and it is suddenly seen to be all atomized into shells, everything but the marble skirting and fireplaces and the floor. The mathematical precision of this shell-work takes the breath away. Even the variations between shell and shell have been reduced to a minimum by rigorous selection, and great taste has been exercised in the choice of which species shall adorn each detail. The walls are all covered with white shells in neat bands like bricks, wonderfully matched thousands, backs outwards, to make a shining scaly pattern that ripples under the hand like a flawless basket of glass. The panels are outlined with masses of tiny black shells set on edge and so thoroughly architectural is the grotto that if one particular species is used to emphasize a vertical corner, it is always carried up to make the rib of the vault, however, complicated an enrichment may be added. Professional help may have been employed in the design, but it seems unnecessary to suppose that the wonderful skill and taste that executed it could not have made the design as well.

Sarah, second Duchess of Richmond, with her daughters and sometimes the Duke, spent some years making the shell-house; worked into the pattern of the ceiling are the initials C.R., S.R., C.F. and E.K. Many of the shells had been collected by an uncle, and more were sent to the Duchess 'by distinguished officers serving abroad', but in 1739 Captain Knowles of H.M.S. *Diamond* brought in a shipload of shells for the Dukes of Bedford[1] and Richmond; perhaps the distinguished officers were not zealous enough, for a grotto absorbs a staggering number of shells—certainly that 'thousand beautiful shells' in Merlin's cave must have been used on a background of pebbles or flint, otherwise a thousand would go nowhere, as the Duchess of Portland must have found

---

[1] The Duke of Bedford's share of the *Diamond's* cargo perhaps made the small grotto at Elmsleigh near Tavistock.

when she killed her thousand snails for a cave at Bulstrode. But seven years, a thousand shells, and ten thousand pounds are all mystic quantities that recur perpetually.

Even the grotto floor sustains the conceit of the commonplace made from the curious, and its star pattern is worked out in animals' teeth, cut level and polished; ivory. Goodwood is one of the finest pieces of shellwork I have seen; other grottoes may enjoy the romanticism of random encrustation, and cleverly display the beauty of special shells, but nowhere else is that beauty so boldly sacrificed to the use of shells as a medium instead of a subject, restraint instead of riot, possible only, perhaps, because of the fantastic plan of Goodwood House itself, part of a huge octagon of flint.

Goodwood is linked by a big group of follies and by another lovely shell house to the two Richmond daughters whose initials appear on its ceiling. In 1744 Georgina Caroline (C.F.) married Henry Fox, so perhaps we may assume that the ceiling was finished before she was made Baroness Holland in 1762. Henry Fox was not made Lord Holland until later, was refused an Earldom and retired to his follies at Kingsgate in Kent (see page 351). Emilia Mary (E.K.) married James Duke of Leinster in 1747 and went to live at Carton in Kildare where she at least supervised the alteration of an old thatched cottage called Waterstown into a shell cottage. It is reached across a red wooden bridge, vaguely Chinese, over a large cascade and is then startlingly a big *cottage orné* with its eaves upheld on cast iron treetrunks set in a pebble floor beautifully inlaid with 1849, V & A, and the crest of Queen Victoria; it was done up for a royal visit. Inside, is a most beautiful and elaborate shell room with a dome whose skylight breaks into the pitched Swiss Cottage roof outside. Some of the decoration is notably like that of Goodwood, though all is less crisp and much more amateur and much more lovable; many of the panels are rustic, filled in with patterns of little branches. Entrance is by 6 feet of passage

Carton. A detail of the rustic work and the interior of the Shell Cottage.

elaborately worked in bark, wood and shells with a mirror door to bewilder; to the left
is the fireplace in carved baroque with twisted columns and pretty blue tiles, then a fine
alcove with three ceramic oriental temples set in ascending and receding grot-work,
with coral on the ceiling, tufa on the floor, and tufts of dyed wool for variety. The ribs
of the coved blue ceiling look much the same but prove to be bunched twigs set with
ormers; everywhere there is variety and surprise. Opposite the fireplace is a canted bay
window almost to the floor, divided from the room by an oriental open screen, and all,
except the big pointed and stained windows, lined with wood in bold starry patterns.
Back inside the screen, set catty-cornered, are two tall alcoves of twig and shell work with
insets of mirror glass and fir cones. Above, some of the finest and most skilful work is
on the ceiling, where perhaps the work began, just as it was probably finished with the
relatively simple woodwork of the bay window.

The room was extended between 1826 and 1834 by the third Duchess, Charlotte
Augusta Stanhope; hers certainly are the painted glass windows dated 1834. How can
the rest be credited? I would say that the fireplace wall and the ceiling are the eighteenth-
century work, and most of the woodwork and the bay end are the nineteenth. Probably,
with repairs needed as well as extension desired, we shall never quite know.

In the centre of it all stands an open pedestal with four twisted columns of shells at
the outer corners and wild gothick ones inside. They support the gesturing statue of a
plump Chinese boy wearing two little flat hats, his feet surrounded by shells. He does
not have to look at a large painting behind him, surely put up for the royal visit, of
another plump but nasty baby dandled by nymphs and a swan.

The furniture parallels the contrasts of the decoration; there are six exquisite sham-
bamboo chairs with seats made of straw, dyed and inlaid, and there is an abominable
barocco Tudorbethan chair. There used to be a rustick dinner service. For further contrast, the external rustic work is enhanced by square openwork panels of Oriental
turquoise ceramic, like those we shall see on the aviary at Dropmore, and therefore
probably part of the later work.

Shells, twigs, wool, coral, mirrors, tufa and tiles do not complete the materials of the
cottage, for there are also birds' eggs to ostrich size, strings of eggs hanging in the large
window, minerals, pine cones and cedar cones. But the diversity of materials cannot disguise the cottage's kinship to Goodwood; they are both hauntingly alike and different.

At Mereworth Castle in Kent is a grotto room with no likeness at all to Goodwood, a
total contrast to the odd house and the clear light grotto lying on the open down. For
one thing, the more diffused light of the weald of Kent illuminates a very different landscape; in Sussex the chalk downs, and even to a less degree the weald itself, are very
clear cut—the trees and hedges there stand more firmly defined against the grass and
corn than anywhere in England; but in Kent, the next county, the vegetation is scattered and veils the landscape, which always seems sewn over (the heraldic 'semé' is the
best, if obscure, word) with apples, nuts, hop bines and the brown seeds of the cow-
parsley plants.

Autumn is the best time here, for the light thickens to a golden haze and such hops
as climbed the hedges instead of their poles, and so escaped picking, turn yellow with the
hazels. Their colours enhance the tarnish of Mereworth's golden stone, whereas the
exhausting riot of Chiltern autumn tints would destroy it for the whole season. Nothing
can be more beautiful than the broad-eaved Italian church in the damp countryside;

its sharp Palladian mouldings, like those of the Castle further down the road, were intended to withstand a stronger light than this, and house and church stand taut in their surroundings; the very air recedes from them. Mereworth Castle is one of Colin Campbell's essays on the theme of Palladio's Villa Rotunda (the word 'copy' is used far too freely of them) and its beauty has just that precision and inevitability that demand somewhere a break, a harlequinade at the end, and, like the nice old simile of the fly in the amber, Mereworth encloses in its gold the dark fly of a sombre shell room. Here the balance is allowed to waver, sometimes the architecture dominates, sometimes the shells. The ceiling would be good in any medium, in shells it is magnificent. Eight dark spearheads of pattern radiate from a central boss of acanthus and round them swing curves of foliage against backgrounds of elaborate diaper. There is a rich cornice of four formal mouldings and then a frieze of dolphins in the waves. All the walls used to be shell work, but now three are papered. In the fourth is a marble fireplace, with a mirror, framed in shells and flanked by low bookcases, above which are two large shallow alcoves with white shell decoration in the dark arches and then the sea bed with waves and dolphins again right down the niches. Against the aqueous arches stand two large free standing cranes, built up in the round from shells to hold swags of shell flowers in their shell beaks. They are a little uncertain in shape here and there, and their armatures bend curiously, but their vitality is superb, and it is nice to see something so unlikely as feathers translated into shells. The bold freedom with which an amateur will turn to an entirely unsuitable medium, beat it to its knees, and produce a masterpiece, must always be infuriating to professionals. Here are the cranes, modelled crazily from things which are complete in themselves and already have form, unlike the amorphous clay, and they are entirely successful. At Hautrives, a French postman made a palace from an olla podrida of stones, village rubbish, coal and bottle-ends; again successfully. Walking sticks are made from stamps, flowers from feathers, and feathers from shells (the making of shells from stone is a professional prerogative); nothing deters a good amateur.

The amateur at Mereworth is said by family tradition to have been an invalid lady; the quality of the work (better, even with three walls gone, than any other) suggests that some minor ailment may have been magnified to provide the peace and seclusion necessary for this ambitious masterpiece. Many women have found no time to work, even in the eighteenth century when there was plenty of leisure for the rich, until they were old or ill, when they suddenly produced a lifetime of work in a few years. Indeed, all the landscaping and building, shell work and county histories produced at the time suggest that many men and women must have used a weak heart, a delicate constitution or even gout to avoid the perpetual claims of sport or family.

Again and again it has been found impossible to get any clear facts about even the most ambitious grottoes; there are dubious costs, dubious stretches of time, 'Italian workmen brought over', and shadowy figures: John Castles, 'late of the Great Grotto', who was buried at St Marylebone church in London in 1757, is known to have finished St Giles (see page 165), but was that the 'Great Grotto'? Josiah Lane, with a varying number of sons or brothers, came from Fonthill or Tisbury or Westbury in Wiltshire, did the grotto at Fonthill, and was also stated in later county guides to have done the grottoes at Pain's Hill, Oatlands, Norbiton House at Kingston, and Wardour. But Loudon in 'Suburban Gardens' claims Pain's Hill, Oatlands and Wimbledon for a man

Barbara Jones 1940

called Bushell. . . . Certainly St Anne's (now gone), Pain's Hill and Oatlands (also gone) had many similarities of style, to make it probable that the Lanes did them all, in which case they must have been among the greatest artists of the eighteenth century.

If indeed the Lanes built it, the grotto at Oatland's Park near Weybridge must have been their masterpiece, the crown of the Surrey grottoes (once best and most numerous), but in January 1948 it was demolished. A number of grottoes were destroyed during the war, not by enemy bombs, but by our own and allied troops, probably from boredom. The destruction of Oatlands, however, was official vandalism, blessed by the Walton and Weybridge Urban District Council and authorized by the then Ministry of Works, which allowed a great work of art to be pulled down on a false plea of 'danger'—so solid was the structure of the grotto that pneumatic drills had to be used to get it down. The Ministry, now the Department of the Environment, does of course preserve with the most loving care any building actually in its charge; nothing can exceed the pains taken with such houses as Bolsover, where the grass floors in the roofless rooms and along the great terrace have produced a most fantastic beauty. How sad that official power, or taste, should be so erratic.

The Oatlands grotto was built for the ninth Earl of Lincoln. It was started in 1747, or (improbably) 1770, took five or twelve years to finish, and cost about £40,000. The work was probably done by Josiah Lane and his son, after they had, again probably, done the grotto at Pain's Hill (see page 42), which certainly, so far as one can reconstruct the hideous devastation, looks like the work of the same artists, though in the form of one large main chamber, while Oatlands, though only 65 feet long was so complicated that after a brief visit one had an impression of great size. Later investigation showed that the ground floor was of only three rooms. A tufa entrance led to three preliminary grots along the front of the building with views over what had been a lake but had become brambles. The way then turned into the centre, the dim and terrifying First Chamber with clams and huge artificial stalactites covered with little teeth of felspar that caught the twisted light from tufa *yeux-de-bœuf*. It is said that there was once a cascade. A short spar and quartz passage, with star patterns made in the changing colours of the satin spar, led to the Gaming Room, where there was a fireplace and a chandelier and Chinese chairs of bamboo; the walls were decorated with tight patterns of spar and here also were the first shells, encrusted thickly on stalactites. The passage wound on, looping back behind the First Chamber to the Bath Chamber beyond it. Here the patterns were all shells and the light greenest and the mystery greatest. Venus de Medici prepared to bathe in the deep sunk bath; surely alone, for the water was an icy spring.

Over the brick vaults of the First Chamber, the Upper Chamber stood to catch the sun, all light and shine, the favourite room of the Duchess of York (the Duke bought the estate in 1790) who took meals there and played with her dogs and monkeys. When they died, the pets were buried outside and the little tombstones marked the edge of the lake. (Queen Victoria ordered their restoration in 1871.)

The main room of the grotto at Oatlands Park, painted before demolition. The wooden cone on the floor had fallen from the ceiling and shows the simple carpenters' work that was the basis of the elaborate shell decoration; most grottoes were made in this way. These are probably the Chinese chairs, made of bamboo, for which the Duchess of York embroidered the cushions.

The Duchess embroidered cushions for the Chinese chairs and there were crystal chandeliers. In 1815 the Duke entertained the Emperor of Russia and the other victors of Waterloo to a celebration supper there; it is pleasant to realize that just for once the clichés of Regency suppers, the gold plate, jewels, white arms, uniforms, were all dull in the blaze of the grotto, for the walls were all waves and stalactites of white spar, and encrustations of pink and white shells supported mirrors and sconces of crystal under wide branches of coral. There was a dado of tufa for contrast to a height of about 3 feet and then it all began, swinging out from the wall and back in loose ogives of shell and coral, shimmering and receding with every movement of the light, the tiny periwinkles and huge conches arranged as Van Huysum arranged his flowers. All gone.

But one grotto in the first flight remains; extremely beautiful, extremely complex, wonderfully preserved, almost as good as my memories of Oatlands, lacking only the furniture—the grotto at Ascot House in Berkshire. Loudon[1] says that it was made to the design of the owner, Daniel Agace, otherwise it seems to have no history. It suggests the Lanes and the 1740s, all spar and sparkle, but is a little less delicate; perhaps earlier.

Fortunately for its safety, it is near the house, from which it can be seen as a fine pile of great rocks and a large cave-mouth across the lake. It is approached by a neat little hump-backed bridge on which one pauses to look to the left at the first grot-work, big rocks breaking a cascade from the lake. Then on, and the rocks appear again, an artificial mount to be climbed. It is high, and skilfully built with a crown of standing rocks at the top which conceal until the last moment a lantern of eight delicately leaded windows to light the grotto. Back at ground level, there is an entrance that has been blocked, and then an open one which winds each side of a rock and tufa pier into the largest chamber which is about 35 feet long contrived with bewildering asymetry of all floors, walls and ceilings except for a fine arch of huge flints with a 10-foot span across a pool with a seat behind, but even this is on no axis, even of the scattered octagons and circles set in the pebble floor. There is another pool and several simple seats; perhaps embroidered cushions like those at Oatlands were kept with other furniture, lamps and candles in a store through the blocked entrance? Certainly the grotto was lit, for all round, both at floor level and high on the walls and niches, are holes in the grot-work, and today there are electric lamps, white below and red above, an effect that the eighteenth century would have loved and that may indeed have been suggested by remaining fragments of red glass. The ceiling is all stalactites of felspar, decorated with zig-zags of a sparkling brown mineral and the spar glitters and shines overhead, under the big arch and off into a corridor beside it. Up among the stalactites are a few eyes for daylight, and the blue sky reflects with the red lamps to turn the glitter of the spar to mauve. Glitter draws one on down the corridor, but the more architectural style, vaulting lined with the dark mineral, gives way to flint, tufa and rock again, and the corridor comes out past another central pillar into a simple pebble-floored rock grotto, opening past more rocks and a pool where there must have been a fountain on to the lake. But the opening first seen across the water was larger, with a big central pier of rock, and what does the lantern on the mount light? There is a third grotto between the two. It can be reached either from the outside by a new gate, or by an open path, or from the first grotto; it is both like and different, equally splendid, lit by daylight through an antechamber of huge

[1] In the *Gardener's Magazine* for 1829, p. 568. The mason's names are also given, Turnbull and Scott.

Ascot. the first
cave

Ascot House. The first grotto room and, opposite, *the roof of the central grotto (and see page 144)*.

rocks on the lake and from, at last, the lantern set in the top of a whole dome of felspar, which descends on to a mass of stalactites, long and short, all zigzagged like the dome, then spar walls with dark clumps of mineral specimens and the ragged grot-work again. From the lantern hangs a copper witch-ball with coloured glass. The first grotto is the most elaborate, this the most startling with the formal lamp giving way to the long teeth of the stalactites biting down; if there were stalagmites as well, this would be a shark's mouth.

Two Wiltshire grottoes in a different style are attributed to Josiah Lane, as well as the almost vanished one at Fonthill. These are mostly open and above ground, all rockwork with no shells, at least as they stand today. One is at Wardour Castle, where according to Sir Richard Colt Hoare's *Ancient and Modern Wiltshire* (Vol. IV) 'about the year 1792 Lord Arundel employed the celebrated constructor of rockwork, Josiah Lane, to form a grotto at Wardour'. 1792 would be about half a century later than Lane's earliest work and it looks earlier, but all the Lane dates are uncertain, and fifty years of grotwork not impossible for one man.

The Castle itself is one of the best ruins in the country; to the north of it is one of the

Wimborne St Giles; a detail of the shell work, photographed by candlelight.

Department of the Environment's wonderful verdant lawns, beyond which is a row of yew trees screening a raised walk, reached by a flight of steps which lead across the walk to the pretty grotto. Built on a brick basis, it is of tufa and stone with the usual occasional ammonite, now covered with green moss and long ferns, for it is in a very sheltered and gloomy situation. The plan is most cunning, turning in and out with many views through jagged holes into other parts. The dark yews and the bank which it is built against and the pattern-book construction make it the most Chinese of grottoes.

The other grotto in the same manner was built for the first Marquis of Lansdowne at Bowood, where the grounds were laid out on the advice of Charles Hamilton and included a 30-foot cascade, inspired by a painting by Poussin. In *Beauties of Wiltshire,* John Britton described the water gushing 'out of several excavations in the rock; and the principal sheet, after falling a few yards, dashes against some projecting masses of stone, and flies off in a cloud of white spray. The dashing and roar of the waters, jumbled confusion of the rock, the wildness and seclusion of the place, and the various sub-terranean passages under the head of the river, conspire to render it a scene strikingly pleasing to every man of taste; but more peculiarly so to the painter and admirer of the the picturesque; for here he may indulge himself in the reveries of fancy, and by a small effort of the imagination may think himself amongst the wild waterfalls of North Wales, or the thundering cataracts of Switzerland'. Later, Josiah Lane built a very long and elaborate grotto winding through the head of the cascade and running down beside it, though part of this has collapsed and everything is heavily overgrown. Lane probably also made the grotto alcove at the head of the lake.

A grotto of about 1750 is at Wimborne St Giles in Dorset, built for Anthony, fourth Earl of Shaftesbury (but the seventh Earl said for the fifth) and perhaps 'finished by Mr. Castles of Marybone', or perhaps made by an Italian who never allowed anyone to watch him at work. The grotto is much smaller and less complex than Ascot, and has shells, but it has something of the same flavour. The description that follows was written in 1951. Bea Howe visited the grotto in 1959 and wrote in *Country Life* that it was being cleaned and restored. Alas, in 1971 it was dilapidated again, and repairs abandoned, but it could still be restored. It is down in the park. One end of the lake fades into a narrow canal, shielded from the house by fir trees and yews till it disappears under an iron-grilled culvert. Set back from the end of the water by a width of grass over the culvert is the grotto, facing down the canal to the lake, consisting of two rooms, each about 6 yards long. The first, nearest to the water, is more of a passage leading through to the second taller and wider room. The building is screened by artificial mounds of earth on three of its sides, so that both inside it and out, there is a sensation of being below ground.

The door is set in a massive rusticated face built of flint and stones, and on either side of this door are two other entrances. The one on the left leads into a short cavern made of large blocks of flint and pieces of old building stone. The roof is of large flints wired to the rafters of curved wood, so that the ceiling is slightly arched. On the right the passage is more complex, leading round to another entrance half way up the length of the grotto and coming out at another rusticated entrance. In this tunnel, though, part of the flint has fallen from the roof, leaving isolated lumps hanging from the dry curves. Except for the front and part of the side passages the brick structure of the building has not been covered, and once we are within the screening earthworks it appears as a plain little house with a slate roof, not holding out any hope of its beautiful interior.

The double grey doors of the main entrance are unlocked with a key engraved with the word 'grotto' in spidery gothick writing. It is dark inside, but the second room is lighter to draw the visitor through a gothick arch curtained at the top with curved branches of dim stone on into the second, higher, room. This is lit with several skylights and a rococo iron window which is above the door and also above the roof tree of the first room. The air is clean, with no smell of must or bones, for on either side of the fireplace deep in the shellwork are two grilles for air. One is bent back, allowing the owls who live here to come and go, to sit at the bottom of the sea digesting, and throwing up the black pellets of skin and bones which lie in the half light by the door. Around the walls are small, curved watery tables of green wood, covered with dust and fallen shells. Their tops have the outline of giant clams and their legs the clumped holdfasts of laminaria. With the light of a torch or candles if it is a winter's day, the plan of this grotto is apparent. The first dark narrow room is dedicated to minerals, the second wider, taller room to shells.

The first is entirely white or grey rock; the floor is of pebbles, and the lower part of the walls is built of white flints and large pieces of spar set firmly one upon the other. There is no encrustation of the decoration here, but higher up the walls and over the curved ceiling the work gets finer, and the pieces of stone in the decoration smaller. On either side of the door is a shallow alcove from the point of whose arches hang pendant curved pieces of wood with small chips of spar, quartz or grey granite plastered to them; they are an indication of what is to come. The room is not decorated with any set abstract pattern, the decoration consisting of every texture of white mirror, smashed wine glass stems, quartz, marble, coral and felspar, enlivened with pale grey granite slate or flint, and, in about three places, pieces of dark red rock. Coral is used predominantly on the ceiling, and huge pieces of it hang like the tentacles of jellyfish, ready to catch one's hair. The light dusty whiteness, white and grey of the same tone, is not reflected in the mirrors. These are mirrors only to return the darkness of the light between the walls, and broken glass to cut the finger pawing the coral and quartz.

The arch of the gothick door into the second room is filled in with twisted boughs, covered with marble and grey pebbles and a few shells. The two side walls, the wall above the fireplace opposite the door, and the walls beside the door, come in and out in haphazard angularities, covered with shells in no set pattern. Most of them are tropical, set to display the pink and white inside; the outsides are used only to give emphasis to this filmy surface, points of violet or black against the pink and white. All over these surfaces, however, are fixed curved branches of wood, writhing and twisting from floor to ceiling with each branch again covered with shells. Sometimes a branch will resemble a fish swimming just clear of the walls. If the first room is the surface of the reef, this is the bed of the sea inside it, the perfect pantomime cavern. Only the skylights through which the dark green yews can be seen reduce this illusion for a moment; directly the eye travels back to the walls, where it must move restlessly over the decoration, one is back under the sea. Candle light is best for this kind of grotto, and gives us the land again, for in certain lights the mother-of-pearl of the shells looks like the trails of huge snails walking slowly up and down. Fans of coral hang from the ceiling, and in a corner behind one of the dusty tables is the vertebra of a whale, dried up, the edges of the bone frayed.

A more carefully documented grotto is at Curraghmore in Waterford, designed in a

Curraghmore

style between the formal architecture of Goodwood and the complexity of Ascot—it is all grotwork with shells, but it is cruciform and symmetrical, the plan instantly clear—a central domed chamber lit from circular skylights, with three large round window-bays, and a rectangular entrance. In the centre of the beautifully patterned dark-and-light pebble floor stands a life-size white marble figure of the artist by Van Nost, on a rock and shell plinth almost black with moss. She holds a shell in her left hand and in her right a scroll with this inscription:

> In two hundred
> & sixty one days
> these shells were
> put up by the
> proper hands
> of the Rt. Hon .
> CATH^NE Countess
> of Tyrone
> 1754

It was a formidable piece of work.

In the south window towards which she looks is a statuette of a seated lady, perhaps another portrait, and here also is a table of specimen shells. The walls are built of large flat pieces of weathered rock to a height of about 4 feet and then the shells begin, small ones clustered into short stalactites and large specimen ones set among them, native and exotic, with coral branches and, an Irish speciality, sea urchins. This is one of the dampest of all grottoes, the chill numbs the visitor to the cold of the marble, but the damp has kept the shells as new, the ormers gleam and the colours glow as though 1754 were yesterday.

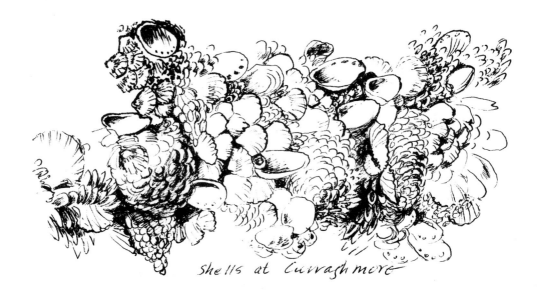

Shells at Curraghmore

At Acton Burnell in Salop a funny little grotto that might have been swept away unnoticed at any time, so little recorded is it, survives in the most unlikely manner on the top of a hill, exposed to all the wind and weather and to every visitor. The stalactites and delicate tracery of more graceful grottoes succumb all too easily to man's desire to pick at things, scabs or shells, and I cannot see any special quality in the shell work of this little brown folly to warrant its survival. Nevertheless, there it is, with no recorded history that I can discover, 8 feet in diameter and 12 feet high, inside a little round stone hut on a bracken-covered brambly hill. The floor is tiled, and charming blue and white Dutch tiles line the lower part of the walls.[1] Visitors are led panting up to it and the

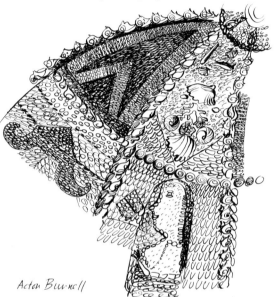

Acton Burnell

stiff little urns and goblets are explained to them as the Holy Grail, so that they are constrained to whisper quietly while they gather breath to return down the hill. The style of the shell work is smooth, like Goodwood's, but there all similarity ends for here the patterns are simple to the point of doodling, flowers, pots, a female head, worked as fancy dictated and not the rule of taste—whoever made it clearly didn't give a damn for the approval of Horace Walpole. Perhaps the vernacular quality of the designs is what has saved Acton Burnell in a world where most grottoes need machine-gun protection; who could destroy something so like all our drawings on the telephone pad?

Now the quality of the grottoes changes, and we begin to lose the light pink and white shells and the glitter of mirror-glass and spar. Later builders take the more sombre shades of Goldney and Stourhead and follow on from there to altogether darker and more badgery grottoes.

At Ware, John Scott built himself a grotto which marks the transition from the airy lightness of the great patrician extravagances to the true morbidity of the less patrician labyrinth builders. In 1860 his estate was sold and split up into building lots, one of which included the grotto. Beside the house a hill rises sharply to a wooded summit crowned with a small octagonal summerhouse reached by winding paths through a typical nineteenth-century shrubbery, while at the foot sunk paths between flint walls covered with ivy and hart's tongue ferns lead to the grass enclosure in front of the main entrance to the grotto. This is built out from the hill; a pedimented porch, with a central door flanked by short lancet windows on each side, then behind a wider front with a curved pediment with three round windows and a door set back on either side of the porch. Behind this is the last wall, which masks the hillside. All this building is of flint,

---

[1] The tiles recall another grotto. On Flamborough Head, the squires of Sowerby once courted the winds from the North Sea with a privy in the garden, lined with Dutch tiles and approached through a grotto of shells.

unknapped, like crochet work, covered with ivy and ferns, gloomy and quiet.

The door in the porch leads into an anteroom, and then into a square chamber, with an arched window in each side wall, and alcoves to cut the corners from the room. All the details of the shell decoration, which covers everything except the floor, are outlined with scallops, and between them haphazard but controlled arrangements of shells cover even the doors. As usual the roof is the most elaborate part; it has four fine shell frames surrounding glass stars, and there is an equally good floor worked in pebbles with the design picked out in wood. Another door opposite the first takes one down two steps under a high slit opening lit by lights in the central façade, and then into the first passage. This is a few feet below a path up to the octagon summerhouse, and is between the last two pedimented walls. Soane could have designed this complicated junction between the shell room and the passage; the narrow slit in the ceiling and intricacy where it is least expected is typical of his style, and he would have enjoyed the sinister black copper slag which immediately succeeds the white shells. A few shells are set into the walls, the last spiral of each cut off so that they are open like ice cream cornets. The passage slopes slightly downhill to a small round room of unknapped flints called the Consultation Room. This is the end of the first shaft, but in line with the axis of the doors is a round opening about 2 feet across, and from it a shaft runs downwards at a gentle angle in a straight line through the Committee Room and on to the Robing Room, 50 feet under the chalk. The room we are in is as far as the central passage goes, the only intimation of the rest of the grotto being the glimmer of candlelight in the other rooms seen down the shaft. The entrance to them is through one of the two doors on either side of the porch. Rooms you can't get into would have been a nice horror; it is a pity that Scott only created the illusion of them.

The passage through the left-hand entrance begins to dip at once; it is parallel at once with the main axis but suddenly turns through a right angle and runs down to a crossroads, where tunnels go to the Refreshment Room and the Second Committee Room. The first of these is circular and the second square, each is covered with simple shells and flints, a covering to the walls more than a full-blooded attempt at grotto decoration. The air is clear, for ventilating shafts run to the surface, and clouds of huge mosquitoes buzz through the candle flames, but they do not bite the visitor; perhaps they are bemused by the sudden light and wait to come out at dusk to feed. After these two rooms the passage is no longer lined with flints, but goes on downhill lined only with cement. Here is the true subterranean horror, it is like the inside of the great pyramid for it has the cold damp of the tomb despite the dryness of walls and floor, yet it only wants a good pungent animal smell to be an enormous sett, with Mr Badger making toast in the next room round the corner.

After the crossroads the passage forks, the right hand leading to the main Committee Room where daylight and the Robing Room can be seen up and down the central shaft. This room is domed and a terrifying echo forces speech back into the brain and the illusion of entombment is complete. The walls are only spotted with shells pressed into the cement. The other fork leads round to the Robing Room on the central axis. This has a higher vault, once supported by a central pillar, covered with hollow earshells though the ribs which connected it to the roof are gone. By lack of shells or by design, who can now tell, the cement walls and ceiling are adorned only with lines, in a flowing pattern of knapped flints and earshells. The passage goes on, sloping upwards: turns and is entirely lined with flints for the next 40 feet, and ends in the largest room, the Council Chamber. This has a patterned pebble floor and, for the councillors, six niches of the usual grotto discomfort in the walls, covered with shells, coal and other minerals, set in circles, stars and octagons. The roof is a dome again covered with the same decoration, though it is above ground and has lights let into it. From outside it is a flattish cone of purple slates. Steps rise from another door to the entrance on the other side of the porch, and if you enter the grotto this way a Soane-like trap leads to a blind, patterned niche while the real entrance is unnoticed.

Scott was a most industrious mole, and his grotto suggests a shell-decorated coal mine. He describes it in his poem, *The Garden*:

> Where midst thick oaks the subterranean way
> To the arched Grot admits a feeble ray,
> Where glossy pebbles pave the varied floors,
> And rough flint walls are decked with shells and ores,
> And silvery pearls, spread o'er the roof on high,
> Glimmer like faint stars in a twilight sky.
> From noon's fierce glare, perhaps he pleased retires,
> Indulging musings which the place inspires;
> Now where the airy octagon ascends,
> Midst evening calm, intent perhaps he stands,
> And looks o'er all that length of sungilt lands,
> Of bright, green pastures stretched by rivers clear
> And willow groves or osier island near.

He does his best for it, but even his own description cannot make it a great work of art. It is, however, the beginning of the labyrinths, the urge to tunnel, to enjoy the musings which tunnelling inspires and about which Scott is not very specific, to have grottoes like black shark's mouths, and prospect towers with tiny windows like Beckford's. Johnson when he visited the grotto said, 'Fairy Hall; none but a poet could have made such a garden'. This is the early eighteenth-century idea of Romanticism, gloom as a gentle titillation, whereas Scott was surely working towards the full exploitation of horror of the nineteenth century. The shell work of his consultation rooms and council chambers is only a cover in the taste of his time for a morbidity which his age had learnt to express in neither literature, art, nor his chosen medium, the grotto.

Follies are comparatively quick and cheap to build and the simple true stories of eccentricity that may attend their creation are quickly forgotten for gaudier legends, but grottoes cost so much time and money that they are usually rather better documented and so less prone to fairy-tales; two at least were made by poets, who not only wrote about them but had friends who kept journals. The romantic English, however, are very kind and rush like air into a vacuum to produce a good story for a naked folly. There are stories of monks of old, nuns of old, secret passages to the folly from a monastery ten miles away, hidden rooms, hidden cellars, wicked lords, silly squires and above all orgies. Truly, the inventors of legends neglected Acton Burnell, but then they had been very busy indeed with a much bigger grotto, accessible in a town, lost, and found again, with almost no history. This vacuum is now not only filled, but overflowing with stories and strife almost on the scale of Borley Rectory, and demonstrating the lure of the orient. Commonsense and the look of the thing itself both suggest that Margate grotto is English work of the late eighteenth or very early nineteenth centuries. But no. The place attracts like a magnet every possible archaeological theory, especially diffusionist, except the Christian ones (very surprisingly no one has suggested that it was built by Joseph of Arimathea); no one seems able to bear the simple thought that Margate might possess a very good English shell grotto—this far-eastern corner of England is determinedly, and widely, exotic. Romans, Danes, Persians, Phoenicians, Essenes, Moors, Mithras, Thibetans and Cretans all jostle for supremacy as the builders, though the Druids and some vague monks uphold the insular claim, and it has been connected with Avebury and Coldrum. The Cretans seem to be the favourite candidates; no attempt is made to prove that they built the grotto—instead the grotto is taken as proof that Priest-Kings were sent from Crete to Kent for instruction and initiation. . . . It is known that the grotto was found in 1834 or 1835 by Joshua Newlove when he was helping to dig a duckpond for his father, a schoolmaster who rented and afterwards bought the land. All attempts so far to find earlier printed references have failed and so have researches into the ownership of the land. Lord Holland owned the Kingsgate area, but as the Powell's land included Whitfield, only a mile and a half from the grotto, as well as Quex, it seems probable that this large estate included Margate. Both families were folly fanciers, and the Isle of Thanet, even without the grotto, is one of the most thickly-sewn folly areas in England. But one piece of plain testimony to the origin of the grotto exists which is always brushed aside, on the lines of how-could-a-poacher-have-written-Shakespeare, by the exoticists: the great grand-daughter was still alive in 1956, of Thomas Bowles who lived with his family in a cottage by the grotto, and, when he was a child, transported many loads of shells with a little cart from Shell Ness nearby to the grotto early in the 1800s. When the Newloves found it in 1835, he told them that the work had been done on an existing excavation by two brothers, his uncles, but even then no one would listen—Mr Newlove wanted it to be *old*; 2800 B.C. seems to be the longest guess so far. I prefer the Bowles brothers. It is certainly odd that the grotto was lost, but not nearly so odd as the Cretans.

The grotto at Margate.

While the first version of this book was being printed and for several years afterwards, I exchanged a series of letters with Thomas Bowles' great-granddaughter Elizabeth Jarrett, and, as the current guide book is still called, unchanged since 1954, '*The Shell Temple of Margate. An Archaic Masterpiece*', although reasonable writers since have all agreed on a date *c.* 1800, I think that Mrs Jarrett's facts should be set out in a small family tree:

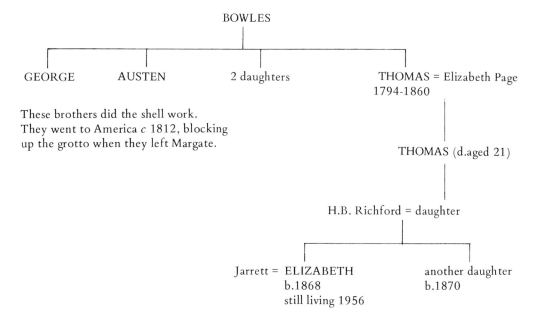

BOWLES

GEORGE   AUSTEN   2 daughters   THOMAS = Elizabeth Page
1794-1860

These brothers did the shell work.
They went to America *c* 1812, blocking
up the grotto when they left Margate.

THOMAS (d.aged 21)

H.B. Richford = daughter

Jarrett = ELIZABETH   another daughter
b.1868   b.1870
still living 1956

Mrs Jarrett saw the grotto with her sister in about 1881—'certainly we heard nothing of Buddha'. (Marie Corelli possibly started the rot in 1888, with a piece called 'One of the World's Wonders', reprinted in *Cameos*.)

The shell work takes the form of pointed arches separated by wide pilasters all the way to the last rectangular chamber. This once had an arched roof but unfortunately Mr Newlove, extending his school, replaced this by a flat plaster roof because the high one would have interfered with his new foundations. Three of the walls of this room, however, are intact (the fourth one was damaged by a bomb and is plaster like the ceiling—on my first visit this was covered with a most distressing mural of purple priestesses performing some ancient rite, but this has gone now) and these walls, except for an arched niche and the entrance, are divided by wide bands of shells into big squares, two deep all round. The designs here are mostly geometrical, stars, diamonds, circles and their various segments, and a few floral arrangements. There is throughout the grotto a small kick-strip of whelk and oyster shells. The designs in the arches are unsophisticated but normal; the medium is handled well but unadventurously—although no great ingenuity is discernible, the shells have been used to the full, within the limits of the design, to make the surface as rich as possible. The little dog-winkle shells that make the backgrounds are used mouth outwards, and the designs are worked with shells set in at all ways and angles, especially on edge in circles to make flowers. (The cement in which they are set of course defies modern analysis.) There are vases with flowering plants climbing out of them, various S and other curves and spirals, two crude representations of human forms, a great number of curving and interlacing plants, flowers and stars. They are indeed just the simple shapes and themes and variations that one would expect an untrained artist to use, the shapes that have been used in decorations since decorations began; they are the universal themes, they are, again, the doodling on the blotting paper.

But here, some curious alchemy in the soil of Margate goes to everyone's head and remarkable transformations occur; photographs have been ruthlessly retouched, so that a vase of flowers becomes the Cretan Mother-Pot, part of an ordinary diamond pattern is isolated as The Double-Headed Axe, a plant is a Sacred Palm of the Bo Tree of Buddha, while every star is Indian, every flower Biblical and every vase Bacchic. 'Isis is here. Pythagoras, Aldebaran with the Ankh . . .'

There is really only one difference between Margate and all the other grottoes and that is its colour. For many years it was lit by gas, and the whole mosaic was smoked brown, shiny here and there from the passing of visitors, but brown all over, a rich, ancient, mummy-coloured, bone-dry brown.

The present proprietors have tried to clean it gently with detergents, and it is certainly brighter than it was, but shells are fragile and soot tenacious. If a safe way of cleaning could be found, and the whole grotto gleamed with the sunshine of the yellow winkles and the blue and white of the mussels, then perhaps the rubbish might be washed away with the soot; but it is very entertaining rubbish.

It will be impossible to consider all the shell work of the nineteenth century; many houses had a little grotto in the conservatory, and many places of entertainment used shells—a teashop in Brighton is entirely grotto, distracting the eye from toast, de Hems Oyster Bar in London, part of the pleasure house under Blackpool Tower, a conservatory in Saffron Walden. A nineteenth-century grotto house used to run half way up the chalk hillside at Riddlesdown in Surrey. It had been a pleasure resort, a gay and slightly raffish place of entertainment, the grotto's inevitable destiny; finally a peeling board over the entrance steps announced in fading letters merely Tea Garden. Past the main building, the grotto, entrance $\frac{1}{2}$d., ran tin-roofed up the hill, with dusty memorials to famous donkeys that had given rides on the downs above, and the tombs of pet monkeys from the menagerie, and of cats, and dogs, all set into the rock and lava work. Children shouted everywhere, and suitably drank mineral-water, and carved their names on the old white paint of the tables or wrote them in very black pencil and purple copying on the open mouths of the shells. That grotto has gone, but hundreds remain; probably no town in England is without its nineteenth-century grot-work.

The nineteenth century also had some very grim caves, but these must be seen later, and so must the last grottoes of all, gardens at the sea where instead of being underground and airless, smoked brown by gas, the shells are bleached yearly whiter by the salt air and the wind. Wherever there are shells to be picked up on the beach, someone will have covered part of his garden with them, substituting them for smooth brown or green paint on sheds and fences. But the atmosphere of these gardens is entirely of the nineteenth century and we must look at them later, or their brisk sea air will blow away too many of the older and darker shells.

For shells in darkness make the special quality of unease in a grotto. Darkness in a house is finite, bounded by flat walls; in a grotto it is less certain, and recedes thickly behind pillars and along the broken walls into the very hearts of the odd shells that catch at it here and there, further and further away, greyed deeper by dust and the thick webs of the spiders that inhabit the whelk shells today just as the hermit crabs once lived in them in the sea.

Augustine Hermitage.

Library.   *Bath.*

Hermits Cell.

The Hermitages

Always excepting the pleasant thought of Minoan chariots in the streets of Margate, the grottoes do certainly lack the racy folly legends: although we constantly hear how many shells, years, or thousands of pounds they consumed, not a single wild peer has been created among them all. This is most sad, for the folly stories are very endearing and some would have been nice for the grottoes, but for compensation we have the ornamental hermits, and the sober fact that men were paid to live in rough robes and seclusion, unshaven and silent in little bothies at the end of a walk in the park.

A Grecian shepherd-boy with pipes and a little flock, nymphs to swim in the ornamental lake, a swineherd in the gothick taste, or a Chinaman in the pagoda, all seem as likely as a hermit, but there is not even a record of a gentleman providing the cowmen with cross garters or interviewing a new Orpheus to play in the Rotondo.

There is only Babs Wyatt, an old woman who pleaded so eloquently when the village at Milton was swept away that she was allowed to keep her 'clay-built cot', which instantly became a picturesque object and herself an Arcadian Shepherdess. Otherwise the collective imagination was fired only by the thought of a tall lean figure with a long beard and flashing eyes, striding in a hairy robe through the park or contemplating in a rocky recess; doubtless if living ornaments were fashionable today there would be a scramble for dwarfs, who would be dressed as gnomes to sit cross-legged on concrete toadstools, grinning.

All the other park buildings may have been gothick or classical, but a special architecture attended the hermit. Picturesque pattern books of the period, as we have seen, show by engravings of elevation and plan how to build an umbrello, a gothick retreat, garden house or shelter, a Chinese temple, a temple of Diana or Venus and, always, a hermitage. Beside it are its special trees, a remarkable species of pine, gently curved and bearing long symmetrical scimitars of branch. In the foreground sits the hermit himself, with one hand following the text of his book and the other pressing the information into his forehead with a long finger. Behind him is the hermitage: it may well be called 'Hermit's Grotto', but it is quite unlike the usual grottoes of shell and rock, for wood, gnarled, is the only material that makes homes fit for hermits to live in. Some of the engravings show mere one-roomed cabins with simple rustic porches and thatched roofs, but there are also splendid designs for two-storey cells fashioned from richly contorted branches knotting in arthritic arcades on the ground floor, going up past rustic cartwheel windows above to support roofs of heather. Porch and eaves are as spiky as monkey-puzzles. Hermitages were sometimes called 'Root Houses'.

Houses like Deepdene were often written of as hermitages, but this simply meant that the owner lived there quietly, not that they were special buildings. An early and

An Augustine Hermitage and a Hermit's Cell, by William Wrighte.

The Hermit's Cell at Badminton

very famous special one was Merlin's Cave, designed by Kent in 1735, for Queen Caroline at Richmond Park. It was not in the true root and rustic style, but stood half-way, a Palladian structure with a thatched roof and ogee door. No description of the interior has been found, but possibly no one noticed it in the excitement of examining its six waxworks of Minerva, Elizabeth of York, Merlin and his secretary, Queen Elizabeth and her muse. Can the portraits of the two queens have been inspired by their funeral effigies in Westminster Abbey, where Elizabeth of York is in wood, but Elizabeth Tudor is another waxwork? The cave was shown to visitors by Stephen Duck, a Wiltshire farm worker and poet, who was later confusingly made Governor of Duck Island in St James' Park; this office was a small sinecure created by Charles II.

For reasons now lost to us, or for no reason at all, Merlin's Cave stirred criticism, abuse, satire, lampoons and praise. In about 1770, Capability Brown, re-landscaping the Old Park, demolished it, to further blame from William Mason in *Heroic Epistle*:

> To Richmond come; for see, untutor'd Brown
> Destroys those wonders which were once their own;
> Lo! from his melon-ground the peasant slave
> Has rudely rush'd, and levell'd Merlin's Cave,
> Knocked down the waxen wizard, seized his wand,
> Transform'd to lawn what late was fairy-land,
> And marr'd with impious hand each sweet design
> Of Stephen Duck and good Queen Caroline.

The Hermit's Cell at Badminton

Fashion and their ephemeral materials have swept away most of these dark caves of solitude, but three survive. The Hermit's Cave at Badminton is the largest, an astonishing work by Thomas Wright, the architect and astronomer. It is wonderfully preserved, a fine room rather than a cell, oddly placed out in the deer park without a yew or a rock in sight, though the park may once have been less open. The cell is about 20 feet by 24 with a swooping thatched roof. A spike on top is probably the remains of the cross that finishes most hermitages in the prints. The door frame is the upturned fork of a huge tree and four more big and particularly knotty trunks make the corner posts and three more at each end the steep pediments, which have sections of hollow tree as *yeux de bœuf* round iron gratings. At each side is a curved bay with a two-light pointed window, and everywhere there is a wild jumbled infill of branches, roots, knots, and sawn ends. Under the rear pediment, which is curved, is a branch bench with an ogee back lettered in nailheads HERE LOUNGERS LOITER up one curve and HERE THE WEARY REST down the other.

The first impression of the interior is classical architecture translated into rustic as at Goodwood it was translated into shells—Carton is the link between them. Opposite the door is a wide alcove with a flat framed back that probably once held a painting. The ceiling and sides of the alcove are lined with moss, still there. The main ceiling is square and coved (now unfortunately depressed at the centre), most elaborately ribbed with knotty wood filled in with the dark moss again. Where it has fallen, the wooden ceiling is revealed, with the ribs drawn in carpenter's pencil, clear as new. Over the entrance a higher area of ceiling, also ribbed and mossed, gives on to the *oeil,* and another window opens into the roof space. There is pretty ironwork over the door that probably held coloured glass. The alcove and the two window bays are arched over with huge trunks which still carry traces of moss and some of the wire and nails that held it—what this must have been like new and green and glowing, watered daily and with fresh moss for parties, is beyond imagining; it is easier to translate it into a contemporary painting, which might have been brownish anyway. So far as I know, though, no one ever painted the interior of a new hermitage. The faces of the supporting walls and pilasters are now almost bare wood, but look as though they were once covered with the flatter pattern of lichen. There are worm holes everywhere.

In the middle of the floor is a table made of a big lump of elm disease, hollow, with gouge-marks where something fitted. In it now lies the centre boss of the ceiling. There is no other furniture, but probably the table was once surrounded by a group of chairs, either built rustic from branches or carved out of the solid trunk, or made from cows' horns, or bamboo; surely the furniture was as fine as the hermitage.

This is, so far as we yet know, Wright's best surviving folly. Twenty years ago, I knew of him only as the designer of his demolished house and the observatory tower at Westerton in County Durham, and of the demolished Nutthall Temple and its surviving gothick summer-house. The researches of Eileen Harris[1] have now shown him to be, with varying degrees of certainty, the designer of Horton Menagerie, the work at Badminton, where much was carried out and more proposed, the rustic work at Halswell, the Shepherds' Monument at Shugborough, some of the Tollymore follies and the superb ones at Belvedere, Codger's Castle at Wallington (and once a Chinese House there), a cataract at Raby and a folly at Rushbrook.

His lovely, but rare, *Universal Architecture* with six designs for ARBOURS and six for GROTTOS, has long been admired, and was thought to be as speculative as most other pattern books of the time, but the Belvedere Rustic Arch is clearly there as the centrepiece of plate M and the Spetchley root-house is clearly the arbour frontispiece. His cheerful drawing for Codger's Castle, flying a huge flag, is preserved at Wallington.

Sanderson Miller emerged long ago; Thomas Wright only lately, though he was a better artist and clearly a more interesting man—the astronomical books should be looked at too. It is now time for discoveries about the grotto builders; we need Josiah Lane's account books.

The small hermitage at Brocklesby in Humberside is said to have had a real hermit who really stayed. It is suitably set at some distance from the house, along a ride past two memorial temples, and down to the left into the woods. The first view is of the back walls of a bare brick octagon with a slate roof (was it always like this?). In front, however, all is changed and the centre wall is open between double ribs of curved trunks and the flanking walls are random rock between more trunks. The elm disease table has around it a rustic bench and four solid-tree chairs. The ceiling follows the pyramidal roof, but the ribs are double and spread out at the bottom, each with a centre boss of bark and disease. The walls still have some of their neat surfaces of pine bark

[1] See her three excellent articles in *Country Life*; 26 August, 2 September and 9 September 1971.

The hermitage at Brocklesby

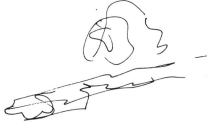

with patterns of branches. About 40 yards from the hermitage is a grotto, a brick curve with a grot-work arch of rock, tufa and slag at each end. Daylight can be seen through, but on the right there is a semicircular vaulted passage round a pillar, neatly groined on to the main tunnel. Probably it was intended to make this more exciting, and probably too, the hermitage was always approached from the house through the grotto and the bare brick never seen, while the temples were visited on a different tour.

Badminton and Brocklesby and Spetchley are our last rustic hermitages, for the Sanctuary of the Hermit Finch at Burley-on-the-Hill in Leicestershire was burnt down by schoolchildren in 1965.[1] This was on the Badminton scale, but purely gothick in style, hidden deep in the woods behind the house. It was circular, 20 feet across, and elaborate, with a sleeping cell behind the main room, and, like the other two, blunter and more cosy than the spiky engraving, a mixture of gnome's house and horror, with a huge chimney and thatch from the fairybook pictures and then, under the thatch, the architecture of bark and disease. The district was perhaps specially blessed with elm disease, for fine bosses of it were nailed all over the Sanctuary, inside and out.

The windows were never glazed; they, like the door, were open gratings of rustic-work.[2] The door was under a forbidding porch of heavy bosses built out on boss-columns under an overhang of thatch. Inside, rather more than half the circle made what was once the living-room of the Hermit Finch, and the door faced the undulating bark dividing wall against which were set four rustic armchairs with their variously-patterned backs built into the wall; one had for seat a tree stump, another half a boss. Overhead was a fan-vaulted ceiling in rustic-work, filled in with bark. The ribs were slats of wood like thin bones nailed thickly together and the pendants ended in elm bosses. To embellish this rich effect still further the junction of ceiling and wall was heavily fringed with twigs.

The floor had a beautiful mosaic of pebbles and knuckle bones, set in various patterns, '1807', 'W', groups of small circles and a large central one. The table was the upturned smooth top of the largest imaginable lump of elm disease sawn in half, nearly 5 feet across scattered with bones. Three triangular stools of remarkable rustic discomfort and an occasional chair completed the furniture; nothing seemed to have been destroyed, the windows were complete, the chairs unbroken, the bones waiting on the table.

On the right of the four chairs, the wall was built out a little way at a right angle, ending in an attached column of wooden ribbing like the roof. Opposite, on the outside wall 2 or 3 feet away was a similar column, and between them through a portière of twigs was the little dark anteroom to the hermit's bedroom. The bark and nails, the bones and diseased wood, the crazy irregularity of the immovable chairs which so startlingly lacked the rickety dangers of the rustic chairs in our own summer-house, all produced unease, but the dim bedroom was really terrifying with tiny windows for warmth, darkened by trees very close to them; much of the faint light came through a fanlight from the other room.

There was a heavily encrusted fireplace with a deep mantelpiece, crowned with a wooden entablature. Beside it under a window was a seat and against the inside wall

---

[1] The family at Burley was called Finch; probably *Hermit Finch* is like *Castle Howard*.

[2] I have been told of cobweb windows in hermitages or grottoes, iron or lead copies of the spider's irregular weaving, but I have never seen one.

The Sanctuary of the Hermit Finch, Burley on the Hill.

the hermit's frugal bed, a wooden rack with some old sacks (he would be coming in again in a moment). There was even a bedside chunk of wood and a stool set into the wall at the foot of the bed for any disciples that might wish to sit there, and overhead again the encrustations and the awful fringes.

Hermits were obtained by advertisement, and it never seems to have been difficult to get one; indeed one young man, Mr Laurence from Plymouth, did not merely answer advertisements but himself advertised in 1810 that he wished to retire as a hermit (to a convenient spot) and was willing to engage (for a gratuity) to any nobleman or gentleman who was desirous of having one. One advertisement demanded a hermit who would live underground invisible, silent, unshaven and unclipped for seven years, in a comfortable room with books, an organ and delicious food. The reward was to be a pension for life of £50 a year, and a hermit accepted, but lasted for only four years. Mr Hamilton's terms at Pain's Hill were similar, again the mystic seven years, again no cutting of hair, nails or beard, again food from the house and no speech. But he could walk in the grounds, and was provided with a Bible, optical glasses, a mat, a hassock and an hourglass. The recompense was to be seven hundred pounds, but the chosen hermit was caught at the end of three weeks going down to the pub.

So what with hermits who were invisible, and hermits who gave notice, and doubtless hermits who were rude to visitors, or posed badly, we must commend the gentleman said to have used a clockwork hermit and also Sir Richard Hill, who built at Hawkstone a very dimly-lit hermitage and solved all employment problems by having his hermit stuffed.

On a high and windy hill outside Pontypool in Gwent is the only shell grotto with anchorite associations. On the very summit of the hill there was an octagonal battlemented tower built by one of the Hanbury family, presumably for the view.[1] The tower was in bad repair in 1935 and is now gone, but down the crest of the hill,

[1]It was an employee of the Hanbury ironworks, Thomas Allgood, who founded the Japanware industry at Pontypool and later at Usk.

The exterior of the shell grotto at Pontypool and, opposite, *the interior.*

among thin bent beech trees stands the little round grotto, started in 1830, a circular wall of rough stone, with a porch and chimney, inside which sits a tiled conical roof. It is a very good grotto indeed, wonderfully preserved and only shown when the custodian is there, so that we may perhaps expect its survival. It is round inside as well as out, and has four stained glass windows, a fireplace, a door and six rustic chairs. The roof is beautifully vaulted all over with small shells, varied with large exotic ones, clusters of sharp spar, stars of glittering crystals, simple patterns of geometry and flowers, false stalactites built up of shells and real ones stolen from some cave. The vaulting springs from six free-standing shell pillars, said to be living ivy trees but actually lath and plaster. They are very slender and elegant, worked in spirals that alternate from pillar to pillar—some of the shellwork here is almost up to the Goodwood standard—and their bases are drums about 18 inches high which instead of making seats have curiosities standing on them, a carving of a quadruple crowned head or a tiny shell house. The walls are writhing with ivy stems, lumps of bark, curious stones, more stalactites, elm bosses, every curiosity that came to hand, and there is a wonderful bone floor patterned with interlacing arcs, stars, and a ring of hearts and diamonds. All this complicated and rich tracery of shells and bones and ivy stems is said to have been done by a hermit who never left the place, finishing in 1844. The story seems pretty definite—one is only shaken by the statement that it took him seven years. Eight or six would seal one's faith for ever.

The shell house, like the tower, was built for the Hanbury family, who used it for luncheon parties. For these occasions fresh moss was brought up from the woods and arranged in the crevices of the walls. Today the estate is a public park and the steep climb to the grotto is an essential undertaking for visitors to the town. The Welsh fully appreciate its curious contrasts, the unpleasant spidery ivy and the clear shells, the mixture of relaxation and distaste; 'ah,' they say, coming in from the tearing wind, 'it's cosy here, look at the bones.'

I wondered at first if this strange fashion for an anchorite in the garden was started, perhaps quite unintentionally, by someone who simply allowed a naturally solitary man to inhabit an isolated building on his estate, and then found his friends jealously sponsoring invitations. But no record of such lucky charity exists, and the hermits occur over too long a period for an accidental fashion; they must have started early in the 1740s, the Pontypool one was a century later, Tong had a hermit till 1822, and Hawkstone had one later still. Accounts of this hermit vary. *Notes and Queries* for 1810 says that a gentleman was shown the hermitage with a 'stuffed figure dressed in the proper professional robe of an Ornamental Hermit, the whole scene being illuminated by the dimmest of lights'. while *Blackwood's Magazine* says that the editor of another magazine had been 'for fourteen years hermit to Lord Hill's father, and sat in a cave in that worthy's grounds'. In any case the hermitage must have existed well into this century, as Miss Cynthia Adburgham remembers that when she was a child visitors paid to tour the grounds and the hotel employed a hermit who sat in the cave fondling a skull; he must have been the last hermit.

The fact that there was no other form of living ornament in vogue all that time, suggests that the hermit satisfied, in the most comfortable imaginable way, the continuing urge to melancholy that inspired much nineteenth century poetry. To write a sad poem is clearly the most romantic way of exorcizing the spleen, and genius is not necessary, for fashion can make very pretty poetry, but if even the slightest talent is lacking, what could be more civilized and comfortable than to pay a hermit to be sad for one? It seems a great advance on the court jester.

Caves and chaos were deemed the fitting setting for anchorites, but sometimes a sociable man wanted to live in twisted stems and the simulacrum of a cavern, and the wildest of these houses is at Eagle Moor, near Lincoln built *c.* 1820. The Jungle is now a farmhouse in a remote and tangled district. It stands without a road in the middle of its fields and is called the Jungle 'because there used to be wild animals here, like kangaroos—a man built it.' Behind a little semicircle of garden cut from the rough field is a sham castle made of encrustations of over-baked bricks, dark purple-red ones all run together, a fanged and snarling façade to a farmhouse. At one end is the front of a square turret, at the other is half a round one, and the window frames and porch are made of oak branches arranged to produce rough gothick arches. On the porch, the branches almost rejoin in another ogee at the bottom, leaving only the narrowest doorstep.

The effect of the dark bricks piling and tumbling, haphazard and full of spiders, round the windows and the arrow-slits is heightened by masses of ivy, its leaves echoing the bricks and its woody stems the porch.

We dismiss the wild animals from the bramble-groves with all the other folly fantasies and then find Major-General J. H. Lofts' account of his visit in 1826:

In Swinethorpe, [Samuel] Russell Collett Esq has had erected a very singular but tasty and handsome Residence. It is composed of overburnt Bricks until they run together in large masses, these are built up in that rough State forming a centre and two circular Corners in the manner of a Castle & has a grotesque but not inelegant Appearance. It stands on the Edge but within an Inclosure of about 7 A[cres] in which are a great number of Trees of different Kinds of Timber, Thorns, several Deer of different Kinds are kept here, the American Axis, which has produced a Breed from with the Does; there are also several very fine Kangeroos, a Male & a Female Buffalo (I think) and their young Calf, all these running loose together; in one Corner of this inclosure a small piece is taken off in which are several very fine Golden Pheasants: in another part of the Inclosure is a large Pond of water in which are kept great Number of Gold & Silver Fish, with the mixed Breed produced by them; the most singular Thing is they are never removed from this Pond in winter, and do not appear to suffer from the Cold.

The Jungle at Eaglemoor.

By 1842 another account indicates the changing taste—'curiously ornamented with clumps of vitrified bricks having a disorderly and metallic appearance.' Mr Collett died in 1850; his Jungle is the only place where the legends were true.

But roots and branches were not always used so wildly; the favourite subjects for rustic work were the neat *cottages ornés* or lodges with thatched roofs, wide-eaved and supported on knotty tree trunks, real, or as at Carton, cast iron—cement rustic does exist here but is much more common in France and Germany. There is a good group of *cottages ornés* at Blaise Hamlet on the outskirts of Bristol; nine cottages, all different, all pure gnome, designed in 1809 or 1811 by John Nash for the banker John Harford. They are grouped round a small green; *Vine, Sweet Briar, Oak, Circular, Dial, Jessamine, Rose, Diamond,* and *Double. Circular* has the most ornate thatch, *Dial* the most elaborate chimneys. There is also an earlier Dairy with a thatched roof in tiers (burnt by vandals but now restored) and various caves, a lovers' leap, a giant's seat, and Nash proposed a Druidical Temple. This seems only to exist in Repton's Notebook, but on top of the hill is Blaise Castle, built by a previous owner, Thomas Farr, in 1766. This is a circular sham castle set between three stout towers. The triangular plan is less successful than usual (the castle has the nasty thinness of Sanderson Miller), but Blaise is nicely picturesque.

The zenith of the rustic style, though, is at Taymouth Castle in Perthshire, where four lodges reach the level of folly. The Castle is an enormous grey ashlar building of 1838–9 designed by Gillespie Grahame, a pupil of Crace, for the Earl of Breadalbane, in place of a house by William Adam. The decoration of the interior was clearly intended to be of unparalleled splendour, and is. All is gothic, elaborately designed and superbly executed, with life-size grotesques and painted knights in armour set in patterned ceilings; a gay and lovely place. Its model village of Kenmore is the same; the cottages have elaborate slate roofs and rustic porches of tree trunks and trellis. The gate is a gothick screen with pinnacles, flanking towers and TAYMOUTH CASTLE in gold over the main arch. The big lodge to the left has a colonnade of tree trunks, fish-scale tiles, and dag-work all round. Through the gates, a long castellated wall runs on the left, between the drive and the river Tay. Behind the Castle is the cast-iron Chinese Bridge, its three arches disappointingly Tudor, but pretty. The large cutwaters may be a relic of the wooden bridge shown on eighteenth-century maps, and that may have been mildly Chinese; it is hard to tell, though the estate map of 1786 has the early follies drawn down the left side. Across the river above its banks is a broad beech avenue; to the left, upstream, is the Cross, or Maxwell's Temple, an Eleanor type, octagonal stone on nine steps, three storeys to a cross, built in 1831 by William Atkinson. Downstream is the Star Battery opening from the drive and overlooking the river, a small sham crennel-lated fort built of rubble, that had two cannon until they went for scrap in the last war. It was once the site of a parish church, and later of a wooden gothick gazebo. On the other side of the park is the Tower, an ordinary eighteenth-century sham castle three storeys high with pointed windows and a side screen which still has its castellations, though they are gone from the tower. Below it in the woods is the Fort, probably done by John Baxter in 1774, a fine folly unfortunately now invisible from the house, a stout screen of simple geometry well over 100 feet long and about 12 feet high, with a central taller gateway and a fat round tower at each end. The side screens are pierced by circular openings with plain flat surrounds. It is a very satisfying object indeed.

Two temples and an urn also remain of the original ornaments that went with the

Font Lodge, Taymouth Castle

Adam house. The other follies are early nineteenth century and outside the park. The Acharn Hermitage sounds the most exciting, but it is only a very ruined octagon two or three miles upstream and overlooking the Falls of Acharn, with a tunnel approach through rock arches.

Rock Lodge is in better shape but battered, an early nineteenth century sham castle with a two-storey circular tower and a one-storey wing to the left; it is made of random rock with long projections. Delarbe Rustic Lodge (which is also rock) shows in mirror image what it must have looked like. The crazy battlements are still in place above triangular projecting rocks, and further complications are added by the writhing roots and stems of dead ivy; the lattice windows are set in wild sunbursts and the wing is to match; no two pieces of rock are alike or at the same angle. The window frames and the door are made of branches and the gatepieces are now solid ivy tods. The rustic work on the door is a simple diagonal infill like veneering; anything more elaborate would have conflicted with the mad rocks.

Rustic comes into its full stride with the other two lodges, probably built in the late 1830s at the same time as the house. Rustic Lodge is a simple rectangular building of one storey built of rubble with metal lattice windows. Then it has long colonnades of pine-trunks down the sides and four deep supporting the porch, undulating eaves below an undulating roof and an elaborate system of vaulting, all of branches, outlined and decorated with circles of sawn branches about 3 inches thick, like bottle-ends, and projecting branches on the trunks. And all painted Indian Red. The rails and stiles of the front door are all branch ends, the top panels had stained glass with a golden pattern and the bottom ones a sunburst of branches held in the structure of a cross path cut from branches chosen for their exact curve. The design on the door is repeated in large pebbles on the porch floor, rather off centre.

Fort Lodge, which is unexpectedly near the Fort, has even more wildly waving eaves; the whole façade to the road is a concave wall of three sunbursts about 9 feet high seen under three eyebrows of the eaves. Two sunbursts still centre on the great disagreeable faces of stuffed stags (one has fallen), whose usually conspicuous antlers fade into the surrounding elaboration. At the side the drip-branches to the windows keep some projecting twigs, and a porch projects on pines, with a half sunburst in the pediment; here one can rein in the racing eye for a moment to see that the rays are cut from birch branches, tapering from about 6 inches across to a point, using the outside of the cylinder all the way, to keep the bark. With careful choosing and sawing, each length of branch would make four rays . . . Here, of course, lies the whole craft of rustic work; to spare no pains in selection. The art lies like all others in seeing its limitations and going beyond them.

The roofs are puzzling—were they perhaps originally thatched in the southern tradition of the *cottage orné* with straw? Or with heather? The thick facing to the eaves suggests this, but no one seems to know, and the slate is perfect everywhere. The Indian Red is a little duller here than on Rustic, but the effect is dazzling—Chinoiserie, Baronial, and Black Forest in one, the Barchinome style.

There is a neat calm essay in rustic at Castle Ashby in Northamptonshire, far removed from the excesses of Scotland; Knucklebone Lodge, no lodge but a circular gazebo in the park, with a thick capped layer of thatch on a conical roof. This is supported on eight fluted columns, classical architecture in a taut and delicate style of rustic, capitals

Taymouth Castle. Rustic Lodge and, above, *Delarbe Rustic Lodge.*

and entablature horizontal, triglyphs shafts and bases vertical, in slender branches chosen from hazel coppice with almost flawless exactness, a miniature return to the wooden Greek temples from which the stone ones derived. The roof is ribbed with branches and the four back spans are filled in for shelter, whole trunks outside, branches in, with wooden seats backed against them. The knucklebones are on the floor, two concentric circles of them with dark pebbles between surrounding a pebble and bone version of that petal pattern produced by drawing six arcs of its own radius inside a circle.

Charming though it is, Knucklebone Lodge indicates the decline of hermitages during the nineteenth century into the rustic summer-houses that were imperative for even the smallest garden. The name is deceptive; 'rustic summerhouse' suggests milkmaids in a rural bower on a May morning, a life-size but still exquisite Chelsea group, with pipes playing and ribbons stirring in the light air. Instead, the summer-houses crouch in the rhododendrons, clearly cheated of their hermits and waiting to catch a visitor instead.

The hermitage at Spetchley Park.

The Moles

Go to it
Hew it
Ye human Moles.[1]

Undoubtedly the caves in Cheddar Gorge, and the similar limestone delights in the Peak District and other parts of England were an inspiration to the grotto fashion; their stalactites (though rarely their stalagmites, which is curious) were everywhere imitated, and spar mimicked the glitter of candlelight on the endlessly dripping water of the natural caverns. The grottoes were both pretty and alarming, offering a nice duality of sensation, infinitely worth all the skill and love that made them, but there were other men who were blind to the charms of shells and made plain excavations, labyrinths and catacombs that plunged down into the earth as far as they could go, ignoring in their progress all decoration and entertainment. After the two very early tunnellers in Surrey, Henry and Charles Howard, the most notable mole was Joseph Williamson who tunnelled far and elaborately under Liverpool until his team, it is said, heard noises ahead in the rock and fled, crying that they had dug down to the Devil. Actually it was a gang of Stephenson's men making a tunnel for the railway and, as usual, utility won the day, so Mr Williamson's tunnels had to stop.

Some of them still remain. Mr David Glover told me in 1972 that a garage now stands on the site of Williamson's old house at 44 Mason Street ('the human mole of Mason Street', they called him). The main tunnel can still be reached by a trapdoor, but most of the other entrances have disappeared with redevelopment of the area, as rubble from demolished houses has simply been shot into the tunnels to save transport charges. But some passages remain, ending abruptly or looping back, with bridges, chasms and arches, also solidly and very plainly built of brick.

There is another city tunnel in Nottingham. Alderman Herbert had a house on one side of the Ropewalk (then Victoria Street) and a garden running down to a park on the other. So in 1856 he had a tunnel driven from his cellars through the rock under the road. There were several pockets of loose earth on the way, and when this was removed, a series of caves was left, several of which overlook the garden. Unfortunately we do not know the name of Mr Herbert's sculptor who was probably local, possibly a stonemason. He carved both along the tunnel walls and in the caves, one of which was a conservatory with animals among the plants and ferns. Another was an Egyptian Temple, with sphinxes, and of course, there were Druids, and the climax was Daniel in the Lions' Den, a spirited group of lions and lionesses, three pairs, roaring and sleepy

---

[1] The refrain of a poem on coalmining by a Scots miner.

The Catacombs at High Beech (see page 197).

The Lions in the Ropewalk.

and Daniel flung back tense at the top of the pile, an acceptable change from the usual placid uncle-with-pussies of the period, cleverly lit from concealed windows of coloured glass; a nice echo of Goldney.

The most dramatic mole was Sir Richard Hill, whose really terrifying black labyrinth at Hawkstone we have already seen, as also Sir Francis Dashwood's less successful attempts in the chalk at West Wycombe.

At Welbeck are the famous underground works of the fifth Duke of Portland. We read of a huge underground ballroom (this tends to get under the lake), a suite of libraries, glass houses and tunnels. The ballroom, three libraries, all *c.* 1875, and a long corridor lined with huge portraits of heavily maned horses are bitterly disappointing at first, as they are sunk only so far that their ceilings are on ground level, and we had expected so much—quite literally, the earth—and there are the rooms lit by normal daylight pouring through the sky-lights. But the walk underground through curving passages, their railtracks giving an illicit feeling of trespassing on the Tube, and then the great empty rooms and the enormous horses, all remain desolately in the memory. The railway lines are set into the floor of the passages, so that food could be driven to the underground rooms. At junctions, there are points levers in the walls and past the last room they still go curving on into the darkness.

There is also more than a mile of tunnel that really does go under the lake by which the Duke drove to Worksop Station in a closed carriage. This went straight on to a truck, and so took the Duke invisibly to London.

In London, privacy continued. The sewers and mains services under the city were already so complex that undoubtedly even a duke was not allowed to tunnel, but I have been told that until about 1905 there was at the south end of Wimpole Street a sham façade continuing the line of houses, its windows thick with dust, that hid part of a garden for the Duke.

After the death of the fifth Duke, Welbeck changed. Virginia Cowles in *1913, The Defiant Swansong* records that the sixth Duke had 'twelve tennis courts placed in different positions so that his guests could play at any hour of the day undisturbed by the glare of the sun'. Still a desire for shade, but guests instead of seclusion.

The fifth Duke and the underground rooms had stirred as much interest as the Friars and follies at West Wycombe and now they could be visited. By 1912, at least three sets of picture postcards had been produced, and two of them would seem from W. H. Smith's serial numbers to have had at least 24 in each. One of those reproduced shows the sixth Duke, the terrace, the fountain and the long conservatory and its lovely cast-iron entrance. (Messages on the backs; 'Our pretty scenery, just a short tunnel'. 'This is one of the Underground Rooms. This ship model was given to the Marquis when a baby and will sail on the lake, I forget where the Sleigh is from, but the Guides tell you when you see round. I don't take the interest in them that strangers do.' Three of the cards were sent to a Mr Arthur Wensley, addressed to Grimsbury Castle, to 'The Cyclist's Rest' Walmsgate, and to No. 6 Ward, Royal Infirmary Sheffield.) The most curious of them show the Ballroom with its cutglass gasoliers, conifers in tubs down the centre, and dozens of sofas and chairs (we can see changing fashion in the shapes and chintzes), not set in conversational groups or towards the dancers, but all facing outwards in a great rectangle to the walls.

No disappointment of any sort attends the Catacombs at High Beech in Epping Forest, an indescribable tumble of masonry into a hole in the earth. It is said to have been made in the 1860s from the stones of Chelmsford gaol, and indeed dentils and entablatures here and there in the chaos were clearly part of some older buildings, but now their original purposes are lost. It is under a mound in the garden of the house and was once a popular show place. It starts quite gradually with a circular court, open to the sky, formed of six pillars carrying an arcading of stone in which holes have been cut as if by a huge leatherpunch. In the niches between the pillars there is some spar and there used to be statues, and once there was purple stained glass in the windows above. Through one niche, the symmetry breaks and the stones begin to spiral downwards. Neither walls nor ceiling nor floor presents a normal surface; the blocks of stone are piled roughly up, and the piles twisted, and the twists pushed over. The instability is emphasised by the use of *almost* normal features—the roof is supported here and there on

2592 Welbeck Abbey. Ballroom & Picture Gallery.

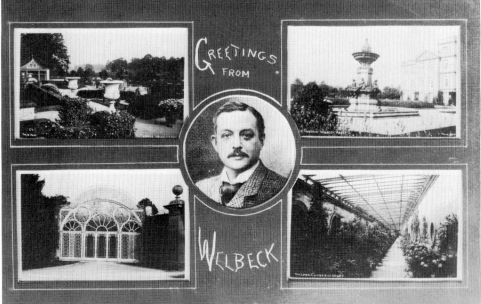

GREETINGS FROM

WELBECK

S 6235 INTERIOR OF LONG TUNNEL, WELBECK ABBEY

columns built of blocks of stone piled one on the other—but they are thin at the base and massive at the top, like Cretan work, and nowhere regular. Blocks of stone make haphazard steps down into the gloom, which is lightened here and there, at longer and longer intervals by light shafts from the ground above. At the bottom, darkness is complete.

The last mole was Whitaker Wright, a financier who promoted mining companies on a large scale in the 1890s. In 1904, he was sentenced to seven years for fraud and killed himself. During his prosperous times in the early 1890s he bought Lea House near Godalming in Surrey and set out to transform it. He pulled down the old manor and built a new one, (later called Witley Park) by R. Paxton Watson, a large but unimpressive half-timbered place, heavy without magnificence, squat in all its proportions. It was gutted by fire in 1952 and has since been demolished, but much of his work in the park remains, and, in a number of *The Royal Magazine* for 1903, *The only Authentic Account that has ever been Published of the Wonderful Way in which Mr. Whitaker Wright 'Improved Nature' at his Home, Lea Park, in Surrey. Full and True Details are given for the First Time of the Marvellous Palace, with its Theatre and Observatory; of the Gorgeous Stables; of the Hills that were Removed and Built again by Hand; of the Construction of the Grottoes and the Great Artificial Lakes, with their Fairy-like Houses under the Water; and of the other Wonderful Surprises that were Prepared for Visitors, which are said to have Cost, in all, £1,250,000.*

. . . wages at this time were at the rate of 14s. a week. It was not long before they rose to 21s. a week—before four hundred men were engaged on the great works that were being carried out by the sombre, silent man in black from the City of London. He strode about his park, carrying a great oak stick, superintending. Everywhere he saw chances of improvement. 'We will have a great lake here,' he said in effect, with a wave of his oak staff, 'this hill blocks the view—take it away. Cut down this wood. Here we will have a grotto. An Italian fountain would look well here. But first have a wall built, ten feet high, all around,' and he waved his stick with an all-embracing sweep. It was a standing joke of the workmen to say, every time they saw that oak stick waving: 'There goes another hundred pounds!' . . . four or five hundred workmen were kept busy, day by day, year by year. Now and again he took a pick and shovel himself.

In the course of six or seven years' hard labour the workmen utterly changed the face of Lea Park, making three artificial lakes, a square lake, a bathing lake, and the big lake, with many statues and fountains. 'One fountain from Italy, representing a grotesque and gigantic dolphin's head,[1] is so enormous, that when it was landed at Southampton, the railway company refused to carry it to Lea Park because it was too big to pass through their tunnels! Mr Wright therefore dispatched one of his traction-engines to Southampton, to haul the dolphin home by road, on a truck that had been specially built for it. All went well, until the traction-engine came to a place where an arch spanned the road. There was not room to pass under. Mr Wright sent down word that the road was to be sunk until the dolphin *could* pass. So the road was cut away, and in due

[1] It was carved from a solid block of marble weighing 80 tons.

Three of the picture postcards of Welbeck Abbey.

time the dolphin reached home in safety. . . .

'But one must go beneath the surface of the big lake to see the wonder of wonders at Lea Park—the houses under the water, the retreats, built of iron and glass, where the Master loved to think of seclusion from the cares of the world, to smoke his cigars in peace.

'On the lawn, by the lake side, is to be seen a little erection sheltering the head of a spiral staircase. Descending the stairs one comes to a subway, 400 feet long, lighted by rows of electric lamps. The passage, which is wide enough for four people to walk abreast, leads into a great chamber of glass 80 feet in height—a beautiful conservatory with a wondrous mosaic floor, settees and chairs, palms, and little tables.

'It is a wonderful place—a fairy palace. In summer it is delightfully cool—in winter, delightfully warm, for the temperature is always fairly even. Outside the clear crystal glass is a curtain of green water—deep, beautiful green at the bottom, fading away to the palest, faintest green at the top, where little white wavelets ripple. Goldfish come and press their faces against the glass, peering at you with strangely magnified eyes. On summer nights one looks through the green water at the stars and the moon, which appear extraordinarily bright and large, for they are magnified quite ten times by the curved glass and the water.

'This submerged fairy-room with appendages cost fully £20,000. It was built, of course, with the utmost care—for if one of the square panes of three-inch glass should break, the place would be filled with water within five minutes.

'But these submerged houses do not exhaust the wonders of the Lake of Surprises. Mr. Wright built a beautiful boathouse of stone by the lake side, wherein were kept a number of boats—electric launches, sailing craft, rowing boats—for he was fond of boating, and has achieved some notable triumphs with his racing yachts.

'Sailing round the lake, one would come unexpectedly upon an opening in the bank almost hidden by shrubs and trees. This gave entrance to a subterranean passage, lined with white tiles, covered in places with creepers, deep water rippling at the bottom. Proceeding cautiously up this strange channel running underground, one was re-assured by the sight of daylight at the end; and, pushing on, came at length to a wond-rous grotto, a fairy-like cavern, with trees, high above, forming a roof with their branches. Leaving the boat, one stepped on to a path carved out of the solid rock, which led, by steps, into an extraordinary labyrinth of galleries and hidden chambers, some of which were beautifully fitted with Oriental decorations.

'Whilst one army of workmen was engaged upon these transformation scenes and fairy effects in the Park, another was engaged in converting the old red-brick house into something akin to a palace. Right and left of the old house two new wings were thrown out, and at one end a domed observatory with a revolving copper roof was put up—Mr. Wright had a taste for astronomy. A little theatre was built in the house, costing about £20,000, and decorated with tapestries, worth about as much, and a wonderful drop curtain.

'When, a little while ago, the order went forth that all work at Lea Park was to be stopped, the labourers, the country people in the neighbourhood, were genuinely sorry.

'The news of the financier's downfall, and of his arrest came to many near Lea Park as a personal sorrow.

'"He never robbed the poor," they said.'

The sad half-tone illustrations of 1903 show the house, the site of the big lake before and after (with a temple on the bank), and also the lake drained of water showing the outside of the submarine passage and the domed smoking room on top of which stands the giant Neptune which normally appeared surrounded by water. The last picture shows the interior with a palm-tree in the middle, a button-upholstered bench, electric lights and a lady and gentleman. The dome is stark lattice; it must have looked better with the goldfish.

Today, the park is still a routine late Surrey one, landscaped with considerable Japonaiserie round a series of big lakes. The weeping birches, small oriental pavilions on the water and the dolphin fountains offered a pretty contrast to the ponderous residence, understandably enough, but in the pine trees beyond the farthest lake is another contrast very difficult to understand indeed, the entrance to the grotto.

A large descending spiral of concrete enclosing a circle of glass lies almost sunk in the ground, like a submerged snail. In the mouth of the shell stands an arched wooden door in a wide concrete frame. Inside, the starkest possible concrete passage sinks slowly round and down, with openings on the right looking into a circular room under the glass into which 15 feet down the passage eventually opens, a bare drum of cold light. The ramp goes on, becomes steps, and opens into another room below the first, semi-circular this time, lit from the room above. Behind the diameter is an echoing vaulted chamber, 25 feet long, bare dark concrete, but now three of the walls are broken with niches, that, utterly plain though they are, seem all Versailles after the bare ramp. The fourth wall opens into a water-floored tunnel to the lake. Once there was a boat, and it was possible to row out and across to a stone octagon pavilion standing in the middle of the water and there leave the boat, descending either to the smoking room to see the ornamental fish or to walk through an underground tunnel to the house.

No record or tradition remains of any intention to decorate any part of the 'grotto' as the smoking room was, or of any use for it; the entrance suggests purpose, extreme utility, a fuel store or an arsenal perhaps, and then at the bottom of the ramp are the odd blank rooms and the water. Perhaps there wasn't time. There is nothing to say except that Whitaker Wright was the last mole.

Lea Park; one of the 'fairy-like houses under the water'.

Towers and Giants

———✦———

Almost every notable hill and beacon in England has its tower and most of them are quite intractable. It would be difficult to call them dull, for each one as it is seen seems different from the others, and rather charming. Probably it is 10 or 15 feet across, 20 or 30 feet high, built of brick, or of flint faced with brick. The door is padlocked and sealed with webs, or gone years ago. The stairs are worn away at the bottom, crackling with birds' nests at the top. Uninteresting little views of the park are framed in round or gothick windows on the way up, and at last we come out on a mildly dangerous roof and can see a little farther. Over the doors a slab carved with initials and date gives a clue that can be followed up in the guides in the county library to give us:

> Erected by Sir Decimus Fandangle, Bart., in 1774 at a cost of £5,000. On a clear day, it is claimed, seven counties may be seen from the summit. While we beg leave to doubt this estimate, we would be the last to deny that Whortle Tower (as it is called locally because of the berries picked here in summer by the village children and made into many a delectable pie) makes an interesting objective, whether for a serious 'hike', or the less strenuous exertion of an evening's stroll.

The walks and plantations of Sir Decimus that once undoubtedly attached the tower to the landscape are overgrown or cut down, while the whortleberries of 1911 are now outnumbered by brambles; nevertheless, gutted and isolated as it is, the little tower has its forlorn charm; the difficulty is the number of towers, and the fact that this forlorn charm, though delightful when spread thinly over years of folly recording, would be unbearable here. A few towers shall stand for all, and also for the giant columns celebrating famous generals, and for the obelisks to the memory of George III, or to the day he shot a stag in someone's park.

Sir Thomas Tresham built his Triangular Lodge in the 1590s. A century and a half later, the triangle became a fashionable plan for ambitious towers, and some fine ones survive in tolerable condition; they were probably too expensive to be thrown away as lightly as the little ones.

The desire to get up higher for the view and to count the counties began long before most of the remaining towers. In 1653 Hollar made an engraving of the hollow elm on Hampstead Heath, a notable specimen with a spiral stair inside, 42 steps up, lit by 16 openings, to the top at 33 feet, where 6 people could sit and 14 stand in an octagon turret. A poem by Robert Codrington was printed with the engraving:

> Six neighbouring counties do on tiptoe all
> Gaze on my mighty limbs and seem to call . . .

and it was sold as a souvenir.

A design for a tower, site and architect unknown.

The first of these triangles was probably Hoober Stand at Wentworth Woodhouse, in 1748, but it is very unlike its successors, and the first fashionable version was probably built in the early 1750s; Shrub Hill Tower, built by Isaac Ware for the Duke of Cumberland as a prospect tower to Virginia Water, but this is now a house, and no more typical than Hoober Stand, so we will start with Racton Tower in Sussex. It is enormous. For once we can believe that it really did cost Lord Halifax £10,000, even in 1772, and it has also achieved a good grey decay. It was designed by Theodosius Keene, who made something much more creepy than Sanderson Miller ever achieved. The plan is a triangle, with a round turret at each corner and a central tower on top. It is nearly 150 feet round the base and still about 70 feet high, though it must once have been more. There are the remains of five floors and a turret staircase. Only the simple shell remains, flint on brick, with raw holes for the doors and windows, and, here and there, brick dripstones over them. On top of the turrets are the stumps of three smaller ones, like half-opened telescopes—perhaps the big tower diminished in the same way? A great strip of old cement, scratched as if for keying, runs down one side of the tower, but most of the flint surface is still beautiful.

It must have been one of the first works of the third Earl of Halifax, who only inherited in 1771. At some time, the interior was dismantled—the history is as usual obscure, but there is an account of it in *A Place in the Forest. The Story of Stanstead in Sussex* by the Earl of Bessborough (Batsford, 1958). Two drawings exist, the architect's original design, and a drawing by Grimm of 1782. Both show a pointed conical roof with a roofed cupola, and this is perhaps the shingled spire 'in the Chinese taste' added just before Lord Halifax died. He is said to have offered the parishioners of Westbourne a spire or the endowment of a Sunday afternoon sermon, and they chose the spire, 'because it would always point to heaven whereas a sermon might not'. If so, how does it appear as the original drawing? Added, perhaps, to save a new sketch. In any case, the additions were taken down in 1860.

The decline of Racton Tower from design to ruin.

The tower is finely placed on top of one of those low hills that are negligible on the Ordnance Map, but contrive from their trifling 100 or 200 feet to command great sweeps and wheels of land. The slipping of the landscape around it from park to farm is immaterial on so good a natural site, and indeed the untrimmed coppice of scrub trees round the bottom of the tower increases the impression it makes; it might soften a lesser folly, but here the fussy trees only throw into greater contrast the bald ruin and the sky.

A neat, almost municipal, tower in yellow stock brick on the same triangular plan, but smaller and with hexagonal turrets on the corners instead of round, stands in Castlewood Park at Shooters Hill above Woolwich, scaffolded for repair when I saw it, preserved and loved, with a tea shop in the bottom and, on the first floor, a hexagonal room with a fine plaster ceiling. The tower is surrounded by little lawns edged with rustic work, ivy and paths, the refreshment room serves excellent tea and beyond the tower the romantically grouped woods open down an enormous vista over South London, a vista entirely in the eighteenth-century taste entirely filled by the clear-cut pink roofs of the 1920s. At our feet, to link the two, are the parterres of a nineteenth-century merchant-princely garden—a feature from each century. There are seats for the view, and someone will tell you about the tower—'In the First World War this belonged to an old German, you know, and he used to sit up on top and shoot the Zeppelins. They rumbled him in the end.'

Not even the truth about the 60-foot tower is unromantic, for it was built in 1784 by the architect or builder W. Jupp for the widow of Sir William James, in honour of her husband who distinguished himself against the pirates of the Indian Seas . . . 'and in a particular manner to Record the Conquest of the CASTLE OF SEVERNDROOG on the COAST of MALABAR which fell to his Superior Valour and able Conduct on the 2nd Day of April MDCCLV'.

The castle was used in 1786 as an observing station for survey; it is 46 feet higher than the top of the cross of St Paul's, and the view really superb; by 1836 it was employed for jollity, and on 12 July the following advertisement appeared:

Mr. John Smith solicits the company of his friends to join a select gipsy party to be held at Shooters Hill on Tuesday, to be continued annually. Tickets 7/6d. each, to admit a lady and gent: and to include a cold collation, tea and coffee, wine, negus, mixed liquors etc. A select portion of the Woolwich Military Band will commence playing at 1 o'clock for quadrilles etc. To keep the party perfectly select, the lady's name to be written on her ticket. The spot fixed on as the resting-place is in the front of the castle at Shooters Hill.

India and a triangle with turrets also inspired Haldon Belvedere, or Lawrence Castle, a magnificently situated tower on the moors near Exeter, 800 feet above sea level, 70 feet high. Again there are three floors and immaculate preservation and a view, but this time the towers are circular again. It was built in 1788 by Sir Robert Palk, first baronet, ex-Governor of Madras, to his great friend Major-General Stringer Lawrence, who is commemorated on three tablets in the lovely hall: it occurs to one here that one of the greatest charms of the elegant (and preserved) follies is that in them we move straight from the wild moor or wet wood into civilization, without the build-up of lodge, drive,

gardens and stables, into a tiny elegant room where no considerations of utility or convenience, warm food or draught-prevention, need stop the decoration from reaching the greatest heights of fantasy and conceit.

The floor of the hall, laid to radiate from the central statue, is, like the spiral staircase in the southeast tower, made of a rare and beautiful marble sent to Sir Robert by the Nizam of Hyderabad as a contribution to the memorial. A rose centres the ceiling and the walls are dark blue. Above is the ballroom with a mahogany floor from the East Indies (said to have been captured from the French), and again the fine gothick plaster-work that is to be seen in so many towers, matched outside by the good proportions of the turrets and their courses, the delicate windows and neat arrow-slits. The dark blue and white staircase is one of the best anywhere; Haldon almost convinces us that the pavilion was the eighteenth-century's chief triumph.

> Quex Park. John Powell Powell Esq a gentleman worth £20,000 per annum in landed estates, at the village of Birchington 13 miles beyond Canterbury . . . has built a large brick tower in his park 60–63 ft. high and 14½ ft., clear within the walls of the belfry, and hung a ringing peal of 12 bells in it, cast by Thomas Mears of London in the years 1818 and 1819. . . . N.B. Mr. Powell will have a lofty spire on his Tower thirds of Cast Iron and to be sprung from four quarter circle arches—then it will be a noble seamark being only one mile from that briny fluid.[1]

The public opening of the Waterloo Tower on 4 August 1819 attracted large crowds; 'the interest was considerably enhanced by its having no parallel—that of a gentleman erecting in his Park, a tower with spire in front of his noble mansion, and placing therein a peal of 12 bells . . . and practising this manly art'. Two ringing societies, the College Youths and the Cumberland Youths of London rang touches and peals on the opening day.

The tower is a very good one indeed, beautifully built of smooth red brick with wide flush joints and restrained stone dressings. It is square, with an octagonal turret at each corner castellated with cast iron. At ground level, there are four wings, each similar in plan to the central tower, and attached to it by the corners, so that the southwest turret of the main tower forms the northeast turret of a wing and so on round the tower: the plan looks like a block of five black squares from a chess board. Gothick pinnacles in stone top the free turrets of the wings, which have, like the tower, elegant gothick windows with white glazing bars. Some dummy windows and the arrow-slits are painted black—the tower is very spruce. From the turrets, as Mr Parnell predicted, springs the cast iron, but 'spire' is too ecclesiastical a word for this exquisite Eiffel Tower, shining in the sun with white paint and a golden weathercock. The tapering girder legs curve inwards to cobweb platforms and then gently out, come together, and continue up in a diminishing spike to the vane. Under it stands another, smaller Eiffel, octagonal this time, echoing the pretty, double-curved taper of the large one, but replacing the weathercock by a white urn. All the girders are braced with square plates, concave-sided and pierced with quatrefoils, but this gothick detail fails to break the pure

[1] J. A. Parnell, *The Gothic Traveller*.

Haldon Belvedere.

mathematical freedom of the whole; it is a remarkably pioneering piece. A belt of trees surrounds the tower, which was restored as a memorial in 1896 and is still perfectly maintained.

Quex has a small satellite tower on the other side of the house, a very plain round castellated one with windows, ivy and a flagpole. It is backed by tall trees and forms the centre for concentric semicircles of old guns, fifty of them, from 2 to 8 feet long, Dutch and English, a little green with oxide. Some of them are very pretty, and ten of the big ones are said to come from the *Royal George*.

The Waterloo Tower at Quex Park (double exposure). Opposite above, *a detail of the interior of Culloden Tower and,* below, *Grimston Park Tower.*

There is a good tower in North Yorkshire that must be mentioned for its beautiful interior. Culloden Tower was built by John York in 1746 to commemorate the Jacobite defeat, and is set on the abrupt edge of the town with lovely views back to it and to the country. It is a very solidly built octagon, with an external staircase turret, a carved lattice parapet and pinnacles. The interior is as fine in its small scale as any work in the country, blending the weight of Kent with gothick rococo, ogee curves and Chinoiserie fretwork—and the tall vaulted roof of the first floor room has a look of Adam. The room above has a shallower ceiling and the same superb quality of carving, which is wonderfully preserved and crisp. Only in 1971 did vandals break in and hack out an overmantle still-life painting of a skull and 'cello.

The general run of prospect towers, though they may be charming from their solitary settings in overgrown woods or cut off from their houses in a stand of trees in a ploughed field, are architecturally extremely dull. This becomes the more extraordinary when one sees a tower like Bettison's Folly, in Humberside, on the coast at Hornsea. Brick, castellated, 1844; one cannot hope for much. But it is tall, simple and slender, 45 feet high, made enchantingly pretty (almost impossible to stop looking at) by the simple complexity of using Flemish bond with every header projecting. It is divided into four drums simply by increasing or decreasing the number of projections but not their depth. The first division is two complete courses of projecting headers: the next, one course of them between two plain courses, then only every other one, then all again, then four of the standard pattern and all again. None, all and none divide drum three from four, and at the top four plain courses take the profile out four stages to a plain band, a short return to the basic pattern, and the castellations. There is a studded door and simple windows, wide pointed and narrow round-headed ones.

It is said that Mr Bettison, who owned a Hull newspaper, built the tower so that a manservant, or a son, could climb it each evening to sight his carriage on Southorpe Hill, hurry down, and see that dinner was hot on the table when he arrived. He was unloved. Soon after the tower was finished a young sailor home from sea swarmed up the headers and planted a placard, BETTISON'S FOLLY, and it has been called that ever since. The house and tower seem to have been bought by the municipality on Bettison's death, for the town band used to play on May Day from the top of the tower.

And there is a curious tapering tower in North Yorkshire at Grimston Park for a very good Decimus Burton house of 1840, and itself built either then or, I would say, some 20 years later. It can be seen as good or bad. In 1953 I described it as 'a square tower 41 feet high from the ground to an overhanging platform upon which sits a classical, octagonal lantern with a flagstaff like a bear pole rising from the summit of its pointed roof'. In 1971 in late evening light it looked much better, well proportioned and in a most interesting style, Milner Square (or Railway) with a hint of China, and sub-Egyptian doors. It is weathering beautifully, and its 82 steps lead to magnificent views over the gently rolling part of North Yorkshire round Tadcaster. Probably, always providing that it is looked after, in 20 more years, it will be seen as a very good tower indeed.

The tallest pleasure tower we have is at Blackpool, 518 feet high, by R. J. J. Read with Maxwell and Tuke in 1891–4, England's answer to Eiffel's 984 feet finished in 1889. Not only is the Paris tower twice as high, it is also at least twice as beautiful, but Blackpool has the luscious Winter Gardens and miles of illuminations every autumn (a folly-fantasy on their own), and it has the sea.

e Tower, Blackpool.

Big Wheel & Tower. Blackpool.

Opposite, *Hornsea Tower.* Above and right, *picture postcards of the Tower and Big Wheel at Blackpool. The sender of the Wheel was* 'staying at Mrs Robertson 17 Central Drive 3 doors below Mrs Southwell bedroom to ourselves'.

All through the nineteenth century men dreamed of towers to reach the magic mountain-height of 1000 feet. Trevithick proposed a gilded cast-iron column to Reform in 1832, C. Burton suggested a glass tower for the Crystal Palace in 1852. Trevithick's scheme was revived as an Albert Memorial in 1862 and another was proposed for London in the early 1890s. M. Sebillot proposed to light all Paris so with electric lamps and at last Freyssinet's aspirations for France reached 2,300 feet in 1937 and Frank Lloyd Wright's for America a mile in 1956. None of them was ever built, but recently the magic 1,000 feet have been reached by the towers and masts of television; Emley Moor Tower in Yorkshire is 1,084 feet high and the elegant stayed mast at Belmont rises to 1,265.

Most of our giants are Neptunes. No Atlases support globes, there are no Vulcans beside any of the folly gorges, and though there are several Temples of the Winds, no colossal Aeolus stands on a hilltop. Only Neptune—he is never Poseidon—was a frequent subject for a statue at a spring or as centrepiece to a lake or fountain. There are a number of very large and handsome or hideous Neptunes, with web-footed horses, tridents, dolphins, shells, water and Nereides according to cost, widely distributed but rarely near the sea, with particularly grand ones at Witley, Cliveden and Twickenham. All these may be called inflated garden-ornaments, but one giant Neptune has become folly. He is very large and very tough, towering now over a caravan site, but once he was in the middle of a big lake and later solitary in the fields. He is made of clinker, with a grotto of clinker behind him and a great deal of ivy. Once indeed, he was entirely ivied over but now the front is cleared and we can see his great cement-faced body. The broken crown and drapery look as if they were originally left as clinker and the effect must have been very fine. Now the armature of the left arm flung across his chest is exposed, and the right arm gone, but the weathered blind face is fierce, and he remains an impressive and defiant figure. He was part of a remarkable eighteenth-century industrial empire now almost overwhelmed by Warmley on the outskirts of Bristol. The Champions were a Quaker family whose spelter and brass works were established in Bristol by 1740. William Champion went to Holland to find out more about the extraction of zinc and the manufacture of spelter and its other alloys, and in 1749 he set up at Warmley large works fo the production of zinc on a commercial scale, using ore mined on Mendip. By 1754 a visiting Swedish metallurgist saw four furnaces for spelter, twelve for brass, fourteen for copper, and mills for making sheet metal, wire and pans—his huge brass pans for evaporating salt were called 'Neptunes'. He had a pin factory, and exported large quantities of brass ware to West Africa, including bars to make slave collars. The empire flourished. He built a fine house (now the Warmley District Council Offices) looking down towards a large lake with Neptune in the middle and, beyond, a canal with a little eyecatcher-boathouse at the end, which still stands. There was a bird sanctuary, and underground tunnels lined with slag, illuminated and decorated with ferns, but I could find no trace of these. Some of the tall model cottages decorated with slag that he built for his Dutch and local workers remain, and so does the clock-tower with slag dressing and steel window frames which must be some of the earliest made.

The empire failed. He went bankrupt in 1768 with everything going wrong at once—

Neptune at Warmley and Polyphemus at Corby Castle.

he bought too much coal while orders were falling against foreign imports, and Parliament would not extend the patent for his process. A rival firm bought the works.

Corby Castle in Cumbria has a fine descent to the River Eden with an unusual crop of statues. It lies in the almost flat country near Carlisle, where the river has cut deeply into the sandstone. The house itself was built round a peel tower early in the nineteenth century of red sandstone with classical details and the lion of the Howards red on top. The descent starts quite near the house, from a terrace with no balustrade, looking down over a beautiful prospect of the river. There is a yew tree, and suddenly another view down to the river through an arch, and then steps lead down into a semicircle-in-rectangle temple, with two pairs of columns at the head of the cascade. There are niches at the back with statues, pretty naïve carvings of nymphs, painted red to match the stone,

one with a dolphin and shell and the other with a pitcher. After the placid charm of these, and twin putti with goat and shell, the exit for the water below is very startling indeed; between the bases of the central columns is a huge monster's head with great back-curved teeth and staring eyes, all in the reddest blood of the sandstone, lichened with pale green. From the narrower spaces between the paired columns, two Cerberus dogs pour six more cascades, and the water plunges through the green and is lost to sight. The path goes on to the left of the cascade and reaches Polyphemus, a sad giant banded to the rock, in rough classical dress with pan pipes in one great clumsy paw and the other gone. He has a sceptical expression, but his third eye looks aspiringly up; Ulysses has not come yet. Almost at river level, a path turns back to the bottom of the 100 foot cascade where the water reaches a large round pool with a bland and handsome Nelson on a pile of rough rock in the centre. From the pool there is a wide stretch of grass and the water runs through a simple arch to the river. On the far side, a castellated barn closes the view, and all is calm. But from below the monsters of the cascade are at their most alarming (the Cerberus heads look like paws to the big grotesque); there is nothing else quite like them in England—did the Grand Tour ever reach Bomarzo? Behind incongruous Nelson are two dark dripping slits hung with long weeds and ferns in the finest grotto tradition. These open into two rock rooms with an arched window between them, and views to the river. Further on, are some man-made caves, but nothing is known of their history—indeed, the very date of the cascade is uncertain, the 1730s, 1780, 1820 . . . Back along the bank to the South is a green walk through the

Sir William Wallace at Dryburgh and the cement sailor at Dalkey.

trees, with picturesque rocks, and the escarpment gradually losing height on the left. A slow rise leads to the 13 mossy steps of a Tempietto, whose steep pediment is carved with two winged sea-horses, four nymphs and a palm tree. Along the bank is Constantine, in monk's robes with a coronet and crossed swords at his feet, undoubtedly by the heavy hand that carved Polyphemus and the monsters. He is bald with a little beard, and might be one of Nelson's sailors, looking across the river at the dressed stone entrance to the caves said to have been his cell. There is also said to have been a hermitage; perhaps it was near the statue.

Sir William Wallace, Scotland's national hero, is commemorated by two giant statues. One is in bronze, 13 feet high, by D. W. Stevenson R.A. mounted high in a niche on the monstrous crumburgerdinger of a 220 foot Memorial which was built between 1861 and 1869 on a high rock above Stirling Bridge which Wallace took from the English in 1297. The giant pinnacled tower can be seen in an unfavourable light from 20 miles away. The other statue is splendid, the first memorial to Wallace, a stone giant put up by the Earl of Buchan in 1814 in the woods above Dryburgh Abbey, a vernacular carving in red sandstone $22\frac{1}{2}$ feet high, designed and carved by Mr John Smith of Darnick. He is square and, like the Warmley Neptune, very tough and determined, wearing warrior's dress, neither mediaeval nor Classical, with helmet, cloak, a shield with St Andrew's cross and an enormous sword. Round his waist is a belt—Wallace was said to have worn one made of an English tax-collector's skin. On the plinth is carved Great patriot hero. Ill-requited Chief, and in front is an urn with the lines

> The peerless knight of Ellerslie
> Who waved on Ayr's romantic shore
> The beamy torch of liberty
> And roaming round from sea to sea,
> From glade obscure or gloomy rock,
> His bold compatriots called to free
> This realm from Edward's iron yoke.

There are staring-eyed, useful giants in Ireland; the Metal Men, dressed as Nelson's sailors, were coloured and indicated dangers at Tramore and Sligo, and a cement one, probably not useful, is at Dalkey.

A final giant. By George Simonds. The Great Lion of Forbury Gardens in Reading, an 1844 tribute to the Afghan War. It is a fine big snarling lion with tail at half-lash and hair sculpted as grass was sculpted a century before.

Plate D from Thomas Wright's *Universal Architecture*.
. . . an Ornithon, or Arbour of the Aviary Kind, Chiefly contrived for
the Reception of singing and other beautiful Birds.

The Method of Executing the Design D.
The Manner of Executing this Design is with the rugged Timbers of
Oak, the more fantastical and robust the better, the Architrave or Eve-
band is of the same unhewn Material, and supports a like rude Cornice,
in some Degree reduced to Order & Design, with large and prominent
regular Nobs instead of Modillions; the Roof is thatched, and of a
Roman Pitch, with a Palladian Projection, and to render it still more
secure of Shade and Shelter, it may be enclosed on three Sides at least,
or five at most, being principally constructed for a Point of View, and
to command a large Extent of the Horizon: on the Inside it may be
fitted up and finished with Ivy-Flakes and Moss, or otherwise with the
roughest Bark of Oak, variegated and comparted with Knots, yet so
as to appear all of one Mass growing together by the Content of Nature.
The Floor may be either Sand, Gravel, or Pebbles agreeable to the
Builder's Fancy.

Useful Follies

By no means all eyecatchers were skeleton scenery on the hilltops—some were useful gothick, acting both as ornaments and as screens to hide utility, giving decorative protection to deer, horses, salmon, farms and children, in descending order of imposing scale.

The British Isles and Ireland are of course scattered all over with stables, gates, aviaries, orangeries, boat-houses and so on, built in the castle style merely as distinct from the Elizabethan, Palladian, classical, cinema or any other style; there is no folly about them at all. But other structures show by their siting and their wealth of arrow-slits and castellations that they were intended to be seen as conceits; their dual purposes may reduce their folly status, but perhaps some of them would never have been built without the excuse of utility.

One of the earliest and most splendid of them is the deer-fold at Sudbury in Derbyshire, facing the beautiful and magnificently redecorated house; a previous deerkeeper has given the date as 1723, thatched in 1750. A mid-eighteenth-century painting in the house shows the deer-fold as four white castellated towers with arrow-slits, just as the corner ones have them now, ogival roofs and crisp weathercocks, all suitably embosomed in trees and one of the front towers does still show traces of white between bricks at the top. The roofs are gone now and it is all red, a fine fiery scarlet standing in a crop of bearded wheat, with two tall half-octagon towers on the face towards the house. These were clearly added later; the original front seems to have had a straight castellated wall of 16 pointed arches which must have been considered dull from the house, so that a central gate was put in with a large round-headed arch and the tall towers. Later more support was needed, so the back of the arch was filled in and the piers strengthened. The brickwork of the centrepiece is unusual, made of projecting horizontal bands crossed by vertical strips, as if arrow-slits in dimensional reverse, and though repairs are needed, the impression from the house is large and splendid.

There is another good deer-fold at Bishop Auckland, County Durham, a pleasant stone gothick cloister, with an arched gateway and a small tower with battlements and crocketed pinnacles in the wall opposite to it. 'The deer-house, a winter-refuge, which stands upon a graceful elevation on the western bank of the Gaunless, beneath the walls of the Castle, was constructed by Bishop Trevor in 1760. There are points of view in which this building, when seen at a distance, has a good effect, but it must not be approached too nearly by an architectural eye. It is said to have cost the small sum of £379.'[1] There is also a beautiful entrance gate to the park in the same style supporting a clock tower.

The distinction between folly stables and castellated stables may seem a tenuous and

[1] Raine's *Auckland Castle*, 1852.

The Deer House at Bishop Auckland, from a lithograph by John Thirsk and, opposite, *the stables at Berkeley Castle.*

over-subtle one, as almost every castle-house had its stable block to match but they were almost always joined to the house, or near it and concealed; the folly ones are either a long way away and definitely used as an object like the deer-folds, or if close have nothing to do with the architecture of the stables behind them and do have the folly feeling. They are more common than the deerfolds, and there is a particularly cosy example at Muncaster Castle in Cumbria, built of red sandstone and weathering softly away as that stone often so pleasantly does. In the centre of the wall is a castellated gable over a big Tudor arch, to the left a taller tower and to the right a square projecting block. There are quatrefoil windows, squares, concave-sided diamonds, circles, a cross, all in the best random folly tradition, and with a surprise to match. Macaws, red-and-blue and blue-and-yellow, come screaming out of the already bright stone, from quatrefoil or cross and away into the nearby trees, where they flash among the leaves in a most satisfactory way; a part of the stables is now an aviary.

The stables at Berkeley Castle in Gloucestershire are again castellated but are quite different, almost black and white, pale random stone with very dark dressing and not a macaw in sight, still used as the hunt stables and alive with the voices of the hounds. The eyecatcher face is two storeys high with a slate roof, in nine bays, carefully detailed with two of the centre three standing a little forward and joining into a high arch for an extra blind storey, with three taller castellations. The windows are pointed and diamond-latticed, and it looks charming across the meadows and water. The back is different but still pretty, with castellations running through the kennels, stables, and the agent's house.

Some estates have small castles for the dogs alone, scaled down below the grandeur for horses and carriages. A particularly good one is at Nunwick in Northumberland, the Gothick Kennels to a fine brown sandstone house of 1760. They are reached through the green and fertile grounds via an odd little twisted column which looks part of something Jacobethan, across a fast stream by a rustic bridge and along the bank. They make a good castellated composition, pointed arches and windows round three sides of a grass plot with an arcade in front. From the central arch a pavement runs through to a little paved court with a circular stone pool in the middle.

The north seems richer than the south in this sort of folly; at Netherby in Cumbria a noble sham castle, tough as a Vanbrugh, hides the salmon coops across the level fields; two three-sided towers of two storeys with a wall between and the largest arrow-slits the walls will hold. The detailing of the stonework on the windows is unusually careful by contrast. Across the river Esk attached to some farm buildings are some more castellated walls and arches for the view from the house.

During the eighteenth century there were landowners in every part of the country who felt that farms and cottages were a little shocking to the sensitive eye. Most of them planted screening trees, but sometimes one of them slapped a camouflaging screen of castellations on to the side nearest the house. Most of these are dull, their utilitarian but useless castellated walls unworthy of the name of gothick. There is a very fine one, though, at Nuthall Hall Farm at Ramsbottom in Greater Manchester. My notebook has only 'gothick screen to farm', but the history of this place would be worth investigation. The farmyard has superb stone barns, one with two storeys of wide round-headed shallow arches; the de Nuthall family lived here for a long time and these look like the

remains of sixteenth-, and seventeenth-century barns altered as farm buildings usually are. On the road is the 'screen', but this surely is one side, or part of one side, of a whole gothick barn; 3 feet behind it is a modern galvanised one. About 40 feet of sombre wall remain with the big pointed arch of the barn door and the arrow-slits for ventilation on each side. Pinnacles and castellations have been lost over the years, for the farm or hall became a dye works, and then a farm again, and was not well cared for.

In this part of the country buildings can be deceptive; industrialized areas may have become rural again. About three miles from Ramsbottom is Tottington, with Tower Farm in Shepherd Street near the edge of the fields, a massive stone castle with a 50-foot tower above the studded wooden gate into the yard, over which is framed J.K. 1840. But it did not start as a castellated farm; Nuthall Hall Farm was turned into a dye works for a time, but Tower Farm, reversing the process, was built by Joshua Knowles as stables for his calico-printing works with its 19 machines. He was first established in 1820, and was a director of the Calico Printers Association which listed 32 printers near Manchester and 14 in Glasgow—the craft was introduced into Scotland from India early in the eighteenth century and reached Manchester later. The rest of Old Tottington Mill has gone completely, only the cobbled ramps for the horses remain, the water levels have changed and the ponds are used for fishing, but the stables must have looked splendid engraved on the writing paper.

The best eyecatcher barns of all are in Ireland. One was built by Mrs Conolly after her obelisk at Castletown. The fine house by Allessandro Galilei and Sir Edward Pearce was built during the 1720s for Speaker Conolly with a layout of the grounds on a *patte-d'oie* plan which seems never to have been finished, perhaps because it was already old fashioned. Mrs Conolly continued to build after her husband's death; his tomb, Celbridge Collegiate School, and then the obelisk, when the winter of 1739–40 saw one of the Great Frosts that occasionally clamp down on Europe, and Mrs Conolly set out to provide work and food for the local people.

The famine went on and so did Mrs Conolly, not only with relief but with a possible remedy, the Wonderful Barn at the end of the northeast vista, a building as strange and beautiful as the obelisk, a stone and brick cone with four tapering drums, a straight one and a little castellated look-out at the top reached by a spiral staircase, an exhilarating turn and a half round the outside. The bottom two drums are the barn, above are four domed brick rooms, with triangular windows for the first three and round ones at the top. Pigeoncotes make two kitten-cones (but with no stair-cases) to corner the grass farmyard at the back. The pediment door to the barn has an inscription on a stone

1743
EXECUT'D
By JOHN GLINn

Corn in years of plenty was to be saved, carried up to the top, to be poured down through central holes in the floors. The barn is said to have been inspired by the great Gola or Golghar at Patna in India, a stone rice store 96 feet high built by Captain John Garstin. But the Gola was not built until 1786, so perhaps the barn inspired the Gola. There is no record of either of them ever having been filled.

A smaller but similar barn called the Bottle Tower stands in the garden of a modern house in Churchtown, Rathfarnham, on the outskirts of Dublin. This has been credited

The pigeon-house beside the Bottle Tower at Rathfarnham and a tortoise detail from Lucan House.

to Mrs Conolly, but also to Major Hall of Whitehall House with a date of 1742. It once had wooden floors to two rooms, with beams 18 inches thick, again reached from the external stairs. Again there is a conical pigeon tower at the side with projecting slates for landing grounds.

Another kind of useful folly, rarely large but often pretty, and sometimes combined with a grotto, is the bath-house. I have found in accounts of the use of these buildings, no invitations to bathe as there are invitations to take tea or a collation in the towers or castles; one can only assume that they were either a heat-wave pleasure or a keep-fit pain as swimming-pools are today.

There is a bath-house built of huge blocks of stone with tufa trim and a rough pediment at Lucan House, Co. Dublin, Classical outside and gothick in. It is about 30 feet long, a blue and white room with a fireplace and a tiny bath down steps in an alcove at the end. In front is the necessary stream and a tiny cascade. On the green path back to the house is the Monument, the burial place of Adam and Eve or of a pet dog, most exquisitely carved in stone, an urn on a three-sided concave pedestal supported by three tortoises each with another support under its chin to help.[1]

After such vista-closers as conical barns, the child-screen called Hartburn Tower in Northumberland is a small folly indeed, but it is a pretty one, a façade to the village school, in three steps with an ogival window, put up by Archdeacon Thomas Sharpe and his parishioners in 1756. There is a small grotto underneath over the stream, now

[1] There are similar monuments at Stanmer near Brighton, 1775, at Brocklesbury in Lincolnshire, possibly by Wyatt, and at Mount Edgcumbe in Cornwall, 1791, by Timothy Butt.

virtually inaccessible in mud and nettles. Dr Sharpe had also built a tower at Whitton in 1720, on a hill for the view from his genuine fourteenth-century peel tower; clearly he was an early gothick enthusiast and one tower was not enough. The folly one is about 30 feet high, plain and round, with round-headed windows and was used as an observatory—the Archdeacon was an amateur astronomer. So the tower was useful too.

From screening deer to screening children the useful follies have become smaller and smaller, but the powerful emotions of rage and jealousy now take us to a large folly, built with passion and purpose—if the stories are true.

At Belvedere House, Westmeath, the stories are so constant and specific that after years of instantly discounting legends, though sometimes writing them down for pleasure in their splendid insanity (Barwick has the maddest), here at last one says, well, perhaps.

The calm villa by Richard Castle was built for the Earl of Belvedere in 1742. A younger brother had a larger house on the next demesne of Tudenham, and Lord Belvedere believed that his wife and a third brother who lived there were lovers, and signalled to one another from the bedrooms of the two houses. So in about 1760 he built the Jealous Wall, some 150 feet of now wildly ruinous gothick to close the view. Lady Belvedere was sent away to live alone for years, unvisited, incommunicado, allowed to walk in the park only with a servant walking before her, ringing a bell to warn away the gardeners. When the wicked Earl died, her son went to find her and found her mad—(Mrs Delany would never have pined, she would have built half a dozen grottoes). Against belief in the story are the facts that both the wall and the Rustic Arch are direct copies from the *Universal Architecture* of Thomas Wright, who worked here—jealousy should not pause to choose from pattern books—and the wall does hide a long low barn. Moreover, the wall looks very good from the Tudenham side—jealousy should have made it hideous. But either way it is fine and sombre, down the grounds to the south, near the house and startlingly out of proportion to it, dark against the sun. It is built of stone; in the centre is a straight wall with three big pointed windows high above the ground and five little round-headed ones above them. Two square wings project at each end, their fronts joined by a lower concave wall with two windows, a door, and much irregularity and ivy. At the end of the right wing is a round tower, at the left two walls of octagon and then more angled walls to break the symmetry.

Belvedere. The Jealous Wall and the Rustic Arch.

Towers Lodge, Penrice

On the other side of the house on a stone bastion is an octagon summer house or gazebo faced with stone, quatrefoils over ogival arches. Then up across the park in the sun is the Rustic Arch, a true folly piece in random stone. For contrast, a tall bay window which can only be described as rising from a vase is made of big round pebbles, and has a tufa crown. More pebbles outline two pointed windows, a course between the two storeys, and a dripstone over the arch, and at the top are wild castellations horned with weathered stone. Ireland has some of the finest of all follies, and two of the best are at Belvedere.

There is a similar, even longer wall, gay instead of sombre, at Penrice Castle on Gower in West Glamorgan, 200 lovely crazy feet of walls, towers, and turrets given a spurious air of utility by a gate in the middle while piers and urns look doubly elegant in the chaos—the ugly sub-art-nouveau gates were made this century in Scotland, but the original ones survive and it is hoped to put them back; the whole Towers Lodge has been well restored—it is believed that the same family has lived in it since the eighteenth century, and it has now returned to a new bathroom and kitchen. The architect was Anthony Keck from Gloucester, who finished the house in 1776, did the Towers in about 1780, and an orangery at Margam, all for Thomas Talbot. The park has a very picturesque drive down to the thirteenth-century Penrice Castle on its mound with the new house below, and the sham castle on the road.

Castled gates on this scale are as surely folly as the deerfolds but they are not so common. There have of course been plenty of routine castellated lodges built in the last 200 years, but even such huge objects as the gates to Eastwell Park near Ashford in Kent are more architectural exercises than follies. In Ireland, though, there are some

This page, *Ballysaggartmore*. Above and below, *the Gothick Bridge;* centre; *the Gothick Gate.* Opposite, *one of the gates at Markree* (*and see pages 426 and 437*).

gates of great extravagance and fantasy, follies to the last stone; a Moghul arch in the Brighton Pavilion manner and period at Dromana, Co. Waterford, almost 300 feet of curved walls, castellations, arrow-slits and towers at Markree in Sligo, by Francis Goodwin in 1832, and the crowning folly of them all, at Ballysaggartmore in Waterford; huge gates, then an even larger bridge, then for economy a smaller bridge, and at last, no house, for there was no more money. The derelict demesne lies heavily overgrown, enclosed, silent, and lighthearted.

The Gothick Gates lie in from the road—the entrance gives no hint, surprise was intended—poor man, no gates, and then round a bend is an ogival crocketed arch with an extravagant finial, between two octagon turrets, between two walls at right angles to each other, between two two-storey square towers, between two tall round towers, with an outwork or two, all castellated, machicolated, keystoned, corbelled, dripstoned, lattice-windowed, and very well built in dressed yellowing sandstone. When this has been wondered at enough, and its symmetrical complexity admired, the lovely overgrown drive runs on, still with the remains of stone curbing, and an avenue of holm oaks, on one side mysteriously new, to a romantic glade sunk in trees near the head of the valley of a stream running into the Blackwater. Across the stream, the Gothick Bridge turns at right angles, about 60 feet of it with curving walls into the banks. Across each end is a castle, hard red sandstone from the local outcrops this time, the first note of economy perhaps, but elaborately worked for rugged grandeur with no economy at all. The first castle is a trifle of a two storey square gatehouse, set in a wall with a window each side, a tall round tower on the left, a lower square on the right, and two round ones behind set against the back of the gatehouse, so that on each side of the arch is a room whose plan might be said to be based on a triangle. Across the bridge, which spans the stream on three pointed arches is a more noble pile, whose gate lies between two square towers and two more triangular rooms of varying heights and pinnacles, all crowned by a tall round tower over the arch. . . . Here the drive divides and falters, but to the left, returning parallel to the stream, a smaller rivulet comes down through the woods and is crossed by a simpler bridge, an arch with buttresses, niches and castellations, drowned in moss and ivy. No one has been able to give me a date for it all, the ogival arch suggests Lacock Abbey and the 1830s, while the ironwork of the gates looks later; but so it may well have been. J. Smith is the only name we have, either as client or architect, and all should be sad with his failure, both to finish and to be a figure, like the wicked Earl at Belvedere, but one is sure that Mr Smith enjoyed it all. The castles appear an end in themselves; perhaps the house would have been the failure.

Cones, Bones and Druids

A decade would seem to be the longest span for which a period can hold its full, distinct flavour, just as a quarter of a century seems to be the longest span which any technique or style in the arts can hold without decline. The decades go back behind us—Thirties, Twenties, Great War, Edwardian, Nineties—each is clear, and quite different from its flanking decades. Undoubtedly this sharp break is superficial, but it must be based on some general truth emerging from the arts and memoirs of the times.

When I wrote the first version of this book, the most curious and neurotic follies, of a peculiarly black and rain-lashed sort, all seemed to fall within the 1820s, but now the strangest group of all must be placed much earlier, proving again the datelessness of amateur architecture, and now several dates set the invention of the cone-shaped folly back into the eighteenth century.

Barwick Park in Somerset has four follies and a grotto. Earlier researches gave them as the work of George Messiter in the 1820s, 1830s or 1840s to provide work when there was a severe depression in Yeovil's glove-making trade. The 1820s seemed most likely. Now, however, Mr and Mrs Messiter have shown me a painting of the house thought to be of about 1780, and two family portraits, probably of John Newman and his wife, whose youngest daughter married George Messiter. They are in the dress of, I would say, the 1770s, and one of the two largest follies appears in the background of each painting.

The follies mark the boundaries of the park and the four main points of the compass from the house; it all sounds rather dull, and the open park does not promise much. A long drive of oaks and beeches leads to the house. On the right is a field which slopes down in a shallow valley and then rises quite sharply again to level ground. The field is typical of Somerset, rank, well-cropped grass, cowdung and thistles, a barbed wire fence, and a thick hedge; here on the ridge across the valley from the drive stands the first folly. This is a new kind, indicating the change which was to come later, in the nineteenth century, when follies were no longer fashionable and therefore more individually eccentric. Clarity and attack detach it from the average eccentricities—it is an abstract work of art, having nothing to do with romantic theories, closing no vista, built for no wager, pure art and the purest folly.

It is a tall slender cone, 75 feet high, a stark spire of rough stone, smooth for the last few feet, with a ball on the top. It stands on a drum in three of whose segments large pointed arches have been cut. There is a plain square-section moulding between the cone and the drum, and the drum in turn stands on a low round base. From almost all points of view, one side of the cone is seen supported on the solid quarter of wall while the other stands as on legs on the piers between the arches. All the way up the tapering

Barwick Park. The conical folly.

sides are cut rings of little square holes. The cone is hollow and, inside, light and sunlight fall through the holes in fading concentric smoke rings far overhead, a hesitant heart to the definite cone.

This architecture is absolutely simple—most follies have decoration, but this is a highly functional structure designed for no function that has yet materialized. In the future there may be a civilization where this will be the most rational of buildings; the holes in the cone are those of a columbarium, but this is no city for doves—it might be a neighbourhood unit for a colony of warrior owls.

The cone stands on its peg leg at the western boundary; the south mark is a thin, thin needle of random rubble above the trees, bent at the top, an obelisk like a scream, a look-out post for the owls' army.

To the north is a calmer boundary called the Fish Tower, an untapered column about 50 feet high on a square plinth, again of random rubble except for a Ham stone, almost art-nouveau, well-head at the top, above whose iron cage was once fixed a fish weathervane. The well-head, a cylindrical cap to the column, is divided vertically by odd little mouldings that make palm trees or ogival arches, according as one looks at stem or space. The Tower is like an Edwardian factory chimney, slightly comic in this setting. There is a door in the north side of the base, and the hollow shaft is irregularly lit by rough slits to show the footholds that go up to the light. The local story is merely that it was built by the Romans; all the love and skill that make folly-stories have been reserved for the fourth folly, 'Jack the Treacle Eater'. This name is not as one might suppose a corruption of some Latin inscription, but refers to Jack, a celebrated local runner who took messages to and from London for the Messiters. He trained on treacle. The Hermes on top of the folly is Jack himself, waiting for midnight before he comes down to the lake by the house to quench the treacle thirst. A more reliable source of local history dismissed this very pleasant account—

Ignorance, pure ignorance—the towers were all built in 1160. Then sometime in the thirteenth century a milkman was murdered. They couldn't hang him because his wife kept him in the tower. He was very fond of treacle. His wife served Barwick House with milk and brought up two churns every day, one for the house, and the other was left by the arch full of food. He was there for seven months and they put the statue on top to commemorate him.

The Treacle Eater is both arch and tower, standing on the crest of a hill east of the house. The outsides of the arch go up in two big steps, and on top of it is a round tower almost as high and on the top of that a conical spire and on top of that Jack, running. The stepping of the arch reduces it to great straddled legs under the heavy superstructure; again, pure folly, but not so fine as the cone, which is unequalled.

As well as four follies, Barwick has the most blood-chilling of all grottoes. Behind the house a narrow path curves through an overgrown garden and woods. Across the path is a jagged stone arch, like a set of jumbled false teeth, with sharp rocks set inwards ready to bite, and long trails of dark ivy. The path goes on past this hazard, and by a decaying rustic bridge, through brambles and fallen trees into a rocky ravine. At last

Barwick Park. The obelisk, the Treacle Eater and the Fish Tower (and see page 245).

it turns sharply out of the sun between yews through another arch into the shell-less grotto, a circular cave of rough rocks. There is another arch in front and one on each side. A faint light comes from the left, where the arch gives on to a stretch of once open, now overgrown, green water enclosed in high fern-grown walls; such sunlight as can reach the scummy water is reflected up to the roof and dies on the rocks. To the right is a rectangular cave, again built of the dank rocks, with a floor of stony mud about a foot below the level of the grotto. This is a water trap; the mud and stones are some way down, and the floor is clear deep water, but the place stirs apprehension so deeply that one looks too closely to be caught. Through the fourth set of vicious teeth is a huge cold vault with the remains of a pebble floor. It smells of sour earth, with earth in the thick air and the jagged stones. The whole dome is utterly dark; the light that strains through an ivy-filled eye at the top cannot touch it, and only towards the bottom of the walls can light begin to grey the tops of the earthy stones, where it is both foggy and curiously intense, with a heavy black shadow under each stone. In the walls are three pairs of niches, for what conversation one cannot contemplate, and the light is strong enough on the stone that frames them to cast long fangs of shadow inside. In the middle of the floor is a cistern of the clear deep water lapping at the sharp, dirty rocks that curb it, a nasty little sound in the silence. There are more rocks under the water, and black branches like starving crocodiles lift out of it. This is the most horrible place the folly builders made. The damp air chills the heart. There are not even the scratched initials of visitors.

 The atmosphere of follies is beyond dispute, but, alas, also beyond analysis. At Barwick the unfamiliar shapes of the follies seem responsible, but Mad Jack Fuller's follies in Sussex immediately confound so simple an answer. True, he had no grotto, but he had a cone, a pyramid tomb, an obelisk, and a hermit's tower, as well as such more normal adornments to an estate as an observatory, and a rotunda, and yet it is all jolly, one cheerful piece of nonsense after another, quite without alarm. The cone is called the Sugar Loaf: one night after dinner John Fuller said that the spire of Dallington church could be seen from his dining-room. Next morning in daylight, he saw that he was wrong, and also that it was something easily set right. Dallington has rather a cobby steeple, and Fuller copied it with a cobby cone just behind the skyline from the dining-room window. It is very friendly and pleasant, solitary in a field, about 40 feet high, built of stone and faced with cement. There is a clumsy porch and a blind window, and, inside, a floor of beaten earth about 15 feet across. Once there was an upper floor— it was used as a cottage until the 1880s—and it has recently been restored.

Dallington. The Sugar Loaf.

*Hill. Above and left, *two of the Fox's Earths*. Below right, *the Cockle House*.

Mad Jack Fuller's tomb is in the churchyard at Brightling, a massive ivy and moss-covered pyramid built in 1810 inside which he, correspondingly massive at 22 stone, is supposed to sit, dressed for dinner with a bottle and a bird in front of him. The official guide book to the Church of St Thomas à Becket most stoutly denies this, protecting the memory of the man who gave the Church a barrel organ of 24 tunes and 12 bassoons, still in use. 'He died,' says the guide, 'a natural death, and is buried in the ordinary recumbent position beneath the floor of the pyramid.' Even if he is sitting just inside the tomb, even if the door flew open before one's eyes, it could not be truly alarming, for the benevolent personality of Mr Fuller clearly never aimed at alarm. He was a patron of Turner, commissioned Smirke to design his Observatory and the Rotunda (or second observatory), built a huge wall around Rose Hill (now Brightling Park) to give employment in time of famine, saved Bodiam Castle from demolition, and refused a peerage. Only one of his works shows an attempt at morbidity, for there is the small tower to which he tried to lure a hermit (seven years, never washing, never cutting hair or nails, all as usual), but he did not succeed in getting anyone to play the part and the tower remains cheerful. It is a very nice one, green all over with moss, standing in a coppice with a dry ditch all round. It is about 25 feet high and 12 feet across, with traces of floors and a staircase. It would have been quite comfortable.

The obelisk is on another hill, very plain and rather squat.

John Fuller died in 1834, aged 77. The folly buildings have no dates, but seem to be of about one decade. They are in any case so like and yet so different from the Barwick follies that it is best to consider them together, for no contrast could be more marked than that between Fuller's unquenchably cheerful nonsenses and the terrible unrest at Barwick.

Mad Jack Fuller obscures the village names of Brightlington and Dallington, but in County Meath the Fox's Earth at Larch Hill has obscured the name of the happy Master of Hounds who built it (to all appearances at about the same time as the Sugar Loaf). Robert Watson was convinced, or pretended to be, that when he died he would be reborn as a fox, and made snug preparations. The Earth itself is under a mound with the remains of an embattled wall, and is entered by three pointed arches. On top is a very odd affair, a group of short, stout plain columns, connected at the core, with a low dome on top. It faces the low simple house which has lovely gates into the garden, very stout circular piers with balls on top and extremely elegant ironwork. By the lodge is another earth with no mound, only the same squat pillars, but open in front. Behind the house is a shelter of three open arches into a room walled with random painted tiles and fine rich windows with purple, gold, clear and emerald glass. It looks north into the sun of a walled garden with crowstepped bits on the walls and, in one corner, a three-storey round tower called the Cockle House. The ground floor has a pointed door with coloured glass and is decorated with cockle, mussel and razor shells, and a few exotics. An external staircase leads to the first floor—there is confusion between the true and apparent floor levels—there are a lot more cockle shells, in bands for economy, and the stair, lined with them, climbs on inside to the roof and the parapet. There are the two bottom storeys of another tower (yet another earth perhaps), the statue of a white lady with a cornucopia, and a statue of Nimrod on a little island in a lake. A place of content and charm, hard to die and leave; one hopes he got back.

There is another strange group of follies with a cone as centrepiece at Aysgarth in

Aysgarth. The folly like a rocket-ship and the sham castle.

North Yorkshire. They stand on high ground above the shadow of a pedimented eighteenth-century house, now a farm; there are balls on the gateposts and in the middle of a lawn become rough grazing, a stone column with an eagle. The cone was described to me as 'a folly like a rocket-ship', and so it is, a cone about 25 feet high with big stone fins, ready for take-off. There are two blind round-headed windows, a stark door and the skeleton of a sheep inside. Along the ridge is a gate, two squat stone cylinders joined by a flat thin arch, and then a smaller cone in three stages, with a cotton-reel waist in the middle. Much higher up the steep hillside and on the axis from the house is the ruin of an excellent sham castle with a curved façade curiously crowned by a pediment, an *oeil-de-boeuf* window repaired boldly with wood, pointed windows and an arch. There is a semi-circular turret at one side and a continuing curtain wall with square turrets. So far I have not been able to find out anything of its history at all, heads are shaken, it has always been there.

A very fine cone is near Dublin in Killiney, Mount Mapas. It stands on a hilltop on two blocks and is very crisp and handsome, even roughcast as it is now. The top and smaller block has a little central pediment on the side overlooking the sea above a marble plaque with a lion crest and the inscription

> LAST year being
> hard with the POOR
> the Walls about these
> HILLS and THIS
> erected by
> JOHN MAPAS
> Esq June 1792

The large cone at Mount Mapas.

On the base block there are four big arched alcoves, one with the door and the others with seats. A marble diamond records repairs by Robert Warren in 1840, and another plaque tells us that Victoria Hill was bought by the Queen's Jubilee Memorial Association and opened as a public park by the Prince of Wales in 1887.

Below, is a much smaller cone almost lost in gorse, standing on two hexagonal storeys with a pointed door in the bottom one and MOUNT MAPAS, well carved.

Then there is a seven-stepped stone pyramid, with a new granite top and some half-steps to make the climb easier added in 1852. Clearly, it has always been loved and cared for here (though the little cone now needs repair), and indeed it is a very fine hill, with two cones and a pyramid, and for view the sea, trees, a coast guard station, a Martello tower on one island and a lighthouse on another.

By the beginning of the nineteenth century, the beautiful natural sites close to London were long gone, every available little Switzerland had been improved and made more wild in the Chinese or the picturesque taste; rocks were piled up, and torrents clashed all over the home counties as tightly as they could be crowded in. Farther out, however, many estates still had great possibilities (though the most promising place of all, Cheddar Gorge, seems always to have escaped notice), and in 1814 the fifteenth Earl of Shrewsbury found that he owned his English Rhineland on the north side of the Churnet valley at Alton in Staffordshire, where we have already seen the pagoda.

It is a deceptive place; the approach from the north is nothing, over high ground dropping gradually from the Peak, with a natural feeling of anticlimax. But from the village or the river there is the true sublimity. Work began on an enormous gothic house with painstaking detail, wonderful stained glass, huge galleries and corridors, and the most crushing gloom and impersonality, as if the Houses of Parliament had been adapted and darkened for domestic use. A picturesque second valley ran down from the house to join the river below the noble heights on which the house could be seen, and this, with the rest of the park, was landscaped with a wonderful collection of exotic trees. Lord Shrewsbury worked hard, and after his death in 1827 his nephew went on, and between them they produced a wonderfully clotted effect.

Loudon, who visited Alton before the pagoda was finished, was stunned by the 'labyrinth of terraces, curious architectural walls, trellis-work arbours . . . stone stairs, wooden stairs, turf stairs . . . temples, pagodas . . . waterfalls, rocks, cottages . . . rock-work, shell-work, root-work, moss houses, old trunks of trees, entire dead trees, etc' as well as all the routine garden ornaments and a Corkscrew Fountain. Much is lost, but however heavily we discount Loudon's disgust, we probably enjoy the pagoda more clearly now.

Little has been found out about the designers of the follies. The pagoda and the startlingly 1740s gothick tower were begun soon after 1814, the pagoda not finished until after 1826. Papworth has been mentioned as a designer, at least of the bridges, and a Mr Abrahams. Pugin worked at Alton for the sixteenth Duke, after 1827, and I can find out no more.

Early in the 1920s the Shrewsburys sold the estate, and a private company opened it to the public. During the war the army had it, and kept it till 1951, and for the last twenty years it has been open again, the garden restored to its trim perfection, and now providing in the park all the usual new pleasures of country house visiting—boating lakes, model and miniature railways, a fairground, sea lions, a pottery studio, bars and cafeterias, and an aerial railway across the gardens.

I first saw Alton when the army had gone but not given up, with a handful of gardeners keeping the main paths clear and the follies safe; it was extraordinarily beautiful and hushed, and I think it worth while to keep my old description of it: 'It was over-planted, is now overgrown, and the rhododendrons down the valley stifle the visitor with their thick airlessness. The paths on the right-hand side, always too close, zig-zagging like a stretched net right down the hillside, are choked with the branches and shiny green leaves, wet underfoot and clattering raindrops in the wet face as one pushes through a yet thicker path; there is an unpleasant level where the path is quite invisible and the rhododendrons breast-high—soon we shall be out of our depth, buoyed up for a little by the beetle-wing leaves and then held down by the branches and choked in the

Alton Towers. The gothick prospect tower and, opposite, *the Druids' Sideboard.*

aromatic greenness. They do indeed at last close over our heads, but after a moment we can walk under them, shrubs like trees, until at last we are out by the lake looking up at the surprising shape of the pagoda in the rain . . . in the middle of the enclosed and silent lake. The ground floor was for the entertainment and comfort of ornamental ducks, and doves were to live in the upper floors, perhaps to make up with their gentle cooing for the silence of the bells. The lake has a very tense atmosphere, one watches the pagoda constantly listening for the bells to stir in the wind and jangle, but they cannot.

'On the top of the other side of the valley is a very pretty gothick prospect tower, eight-sided, in three diminishing storeys of open arcades, with a spiral staircase to the crocketed ogives of the top and a lantern of stained glass for the view. The walls are painted red and the elegant arcading of gothick arches is left in its natural grey stone: no stucco here. At first sight the graceful lightness of the tower suggests the eighteenth century, but the accurate detail is clearly later.

'The closely crowded trees hide almost everything that might be seen from this height, and indeed only the Choragic Monument and the glasshouses under their rich coloured coronet are really easy to find, being clearly visible on a terrace with tight flower beds.

On the way back towards the house past the glasshouses there is more open gardening in paths and terraces up the hillside, and at the top of it, against a heavy background of trees, is a new folly, a sort of sideboard made of big dark stones. Four piles of neat rocks stand in a row, joined by big slabs across their tops. In the centre, the edifice rises another storey in the same way, the whole finished by the addition of two smaller slabs on top and a last one on top again. A very small bell rings in the mind; faintly and far away, minimized almost out of recognition, but not quite, this is Stonehenge. Older than hermits and so surely even more romantic, suggested not by gnarled roots and heather thatch but by durable and practical rocks, not foreign like pagodas but thoroughly British and patriotic; the folly builders have found the Druids.'

A curious feature of the Druid vogue is that the construction of Stonehenge has been imitated and not its gigantic scale; with two exceptions all the Druids' circles are tiny. The Tetralithon for instance is a dwarf beside the Petersfield–Winchester road. On one side there used to be a large heap of stones in a beech copse, the tomb of a racehorse with silver shoes, and across the road there is still a little 4-foot henge, three groups of boulders overgrown with brambles: 'someone brought them there'.

Temple Combe at Henley-on-Thames has a more ambitious group, and real.

'Cet ancien Temple des Druides découvert le 12me Août 1785 sur le Montagne de St. Helier dans l'Isle de Jersey: A été presenté par les Habitans à son Excellence le General Conway, leur Gouverneur.

> *Pour des siècles caché, aux regards des mortels*
> *Cet ancien monument, ces pierres, ces autels,*
> *Où le sang des humains offert en sacrifice,*
> *Ruissela, pour des Dieux, qu'enfantiot le caprice.*
> *Ce monument, sans prix par son antiquité,*
> *Témoignera pour nous à la postérité,*
> *Que dans tous les dangers Cesarée eut un père*
> *Attentif, et vaillant, généreux, et prospère;*
> *Et redira, Conway, Aux siècles à venir,*
> *Qu'en vertu du respect dû à ce souvenir,*
> *Elle te fit ce don, acquis à la vaillance,*
> *Comme un juste tribut de sa reconnaissance.*

The site of the Circle is fantastic. Temple Combe when I went there was empty, a large yellow brick mid-nineteenth century house, more huge villa than mansion, upright and crisp. Most empty houses sink back passively, but occasionally one of them feels that, denied human protection, it must be extra vigilant on its own account, and Temple Combe watches the visitor up to the front door, round to the back and down the long

Templecombe. The Druids' Circle.

grass of the lawn to the stones. Here it is difficult to stop looking back at the alert house, so intense is the vitality of each pale separate brick.

The circle on the grass is 27 feet in diameter and was accurately re-made though the original circle was only 21 feet. It is entered through a stone passage 10 feet long and only 4 feet high. However, upright again and in the centre of the stones, we are cut off from the yellow eyes of the house, and can look at the sharp monoliths, 7 to 10 feet high, and the five smaller, precariously balanced trilithons that alternate with them. A few small shrubs grow round the stones, and on the outside of one monolith is the inscription quoted above. Away round the edge of the lawn is an Aubrey-circle of trees. The house makes a hele-stone.

The dubious but endearing archaeology of the early nineteenth century, enthusiasms, muddles, and jolly leaps at pleasing conclusions, finds its best expression in terms of follies at Banwell in Somerset. George Henry Law, Bishop of Bath and Wells from 1824 to 1845, was a fortunate man: one of the most important early finds of prehistoric bones in this country was made on one of his estates. Who knows but that the well-known connection between the Protestant Church and archaeology was founded by this very Bishop, to whom hundreds of keen vicars may owe their undisputed authority on antiquity. If Banwell Bone Cave had been otherwise owned, the tradition of Sir Thomas Browne might have continued and old bones be regarded as perquisites of the doctor. However, Bishop Law treated his caves handsomely.

Banwell village is at the foot of a ridge of hills lying close to the sea on the north side of Mendip. In 1780 miners started to sink a shaft at the west end of this hill in search of ochre and lead. Instead of minerals they found a large cave 150 feet long and 35 feet high, with the usual stalactites and stalagmites, which were of no use to them (presumably no gentlemen even came to shoot down the crystal decoration of this faery hall for their grottoes), so the miners closed the shaft, having found neither ochre nor lead, but the memory of the underground chamber survived. A farmer called Beard discovered in 1822 a skeleton near the entrance to the old shaft, and in 1824 he decided to reopen it, and in that year rediscovered the cave. Next year with two miners he started to make another entrance to it by sinking a shaft down a fault in a quarry about 75 yards to the west of the original entrance. Here he found a smaller cave with a sandy floor rich in the bones of Arctic Fox, Wolf, Reindeer, Bison and Glutton. Bishop Law immediately became intensely interested, and so that he should be able to spend his time there comfortably he built a cottage on the steep slope of the hill between the entrances to the two caves.

As Bishop of Chester before his translation to Bath and Wells, he must have found little scope for improving an already overpowering clutter of mediaeval and Roman remains, but at Banwell, where there was only the remains of the civilization of Glutton and Fox, his gentle morbidity found ample means of expression. The improvements to his estate here continued for the rest of his life; the house was enlarged in 1833 and his son Mr Chancellor Law continued the work, as they meant their elaborate layout of paths and improving inscriptions to become a public park for the people of Banwell. It is, however, still private property.

The entrance to 'The Caves' used to be through a great semicircular arch of worn stones, perhaps tufa, now gone. Most of the buildings in the garden here are built of this stone, water-worn or deposited, a dark yellow colour with ferns and ivy growing in the interstices. Beside the arch are two massive piers supporting pyramids, the dominant architectural motif at Banwell, used by the Bishop and his son to emphasize every angle and entrance. The drive curves round a khaki-coloured barn, passes below the front of the house and fades away in a clump of trees. Just beyond the house the gardens begin. On the right is a tufa retaining wall. It curves back slightly into the hill making a recess, and in the wall is a niche arched over with stone and almost obscured by ivy and hartstongue ferns; on a stone slab forming a seat is the head of a statue and above the niche is a tablet, with the Bishop's arms under a little pediment, and this poem:

> Here let time's creeping winter shed,
> His hoary snow around my head,
> And while I feel by fast degrees
> My sluggish blood wax chill and freeze
> Let thought unveil to my fixed eye
> The scenes of deep eternity.
> Till life dissolving at the view,
> I wake, and find the vision true.

Farther on past a path leading up the hillside is a coffin-shaped contemplation cosy, with a gothic façade of sandstone and plaster:

> Here mid diluvial relics in this cell
> Let musing heavenly contemplation dwell
> And hence beholding him who reigns above
> Adore a God of mercy and of love.

The path which we passed goes between low walls of stone overgrown with harts-tongue, spurge laurel, holly and brambles to a terrace where it divides; to the left, on up the hill, and to the right between two pyramids down into a cutting. This is the way to the cave discovered in 1780 and opened by Beard in 1824.

One goes about normally prepared only to cope with life above ground; ladders and skindiving equipment seem superfluous. Here at least a powerful torch is needed. A crude stair cut in the rock spirals steeply downwards, and, after a few confident steps before daylight is lost, any party is sure to be divided into the prudent who stay crouched against the walls of the shaft and the foolhardy who continue the descent, shouting as they go in the vain hope that the concussion of their voices will bring down any loose rocks before they come to them. Eventually the light going down disappears, but the wail marking a death plunge is not heard, and at last they return after not reaching the cave, saying that it was no trouble at all, and couldn't have been easier.

The path we left to get to the cave continues between stone walls hung with a wonderful profusion of ferns and ivy. An arch with its wooden, studded door on the ground with tendrils of ivy creeping over it is the way into the garden above and behind the house. (The path, however, goes on along the ridge of the hill to the tower which Bishop Law built between 1835–40.) In this garden is a charming little summer house. The back wall has three shallow niches and above them is a gable rising between two mediaeval carvings. The front is open and the roofs of the house can be seen between gothick arches which are covered with a fine encrustation of evenly matched pebbles. Inside there is a stone seat, and the ceiling is covered with small stone chips, not over-lapping as in most grottoes, but sticking straight downwards, like Barwick on a smaller scale, giving that toothy jagged look popular in the 1820s. The corner piers this side support a lion and a very sinuous camel. The Tower is a better belvedere, so this little building must be for intellectual rather than visual contemplation, musings on bones, the origin of man, the reconciliation of the Bible with archaeology. We are a long way here from the seventeenth-century metaphysician's thoughts on bones, on death and on God, a long way from the bell striking out the minutes in Mr Tyer's wood. These are some of Bishop Law's thoughts on bones, written to mark the spot where Beard buried the skeleton:

> Beard with his kindness brought me to this spot,
> As one unknown and long forgot,
> He dug my grave and laid me here
> With no kind friend to shed a tear
> My bones are here, my spirit fled
> For years unnumbered with the dead.

On the way to the tower there is another little cell, square with no roof, and the walls plastered with Roman cement, the doors and windows made of carefully chosen branches to make natural gothick arches. The path now enters the woods which the Bishop planted when he first came to Banwell, and every 50 yards are pairs of standing stones one on each side, leading to the tall and clumsy tower. The elegance has gone from gothick towers by now; they reached their peak at Alton and are henceforth a little dull. Banwell tower has three storeys that instead of diminishing one above the other with clarity and

*The Caves, Banwell. The contemplation cosy
and the tower, two of the grotesque animals,
a bone chalet and the old entrance arch.*

precision as they do at Alton, lessen in a sleazy, indeterminate way. On the top is a belfry with a pointed roof; the tower is now in poor condition.

To see the bone cave we must go back to the beginning of the drive; on the left is a large roughly circular open space, the site of the quarry, surrounded on both sides with two beautiful folly screens. The semi-circle on the right is a low stone wall with piers at each end and niches in all its length, sweeping up to a higher stretch supporting two pyramids of rough stone. On the left, however, the wall is higher, to screen the sides of the old quarry, and much more elaborate. Its length is punctuated with the same niches as on the other side, an elaborate arch leads to the bone cave, and in the centre are two gothick arches under a series of diminishing entablatures. They lead into a semi-circular room with five niches cut into the rock, coffin-shaped and making quite comfortable seats. In the centre of the room is a round stone table supported on one random rubble leg. On the outside wall between the two arches is a marble tablet with the Bishop's explanatory verse:

> Here where once druids trod in times of yore
> And stain'd their altars with a victim's gore
> Here now the Christian ransomed from above
> Adores a God of mercy and of love.

Before the war a tetralithon stood in the space between the two screens, but it impeded the drivers of army lorries, so it was removed.

The bone cave rouses all the fears and fuss experienced before, but this descent is more rewarding for not far underground is a ledge cut out of the rock, and upon this are collected some of those bones which were not worthy of Taunton Museum. They are not lying in haphazard piles, the Bishop's love of building prevailed, and they are used as the logs for little chalets, with bone gables, knucklebone chimneys and knucklebone carving over the door; a skeletal cuckoo might pop out at any minute. However old the bones may be they seem new, for the earth upon them is like flesh in an advanced state of decay, and the imagination supplies a smell of carrion, so a visit to this cave is not likely to be a lengthy one.

The second drive which runs through the space between the screens comes out on to the road by a lodge, behind a façade of dream architecture. A white door with black studs, set in an arch of rough stones is flanked by two pillars with pyramids of tufa on top. A triangular pediment is between them over the door. More walls, pediments, pyramids and arches are on each side of the gate, with clumps of ivy further contorting the grotesque rocks.

At Banwell, the Druids have five seats round a stone table, but on the Yorkshire moors at Ilton is a complete temple for them, built in the 1820s (the Druids' period of ascendancy in England was short, only about 50 years) by William Danby of Swinton Park.

A folly tour must be based on the sound military maxim that time spent in reconnaissance is seldom wasted. Here the notebook in 1949 said simply 'Masham in Uredale. Model Stonehenge on moors', and, as we did not reach Masham till dusk, late on a

Swinton Park. The Druids' Circle.

summer evening, anyone with a grain of commonsense would have admired the stone town built round a big square and gone to bed, leaving both reconnaissance and folly till morning. However, we had had a very good day, long and energetic, the follies well above average, so when the pub closed, confident in the authoritative directions of half the saloon bar, we drove on up the narrowing roads to the moor. No one had mentioned that Ilton is one of those villages on a circular road, but after a while we got free of it and up a narrow lane—can't miss it. The car stopped at a field gate, the folly would be in the plantation across the stubble, an extra dark patch in the night, that finally became a solid black wall of young conifers, 40 feet high. Hand in terrified hand we quartered the wood. Ernest Griset's owls sat silent in every tree, daggers ready in their belts. At last it was decided that this could not be right and we drove on, higher up the moors, to an isolated cottage with a light shining. 11.30 p.m. I said, 'Forgive me for disturbing you so late, but could you please tell me the way to the Druids' Circle?' 'Why, of course. Straight on, turn left . . . you can't miss it.' The lane ended at a gate and only a footpath ran ahead over the moor. We left the car and went on through high bracken, past a standing stone, and then another, on the right track. The moon was up now and the bracken in sharp relief against its own dense shadows, the death of the moon reflected on the landscape, all the cold terror that keeps one indoors at night. Monoliths, and another black wood on the right, and there is the stone circle in full moonlight on the hillside. All effort and owl-terrors fall away; once inside, past the heavy shadows of the entrance, the warm stones enclose a different moonlight, the lovely tranquillity of Palmer and the poets, a very rare moonlight indeed.

The stones hold back the bracken as well as terror, and preserve a fine springy turf that is for once the true dark green carpet of the similes, and on it stands the tightly-knit henge of trilithons and monoliths, not in a circle but a big ellipse, 10 or 12 feet high, 75 feet long, still a little huddled against the awful winter weather. In the centre though, a tall monolith stands on three round steps as though no wind ever reached it; a slip, too, from Druidical research into the Roman taste, for in a prehistoric circle or horseshoe the 'altar stone' is back from the centre, and so it is here, but the monolith dominates the scene like a commemorative column in a forum and the altar takes second place. Beyond it, through a screen of cobby trilithons is a second, smaller ellipse of stones, surrounding a slab like a tortoise, and ending a last enclosure, a black cave in the hillside.

Does the Englishman exist who never to himself has sworn to see Stonehenge just once at dawn? It occurred to us that here was a nobler opportunity, to see the sun rise, not over that common circle in Wiltshire where charabanc parties stand bewildered under a sky of solid cloud, but over a private Stonehenge, in perfect weather, in peace. Two journeys over the silent moor to the car, and there was the white tent set up in the circle on the turf, a last look at the night, and sleep. Just before dawn the black and silver was gone, replaced by dull darkness. Then the sun rose, all in the wrong place, but quickly warm and golden, and we had breakfast on the sacrificial stone in the transformed circle. By day the stones and bracken, all of one tone, separated only by colour, dazzle together, and the circles are seen not quite to have repelled the bracken, for the pale croziers are creeping in. An isolated tree outside grows on the roof slab of a group of stones, flourishing but disturbed by the wind which has also torn the outer trees of the wood—it is hard to imagine, under the calm moon, what winter is like up here.

By 1971 a large reservoir had been built below the henge, and the Forestry Commission has planted all over the hillside; the little firs are springing up where the bracken was, and will soon overcome, but the henge is preserved and there is an easy road past the reservoir to the car-park, and DRUIDS PICNIC PLACE on a rustic notice board. There are four Druidical seats of asymmetrical picturesque design, two rubbish bins and some stones to whet the appetite. A notice board points the footpath on to Druids' Temple, with no word of the 1820s, and there is the henge just as it was, though now with a nasty conifer background, a little more worn and reverently visited; the awe of isolation and moonlight has been replaced by the awe given to works B.C.; like Margate Grotto, it has been taken very seriously—in 1936 it was analyzed in terms of Tyrians, Phoenicians, Romans, the Eucharist, and Freemasonry. It is now a bit comic, but it is safe and still amazing.

The other large Druids' circle is much more like Stonehenge in design, but seems to have attracted little attention and no legends, a curiously unimpressive ring of slender dark stones, standing in a field at Weston Rhyn in Salop. Summer or winter, sun or rain, they retreat into their background, and have no picturesque aspect at all. There are more than 40 stones in a circle about 45 feet across, the tallest about 14 feet high. The edges of the stones are made interesting by the drill-holes of quarrying, but the circle remains a bore.

Wales has a pleasant little sham circle at Reynoldston on Gower, about 20 feet across, made early in the nineteenth century, at the height of the vogue for Druids, by the Lucas family of Stouthall Park, with a grotto now gone, and another stone, a pre-Norman pillar in another field. A central engraved stone lying in the middle of the henge as footstool to a small mossy stone throne, may be ancient too, but otherwise it is as described by a guide to West Gower, 'nothing more than a whim of that gentleman'.

Elsewhere in Wales, one must beware of stone circles. One may see here and there a green field with dark stones standing in the rain. The map does not mark them in that gothic lettering which proclaims an ancient monument, nor do they embellish the local estates. They are nevertheless druids' circles, even newer than the ones we have been looking at: they mark the site of a Gorsedd, the meeting of bards and Druids before an Eisteddfod. One feels very cut off from the Welsh at these festivals, the long poems, the harps, and the unfamiliar penillion singing. The trouble is that other nations have a visible culture, and we can enjoy their painting, sculpture and architecture with little difficulty, while the Welsh have, uniquely, no visual arts at all, being confined to singing, brass-bands and poetry which, however magnificent it may be, is in a language which one has no other inducement to learn. The blank gap in Welsh life where the visual arts should be is nowhere better illustrated than by the bardic druidical costumes, like crumpled nightdresses, with trousers and boots sticking out underneath, and draped wimples so unbecoming that it is cruel to believe that someone actually designed them. They should be changed to achieve some of the dignity of the commemorative stones.

Barwick Park. The Treacle Eater.

Folly Gardens

After 1840, there are few romantic follies; the fashion was over. There are some remarkable eccentricities, and thousands of romantic houses built with no regard for comfort or expense in any of a hundred styles, including some gloomy varieties of gothic undreamed of in the eighteenth century, but when people began to live in their follies, the gardens began to grow rationally: 'Everything in the shape of *grottoes,* when they take the form of a cavern, is disagreeable, and injurious to health. . . . Grottoes are very rarely to be coveted, either as picturesque objects or resting-places; a good summerhouse being capable of quite as much rusticity, and far more comfort.'[1]

So the building of exotic conceits passed from our hands; the young man who took his own folly from England to Constantinople with him, a whole sham library of false books, and set it upon an island in the Bosphorus, is replaced by the Shah of Persia who was so charmed by the Albert Hall when he visited London that he ordered a copy to be built at Teheran.[2]

Such grottoes as were built are made of concrete, plain and hygienic places, infinitely more mysterious than the pretty caves of shells and felspar. New gardens and parks were still scattered with embellishments, though these again are spare and unloved, as if built for tokens, merely to indicate a temple or a pavilion, or to inform that this is their pattern; the planting, on the other hand, is more lush and much more coloured, the green eighteenth-century landscape thickened not only with flowers, but also with coloured shrubs and trees. Wood was the thing now, alive or dead; more trees in the park, more rustic summerhouses in the shrubbery.

Stancombe Park was built at the time of the Chartist riots, during the 1840s. With it was built a garden, far down the park, hidden and tight. In 1880 the house was burnt down and later rebuilt, but the distant garden and two remarkable picturesque cottages remained intact. One cottage is visible from the road, an exotic surprise at the top of a baked field, like the top storey of a rather Swiss pagoda showing above the hill, with a smaller one for a shed pushing up beside it. It is built of bright yellow stone, with gables and panels of diagonally-worked red brick. The roofs curve, but the chimneys are richly Tudor, and there is a lot of Cotswold detail, as if the local builder had interpreted a drawing from a pattern-book on village architecture.

The house itself is built high, and from it a dark romantic glen falls through ferns and rhododendrons. At the bottom, traces of a round flower-bed mark the centre of a glade of pine needles. Paths run from it in several directions, some to be overwhelmed by

---

[1] Edward Kemp, *How to Lay Out a Garden,* second edition, 1858.
[2] When the walls were finished, it was suddenly found that they would not take the weight of the roof, but luckily by then the Shah had forgotten all about it.

The folly garden at Frome (see page 384)

towering nettles on their way to overgrown doors in a corrugated iron fence, plum-coloured and cut zig-zag at the top like a fence round a greyhound stadium.

Inside the palisade is the garden, round a lake. A stiff door opens to it in the damp back of a stone building set in the fence, a Doric temple overlooking the water. The lake runs north and south, an irregular oval almost 150 yards long, and the temple is on the southeast corner; the edges are grown over with rushes, lilies and willowherb. There are some huge trees, oak, copper-beech, chestnut and mountain ash; ferns are everywhere.

The steps from the temple go down through that uniform grey-green tangle into which formal beds always disintegrate, to a semicircle of stone jutting into the lake, enclosing a little round pond with a fountain. Crumbs call up enormous goldfish. A flagged path runs north along the verge, almost crowded into the lake by great bushes and closed above by a naked iron pergola in the precise arch of a railway terminus. At the end of the lake the path curves to the left, and the skeleton tunnel takes on grotto flesh and encloses it in abrupt darkness. Water drips traditionally ahead, and we pass a little slit through which a thin cascade can be seen trickling into the lake. The chink faintly lights a cul-de-sac tunnel ending in one of the disused doors. Everything is so narrow that the walls seem to touch one everywhere. The dark path turns left and goes out up steps on to a rough path, but quickly into another grotto, another skimpily-rocked entrance to coffin-narrow passages of plain, untextured, practical brick. A hundred years have spread over some of the walls a thin yellow-green stain; otherwise they are smooth and bare, with no sign at all of more romantic intentions.

Stancombe Park. The square court and the vaulted niche.

Four tunnels meet. High in the vaulting is a round eye of green light which shows another dark door into the nettles and a spare vaulted niche with pantry shelves, its whitewash lightening the gloom to display a little collection of ammonites and fossils. The fourth tunnel returns us to daylight on the other long side of the lake with a path so closely hedged in that only the charming perspective down the sunny flags is visible, with arches of iron overhead to centre the eye. The end of the vista is gloom again, a small square court closed on three sides. In the middle is a stone urn, barer than the palm of any hand and three exotic but bare doorways breaking the walls. Every ingredient of a romantic garden is here, water, winding walks, fine trees, gloomy grottoes, mossy cascades, pavilions and a temple, shudders and surprise, and everything is more than a hundred years old, but everything is wrong, thin and entirely unmellowed; the urn in this little court is the focal point of a long perspective from one direction, while from the other it is the first thing visible from another dark passage, yet it has neither interesting detail nor elegance of shape. Nevertheless, this is a most compelling garden; this place, that must have been designed by someone who knew what and not quite how, stays in the mind, especially the three doorways in the court. The Stonehenge-shaped one on the left frames a winding path leading to a seat under a tree, the only place on this side from which the lake is visible, a touch of skill. Opposite Stonehenge is a deep wooden porch like half a boat on end. At the back is an Egyptian door, of wood, and farther in and darker still is an opening in a stone wall, empty. The third door is Moorish, completely undecorated, and leads through a black brick passage to a path between castellated hedges of thick box, ending at the temple. From here a path just inside the corrugated fence starts out again as if to make a second circuit of the lake at a higher level. This path is lined with low brick walls and little sumacs in delightful wire cages (under the temple, at the back, are lying other wire embellishments; towers, flower-baskets and auricula theatres). At the far end is an open square of flower beds under grass enclosed in a trellis cage whose trellis piers are crowned with wooden steeples. On two sides of it are pavilions of glass with conical fairy-tale roofs. Inside they have narrow shelves in stadium rows for a display of the parti-coloured, fringed, and curled elaborations of hot-house flowers. One pavilion has a fountain, and another fountain stands in the centre of the square, with birds bending their heads to support on their looped necks a basin, in which stand more birds, and, on their smaller necks, a smaller basin.

Stancombe is transitional. The choice of site for the house at the head of a pretty valley, the flowing, informal landscaping and planting, the use of cottages as part of the design, the building of exotic conceits, all belong to the romantic tradition. The enclosure of the lake in a tight belt of garden; the beds, theatres and pavilions for flowers; the chalet air of the cottages; the static tightness of the fountains; the choice of Egyptian and prehistoric themes for the conceits instead of Chinese, all anticipate the second half of the nineteenth century, the gravel and the elaborate herbaceous borders; still beautiful and still romantic, but with a changed focus, the eye looking close instead of across the valley, not at a plantation but at a rose.

Since this was written the garden has been cleared and replanted by new owners and the extraordinary corrugated iron fence that parcelled it so tightly together has been taken away, but otherwise all remains. This garden and Biddulph share the same date and something of the same atmosphere, so that water-lilies in their lakes look quite different from water-lilies in eighteenth century lakes, and they share with the earlier Alton the qualities of transition from the romantic landscaped park to the formal flower garden near the house.

At about the same time, a very different garden was being made by Thomas Bland at Reagill in Cumbria, set behind the drystone walls of a slight and straggling village on the moors. Very little is known of Thomas Bland, whose grandfather was a yeoman farmer, except that he taught himself to sculpt and draw and write music, and stayed up here at work on his garden unimpressed by an offer from the younger David Cox to introduce him to the art world in London. He seems to have been one of those artists with new ideas all the time, who prefer to rough in a thought and get on with the next one, not a popular way of thinking in his part of the nineteenth century, when finish was important, and Impressionism still to come.

His garden is small and in the Italian manner, rising in three terraces beside and beyond the farm, each surrounded in carving in local stone joined by drystone walls. Plinths support urns, balls, snake-twined vases, classical and vernacular statues, dogs, a deer, a sphinx, a king holding his own wrist, a prince, everything mossy, tilting, falling, unloved but undestroyed. Some of it is very good.

One piece may be seen that shows his gentle classicism finely finished; it has a loving quality that he probably knew would not survive the competition for official commissions, for a place painting murals in the House of Lords or sculpting the Royal children. This piece is at Shap Wells near a spa built by an Earl of Lonsdale sometime after 1830, but presumably before the Earl commissioned from Bland a monument of 1842 to commemorate the accession of Queen Victoria. It is perhaps 25 feet high, an octagonal pillar on a square base, designed by Mr Mawson of Lowther. On top is a statue of Britannia rather smaller than lifesize, relaxed but dignified, with her shield, carved by Thomas Bland who also carved the bas-reliefs on the sides of the plinth. On one is a wreath, on another a girl in draperies pours water into a bowl held up by an old man and on the third a charming lion fails to prefigure Empire.

In the middle of the nineteenth century there was a recurrence of the fashion for putting up mediaeval stones into sham ruins for the park, though now they were usually unwanted pieces left over from the great tide of restoration, and not the results of vandalism or change of fashion, as at Milton and Shobdon. The finest of these later re-arrangements is at Kettlethorpe Hall in West Yorkshire. The 1460 chantry chapel of St Mary on the bridge in Wakefield was restored and later renewed completely—it may look passable in another 200 years—and the ruins of the original were bought by the

Opposite, *the memorial at Shap Wells and,* below, *Kettlethorpe Hall boathouse.*

Hon. George Chapple Norton in 1847 and made into what Nikolaus Pevsner rightly calls 'the most precious of all boat houses', under the supervision of William Fox, sculptor. Today, it is in a public park, separated from the hall, which can be seen from the far end of the lake, a ravishing small specimen of Early Georgian to contrast the lovely flamboyant gothic of the boat house. The five bays of ogival arches—three doors and two windows, with buttresses to match, and the remains of the first floor bays above—have suffered badly, but are now resin-coated and may be hoped for.

Pieces of the ruins of Abingdon Abbey in Oxfordshire were re-erected in about 1860 with a lot more bits from other sources by Mr Trendell who lived in Abbey House and, again, the grounds are a public park. The work was so well done that a new A.A. guide book refers to them as the ruins of the ancient abbey, though that is an entirely different building which has suffered continuously, being deplored by Anthony à Wood as the ruins of a ruin in 1662 and still being smashed up in the Second World War to make a food-store.

The big sham ruin is faring better, in spite of the clambering children. It projects from the wall of the park, which itself has some inset windows, with a variety of windows and doors from Norman to Perpendicular and other fragments, arches and columns, petrified logs and some rock-work. It is a splendid and most convincing sham.

It would seem that follies continued to be a rich man's occupation until about the middle of the nineteenth century; this makes the time-lag before general distribution so long that one wonders if there were more vernacular follies earlier than we know, now destroyed. Certainly a lot of older trifles have a vernacular air, but this is only because the local men who built them had a fairly free hand when carrying out commissions, not because those local men built follies to please themselves.

The vernacular folly when it began did not merely stand in a corner of the garden—it swallowed small gardens whole, just at the time when follies were leaving the big gardens of the rich. The favourite materials were the aristocratic ones, flint and shells again, all over the bottom of the cottage, the garden walls, edging the paths, covering urns and seats, eked out with broken china, glass and coal, reaching in at least one place the climax of a brass bedstead set among the shards. Even in London little curiosities come and go; Chelsea used to have one called Casa Pussy, a shell summerhouse and garden making a private pleasaunce for a nice fat cat.

The sham ruins at Abingdon.

Water was too expensive for the poor to play with, at least for movement, and although there is often a pond, air is the element harnessed in these gardens; wind-toys take the place of fountains, vanes and propellers spin to replace the curve of the water, and creak on their posts to replace its sound.

There must be one or two of these gardens in every town in England, sometimes in front of the house (bowers of broken china inland, of shells near the sea), enclosing Kitchener, or George and Mary, or Churchill. Or at the back, only visible from the railway, a garden shed encrusted and castellated, with concrete sculpture and a wooden aeroplane on a wireless mast. Its influence will have spread to a garden or two on both sides, and then the smooth pattern of lawn, flower beds down each side, shed at the bottom, starts again. When the train reaches a rather richer suburb, the beds are wider, called herbaceous borders, there is a central oval or diamond bed, standard roses in round ones to enliven the corners of the lawn, and fruit trees at the bottom. A folly garden here will be very, very rare.

Scale is almost always well preserved—these are little gardens and their follies are miniatures. At Yarm is a beauty which is both reduced from the originals and surpasses them. It stands, 2 feet high, on a garden wall, but instead of being merely a small sham castle, it is a microcosmic city, keep, ramparts, bastions, town hall and obelisk. David Doughty, a builder (1866–1938), began making it when he was eighteen. Later he worked on the back garden as well. He went to London as a young man, and to the Tower, and when he came back modelled three concrete knights in armour, 3 feet high, very elegant and slim, from sketches he made in the Armoury. Only two of them survive now, but there is a ruined church on a mound of shells and stones and rock plants, its leaning Gaudiesque tower no taller than the roses growing round it. And there is a castellated screen to the coal house with a cherub's head and, set in a window, a bas-relief of another ruined church with tombs in the grass. Concrete caryatids support urns to break up the trellised fence. The professional eye for proportion has been defeated here, however, for beside the garden is a dwarfing gas-holder and, to minimize the gas-holder, the great arches of a viaduct. Scale comes and goes with the focus of the eye—the viaduct dominates the garden and the church is a walnut-shell toy, or the millimetre bricks of the church are reality, and the viaduct invisible.

A very big decorated garden, a shell one, is at Leven in Fifeshire. The old man who made it was still alive in 1945 and still at work on it. The first piece of it was made during the First World War, the decoration of his cottage garden, which was filled by a circular tram rail, as it were, of shells laid on the earth, with a great variety of embellishments growing up along it; arches, peel towers, groups of large cowries and a china hen, with, facing the garden gate, a lump of naturally grotesque wood, mounted on a shell pedestal and set with shell teeth and eyes. In the middle of the circle was a large version, still in shells, of the thin white rocky grottoes through which goldfish swim in bowls. At the back was an aviary to match, the top castellated with bricks set on their corners, diamond-wise, alternating with green glass floats. There was also a pigeon loft, and the birds cooed and walked among cockles set on edge like fans.

This garden, though, was not enough, and he bought a piece of land by the sea to decorate, a local wonderland, entrance fee two-pence. The garden walls are covered with shells much as they would have been in the eighteenth century, the small specimens neatly set for background and the large ones, native or exotic, arranged among them for emphasis or pattern. Walks lead to special features, the bas-relief of Burns or a huge bullock's head with real horns and a third unicorn spike made of a twisted shell in the forehead. A whole single-decker bus, with a Special sign on the direction indicator, and a shell coat that even includes the wheels, has a bird cage for passenger, and there is a small menagerie of pheasants, goats and monkeys. The grey-white old man who made it

The shell bus at Leven and, opposite, *the shell garden at Southbourne.*

all looked after the animals with the help of his children, while they went on collecting and encrusting. Quantities of material were still awaiting inclusion when I first went there, with dozens of Staffordshire dogs, some bad, some good, staring in a pile behind a shed. The owner, scraping a grey-white owlet towards him with a stick so that he might push bread and milk down its beak with a match-stick, angrily refused an offer to buy a pair. 'But some of them are beauties, much too good,' complained the visitor; 'So's my garden a beauty, sir. The dogs'll look well,' and he abandoned the owl to consider the arrangement, in tiers, friezes or zig-zags, of nearly 200 pop-eyed spaniels.

Walter Bissett died in 1964, aged 95, having spent the last 20 years wholly devoted to his shell garden. The garden to the house has alas been returned to normal, but the bus-garden remains on the sea-front, kept by Mr Bissett's sons with a nice taste in succulent plants—WELCOME TO SHELL HOUSE is written in them—but the fierce creative urge has gone.

It remains, though, with Mr G. E. Howard at Southbourne, who also has worked hard at his garden for 20 years, starting in 1948. So far, he says, he has spent over £7,000 on it, and has given it every ingredient that a shell garden should have, except a coat of shells over the house and some major variation in height. There are shells from every ocean; Mr Howard was in the Merchant Navy and got them himself—'no boozing but collecting,' and he has had a new thought in keeping with the best traditions of grotto building; the large shells are decorated with artificial pearls and gem-stones; the eighteenth-century grotto builders missed artificial pearls by about a hundred years.

A long grottoed garage is the Cave of Curios. There are rock-specimens named in incised letters filled with a mosaic of broken coloured glass and beads. The Davy lamp Mr Howard used in a Welsh coalmine as a boy is here, and so is the woolly hat Sir Alec

Rose wore on his voyage round the world. There are stuffed birds of paradise, model ships, cameoed shells, a model windmill, a babbling brook and a little square descending grotto of shells. Outside a marble Dante broods with his back to a naked nymph, and there are mountains, tables, shrines and pools, made of shells and broken china and glass with large patterned dishes inset, statues, mosaic paths, and mottoes.

The Larmer Gardens at Tollard Royal were made in the 1890s by Lieutenant-General Pitt-Rivers, F.R.S., founder of the Pitt-Rivers Museum, who died in 1900. They remain unchanged. The grounds are divided into Quarters, named for Owls, Cats, Yaks, Stags, Hogs, and Hounds. The Vista and Band View were reserved for parties of eight or more, and until 1939 the gardens were open to an appreciative public for picnics and concerts.

By the entrance is a small oriental garden, sunk in a dell; here is the Larmer tree after which the gardens are called, and there is an ornamental lake with a cave and Japanese bronze cranes. Beyond is a great open lawn surrounded by trees and the didactic ornaments of Victorian junketings, like the prehistoric animals at the Crystal Palace.

The open air theatre came first in 1895, the usual design of a high pilastered proscenium of dark wood filled in at the back with a great curved sounding board, one of the most delightful architectural inventions. The Dining Hall, where elaborate catering fed those who had not brought their sandwiches, followed during the next year, and in 1897–8 the Indian Temples from the Earl's Court Exhibition of 1890 were put up at the end of the clearing. Then the Oriental Pavilion, and a bronze horse.

The atmosphere is expectant, even after 35 empty years; there is a feeling that suddenly a brass band will appear on the platform of the theatre and then, to the resonant pom-pom-pom-clash under the sounding arch, a crowd will hurry in, to look at the Pavilions, moving from one to another in a dancing gesticulating run, as if the people from an *Illustrated London News* picture of the crowds waiting for the Queen's Jubilee were to dance Petrouchka.

Exotic gardening inspired by travel with the Army can be seen on a smaller scale in Lincolnshire where Major Fitzwilliam planted and modelled an enchanting garden behind The Hall Cottage in Greatford. It was made in the 1930s and follows the Japonaiserie style of the time with the addition of a very large number of concrete garden ornaments. Elephants and crowns for the Coronation are the most frequent themes; one serpentine path by the lake is bordered on one side by semi-crowns filled with irises. There is a little bridge with dogs-heads in spandrels, an Indian figure, a St Francis, two curved seats each with a snake coiled at one end for company, sofas, gothickry, giant chess pawns guarding another bridge, a wooden baroque gate, a portrait and a nice mossy bear. No gnomes.

Major Fitzwilliam's garden at Greatford and, opposite, *some of the animals at Mount Stewart.*

STEGOSAUR

DINOSAUR

There are also amiable animals at Mount Stewart in County Down, in a garden started by Lady Londonderry during the 1920s. She designed them, and they were carved by Thomas Beattie from Newtonards. There are three pussies, a gnome, a mad cat-and-fiddle, some gryphons, two lions, two googly birds, an owl and a group of two fond cats with their kitten; all small, some under bushes. Larger; two baboons, a horse and monkey, a rolling horse chewing a back foot, two large indistinct felines, two hogs, one hedgehog, the Mermaid of Moher, two fox-and-grape groups crowned with cormorants above consoles of pterodactyls, fourteen monkey-terns, four more gryphons, two lions with shields behind a basin upheld by dogs, another dog, one Noah's Ark, with two small squirrels, three crocodiles and two rabbits, four dodoes, several dog memorials, a bird, a dinosaur, a stegosaur, a fox, and a fox confronting a giant frog. . . .

And there is the Shamrock Garden, enclosed by two sets of part-circular walls of yew 12 feet high. Round the top is a topiary family hunt in full cry, taken from a painted hunt in a psalter that belonged to Mary Tudor. Everything from the book is said to have been copied in tope. The people arrive in a boat, chase a stag which is saved by the devil, and at last return with a rabbit. And there is a Temple of the Winds by Athenian Stuart, which is of course much better documented.

Stancombe Park (and see page 247).

Concrete and Engineering Bricks

The whole folly scene is changed, we have said, by 1840; the percentage of ducal grottoes to the acre has decreased while the percentage of *nouveau riche* extravaganzas has steadily grown. The blue and pink and white glitter of the 1740s, and the morning charm of Pain's Hill, has changed to solid stone, cement, and brick. There will still be some castellations, but they are not so often on real sham castles as on useful buildings masquerading behind gothic façades—a bridge, a bear-pit, or a booking-office. Rivalry is more open, much less gentlemanly; a tower will be built, proclaimed to be insultingly overlooking a neighbour's grounds, and unashamedly competed with. There were hardly any folly houses in the eighteenth century; the nineteenth is full of them, houses that look like Blois or Zimbabwe, houses like cathedrals, houses with 365 rooms or windows and so on, in the Knole tradition, houses with no doors, houses with the bell push in the mouth of a monk, houses like nothing on earth; lovely houses, but lacking the fantasy of follies. That comes again in the twentieth century, but for the next eighty years the follies are more moral and utilitarian than ornamental.

Folly history is as perverse as all history; we have more than enough letters concerning Sanderson Miller and Walpole, but never by any chance does a single word appear to tell us how any of the folly fashions started. Suddenly there were grottoes, suddenly stonehenges, suddenly they fell from grace and just where a few letters might be entertaining, there is nothing. The 1840s change of fashion, though, is clear enough—shells and Stonehenge probably became fascinating through the enthusiasm of individuals, but the influence of the Industrial Revolution was almost nationwide, and certainly spread to follies—about a third of the 1840s follies are industrial, and the rest very coloured by the engineering architecture of the time, blue bricks and no pinnacles, and by the railways.

Railway taste is austere—St Pancras is a beautiful exception—and most railway architecture has a calm style peculiar to itself, sometimes pure functionalism, sometimes monumental, sometimes decorated with romantic wooden dags and spikes, but always recognizable as railway. The monumental examples are essays in period style, great granite demonstrations of Greek or gothic, noble and soothing. Euston Arch was the most famous of them, but there are also many stupendous tunnel entrances, at Primrose Hill and Tottenham in London, and here and there on almost every line. Some of them are very near the folly border; Euston Arch, in fact, fulfilled all the folly requirements but yet seemed not to be one, undoubtedly because it was in the Doric style; Decorated might have pigeon-holed it. One of the tunnel entrances, however, at Clayton in East Sussex, is certainly a folly, though built to be lived in. A huge brick tunnel entrance, turreted, castellated and machicolated, black with soot and shaken constantly by the

Euston Arch. Philip Hardwick's superb entrance to the station. Demolished in 1962.

Ironbridge. A castellated forge, now a garage. Opposite, *Jezreel Temple as it was designed to look when finished.*

Brighton trains, was felt to be an admirable site for a house, and the tunnel-keeper's cottage is inset between the turrets right over the arch, a rocking-home to lull the keeper's children to sleep.

The spread of the railways in their great net all over Britain, new architecture and smart stations, induced a minor outbreak of smartness in the servicing of the rival form of transport; there are a number of fine castellated forges and at least three with large horseshoes round or over the door, looking very Moorish. The number of nails is generally wrong, but at Belton in Lincolnshire there is a chestnut tree outside to make up for it.

Engineering building materials were to be widely used; one splendid tough ruin, now destroyed, defied picturesque decay and stood roofless and stark high on the out-skirts of Gillingham in Kent, the Jezreel Temple of 1885, still a legend. It was a 110 feet square, with the walls at ground level 4 feet 6 inches thick; they were to have been 100 feet high. The windows were so large that the areas of yellow brick were reduced almost to the thickness of girders, and there were recessed horizontal panels of blue engineering bricks framing large bas-reliefs in orange faience tiles, a trumpet with a scroll attached, and crossed swords with a crown and the Prince of Wales' feathers. Inside, the girder suggestion was fact, for the bricks were only a facing on a steel and concrete structure, with nearly a thousand tons of girders framing three great circular galleries.

The design and construction of the building were far in advance of its time, and,

finished, it would have been a textbook forerunner. Unfortunately it became a folly, coloured by failure and by the legends of its purpose. It was certainly intended for the 144,000 descendants of the twelve tribes of Israel, but there was no intention for the tower to reach heaven, or for sermons to be preached in all languages at once, and the architect did not forget the stairs.

Most of the later nineteenth-century follies follow the railways towards the more austere of the many styles in fashionable favour; the sham castles and towers of the eighteenth century were very simple outside—English taste at the time being for concealed richness—but many Victorian buildings were iced all over, like Holloway College, with a very fancy assortment of ornaments indeed, and the follies might well have been like them, but no, they are austere to starkness; a nice change again, no doubt. A few of the prospect towers are lavishly decorated; otherwise only the folly gardens echo the elaboration of the age. The other towers are spare, the rare sham ruins like Knebworth have lost heart, and the traditional folly patterns gradually give way to experiments with ferro-concrete, although there are some notable excavations, the Epping Forest Catacombs and the grottoes at Friar Park, Henley-on-Thames.

Jersey Marine in West Glamorgan must have been a model small seaside resort of the middle of the century. A water-colour painting by W. Key dated 1867 shows it in its heyday with a tall-stacked train drawing out of the little station—other visitors came by canal from Neath. In the centre are the romantic barge-boarded roofs of the Marine Hotel, with trim flower-beds in front, and at the side its brick octagonal prospect tower, complete with the shallow cupola and lantern of a camera obscura, and an enormous

Jersey Marine, from the watercolour by W. Key and, opposite, *Sway Towers.*

flag flying over all. Away to the left can be seen the curved walltop of the ball-court and in front there are four bathing machines, a line of drying swimming things and Boudin-groups of ladies in crinolines with little sunshades. Nothing could be more idyllic.

Today it has the most remarkable atmosphere; the hotel was demolished in 1965 except for one of its tea-rooms, the tower has lost its coloured glass and is used as a stable, the skittle alleys and forge have gone and the ball-court has only its wall with 1880 and the crowned motto of the builder, Sir Evanson Bevan, and racquet-shapes in the brick; but a charming little garden leads down to it, the old ballroom lined with mirrors is remembered, and, even cut off as it is from the sea by the main road from Port Talbot to Swansea, it is unconquerable, a little raffish and gay, with the red, white, blue, yellow and green poles of a small riding school round the tower.

The beloved influence of the orient appears again in concrete, in the towers at Sway, built between 1876 and 79. The desire of A. T. T. Peterson, Judge of the High Court of Calcutta, retired 1868, to introduce Hindu burial customs into England, or the desire of Judge Peterson to be buried at the top of the tower with his wife at the bottom fade on investigation, and so does Judge Peterson's autobiography recording his working directions from the spirit of Sir Christopher Wren, who was impatient to see concrete take its rightful place as a building material. A copy of this exciting work was stated to be in the British Museum, and another in the library of the London Spiritualists Alliance; who could doubt such definite statements? Truth would be stranger than fiction, the autobiography would outshine the ritual burials, but neither copy exists, and we return to the solid information that Judge Peterson was interested in the use of Portland Cement concrete for large buildings and made his slender tower 218 feet high, with a smaller one beside it, to prove its efficiency. The gravel came from Milford, four miles away, and the local workmen, who used no scaffolding, were generously paid.

The tower is Indian, with undertones of gothick, built with precision of sandy-grey concrete blocks very rough, with the aggregate showing, and the mouldings cast in a darker, red-brown colour. It is 22 feet square with porches on the east and west sides and a small hexagonal turret on the north wall taking up a spiral staircase of 330 steps, each one moulded separately and built in. There are 11 rooms in the tower, and on the top is an octagonal open lantern for the view—a light in it was refused by the Admiralty as confusing to shipping. The smaller tower is square and quite unoriental in style, but there is also a range of farm-buildings with curved roofs, all of concrete, as are the pig-styes, walls and watercourses.

The elegance of the tower in the flat Hampshire landscape is virtue enough, but as an advertisement for concrete this height and thinness without reinforcing bars seem unsuitable, for the tower has already had to be strengthened. Judge Peterson died in 1906, aged ninety-two.

The Twentieth Century

———————◆——◆◇◆——◆———————

This century has produced few follies of the true compulsive sort, though the fashion for model villages and shell gardens flourishes.

It begins, however, with a bang, one of the largest, ugliest, most famous and most impressive of all follies, McCaig's Tower at Oban. It is not in fact a tower but a great hollow granite drum built on top of a rocky hill above the town, about 200 feet across and in places 40 feet high. It was inspired by foreign travel, for Mr McCaig, yet another folly-building banker, went to Rome and was inspired by the Colosseum, but he was not, like the eighteenth-century travellers, content with a painting or a Piranesi ruin-engraving; he made his own Colosseum and he made it perfect. The intention, it is said, was not only perfection but improvement, and the elaborations on the Roman design were to include a central tower, but he died before it all could be completed; observation point, museum, and art gallery. (There is another unfinished building on the hill, the shell of a hydropathic establishment, unfinished for lack of funds.)

The main structure of the drum is two tiers, each of 50 plain pointed arches, the top ones taller than those below. Where the land falls away towards the sea, a third tier below has three more arches, two pointed flanking one square, with fine views over the harbour, the grey town and the island with its obelisk. The entrance is through a round-headed arch the width of two of the pointed ones; above are six castellations and there is an inscription on pink granite:

ERECTED IN 1900

BY

JOHN STEWART MCCAIG

ART CRITIC

AND PHILOSOPHICAL ESSAYIST

AND BANKER, OBAN

Before 1914 there were some other expensive exercises, notably the Ashton Memorial in Lancaster, built between 1906 and 1909, a folly for the future. It is a huge Portland stone fancy piece with a copper dome on the lines of St Peter's, four smaller ones, coupled columns and every variety of classical ornament standing at the top of an elaborate staircase in Williamson Park. It is 150 feet high and cost £87,000. The architect was Sir John Belcher, R.A. There are various accounts of the intended purpose of its white marble and mosaic octagonal interior—natural history museum, concert hall and Temple of Learning—but it does not look as if it can have been made for use, as the architecture infinitely out-elbows the living space.

Heaton Park (see page 334).

McCaig's Folly at Oban and, opposite, *the Ashton Memorial in Lancaster.*

Williamson Park is magnificent, and should be seen quickly while it is still in the hands of a head-gardener who understands the best principles of late nineteenth-century gardening. It is at the present time the crown and zenith of municipal planting. Part of it was made in 1862–3 from old quarries to relieve distress in the cotton famine, and in 1878 James Williamson went on with it and gave it to the town. It was finished by his son, later Lord Ashton, who provided a maintenance fund and built the memorial.

Both nature and artifice make the park hilly; it has green privet, rhododendrons, variegated laurel, cotoneaster, cypress, tamarisk, sycamore and every kind of conifer. The dark shrubs are tightly clipped into the typical municipal phallic shapes, and some of the golden privets are trimmed into balls. The paths winding up and down the real and artificial hills to the memorial are wide, coated with rich black asphalt and bordered with rows of white pebbles, the *art-nouveau* lawns are pea-green and flawless, the earth black and weedless; curved and serpentine flower beds are cut into the lawns with lobelia and its white shadow in alternate clumps, calceolaries (yellow and brown), fuchsias, gladioli and all possible varieties of dahlias and begonia; the beds by the entrance gates are absolutely superb. There are cast-iron rustic seats, a bandstand, a conservatory, and an Edwardian baroque monument with baskets of roses carved on it.

There have been several pleasant and worthy removals this century; one was the beautiful Ionic screen of a Manchester hospital in yellow sandstone, set up across the lake from Wyatt's Heaton Park in 1912, and another was a large piece of Trentham Park to Sandon in Staffordshire in 1910. For sentiment or taste, Lord Harrowby paid £100 for the top of a belvedere tower in the Italian manner when the Duke of Sutherland demolished Trentham. The stones were numbered, and the belvedere moved piecemeal to a solid brick base at Sandon, among thistles on rising ground. It is square and very large, an open cube of twelve high arches with pilasters and half-columns. Balustrades protect the floor and roof, and at the top corners are four groups of four urns; fussy, but impressive.

Original fantasy revived after 1918, and between the wars we have several small castle-façades on suburban houses, a helter-skelter and a villa in the sky.

At Thorpeness on the coast of Suffolk is a holiday garden village built in the 1920s, mostly in the Tudor style. There is an hotel, a country club, two guest houses, and a hundred or so furnished houses and bungalows let to visitors. The country is flat with gorse and sand, and the amenities are carefully preserved, for 'Thorpeness is the outcome of an ideal. Its creator planned a village where those in search of rest and relaxation might find it in charming surroundings, and in the course of years of careful planning that ideal has been realized. There is no cinema. Thorpeness is a village and will remain a village when the last of its houses has been built, so there are no piers, no pierrots, promenades or picture palaces! No trippers and no charabancs. But for those who like cinemas there are several in the immediate locality.'[1] The sightly provision of water was a difficulty, but the planners have produced two delightful water tanks. One is part of the Country Club annexe, between two black and white half-timbered houses, in a tall square church tower, castellated, arrow-slitted, in a new and unlikely place, with large belfry windows, slatted.

The other is a fantasy unmatched in England, The House in the Clouds, a complete weatherboarded twenties villa, steep roof, chimneys, drainpipes, windows and all, raised on a pedestal some 40 feet above the gorse bushes. It can be seen for miles, sometimes appearing to sit on the chimneys of other houses and sometimes floating over the trees.

A large boating lake adds a minute folly in an older tradition that can be reached by water in one of the very safe boats provided for children. After passing the Spanish Main, Peter Pan's Property, Wendy's House, the House of the Seven Dwarfs, and the Magic Pavilion, Otter Isle and the Smuggler's Cave, there appears among the rushes on the bank of Pirate's Lair a little

[1] From a prospectus.

sham fort, with guns. Further on there are concrete crocodiles.

Some gardens contain model villages. The best of them that I have seen so far is at Bourton-on-the-Water, behind the Old New Inn, a scale model of the village itself, so that the visitor walks out of the real Cotswold beauty spot, the Venice of the West, into a remarkably good replica one-ninth the size. Behind the model of the inn is a model of the model village, and in that behind the model of the inn is a model of the model of the model village, with a choral service sounding from the smallest church but one, just as it is from the big model church, just as it is on Sunday, from St Lawrence's magnificent tower up the street; a good Chinese-box sensation. Eight men worked on this for about four years, with loving local co-operation over the details of houses and gardens; they used old local stone and the effect is very faithful, less so, oddly, at first glance that at a more careful survey, for the aerial view is so unfamiliar to most of us that we can hardly judge its correctness, but the most wonderful care has gone into the little dry-stone walls, doors, gates, cast-iron railings and gardens of dwarf plants: the eye has to have time to change its scale. To aid this, at the far end is a turning periscope which lowers our eye to the eye-level of the model and also cuts out the big pub, and the surrounding houses and all but an occasional giant visitor's foot. Then the accuracy of the shop-fronts, with all their varied styles of lettering comes within our power of concentration.

The model has one almost exclusive charm—except for a stone miller (a statue instead of a miniature man) there are NO PEOPLE. Usually the creation of mannikins, difficult enough for a sculptor, overwhelms the amateur completely, and he buys them ready made, lead or plastic toys, always a little too large or a little too small.

There is a good curious tower at Wappingthorne in Sussex, an octagon with an outside stair up to a summer-house with a pointed roof. The tower does not taper but the walls of the narrowing staircase do, so it looks just like the big helter-skelter at a fairground. It was designed by Maxwell Ayrton who built a new farm in 1928 around a 1609

Opposite, *the House in the Clouds at Thorpeness and,* right, *the water tower at Wappingthorne.*

one. Two new silos distract the eye, but the whole is a most interesting group of buildings, imaginative, a little Voysey, a most successful twentieth-century farm (where are others?). There is an octagon dairy and two good towers with green shutters at the top, and to the north the helter-skelter which combines a prospect tower with a water-tank. It is built of reinforced concrete covered with fine-grain pebbledash, and the stair-case of 94 steps has a wooden handrail. The summer-house has a domed ceiling and triangular light fittings that look as if they were designed for it.

Also between the wars one last traditional folly tower, and a superb grotto. The tower was built in 1935 by the fourteenth Lord Berners, traditional both in its mildly gothick style and in the stir it created. Just outside Faringdon in Oxfordshire is a hill, which Lord Berners found already crowned with a good *feuillée*-folly of pines and beeches planted, on the remains of a long series of fortifications, by Henry James Pye, who was made Poet-Laureate in 1790, and built Lord Berners' house in Faringdon; he wrote a poem at Eaglehurst. The fuss started before the tower; the local Council vetoed it, plans unseen, on hearsay, which went so far as to say that Lord Berners intended to mount on the tower a very powerful siren. However, the Ministry of Health, which did see the plans, held an enquiry at Faringdon, not without strife. The battle produced some excellent folly material; Admiral Clifton Brown, who evidently lived some way from Faringdon, objected that the tower would spoil his view. The architect replied: 'But you could not see the tower from your garden without a tele-scope,' to which the Admiral answered: 'It is my custom to look through a telescope at the view.' Later the architect pointed out how magnificent the view from the tower would be, at which the lover of views demanded how it could be reached, giving the architect the chance of a return thrust—'By the stairs.' The Ministry passed the plans.

Luck held right through, for even the digging of the foundations in the middle of the clump turned up the bones of Cromwellian soldiers, so that one way and another, the newspapers were able to keep up interest all through 1935. The architects were Lord Gerald Wellesley[1] and Trenwith Wills; the main structure is square, 140 feet high, built of brick, colourwashed cream. A staircase goes up inside to a belvedere room with nine large Georgian round-headed windows, for the appreciation of the view (six counties claimed). Above is an octagonal tower, slightly castellated, with eight pinnacles and, in Lord Berners' time, a flag. It is a pretty tower; the octagon alone is visible from a distance, closer the tower disappears altogether, and then appears again through the trees of the *feuillée* on approach.

On Guy Fawkes Day, 1935, Lord Berners celebrated the completion of the tower with a big party and fireworks, reported in the *Tatler* with a full page of photographs, one of the tower, and five of the fashionable guests. After this the excitement subsided, but everything is going according to pattern, for the tower now seems to be always locked. It will soon be ready for the next folly stage; a cow must climb up and get stuck half-way, or someone build another, higher, tower nearby, or a new owner desire to be buried at the top. Faringdon Tower should do well.

The grotto is magnificent and dazzling, at Dinmore Manor in Hereford and Wor-cester, an addition to an ancient foundation of the Commandery of the Knights Hospital-ler of St John of Jerusalem which was started sometime in the twelfth century. The long

---

[1] Now Duke of Wellington.

Lord Berner's Folly at Faringdon.

history, with the addition of other manors when the Templars were suppressed, the Dissolution in 1540, and the building of the present Manor in the late sixteenth century are not for us here. The modern work was done by Richard Hollins Murray between 1932 and 1936 with local labour (everyone's name is recorded), stone from Hereford gaol for the outside and Bathstone for the inside, in a simple mediaeval style. The architects were Bettington & Son of Hereford and all the stained glass was the work of W. Morris (Westminster) Ltd. There is a large Music Room, an octagonal South Room, a Tower and two lengths of cloister joined by an octagonal court from the west side of which opens the grotto. At the back of it is a large gothic window in keeping with the cloister-architecture but this is filled with a bright stained-glass scene of sunset in the desert, palms, mountains, and blue sky, perhaps to recall that the Hospitallers went to the Crusades. The grotto walls and ceiling are made of concrete on wire mesh, stained with earth colours, and the rocky ground, with pools to reflect the oriental splendour of the window at sunset, is piled with stones and grown with ferns. There are more stained glass windows in the two rooms and the cloisters; figures of knights from the history of Dinmore, rural scenes, flowers and birds, marine marshland, flowers, night, prehistoric life and Blake's Jerusalem, but the grotto is the thing, unexpected and spectacular; certainly to be seen at sunset.

Possibly in two hundred years time the mid-twentieth century will appear richer in follies than it does to us, for there will be the pill-boxes of the Second World War. A lot of these were built, and a number have escaped demolition. If they survive for a century or so their purpose will probably be forgotten, and the thick concrete rooms lit only by slits will seem very curious follies indeed. Or, if their purpose is remembered, certain examples will be held parallel to the canvas follies of the eighteenth century—shells of thin brick, ringed with gun-slits and painted to resemble cottages.

Dinmore

The Second World War produced one small but charming folly, beside the A39 on the hill above Wells. It stands behind a low dry-stone wall, a statue from the Roman, the wolf suckling Romulus and Remus. She stands about 12 feet up and has a crazy-paving mane. Four scaly piers support a slab inscribed GAETANO CELESTRA. It was made by an Italian prisoner-of-war, one of a number who worked here and were happy. This one was a mason, and made it for a thank-you, with a fish pond and a flower basket in front of the house.

In 1950 came the memorial arch at Pitlochry in Perthshire, a massive crazy-paving block to commemorate the completion of a hydroelectric scheme. Again, only time will produce the folly atmosphere, but it has all the ingredients; obelisks, an arch pierced through in exact representation of the cross-section of the Clunie tunnel (1946–50), plaques to the memory not only of five men killed on the works but of every contractor, the architect, the members of the board and full details of the 400,000 slabs of quartzitic schist that made the tunnel from Loch Tummel and lined the 22 foot 6 inch arch.

Romulus and Remus and the wolf and the arch at Pitlochry.

Peacock Place. The boy Shakespeare, a lion and two monkey musicians.

In 1956 there was a last light-hearted garden, at Peacock Place near Basildon in Berkshire. It sounds intimidating, the Child-Beale Nature Reserve; perhaps only accredited members of the suitable societies will be let in? And what can there be on this flat land between the road and the Thames, so near to Reading? Just as it should be; peacocks. Free and caged, white and coloured, tails folded or displayed, everywhere.

It was founded by Gilbert Child-Beale who was a director of Carter's Tested Seeds, to keep this stretch of the valley unspoiled, in memory of his parents and for public pleasure. The Peacock Pavilion, pedimented with Ionic columns was built in 1956 with stonework from Adam's Bowood and is richly furnished with silk armchairs and horse-restraining bronze statuary.

Outside is a most fascinating collection of larger statues; a big 1890s fountain from Whitaker Wright's Witley by Spalmach, a Valkyrie at full charge, lions playing with balls, urns, bronze cranes, gryphons, Shakespeare as a boy by A. Salara and a fountain of giant frogs. Best of all, sculptor so far unknown, but recent, a monkey orchestra; Pan laughs on a column in the middle of a 40-foot wide circle of twelve monkeys, each on his column, glass eyed and vivid, with violin and smoking cap, roll of music, cello, panpipes in two versions, drum, double-bass, two concertinas and two pairs of cymbals. So far as I know there is no other such monkey orchestra; it took two centuries for *singerie* to get from the drawing room out on to the grass.

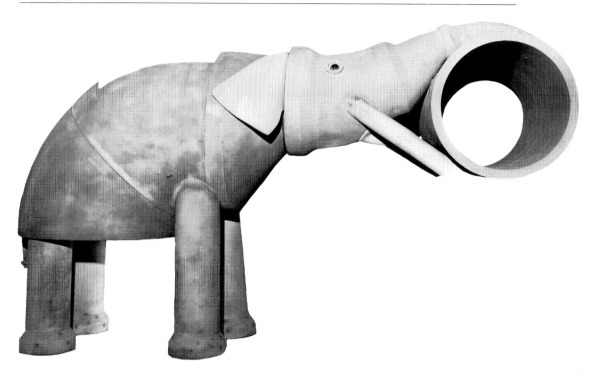

The elephant at Camberley under construction.

An elephant stands over the entrance to Messrs Trollope & Colls concrete pipe works at Camberley in Surrey. In 1963 the author designed the Lord Mayor's Show on the theme of building. Other floats showed other materials, methods and services, steel with a steel band, electricity, stone-age men, timber, glass, and as much giant earth-moving equipment as the City streets would bear. Only the elephant survives. It was designed to be made, all but the ears, out of standard concrete pipes, holding another section of pipe between trunk and tusks. It was constructed at the works and the staff also provided a driver, and attendants for it, who were very brave about the wet London weather on a November day. Today the elephant, although not designed for the site, and so too small, looks reasonably folly above the gate.

One last folly is at Hodnet Hall where a fine eyecatcher was put up in 1970 on a perfect site, up an avenue on the skyline across the road from the house. Two 20-ton cranes took two weeks to put it up; a row of complete and ruined columns and a piece of pediment on a new podium. Brigadier Algernon George William Heber-Percy, who also made the lovely gardens, brought over the portico of Apley Castle near Wellington when this was demolished in the 1950s, and decided where to re-erect it. Now his friends and family have finished the work in his memory. It looks just as it should, surprising but assured, in the best tradition of follies.

Nothing on the really grand scale has been built here since Oban; the folly instinct

The folly at Hodnet Hall.

that was so strong for 200 years may take a new form or start somewhere else. There is some hope for America, where from 1921 to 1954 Simon Rodia built the most beautiful folly in the world, a gift for the United States from an immigrant Italian tile-setter who wanted to do something big and did, less a building than a glittering sculpture at Watts, Los Angeles. It is made of tiles, broken china, glass and shells set with cement on thin steel, concentric towers, or cones of spirals, circles and arcs, on a gigantic scale for one man's work and so beautiful that it must, with the palace of postman Cheval at Hautrives, be held superior to all but the finest work of the eighteenth century; we have only Josiah Lane to rival him.

Rodia was a genius, and it would be too much to expect another sculptor of his status in the Los Angeles area this century, but at least a very splendid attempt is being made. At Cabazon on the San Gorgonio pass Claude K. Bell, who was once a sand sculptor, is building a brontosaurus 45 feet high and 150 feet long; 'If we make it into a restaurant we'll be able to accommodate 80 diners . . . it will be the strangest dinosaur ever built . . . At night the eyes will glow and the dinosaur will spit fire.'

It is very encouraging; there is a 62-acre site, and there are to be more dinosaurs on it, and they are being built for fun.

We invented here in the follies of the eighteenth century a form of architecture almost entirely our own, and most bewildering and curious to study, but from about the middle of the nineteenth century until the middle of our own it fell under a cloud, and although a few folly-lovers have always praised and protected the buildings, they were generally felt to be a little shameful, better pulled down than kept up.

Today, though, many notable follies have been restored, and more will be; they are seen to be as real a part of the great landscaped parks as the trees and the walks and the water. We must hope that the wilder follies, the rocket-ships and the lonely grottoes and the houseless gates, will attract some benefactors before it is too late, and, more important still, that some new follies will be built using the still wilder opportunities of our new building materials.

At least one splendid chance has recently been lost. Sir William Burrell died in 1958 and left his art collection to the nation, to be housed in a rural setting for public enjoyment. Two young architects, Ray Bryant and Peter Mason, submitted a scheme housing the museum inside three gigantic black and white cows, one lying and two standing, to be built with aluminium monocoque construction in three cylinders with the cow-cladding in fibreglass. The assessors threw away the chance of giving Scotland a unique museum, as fascinating in itself as any exhibit, but still the cows were invented, and carefully designed, and another chance may come; the folly spirit remains undimmed.

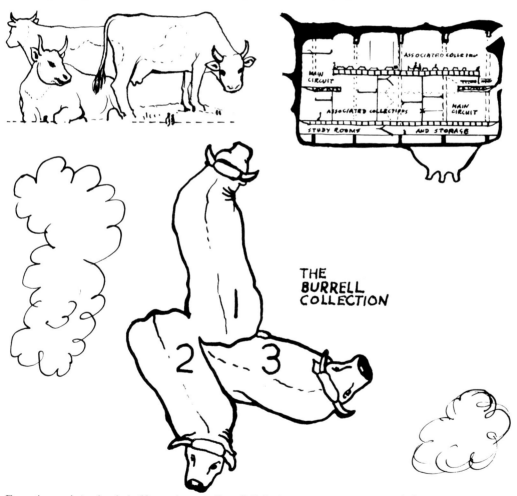

From the cow design for the building to house the Burrell Collection; perspective, a section and plan.

Follies by County

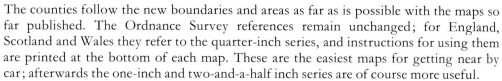

The counties follow the new boundaries and areas as far as is possible with the maps so far published. The Ordnance Survey references remain unchanged; for England, Scotland and Wales they refer to the quarter-inch series, and instructions for using them are printed at the bottom of each map. These are the easiest maps for getting near by car; afterwards the one-inch and two-and-a-half inch series are of course more useful.

An asterisk means that I have not seen the folly myself. A dagger means that the folly has been demolished, though I thought details of it worth preserving.

Wainhouse Tower, Halifax; from a lithograph by John Thirsk (See page 403)

Avon

A new county with good follies and Bristol in the middle, keeping its character and beauty in the teeth of the developers, with an astonishing number of pleasures; not only a *camera obscura,* a superb suspension bridge, good warehouses and a zoo with white tigers, but also an exceptional grotto, a model village with a sham castle, and a giant.

Banwell *Banwell House*
Bone caves, early nineteenth century ST 4059
See page 238.

Bath *On hill to east*
Ralph Allen's Sham Castle, 1762   ST 7565
See page 58.

Lansdown
Beckford's Tower   ST 7565
Unlike Fonthill (*q.v.*) this tower survives with part of Beckford's extensive gardens for it, and will be restored. In 1822 he saw that even the enormous sugar fortune his father had left him could go only so far and he left Fonthill for Bath, where he bought two houses, with land and a hilltop more than a mile away. Here he built the tower to the designs of H. E. Goodridge, for the views to be obtained from the belvedere room and the top of the lantern. At the foot of the tower, and connected to it, is a building with several small rooms. One of them, the Sanctuary described in the *Illustrated London News* of 22 November 1845, just before the contents were sold by auction, had 'an air of mystic gloom and magnificence', while the others were all luxuriously furnished, and embellished with works of art. The garden was a 'shrubbery, kept with strict adherence to the wildness of nature: no trim walks, no nicely-edged borders are there, the paths being only such as are worn by the passenger's feet'.

Inside the tower the stair begins to climb with a shallow sweep to the first floor. Suddenly everything above is black, burnt out, with the stair and railing spiralling up in a suitably stygian gloom. As the stairs ascend, the climb breaks for the view, first at the belvedere room from which the magnificent outlook is diminished by too much wood and stone. Then another stage with tiny recessed windows through which almost nothing shows, and lastly at the top the lantern, where a narrow platform is pushed up under the roof and the windows are behind heavy wooden frames, through which only the head will go to peer through panes one foot square, further frustrated by iron tracery outside. The lantern is made of cast-iron filled in with wood, and is a reproduction of the Choragic Monument of Lysikrates, a building which fascinated many folly builders.

To those who like to get out of the car at the exact spot indicated by the view sign on the touring map, this tower should be the perfect belvedere. Here one is not inconvenienced by a high wind—Beckford prudently had hot air pumped up by a furnace—and the views were chosen by a connoisseur. But the modern traveller may be troubled by Beckford's treatment of the views when he has found them; each is tightly enclosed and adjusted like the composition of a painting or a photograph, while today the great sweep of amorphous distance is more *à la mode*.

The garden near the tower is now a cemetery, and in the passages there are bicycles and elegant handcarts for pushing coffins down the trimmed walks to the grave.

Further away, there remain the ride to the stables from the Embattled Gate, with one of Beckford's three coats of arms, a lime avenue, part of the planting of an old quarry, and a grotto-tunnel 70 feet long.[1]

Monkton Combe
Allen's Memorial, 1765†   ST 7662

[1] See Peter Summers' *William Beckford.* Some notes on his life, etc. Privately printed 1966.

Bristol

Arnos Castle, Goldney's Grotto, etc.   ST 5874
Arnos Castle, the Devil's Cathedral, 1760s
See page 63.

Cabot's Tower, 1898
In gardens on Brandon Hill, with superb views, an elaborate tower 105 feet high in red sandstone and Bath freestone, to commemorate John Cabot's landfall in America in 1497. It has square angle turrets cutting off the corners, flamboyant ogival windows and a pyramid crowned by a golden figure of Commerce, and, I am told, BRISTOL flashes out in morse at night from the top.

Clifton, Cook's Folly story,   ST 6074
late sixteenth century†
Now demolished; the tower was built about 1696 by John Cook, an ex-Master of the Merchant Adventurers, as an ornament to his country residence. An extract from Arrowsmith's *Dictionary of Bristol* published in 1906 tells the story attached to the tower with a relish which justifies a vanished folly:

> A story invented about a century and a half ago alleges that a gipsy foretold Goodman Cook that his unborn son would not survive his twenty-first birthday, but die from the attack of some silent secret foe. To avoid the catastrophe the father built this tower and immured his son therein on his twentieth natal day. Huge were the walls, massive the locks, and strong the bars that guarded the old man's treasure, his only son. Round rolled the year without incident, the dawn of the last day found the youth hearty and well; singing like a bird at the near prospect of escape from his wearisome cage, he hauls up his last faggot of sticks to cook therewith his parting dinner and cheer the sombre night with a flickering flame. The father bids him goodnight with a joyous heart, and is early astir on the coming morn. Alas! all too soon is the gipsy's prediction verified. There on the threshold of maturity lies all that is left of his son—a pallid corpse. A viper from the faggot had bitten him, and his destiny was fulfilled.

Goldney's Grotto, 1737–64   ST 6074
See page 152.

Dodington *Dodington House*

Cascade   ST 7580
This is admired because Capability Brown designed it. There is a square castellated tower with thin buttresses and a central pointed arch through which water cascades down over rocks between long hanks of green moss hair. On each side is a short stretch of wall over flatter arches and then two lower towers with battered bases. It all looks very crisp and new, and except for the green hair, most unpicturesque—dressed stone is no material for this sort of thing—it must be counted one of Brown's rare failures. Behind the top lake is a matching icehouse, mysteriously in the sun beside a rectangular tower with a curious and elaborate window and a tiny pigeon hole.

Doynton *Tracey Park*

Four Columns   ST 7274
At each main gate is a pair of pillars. Those nearest the house are square with elaborate double masonic crosses on top. The others are circular, made of half-dressed stone bricks. There are more symbols about the solid house which has a tower tied up with carved ropes. Near a farm on the estate, three rocks make a tiny henge on the site of a Roman villa.

Hawkesbury

Tower, 1846   ST 7787
A tall, rather Chinese stone tower in memory of the Duke of Somerset of the time; altogether a bleak piece of design with some gilding, a barbaric portcullis and a chain railing round the top.

Henbury *Blaise Castle*

Sham castle, village and dairy,   ST 5778
eighteenth century
See page 188.

Long Acre Screen   ST 5778
In November of 1819 the Common Council of Bristol decided to repair and beautify St Mark's Chapel. In 1822 the very good late Decorated west window was taken down and a copy put back in its place. The old window

One of the cottages at Blaise Hamlet

was given to Mr Cave, a member of the Council, who used it to make a screen in his garden. The window is set between two very amateur towers of rubble, one is slightly taller and capped with a little steeple and weathervane, the other has a flagstaff. Beside the lower tower is a wall pierced with a tall gothic arch. This is a most touching piece of amateur folly work.

Kingswood *Warmley*
Giant Neptune, eighteenth century   ST 6873
See page 212.

Long Ashton
The Bungalow, ex The Observatory ST 5471
A house too amazing to omit. Peacock gates to the drive, and then a high mound of rockery with steps straight up to a rustic porch. House square, on a concrete platform with posts and chains and tri-quadrant windows on the front corners. The centre of the roof is flat with a castellated lantern room, dome and weathercock. Once it was thatched, but is now crinoline-ruched with tar on top.

Marshfield *Beck's Lane*
Pillar, eighteenth century*   ST 7774
A stone pillar with a ball finial.

Monkton Combe *Midford Castle*
The Priory, *c.* 1780   ST 7662
Midford Castle is one of the most beautiful houses in Somerset; the best view of it is from the eastern side of the Wellow–Limpley Stoke railway, when it is seen standing above a small but well-planted park. It was built by Henry Woolhouse Disney Roebuck, and is sometimes referred to as Roebuck's Folly. The story, probably apocryphal, is that Roebuck won a large fortune by betting on the ace of clubs and built the trefoil-shaped house to celebrate and commemorate his luck. On the north side in a wooded glen is the Priory; Collinson in his *History of Somerset* describes it as 'an elegant building called the priory, with gothick windows and a circular embattled tower, in which is a commodious tea room, and offices below. At a little distance from this, under a thick mass of shade, stands a rustick hermitage on the brow of the steep descent. The whole surrounding scenery is highly picturesque and romantick.' This description appeared in 1791; there is no date for the building of Midford Castle, but the architecture of the Priory would suggest a date *c.* 1780.

It is a single apartment with the tower at one end, and at the other an apse with a fireplace. There are niches in the wall under high windows—the story is that it was used for gambling, and the windows were put at this height so that no one could see in. Unfortunately the roofs of both tower and room have collapsed, and the hermitage has completely disappeared. The Knight of Glin has recently designed a castellated screen with outside cross-slits to hide the swimming-pool pump.

Nympnett Thrubwell
A small routine obelisk near   ST 5360
Rookery Farm

Stoke Gifford *Stoke Park**   ST 6380
Thomas Wright is said to have worked here, on follies now gone, but there is an obelisk of the 1730s and a sarcophagus in one of the woods to a St Leger winner of the 1830s.

Weston in Gordano

Walton Castle, eighteenth century ST 4575
A square of curtain walls interspersed with small rectangular towers enclose a piece of ground about 30 yards across. It is not very exciting.

Worle *Worle Observatory*

Tower ST 3562
This was Worle Mill, working until 1875. The last miller was Mr William Rogers. It was confusingly converted about the end of the last century by a Mr Baker into a prospect tower, cemented over, given castellations and some debased Owen Jonesy decoration over the door. There was a very pretty octagon lantern on the roof with an ogival roof, and a postcard of about 1905 shows a flag-post flying the royal standard at half mast, but lantern and post have now gone.

Worle Observatory

Bedfordshire

A remarkably poor county for follies, even allowing for its flat, low-lying and generally unencouraging terrain; there is only one good group, at Woburn, but that is very good indeed.

Ampthill TL 0438
A trifle; an obelisk-pump designed by Sir William Chambers in 1784, giving distances and directions.

Flitwick *Flitwick Manor*

Grotto-Bridge, eighteenth century TL 0435
A nice wide grass bridge crossing nothing, built of clinker trimmed with brick; one face is cobby gothick with a big *quatrefoil* on each side of the arch, and the other is cobby classical with alcoves. The roof is decorated with very simple pebble patterns and there is also a pebble floor.

Shefford *Chicksands Priory*

Two Obelisks TL 1539
One commemorates the peace of 1815 and the other is in memory of the second Duke of Hamilton who died in 1771. It was put up by his brother-in-law.

Woburn *Woburn Abbey*

Shell room; large group, SP 9534
seventeenth to nineteenth century
Shell room, see page 145.
Untouched by the addition of a fun-fair, antique shops, aerial railway and wildlife park, a large group of varied and interesting follies continues undisturbed and well preserved in the park at Woburn, including no less than three pretty pieces of Chinoiserie, two rustic works and a sham half-timbered house.

The most notable piece is the Chinese

Dairy, by Holland, with painted decorations almost certainly by Crace, and delightful windows of figures, flowers, birds and butterflies in both etched-and-clear and painted glass by John Theodore Perrache, dated 1794 and 1795, which probably dates the whole building reasonably closely, and the other Chinoiseries as well. The Dairy is set in a long curved arcade painted scarlet, by a lake very near the house, surely designed for walking on wet days, adding to the fashionable late eighteenth-century dairy-maid dream, the pleasure of watching the rain make yachts on the water.

The little Pagoda is set in the centre of a maze of yew, beech, box and holly, on an octagonal stone platform, with an elaborate curved roof with dragons, and another roof to the lantern. Both buildings have the most bewildering complexity of painted decoration—*trompe l'oeil* fretwork painted behind or within frames of 3-D sham bamboo—and the dairy adds this to a very complicated ceiling plan of octagon via rectangles, triangles and square to octagon again. There are marble shelves all round on pretty fretwork supports with a central table to match and fretted shelves on the walls.

A Chinese-gothick Pavilion stands on an island in a distant lake, an open octagon of ogival arches with quatrefoils and a flaring three-tiered roof. It has been newly painted white with red and blue stripes and its exotic charm is embellished with flamingos; a crude shelter for the birds cries out for improvement.

In the woods are two minor follies; a sham Roman gate now reduced to a pile of columns and pieces, and a rectangular roofless building of stone and flint with a round arch and two doors. The back is rendered brick which might be a later addition; the front suggests 1740.

The Thornery, in a clearing in another wood and ringed by hawthorns recalls Queen Charlotte's cottage at Kew, although it is probably later. Again, as in the dairy, there is an extremely complex ceiling in a simple building. Outside it is square, thatched, with four steep thatched gables; the eaves are held

The Thornery at Woburn Abbey

up on pine trees, and the stone walls look new— possibly they replaced bark ones early this century. Inside, the corners of the ceiling are filled in to make an octagon on which is set the inside of an umbrella with an umbrella lantern. All this is lined, outlined and crossed with painted trellis and flowers that become a herbaceous border by the bottom of the walls. There is stained glass, some pretty bamboo furniture and two convex mirrors to reflect it all.

The Log Cabin is just that, cruciform in plan and built of pine trunks, but the crossing of the logs at the corners has been faked.

The Paris House is sham Tudor, 'Built at London by William Cubitt & Co for the Universal Exhibition holden at Paris'. (1878)

Wrest *Wrest Park*   TL 0836

Not really a folly group at all, very serious and rather sad, but interesting because all the ingredients, with the exception of Archer's superb pavilion and Cléphanes orangery to match his house, have folly possibilities. There are: an exedra with pavilions, a bath house and bowling green by Capability Brown of *c.* 1740, and a column to his memory, which is a rare thing and very encouraging, an urn on another column, rusticated, but with only two rusticated blocks, a third column of 1831 to Jemima, Marchioness de Grey and a Chinese bridge for a willow-pattern composition. Robert Walpole was lukewarm about Wrest, and no one has liked it much since, except for the Archer pavilion.

Berkshire

Basildon *The Grotto†*   SU 6179

A house built by Lady Fane, with a very famous grotto (eighteenth century) in the grounds, which has now gone, but it is often mentioned in contemporary letters and diaries.

Peacock Place
Garden, twentieth century   SU 6179
See page 276.

Bray *Monkey Island*
Fishing pavilions, rustic lodge,   SU 9279
eighteenth century

I have often been told that Monkey Island is covered with follies; in fact there are two eighteenth-century fishing pavilions on the island in the Thames, and very idyllic it must have been. The Rustic Lodge has a good second-storey octagon room with singeries by Clermont but it now stands engulfed in a hotel, and the pavilion of the third Duke of Marlborough, *c.* 1744, with a room of tough fishy Thamesis plasterwork, has been added to disastrously.

Chieveley *Hop Castle*
Grotto, early eighteenth century   SU 4874

A charming nonsense isolated in the fields, with no ascertainable history and plenty of legends—it was a hunting lodge for King John, it has a secret tunnel running to the Blue Boar on the Newbury–Wantage road, and a King kept a Queen in the coal cellar. It is built of brick faced with unknapped flints and bones, an ogival octagon roof and short curtain walls with acorn finials. There is a half-basement floor with kitchen, larder and a cool cellar, and above a central octagon room with four little ones under pyramid roofs opening off it. The entrance and stairs have grotto-work of pebbles and shells all over the walls and ceiling.

Coleshill *Strattenborough Castle Farm*
Eyecatcher, 1792   SU 9595

A false façade to the farmhouse to act as eyecatcher to Coleshill House. It is very imposing and grim, crouching behind a monkey-puzzle. There are some blind windows, always disturbing, and enormous arrow-slits, all in stone with brick towards the top—it seems to have been much altered. One tower-front is flat, with a plain castellated top and the other is three sides of an octagon.

The back of Strattenborough Castle

Erleigh *Erleigh Park*
Sham Ruin, eighteenth century   SU 7573
Two negligible pieces of red brick gothick ruin, one with a window, standing in the park.

Purley *Purley Hall*
Flint Pavilion, 1746   SU 6677
The Hall has very pretty low square castellated lodges of brick and flint with curved walls extending on each side. Once there was an arch between them with their joint central chimney, but a truck swept it away.

Down the axis from the house is a Palladian pavilion of knapped flint with unknapped rustications, etc. It was built by Francis

Hawes (who had gone broke with the South Sea Bubble) to commemorate Culloden, for his wife was a Jacobite. The folly feature, unusual in a gentry folly, is the keystone of the arch, a huge unknapped flint with its natural grotesquery stepped up by great shining eyes of polished agate.

Reading *Forbury Gardens*

'The largest nineteenth century   SU 7374
lion in the world'
See page 215.

Remenham Hill *Park Place*

Grotto, cyclopic bridge and   SU 7784
obelisks, eighteenth and nineteenth centuries
General Conway bought Park Place in 1752 and improved the grounds. There are obelisk piers at the entrance, another west of the house and a fourth to the east. This one is the top of the spire of St Bride's, standing on a pediment of brick faced with stone, and prettily placed on a ridge overlooking a shallow valley with tall trees on either side of it. Nearby is a brick-faced flint tower, in ruins. It is said to be the remains of an ice house, but looks much more like the relics of a folly tower, very Buckinghamshire in style, like Lord Boston's Folly, and St Crispin's Cottages. A Chinese house has gone. At the foot of the Happy Valley and now in the grounds of *Happy Valley House,* is the Cyclopic Bridge made between 1781 and 1786 of huge rocks from, it is said, 14 different counties, with other pieces from the ruins of Reading Abbey, but I saw no definitely ecclesiastical stones. Similar rocks make the grotto at the head of the valley, six arched entries into a cross-vaulted sombre chamber with empty niches. It is difficult to find this a good grotto; the General was heavy-handed with his follies. He did better next door at Temple Combe, but there used to be shells all over the grotto, with the sound of the sea in some and a knucklebone floor.

Temple Combe
Druids' Circle, 1785   SU 7784
A real stone circle from Jersey. See page 237.

Sulham

Tower, probably eighteenth   SU 6574
century
A circular red brick tower, castellated and inhabited by jackdaws, standing in a field north of the M4; probably built as something to see from Sulham House. (Across the River Kennett in Sulhamstead, Folly Farm is a name alone.)

Windsor *Windsor Castle*

Grottoes and Sham Ruin,   SU 9777
eighteenth century
The grottoes, probably of the time of George III, are cut in chalk in the private gardens. They seem designed to be seen with the most distant one first; this is a round-arched passage lined with knapped and unknapped flint, and about 45 feet long. The open path here lined with marble, flint, pudding-stone and over-backed brick-clumps, skirts a small cliff and leads into a circular grotto about 10 feet across and 8 feet high, entirely lined with small pebbles. The ceiling is slightly domed with a central clump of minerals, above another clump on the floor—they may have been joined by a pillar. For seats, there are ten chunks of solid oak with rock-work between, and there are fine ammonites in the rock surrounds to the windows.

The sham ruin at Frogmore

On towards the Castle is a skylight by the path; at a lower level is another grotto, a curved tunnel in the shape of a high narrow pointed arch leaves the road and returns to it, cut across in the middle by a straight tunnel from road to grotto. Both are entirely lined with pebbles. The grotto is an octagon about 12 feet across, very high and breathless, with stout mineral-covered columns between the walls, which have blind pointed arches filled with pointed scale-shapes cut in the chalk. The ceiling is a high dome in eight sections, now bare brick, but said to have been covered with mirrors when used by Queen Charlotte's daughters. At the top is a brick lantern under the skylight about 30 feet up. All new and mirrored it must have been dazzling on a sunny day but now it is very forbidding indeed.

The sham ruin or Gothick Temple is in the grounds of Frogmore, which were designed by Major William Price for Queen Charlotte and redesigned by Queen Mary. Work started in 1793, and the ruin was designed by James Wyatt. There is a pavilion for use as a summer-house with a pointed two-light central arch and two smaller ones, elaborately carved and filled with patterned glass, facing across the lake. There are seven fretted castellations above and a pinnacle at each end. The truly ruinous pieces run out to the sides and are made of older stones. It is much overgrown with wistaria.

The Indian Kiosk was taken by Lord Canning from the Kaiserbajh at Lucknow in 1858 and given to Queen Victoria. In the same year, Prince Albert designed the dairy which has the cool charm common to dairies, and fountains with herons and shells by the Consort's favourite sculptor, John Thomas.

Winkfield Row *Ascot House*
Grotto, eighteenth century   SU 9271
See pages 144 and 160.

Buckinghamshire

Amersham *Woodrow Hill House*
Grotto, early eighteenth century   SU 9498
On the far side of the field in front of the house, there is what can only be described as a dingle, and cut into the side of it is the grotto. This is a domed octagon 10 feet across, and in one of the walls there is a little fireplace; the decoration is in pebbles, bold patterns of black and white.

Beaconsfield
Bekonscot Model Village, twentieth   SU 9491
century
'Bekonscot' was started in 1929, and work was continued by the artist, Ronald Robert Callingham, until his death in 1961. It is the first major attempt to record the physical aspects of the suburb. The garden is planted with the most favoured shrubs and bedding plants round flawless lawns, and the whole thing is laid out with the most serpentine and elaborate planning as a model village, with the shrubs and plants as trees. The miniature villas are mostly half-timbered, with one or two small Georgian houses. There are model inhabitants, horses and carts, varying like the bricks and tiles in scale, four or five churches (stained glass, choirboys, sacred music playing), shops, Town Hall, castle, racecourse and a railway running busily all around. Only the docks, lighthouse and a very industrial bridge are out of key. Certainly the scale is often wrong, and the use of cyprus bushes, which always seem themselves and not miniature trees, aggravates this failing, but scale is often wrong in the proto-suburb.

A hunt in full cry after a fox stands for tradition, and an airfield for progress: there seems to be no aspect of well-to-do suburbia left unrecorded.

Hedsor Priory

Bourne End *Hedsor Priory*

Sham Castle, late eighteenth century SU 9287
This is a large flint folly, three towers, circular, hexagonal and square, connected with curtain walls; the hexagonal tower was used as a lodge, and the circular tower, which is the tallest, must have been its outhouse, as there is a copper and fireplace against one wall. The square tower which is hollow stands on open arches and is completely covered in ivy, like the round one. When it was new, gleaming white flint and crisp red brick castellations, seen from the house it must have been one of the most imposing follies in England. Now when seen from this side it is just a great bumble of vegetation, an elaborate topiary folly. Only the complex castellations of the hexagon tower rise fairly free of the ivy, brambles, elder trees and tall burnt grass, and on top of it are fragments of some wooden conceit, nameless and full of nails.

Buckingham *Lord Cobham's Castle* SP 6934
A big sham castle (1748) built at the north end of Buckingham Market Square, right in the middle of the wide road. It was desired to bring the County Assizes back to Buckingham, and as there can be no assizes without a jail, Lord Cobham gave the town one, so truly mediaeval in appearance that local guides and postcards cheat unblushingly, leaving out the date. The front was added by George Gilbert Scott (his first work) in 1839, a semi-circular addition to make a warder's house. Inside are cells, a fire station with a beautiful old engine, and at the back are ladies' and gents' lavatories and 'Stick No Bills'.
Stowe (2½ miles N.W.), SP 6934
eighteenth century
See pages xx and 135.

Bulstrode

Grotto, eighteenth century† SU 9989
This very famous grotto by a Duke of Portland and Mrs Delany crops up constantly in memoirs and letters; unfortunately it has been demolished.

The aviary at Dropmore

Burnham *Dropmore*

Aviary, etc., nineteenth century   SU 9387

A beautiful aviary (no birds) set in a considerable pergola. The base and supporting pillars are made of fretted Chinoiserie ceramic tiles in a turquoise glaze, and iron and wire, painted red, make a central hexagonal lantern and a little dome at each end. The house was built in the early 1790s; I would place the aviary with additions made to it in about 1810. Dropmore has one of the finest, and most beautifully landscaped collections of trees in the country, and several other conceits. There is a Chinese summerhouse, and a small sad pedimented bark temple of any date between 1740 and 1820. It has two columns (with the echinus cunningly made of rope) and a red, black and white tiled floor. A bark shelter looks later and has been restored, but is much less attractive.

The Vache

Chalfont St Giles *The Vache*

Cook Memorial, eighteenth century   SU 9894

The monument stands on a mound ringed by trees and a small moat with a wooden bridge. It is a charming small square flint tower trimmed and castellated with red brick, with a big round-headed arch in each wall to show the marble plinth and globe of the world. On the plinth is a very long inscription, which starts:

> TO THE MEMORY OF
> CAPTAIN JAMES COOK
> The ablest and most renowned
> Navigator this or any country
> hath produced.
> He raised himself, solely by his merit
> from a very obscure birth, to the rank
> of Post Captain, in the royal navy, and
> was unfortunately killed by the Savages
> of the island Owhyhee, on the 14th of February
> 1779; . . . .

For a wonder, not one line in an inscription at least eight times this length, mentions the donor, who even provided stairs and a flat roof for the view, 12 feet up.

Chalfont St Peter *Passmore Edwards Colony*

Obelisk, 1785   TQ 0289

This was built by Sir H. T. Gott to commemorate the spot where George III killed a stag. It is made of flint and stands on a brick base; the edge at the top is banded with brick where it was restored by W. Brown in 1879. A plaque let into it records the distances to Chesham, Denham, Uxbridge, London and Newland 1 mile III furlongs. It was also a beacon.

Dinton

Sham Castle, 1769   SP 7711

A most charming, innocent folly, standing on a little mound by the Aylesbury–Thame road and circled by pine trees. It was built in 1769 by Sir John Vanhatten to house his collection of fossils, some of which are let into the random rubble walls. The plan is a hexagon with towers at two opposite corners, one for fireplaces and the other for a spiral staircase. It had a cellar, a kitchen ground floor reached from it, and a piano nobile at the top of a flight of steps from the ground. Only sockets and splinters remain of the floors and the whole building is in decay, stucco dressings fallen from their bricks and ivy everywhere.

Dorney *Dorney Court*

The Hermitage, eighteenth century   SU 9379

A pretty lodge carried beyond the normal call of lodges. A cruciform plan on one storey with a central octagon tower of one room under a flaring pyramid roof and an unusual reversal of materials; it is made of dark random stone and brick dressed with the white of unknapped flints. There are three mad thin chimneys as tall as the lodge, a terracotta plaque set in a ring of bottle-bottoms and very elegant windows.

Ellesborough *Chequers*

Grotto, nineteenth century?   SP 8406

The six-inch Ordnance Survey map marks a Druid's Maze to the north of the house, and until recently there were traces of a circle in the fields, but now nothing. However, it is prominently marked on an estate map of 1629; perhaps there were ancient stones, perhaps a grass maze, perhaps an early sham circle.

Nearer to the house is an open grotto walk of rocks piled up under yew trees with some ferns and a modern statue of a fawn. Nothing is known of its history or date. I would think the second half of the nineteenth century.

On Combe Hill

Obelisk, 1902

An obelisk crowned by a flaming grenade to the men of the Royal Artillery killed in the Boer war.

Fawley *Fawley Court*

Sham Ruin, nineteenth century   SU 7587

A most impressive folly, so surrounded by yews and firs that it is difficult to see or draw and almost impossible to photograph. It looks in the West Wycombe tradition, built of flint with brick and stone trim but nothing seems known of its history.

Down the walk from the house the ruin appears as a big perpendicular window that may be a real fragment, built into a flint pediment with three remaining castellations of brick. Below is a porch with a pointed stone door and through this is a most beautiful and impressive circular flint room with a

The sham ruin at Fawley Court

flint and knucklebone dome of 16 ribs that taper from five lines of bones to two. The floor is tiled in black and white with a complex pattern based on swastikas. Opposite the entrance is an alcove with big specimen flints and to right and left are exits to the park, one a pedimented door, in a larger plain arch. Outside, the tiled dome can be seen, and a variety of blind windows, alcoves and buttresses. Once there were a great many statues and busts but those that survive have been removed for safety and only a headless tern remains.

Nearby is a charming but dilapidated covered bridge with pediments and flint rustications.

From the garden front of the house a canal runs to the Thames down an avenue of poplar and ilex. At the end to the left on a bend of the river can be seen Temple Island, which used to be part of the Fawley estate, a most picturesque composition with big weeping willows and an elegant Fishing Temple, once visible from the house. The architect is unknown, though it used to be attributed to James Wyatt. A painting by Copley Fielding shows the island much as it is now, but without the cottage which was added to the temple in the nineteenth century. The main room is decorated with paintings by Biagio Rebecca, and restoration is under way.

Haddenham

The Bone House, 1807   SP 7409

A double-fronted whitewashed cottage decorated with sheep's knucklebones set into the
walls; they make faces, the date, crossed
spade and forks, hearts and diamonds. One
of the faces has the bowl of a clay-pipe for a
nose.

Hartwell   SP 8012

Hartwell has a real ruined gothick church
(1753–5) of the utmost romantic melancholy, an octagon with ogival doors and
windows, roofless and full of young trees,
though the tower still stands, its dead clock-
face visible from the house. Near the church,
which rivals every sham in the country, is a
simple round limestone tower, perhaps 30
feet high, with a pointed door at the top of
five narrowing steps and three quatrefoil
windows. It is plainly domed and very well
built, with the curious number of 14 castellations.

There is also in the park a column with an
over-large statue of George II on top, flanked
by more statues, and a fine folly wall for the
main drive, made of random stone with
occasional squares of flint, fossils, etc., 1855
and J C 1853 in stone set in big flint panels and
a bridge with some odd old bits added. This
takes the road over an underpass in the
grounds with folly façades, triple arched, with
gryphons, stone shells and bits of urns and
carving that can be seen to come from some of
the complicated rebuilding of the house.

The Egyptian Spring, Hartwell

Near the east face are some decaying palm
trees to prepare us for the Egyptian Spring,
a trifling well-head in the Egyptian taste
designed by Joseph Bonomi. It is made of
squared rubble and backed into the cutting of
the road. The lintel is banded with a strip of
perhaps hieroglyphics; a bumbling contrast
to the church.

Hughenden

Column, 1863   SU 8595

A memorial from Benjamin Disraeli to his
father Isaac ('Curiosities of Literature').
Fifty feet high in red granite, designed by
E. B. Lamb.

Iver *Richings Park*

Cascade and Grotto, eighteenth   TQ 0481
century*

These are said to be the remains of these.

(Ivinghoe) *Hamlet Seabrooke*   SP 9317

Not a folly at all, though often reported as
one. See page 4.

Langley Marish *Langley Park*

Grotto, nineteenth century*   TQ 0382

A big grotto-wall in a conservatory attached
to the house.

Mapledurham *Mapledurham House*

Eyecatcher, eighteenth century   SU 6777

A small, tall façade two bricks thick of three
plinths and two shallow niches to uphold a
statue of Pan. It was designed, possibly at the
inspiration of Pope, who often stayed here, to
close a yew walk up from the house, passing a
statue of the God of the Meadows in the
garden. It is now almost invisible among
young beeches, though some of the yews
remain, and has lost the pinnacles from the
smaller plinths. Most of its Roman cement
has gone too, leaving pink brick patterned
with the warm green of lichen.

Medmenham *Medmenham Abbey*

Screen and Tower, *c.* 1760   SU 8184

This is where Sir Francis Dashwood lived
before he went to West Wycombe. If he ever

made extensive folly works here as he did there, they have gone for now there is only a gothick colonnade and a ruinous tower. See page 100.

Stoke Mandeville *Elm Cottage*   SU 8310

A bright trifle if passing by. A front fence of painted agricultural implements (twentieth century), including a plough, and a gate made of two big iron wheels. Two peacocks, one red and one yellow, have fantails of laths painted white.

Stoke Poges *Stoke Park*

Column, 1800*   SU 9984

A column to Sir Edward Coke, designed by James Wyatt. It is 60 feet high, in Roman Doric style, with a statue on the top.

Taplow *Cliveden*

Iron Pagoda, nineteenth century   SU 9186
See page 117.

Waddesdon *Waddesdon Manor*

Aviary, nineteenth century   SP 7417

Some very small fragments of rocaille in the aviary to a Rothschild house of 1880–9 (a big château). Trellis and debased baroquery of the most delightful and typical sort with free-flying macaws screaming through the trees. Also rock-work with a small rock grotto near the main drive.

West Wycombe *West Wycombe Park*

Group, eighteenth century   SU 8395
See page 100.

Wotton Underwood *Wotton House*

Turkish Temple, etc., eighteenth   SP 6916
century

The Turkish Temple, or Crescent Moon, which was illustrated in *Country Life,* 8 July 1949, has been dismantled for restoration and repainting. The Chinese Pavilion is at Harristown (*q.v.*).

Cambridgeshire

New Wimpole *Wimpole Hall*

Sham castle, eighteenth century   TL 3351
See page 56.

Norman Cross

Column, twentieth century   TL 1692
Just north of Norman Cross on the A1 is a column with a bronze eagle on top which was put up early this century by the Entente Cordiale Society to commemorate the French who were prisoners-of-war between 1796–7. One sees it from the car and stops because the situation is so unlikely and then drives on again, puzzled.

Wimpole Hall sham castle, perhaps as intended, from a print at Radway

Cheshire

Bollington

White Nancy, nineteenth century   SJ 9377
White Nancy, a beautiful gleaming landmark for all northern Cheshire as it stands on the edge of the High Peak, is a circular stone building conical in shape and painted brilliant white. Inside there is a stone table with seats surrounding it. White Nancy was built as a boundary mark by Colonel Gaskell to commemorate the victory at Waterloo; in places the whitewash is covered with a thin pattern of initials, erased and replaced every time it is repainted.

Congleton *Mow Cop*

Sham Ruin, eighteenth century   SJ 8664
Mow Cop is a particularly good and dramatic sham ruin; there is a big round stone tower, joined by a curtain wall with a high pointed arch in it, to a cluster of picturesque ruined walls. It was built in 1750 by Randle Wilbraham of Rode Hall, in the valley to the west.

Most follies relapse into quiet melancholy between the excitement of their building and the lust for their destruction. Mow Cop, however, is a rallying ground for Methodists, possibly because of the stony and Sinai-like hill on which it stands. On 31 May 1807, the first camp meeting in England was held here, and there was a great revival of Wesley's open air witness all over the country. In 1812 Primitive Methodism was founded at Mow Cop: hundreds of people arrived on the hill all day from dawn onwards to pray and testify. Many meetings have been held there since, but the influence of Christianity has not purged the village children of their desire to heave half a brick at an artist.

Disley *Lyme Park*

Eyecatcher—Lodge, eighteenth   SJ 9685
century
When Giacomo Leoni altered Sir Peter Legh's Elizabethan mansion at Lyme in 1726 he refaced the Cage and added four towers. This is a stubby square building about a mile from the house standing on a rise in the park; it was originally built in about 1520 as a combination of hunting lodge, and of prison for local delinquents before they were sent for trial at Chester. The eighteenth-century intention, however, must have been to preserve it as a folly gazebo, though the view is less lovely than the elevated windy walk towards it.

Mow Cop

Cleveland

Saltburn by Sea *Valley Gardens*
Albert Memorial*   NZ 6721
This was the classical portico of Barnard
Castle railway station, re-erected here by
Henry Pease, who started the resort when the
railway reached the sea in the 1860s.

Sedgefield *Hardwick Hall*
Sham Ruin, eighteenth century*   NZ 3630
The gatehouse to Hardwick is a sham ruin by
James Paine, an elaborate one, with real
pieces from Guisborough Priory and a big
round gothick castellated tower. It was
probably built between 1748 when John

Burdon first came here and 1760 when he
built the now ruinous Banqueting House.
There is also an octagonal Paine temple with
a square colonnade round it, again ruinous.

Wolviston *Wynyard Park*
Obelisk, 1827*   NZ 4326
To commemorate a visit of the Duke of
Wellington.

Yarm
Folly garden, twentieth century   NZ 4213
See page 253.

Cornwall

A rocky county, with suitable materials for
making obelisks and columns, and hills to
build them on. The south coast is warm, and
in places like St Just in Roseland hot and lush,
but given to sub-tropical plants rather than
to the grottoes one might expect.

Boconnoc
Obelisk, 1771   SX 1361
This one is 123 feet high, a very fine obelisk
to the memory of his uncle by Lord Camel-
ford who decorated the gallery at Strawberry
Hill for his friend Walpole.

Bodmin
Obelisk, 1856–7   SX 0768
This one is granite, 144 feet high, 'To the
memory of Walter Raleigh Gilbert, Lieutenant-General in the Bengal army'.

Botusfleming
Obelisk, eighteenth century   SX 4161
This one is 12 feet high, on top of a tomb in a
field which bears this complete explanatory
inscription:

Here lieth the body of William Martyn
of the Borough of Plymouth in the County
of Devon, Doctor of Physick, who died
the 22nd day of November in the year of
our Lord Jesus Christ, 1762, aged 62 years.
He was an honest good-natured man,
willing to do all the good in his power to all
mankind; and not willing to hurt any person. He lived and died a Catholic Christian,
in the true and not depraved Popish sense
of the word, had no superstitious venera-
tion for Church or Churchyard ground, and
willing by his example if that might have
any influence to lessen the unreasonable

esteem which some poor men and women through prejudice of education often show for it in frequently parting with the earnings of many a hard day's labour, which might be better bestowed in sustenance for themselves and their families, to pay for Holy Beds for their kinsfolk's corpses, through a ridiculous fear lest their kinsfolks at the Day of Judgement should some way or other suffer because their corpses were wrongly situated or not, where the worldly advantage of their spiritual guides loudly called for them.

His will provided that the monument must go with the field in perpetuity, lest at any time the parson should remove it.

Pentillie Castle (2 m. N.)
Tower, *c.* 1800   SX 4164
The burial place of Sir James Tillie.

Bude *Stratton*
Monument, seventeenth century   SS 2207
An arch with knobbly obelisk, or octagon pyramid, or spire with crockets, on the site of the Battle of Stratton, where YE ARMY OF YE REBELLS UNDER YE COMMAND OF YE EARL OF STAMFORD RECEIV'D A SIGNALL OVERTHROU BY YE VALOR OF SR BEVILL GRANVILLE AND YE CORNISH ARMY ON TUESDAY YE 16TH OF MAY 1643.

Caerhayes
Caerhayes Castle   SW 9642
A very highly castellated and turreted house by John Nash, with a circular two-tier tower of 1808 joined on by a castellated wall.

Calstock *Cothele House*
Tower   SX 4268
An unusual prospect tower, not only triangular on plan but with dished sides, made of local slatestone with granite pinnacles and massively dressed pointed sham windows. Three clumsy storeys, 60 feet high, no date, no history except stories that Fanny Burney was told that obelisks were planned and that it was used as a signal tower to Mount Edgcumbe.

Carnbrea
Castle and Column, eighteenth   SW 6942
and nineteenth century
First a hunting lodge and then a sham castle, on an ancient earthwork, altered and added to by the Bassetts of Tehidy. The 90 foot monument was put up by the County of Cornwall in 1836 to commemorate the defence of Plymouth in the Peninsular War by Lord de Dunstanville and Bassett (1753–1835). Builder, Joseph Pryor of Gwennap.

Falmouth   SW 8033
A pretty octagonal Oriental Summerhouse† with a crescent on the roof has gone from the grounds of Marlborough House, leaving Falmouth with a dull obelisk of 1737 to Sir Peter Killegrew.

Fowey *Menabilly*
Grotto, *c.* 1780   SX 1151
Philip Rashleigh built his grotto as a repository for the discards from his colossal collection of minerals. Gilbert in his *Survey of Cornwall* gives an exact description, but he gives no conception of the scale of this building, which is very small, about 10 feet across, now not as glossy as it was.

The Grotto is of an octagonal form, erected some years ago by Philip Rashleigh esq., with the assistance of only one tradesman. The outside is composed of enormous sea pebbles, and the intermediate spaces are filled with various shells, and rising on the top into eight pediments, it has in each of them a small window formed of one large pane of glass, bordered with various specimens of granite, shells, etc. These support a roof, of a conical form, bearing on its centre a vase, which is also formed of shells, and the lower part of the covering being hung round with a species of stalactites, resembling icicles, produce, at all seasons of the year, an exact imitation of a severe frost. The entrance is at a rustic door, formed of the yew tree on the eastern side, facing which is a large window, that

The grotto at Menabilly

takes a view of a sloping lawn, terminated by an expansive sea.

In the centre of the interior is placed a table, of an octagonal form, composed of thirty-one specimens of Cornish Granite, and divided into thirty-two compartments. This beautiful stone, raised in the parish of Lanlivery, was polished in London and displays in great perfection, all the varieties of its natural composition. The walls of this splendid fabric are adorned with shells of almost every description, minerals and a great number of stones of great brilliancy, which are reflected from the opposite sides by the help of glasses, whilst the ceiling presents all the appearance of a hanging mass of congealed water. Among the profusion of natural beauties here displayed, are various specimens of tin, copper, lead and iron, separately classed. In the other sides are displayed organic fossils, jaspers and polished agates, which are interspersed with coraloids, a variety of quartz, and a large collection of peculiarly fine shells. The chief artificial curiosities are two links

of chain found in Fowey Harbour, supposed to have been a part of one which formerly extended across the entrance for its security. They are about sixteen inches in diameter, and are incrusted with shells. On the northern side of the grotto is a door, which opens into the lawn. The arch is formed of the jaw-bone of a whale, and the sides constructed with large unshapely stones, laid loosely one upon another, over-run with lichens, and shaded with hardy foliage.

This was written in 1817. The entrance is now walled up, but the outside is the same.

Morwenstow *Hawker's Rectory*
Chimneys, *c.* 1860   ss 2115
Robert Stephen Hawker wrote the poem, *Song of the Western Men,* with the refrain 'And shall Trelawny die?', which is for Cornish nationalists the best poem in the language.

When he built his vicarage at Morwenstow, he decided that the chimneys should be

Morwenstow Rectory

replicas of the towers of his favourite churches; there are five church towers, and the sixth, the kitchen chimney, 'perplexed me very much', said Hawker, 'till I bethought me of my mother's tomb; and there it is, in its exact shape and dimensions'.

Over the front door is carved

> A House A Glebe A Pound a Day,
> A pleasant Place to watch and pray:
> Be true to Church, Be Kind to Poor,
> O Minister, for evermore.

Mount Edgcumbe
Sham Ruin, *c.* 1750   SX 4553
One of the most spectacularly placed of all ruins, on a cliff overlooking Plymouth Sound. A clunch-type ruin in stone, rectangular, with two big windows and plenty of ivy. There are gardens in three styles to see here, a temple, a garden-house, early eighteenth century with late eighteenth-century wings, and another of the nice little Coade stone triangular memorials. This one is 14 feet high, to Timothy Brett. There used to be a grotto.

Penzance *Castle An Dinas West*
Rogers Tower, *c.* 1800   SW 4936
A square tower built on the ramparts of an Iron Age fort, with a turret at each corner standing on the outer ramparts of the fort. It is a very small folly indeed, built of rough stone, the pieces getting bigger towards the top so that about half a dozen enormous boulders make a complete course at the top of the turrets. There is a gothick doorway in one side and gothick windows on the ground floor; on the top of each turret is a great knob of stone. It was built for a Mr Rogers, a local landowner, and is more an elaborate stone hut than a tower.

Legrice's Folly
Tower   SW 4730
A minute tower about 10 feet high with a castellation of single great square stones. It was supposed to have been built as a look-out for shipping; it is very Cornish and wind-resisting.

And there is Foulston's lovely Egyptian House of 1830 in Penzance itself.

Legrice's Folly

Early in the eighteenth century, the Connoc family built a new house on to an existing farm and laid out a garden with lawns, statues, yews and a box-garden with beds in the shape of hearts, diamonds, clubs and spades, adding a pretty and distinctly Chinese clocktower in three diminishing storeys. The ground floor is stone, and the upper two shingle, all with slate roofs. The octagonal one-handed clock (also slate) is dated 1733, the bell is older (1620), and, hopelessly on the west wall, is a sundial of 1773. 'Every hour shortens life.'

Polperro

The Shell House   SX 2151
A house in The Warren with good restrained shellwork on the façade, embellished with a cast-iron stair-rail. Most of the decoration is in abstract patterns of circles, diamonds, stars and the other basic shell arrangements, but there are also sailing boats in semicircular frames and the Eddystone Lighthouse. It was made by Mr Sam Puckey, who started work on it in 1937 and went on, changing and adding, for about five years.

Port Isaac *The Birdcage*

Tower, eighteenth century   SW 9981
A hexagonal tower, one storey stone and another stone and slate.

St Ives

Knill Monument, 1782 or 1811   SW 5140
A pyramid like a church steeple, built by John Knill probably in 1811; at his death he left freehold property to defray the expense involved in having every five years, an old woman and ten girls under the age of 14 (or ten little girls under ten) parading from the Market Place to the pyramid where they were to dance and sing the 100th Psalm: 'Make a joyful noise unto the Lord all ye lands.' He also left ten pounds so that the port collector and the minister should have a dinner.

Treworgy *Treworgy Manor*

Clocktower,* early eighteenth   SX 2566
century

Truro

Column, 1835   SW 8345
A massive Doric column to commemorate an explorer called Lauder stands high above Lemon Street's pretty houses.

Veryan

Round Houses, early nineteenth   SW 9239
century
A pretty village with five round, whitewashed cottages of great charm, sometimes called Parson Trist's houses. There are two at each end of the village, like lodges, all thatched and crowned with crosses, with gothick windows. The fifth is near the church with a mediaeval detail or two incorporated, and has a slate roof and a central chimney. They were put up by a builder from Lostwithiel, Hugh Rowe, but are often said to be mediaeval (no corners for the devil to lurk in) or to have been designed by the lord of the manor when he returned from travels in Africa early in the nineteenth century; possibly Mr Rowe built them for him.

Werrington *Werrington Park*

Eyecatcher   SX 3488
A stone podium on a hill with a big round-arched recess with a seat for the view. On top are The Sugar Loaves, three stone cones, set two forward and one back, in the simplest and most bewildering folly architecture. The owner believes them to have been built by the Morice family in about 1704, 'a model of the tomb of Horatii and Curiatii', while

The Sugar Loaves, Werrington Park

Nikolaus Pevsner suggests that they might be derived from the Daniell's Indian drawings *c.* 1800 or shortly after. I think just cones, and on the evidence of Barwick (on the way to London from Werrington) possibly the last quarter of the eighteenth century.

There was another folly here, in brick, built by the Duke of Northumberland after he bought the estate in 1775, to rival the Duke of Bedford's folly at Mount Edgcumbe. The present owner's father blew it up in the 1880s or 1890s because it wasn't real, so it was probably a sham ruin.

Whitesand Bay *Sharrow Grot*   SW 3527
Gilbert described this grotto in 1820.

Situated in the cliffs of Whitsand Bay between the Rame and Looe, East Cornwall. This singular excavation, which is in Whitsand Bay, opens to an Immense Ocean, and is placed in a romantic position. It was hewn out of the solid rock by the uncle of the late Joseph Lugger Esq., and he is said to have escaped the gout for many years in consequence of the laborious exercise required in its formation. The depth within is fifteen feet and the height nearly seven, with breadth in proportion, and has an arched roof. The benches are of stone and sufficiently commodious to entertain twenty persons, poetic effusions principally descriptive of the surrounding scenery, are chiselled in the room which forms its back and sides.

Cumbria

By the lakes and fells which were fashionable in Wordsworth's time, the picturesque was not felt to be enhanced by sham ruins, eyecatchers or pagodas, but nevertheless the Cumbrian follies are good ones, very personal and strange. Ordinary obelisks at Burneside and Kendal, and a special one at Lindale.

Allithwaite

Kirkhead Tower, probably early   SD 3878
nineteenth century
A small square stone tower with castellations, and a big lump of weatherworn rock on each corner.

Appleby *Appleby Castle*

Lady Anne's Bee House,   NY 6921
seventeenth century
Let us get rid of Lady Anne Clifford as quickly as possible. She was an inveterate and boring builder; the Bee House is a small square building with a pyramid roof.

At *Brougham Castle* NY 5228 is Countess' Pillar, a small thing put up in 1656 by Lady Anne to her mother, 'where they parted'. At Mallerstang is the stump of Lady's Pillar, 1664, and I expect there are some more little oddments elsewhere.

Bardsea

Bradyll Mausoleum   SD 3074

See page 94.

Bowness-on-Windermere *Storr's Hall*

Fishing House, 1804   SD 4096
On the lake shore on a little neck of land the smallest possible octagon with four open arches and four tablets to four admirals, Duncan, St Vincent, Howe and Nelson.

Corby *Corby Castle*

A magnificent grotto-cascade,   NY 4755
a giant and other statues,
eighteenth/nineteenth century
See page 213.
In the village, two charming sad dogs on Grove Cottage and a massive façade to the smithy, a huge arch on squat romanesque pillars, 1833.

The head of the cascade, Corby Castle

Drumburgh *Drumburgh Castle*

Tower   NY 2760

A negligible square trifle; no known date.

Greystoke *Greystoke Castle*

Group, 1780   NY 4431
Charles 11th Duke of Norfolk, who lived at Greystoke Castle, was a great admirer of America; he called a farm and a cottage which he built 'Jefferson', but his more elaborate commemorations of American independence are Bunker's Hill and Fort Putnam. Fort Putnam is the most ambitious, a farmhouse and outbuildings entirely enclosed within a system of fortifications. The best part of this is the outside wall of the cow house, which is a row of blind gothick arches separated by semicircular piers; these are ringed at the top by coronets of stiff stone petals from which rise cones with balls on top, very like chessmen. The wall round the rest is castellated, and at one point there is a hexagonal watch tower built into the line of the walls. Bunker's

Spire House, Greystoke Castle

The cowhouse wall, Greystoke Castle

Hill is less complicated; again it is a farm, but this time only the three outside walls of the farmhouse have been castellated and given rather pleasant gothick windows with very simple glazing bars. Spire House has nothing to do with the American War of Independence, but there is the story that Charles Howard when commissioning his architect told him to build him anything so long as it did not look like a church. This, the prettiest of these follies, is again a farmhouse with an addition, three sides of an octagonal tower with pretty gothick windows; at the back is an ordinary building, and on top a small turret (with a lead steeple and weathervane) built of the most beautiful dark tobacco-coloured stone.

On the Penrith–Keswick road is Greystoke Pillar, a tapering octagonal obelisk or spire about 20 feet high, banded near top and middle and standing on a square plinth. No more charming group exists anywhere; the Howards probably come out top on the list of folly-building families.

Lindale

Obelisk, 1808   SD 4180

The valley of the River Winster is full of relics of eighteenth-century industry. Lindale has a most beautiful and special cast iron obelisk, painted red, with a small ball on top, to

JOHN WILKINSON,
IRON MASTER,
WHO DIED XIV JULY, MDCCCVIII;
AGED LXXX YEARS

Wilkinson built the obelisk with its once-gilded portrait medallion, and his own iron coffin. He started in his father's ironworks at Backbarrow, with domestic ironware, and later, it is claimed, built the first iron ship in Vickers' yards at Barrow-in-Furness. The remains of this are said to be 'buried in the moss up the valley'.

Muncaster *Muncaster Castle*
Screen and tower, eighteenth and   SD 1196
nineteenth centuries
For the stable screen see page 218.

There is also a massive three-storey stone octagon tower with a pyramidal roof on a hill 1 mile to the north-east. This was put up by the first Lord Muncaster in about 1800, to commemorate the meeting of Henry VI, who was fleeing, with a shepherd who took him to safety in the castle in 1461, clearly a great day in local history.

Netherby
Sham Castle Salmon Coops,   NY 3972
eighteenth century
See page 219.

Newby Bridge *Pennington Tower*   SD 3786
To commemorate naval victories over France, Holland and Spain.

Penrith
Beacon Tower, 1719   NY 5232
1719 seems late for a real border-raid beacon tower, but it has the utility look. A square squat red sandstone tower with a plain pyramidal roof and big round-headed windows with projecting keystones and sills for sole ornament.

Reagill
Folly garden by Thomas Bland,   NY 6118
nineteenth century
See page 250.

St Bees Head (Inland) *Windscale*
Atomic Plant, twentieth century   NX 9514
Surely this will be seen as a folly in 200 years time? The pile leaked, cows died of radiation sickness, and the plant was filled with concrete and abandoned.

Sawrey
A small tower*   SD 3795

Shap Wells
Monument by Thomas Bland,   NY 5811
nineteenth century
See page 250.

Ulverston *Chapel Island**   SD 3379
On Chapel Island, and visible from Ulverston, is a small gothick folly chapel. In 1774 the ruins of a mediaeval chapel were still here; they were taken down and put up again properly in 1823 by Colonel Bradyll, with a gabled wall pierced by lancet and circular windows. The island can be reached by boat during the summer season. See page 94.

Conishead
A small octagon tower on a hill   SD 3076

The Hoade, 1850 (*Ulverston*)   SD 2978
A large lighthouse in dressed pale stone, weakly detailed. The foundation stone was laid by Sir John Barrow's sons on 15 May 1850. It was a very grand day, recorded in the *Illustrated London News,* and celebrated by the Ulverston brass bands and two triumphal arches at the school, one inscribed BE HIS THE PALM THAT MERITS IT and the other VIRTUE SURVIVES THE GRAVE and the Barrow coat-of-arms. The Hoade cost £1,250 of which Trinity House subscribed £100 on condition that it could become a real lighthouse if ever needed. It was finished, but struck by lightning in January 1851 before the lightning conductor went up. None of it sounds right for Barrow, who was born in a cottage preserved at Dragley Bank in 1764, went to China and South Africa and was Secretary of the Admiralty both during and after the Napoleonic Wars, when he helped and encouraged Arctic exploration. Barrow Point, Sound and Bay are all named after him.

The tower at Conishead Priory

Wetherall

Caves   NY 4655

Three small man-made caves connected traditionally with the fourteenth century and St Constantine, whose statue is opposite them across the river at Corby (*q.v.*).

There is a tower on Cote Hill.*

Wray *Wray Castle*

John Longmire's Folly, nineteenth   NY 3702
century

The castle is now a naval training college, overlooking Lake Windermere. It was once embellished with several stark little stone shams. One, and an arch, were demolished as unsafe quite recently. One remains; square, battered, castellated, machicolated, two quatrefoils, two slits, pointed door. John Longmire lived at Troutbeck and seems to have had nothing to do with any of it, except that he carved messages on stones and that some of these were later used for the castles.

Wreay *St Mary's*

Sarah Losh's Church, 1840–2   NY 4449

Usually when an old church decays it is restored, or an architect designs a new one. Here, Miss Sarah Losh of Woodside, widely travelled but untrained, built a new church for £1,200, with local stone and local craftsmen, modelling in clay the conceits they carved in stone and wood, and herself carving at least the font—an uncle carved the cover. Most of the stone-carving was by William Hindson. The church itself is simple; almost without style, no transepts, a semicircular cobby apse, and tall windows. The decoration is the thing; two big wild lecterns—an eagle and a flapping pelican in chestnut wood on contorted boles of bog oak, two bog oak chairs and a pulpit with a palm-tree candle-holder. Over the chancel arch are angels between trees, and round the west door, carved by Miss Losh's gardener, runs a gourd, gnawed by a caterpillar. The font has wheat, a dragonfly, moths, a dove, and today is piled for harvest festival with the fruits of the Cumbrian earth—a plaited loaf, cabbages, flowers, cartons of eggs, pots of shop jam, bananas and tinned fruit.

There are a number of big pine cones, and half-cones make the door pulls. Major William Thain, a friend of Miss Losh, was killed by a poisoned arrow in the Khyber Pass; she grew a tree from a cone he had sent, and adopted cones for resurgam. Outside, they support the round arch of the door, and join for the decoration of windows and wall tops with squids, ammonites, insects and an owl. Serpent, crocodile, turtle, a huge bat and a dragon are gargoyles. The whole church has a happy atmosphere of love and care; it is the centre of village life, and everyone is rightly proud of it.

John Longmire's Folly

Sarah Losh's church

Derbyshire

A county of rock; most of the follies are based on the Trent and the Derwent and the paths they have cut for themselves. The northern half of Derbyshire is in the beautiful Peak District, and this of course is exploited at Chatsworth, but the best follies are in the flatter country south of Derby, at Elvaston, Bladon and Sudbury.

Birchover *The Druid Inn*
Rowter Rocks, 1717   SK 2463
Just behind the Druid Inn is an outcrop of rock with gritstone which has weathered to the appearance of an enormous boulder on top of a sheer cliff, so that one looks down on the tops of large trees below from a great pile-up complete with blow-holes, rocking-stones and the ruin of a house. In 1717 the Reverend Thomas Eyre improved it with steps, retaining walls for paths, and rooms, a table and three bears' chairs cut in what is always called the living rock.

Between two of the largest overhanging lumps a scramble goes to the summit, a bit of pole and a dark rectangular room about 10 feet long. An alcove has a long round peep-hole to the treetops. The walls show the scars of blasting, but have also been worked all over with chisels, a lovely surface of random herring-bone.

Back in the pub is a pretty tinted engraving of 1853 showing the rocks with a pennant on the pole and a picnic party on a vanished greensward, several graceful ladies and a man in a very tall hat.

Not far away, west of the A524, off the path between Gratcliffe Rocks and Robin Hood's stride is a Hermit's Cave with a rough crucifix carved, for which no date can even be guessed.

Buxton
Solomon's Temple   SK 0674
Another windy hilltop tower, on Grinlow Barrow, 2 miles south of Buxton. Solomon's Temple, built in 1896 but looking older, is only about 20 feet high, a hollow circular bandbox with a battlemented top. It is absolutely charming, very solidly built of light stone faced with dark.

There is a round-arched door and windows to match, unglazed now, for the view, and a fine open-string spiral stair leads straight up to the roof, though there is another band of windows, blinded with stone, on the outside. The view is superb.

There was an earlier Solomon's Temple on the same site, 'built by public subscription to relieve unemployment' like so many other towers, on ground belonging to a farmer called Solomon Mycock. It would be interesting to solve the mystery of 'public subscription' here: it is easy to understand a landowner giving work to the unemployed on a fantasy for his own amusement, but it is difficult indeed to visualize the subscribers' meeting at which it was decided that Buxton was perfect, and needed no road, school or even drinking fountain to enhance it, so that the miserable unemployed must climb the steep hill two miles out of town to build a prospect tower.

Solomon's Temple, Buxton

Carsington *Hopton Hall*

Tower, Tufa Cottage, Iffe's Folly,   SK 2554
eighteenth century

All the work of Lord Gell, in about 1790. The Tower is in the lovely peace of the walled garden, facing south from the shallow arcs of a semi-serpentine wall. Two storeys in warm red brick with two pretty doors. By the time these were finished Lord Gell was impatient for Town, but the builders pestered for instructions, so he said 'Oh for God's sake go on *building*', and they did, no windows and no decorations, and Lord Gell came back and said, 'Nothing to do now but put a roof on it', so they did, and a pear tree is espaliered up the front to hide the shameful blank.

Near Bonsall, Lord Gell made a stretch of road called Via Gellia (A5012), and on this are the remains of his waterworks and also Tufa Cottage, a solid villa in solid tufa. Iffe's Folly was up in the woods nearby, but is now only a pile of rubble; Bonsall, though, is a pretty village and has a well dressing, so on a lucky day everyone may be found in the village hall setting down flowers in the big frames of damp clay, geranium petals like the scales on a butterfly's wing, and lichen to outline the Bible picture.

Chatsworth

Rockwork, etc., eighteenth century   SK 2670
A splendid house with lovely gardens full of interest, and an excellent model village; everything but a true folly. Even the cyclopean rock-work does not quite qualify. The Stand is probably of Bess of Hardwick's time, carefully preserved and dull, like Queen Mary's Bower nearer the house; all that remains of the mid-seventeenth-century work. The first Duke of Devonshire inherited in 1684 and most of the marginal follies are of his time. There is a grotto in the house; Tuscan columns, a fountain and a French carving of Diana under the stairs, not a shell in sight. Outside, a canal, a temple to Flora and a big cascade begun in 1694. Right at the top of the grounds behind the house is the Wilderness and here the water from the hills was gathered into the Aqueduct, four massive rusticated arches and stop. The water then falls over rocks to Archer's beautiful Cascade House, with water-rustication, dolphins, a sleeping river-god, nymphs, spouting lizards, ferns and stone shells. Hence the water descends calmly in shallow terraces, a good place for a picnic with the feet in the water on a hot day.

The rest of the gardens lie to the south, mostly the work of Capability Brown with the fourth duke and of Paxton with the sixth. The early picturesque landscaping is good but uninspired in spite of boulder work on a very grand scale indeed, part natural, part artificial —there is a good piece of gigantic tooth-work west of the waterfall, quite out of scale with the pretty Willow Tree (presumably nineteenth century), a fragile spiky bronze tree fifteen feet high which throws thin jets of water in the lines of a weeping willow.

The grotto, alas, has none of the atmosphere proper to a good grotto, in spite of a dead tree beside it. It lies behind the water-lilies of an open pool, a stolid arch of big rocks, tufa and stalactites. A short tunnel, now concreted, leads to a round domed chamber lined with minerals, copper ore, flints and spar, monotonously arranged. In the middle of the dome remains the spray nozzle from the water-joke; undoubtedly there were others concealed. One can climb up at the side on to the roof which is much nicer than the inside, rustic under slate.

Paxton's Great Conservatory, that forerunner of the Crystal Palace, was destroyed in 1920. On its 276-foot site is a sunk walled garden divided into three parts, for lupins, a yew maze and a paved bit. Two life-size Egyptian puss-goddesses sit side by side looking across the maze.

The head of the cascade at Chatsworth

Depedale

Rock Hermitage of the Pious Baker   SK 4439
A pious baker was told by the Virgin to go to
Depedale and there build himself a hermitage;
he did so and carved out this curious little
cave in the rocks, a well-authenticated story
of mediaeval life. Later in the eighteenth
century Sir Robert Burdett extended the cave
and used to give dinners there to his friends;
at the moment there are four cells, and one
commands a fine view down the valley of the
river Trent.

Elvaston *Elvaston Castle*

Moorish Temple, nineteenth century SK 4133
See page 129.

Foremark

Rock Hermitage   SK 3527
The Anchorage Chapel at Ingleby, the Rock
Hermitage at Repton and the Chapel in the
caves at Foremark are all one, a series of caves
in a low cliff of sandstone and pudding stone
on the south bank of the River Trent. It is
said that they were excavated in the middle
ages (and *Anchor Church* is in gothic type on
the Ordnance Map) and embellished in the
eighteenth century by the Squire of Foremark
Hall. The largest of the caves has been dug out
round several rough columns with light shafts
and two entrances, very impressive in a
thunderstorm.

Matlock *Heights of Abraham*

Prospect Tower, 1844   SK 3060
One of the plainest of all towers, circular,
random stone, slight machicolations, no
castellation at all, above the Derwent. Put up
by John Petchell to provide work for local

stonemasons and dedicated to Queen Victoria.
There are caverns and Roman mine workings
in the hill underneath the pleasure-grounds.

Newton Solney *Bladon Castle*

Hoskin's Folly   SK 2926
See page 68.

Renishaw

Gothick Arch   SK 4578
A very pretty borderline folly—in the classic
taste it would be garden ornament—built of
golden stone with crocketed pinnacles.

Stanton

Tower, 1832   SK 2565
Again near Rowter Rocks. A tower to com-
memorate the Reform Bill and honour Earl
Grey.

Sudbury

Deerfold   SK 1632
See page 217.

Swarkeston

The Stand, seventeenth century?   SK 3728
This has many names and purposes. It is
hardly a folly but one keeps being told of it;
two octagon towers with ogee lids, a castellated wall between and curious brick ogee
arches to a loggia. An arena called the Cuttle
lies in front of it, probably for baiting something.

Two Dales *Sydnope Hall*

Eyecatcher   SK 2863
A hunting-stand given castellations for the
view from the house; now a cottage.

The gothick folly at Renishaw

Devonshire

A warm lush county with the bleak island of Dartmoor in the middle; it has some pleasant follies, many more than Cornwall, but falling far short of Somerset. The best things lie round the estuary of the Exe away from both the lush and the bleak, and there are also a number of cottages ornés and rustic lodges.

Ashcombe
Tower*   SX 9277
Two miles to the south, a tower on Little Haldon Hill.

Babbacombe Bay *On road to beach*
Grotto*   SX 9368
There is a small shell grotto with a pebble floor, white star on grey, behind a gothick house.

Berrynarbour *Watermouth Castle*
Sham Ruin, nineteenth century   SS 5647
The coasts of Devon are very picturesque and catch the Gulf Stream; there has been much ambitious sub-tropical gardening. This was a famous one, very overgrown and steamy when I saw it, with an arch made of elaborate flamboyant gothic relics of 1525, from Umberleigh House 20 miles away, which was demolished in the nineteenth century.

Blackawton *Oldstones*
Grotto and Hermitage, eighteenth SX 8151
century*
Oldstones is the ruin of a burnt out Palladian house, whose decaying little follies have been described to me by Mr F. L. Burt: '. . . most of the parkland is given over to farming. We followed a path from the mansion, through a decayed avenue of trees, to a wood, growing on the slope of a hill. In the valley, we found three artificial lakes. . . . Beside one . . . was a small grotto, containing two alcoves. On the outskirts of the wood we found a crazily constructed stone archway, to the right of which, set in a stone wall, was a granite plaque—

Within a Wood unknown to Public View
From Youth to Age a Reverend Hermit grew
The Moss His Bed, the Cave His Humble Cell,
His Food the Fruits, His drink the Crystal Well
Remote from Man with God he passed His days
Pray'r all his Business, all his Pleasure Praise.

'Through the archway, leading into the wood, was a narrow path in a cutting about 7 feet deep and we found, hollowed out in one side of the cutting, a little cave lined with stone set in mortar. . . .' The Cholwich family seems to have been unusually fortunate in its hermit; long-lasting and economical.

Braunton
Tower, *c.* 1846   SS 4936
A tower built by Thomas Mortimer to celebrate the repeal of the Corn Laws.

Buckland Beacon
The Tablets, 1928   SX 7374
'The Tablets' are not an architectural folly at all, but they are new, and individualism of this sort seems rarer today than it was in the eighteenth and nineteenth centuries, so they must be recorded, though monuments of such durability are unlikely to pass from us easily. Two huge slabs of rock on the top of the Beacon have been smoothed on the upper face and inscribed with the ten commandments. This was done by Mr Whitley to commemorate the defeat of the proposed new Prayer Book in 1928.

In the valley below is Ashburton, where one house has a façade decorated with playing card designs. It is not as exciting as the prominence given to it in tourist literature leads one to expect: one pictures at the very least a house built of blocks set up like a castle of cards, but the thin graffito ornament falls very short of the cardboard dream, the folly everyone makes, though most of us unfortunately lose the taste for it.

Chagford

Rushford Tower, 1870–85   SX 7188
A small sham castle on a hill, utterly submerged in a dying overgrown wood. It can be reached through brambles and bracken five feet high, but it is very easily missed and very forlorn when found. There is a round tower with arrow-slits and battlements and a lower square tower beside it, with steps up to the other, built by the Hayter-Hames family.

Combe Martin

The Pack of Cards Inn   SS 5847
Very much better than the house at Ashburton; this one really has a stacked-up house-of-cards appearance, a diminishing pile with eight chimneys to match.

Devonport

Column, Tower and Chimney,   SX 4655
nineteenth century
There is another Egyptian House by Foulston here but not so good as the one in Penzance, and his column in ordinary Doric to commemorate Devonport's achievement of town status in 1824. At Leigham, a two-storey grey stone octagon tower, of no known date or history.

And I am told that there is a drain vent in Wyndham Lane, Plymouth, disguised as an ornamental factory chimney.*

Doddiscombsleigh *Haldon House*

Belvedere, eighteenth century   SX 8687
See page 205.

East Budleigh *Bicton House*

Shell Cottage, Hermitage, etc.,   SY 0785
nineteenth century
Here are the results of almost two and a half centuries of steady gardening. The main impression is of the nineteenth century; undoubtedly we still feel the influence of James Barnes, who was head gardener from 1839 to 1869. There is an amusing account of his activities, his iron hand and his system of fines (as well as details of the whole arboretum and planting) in N. D. G. James' *The Trees of*

Bicton (Blackwell, 1969) which quotes the notice on the Palm House doors (surely by Mr. Barnes?).

> The Gardener at a hole looks out
> and holes are plenty hereabout
> A pair of pistols by his lug
> One load with ball the other slug
> A blunderbus of cannon shape
> Just ready to discharge with grape
> Let midnight thief or robber stand
> And pause ere he puts out his hand
> While those who came in open day
> May look but carry nought away.
>   Bicton 1850

The gardens near the house were laid out in 1735 for the first Lord Rolle to a design by Le Nôtre, who had died in 1700, and it is therefore a very late piece of axial planning leading to an obelisk beyond the grounds put up in 1743. Then no further great works are recorded until Lord John Rolle began the arboretum in 1830 and the pinetum in 1839, when Lady Rolle built the first two follies, the hermitage, and also the China Tower in a distant wood as a surprise birthday present for her husband; its name comes from her collection of porcelain kept there and not from the style of the tower, which is a three-storey octagonal stone one, rendered, about 70 feet high.

BICTON HERMITAGE

The Hermitage is at the edge of the pinetum, in the Hermitage Garden, overlooking a lake. It is an octagon again, but this time of wood, in fish-scale shingles with coloured glass windows and a two-tier pyramid roof in bigger shingles. On each side is a small pavilion with heavy gables held up on tree trunks; the Hermitage is really a nineteenth-century rustic summerhouse, but with an odd throwback—a knucklebone floor and an uncommon basketwork lining nicely free of the spiders and earwigs that usually attend the rustic style.

The Shell House in the American Garden followed between 1840 and 1845. Probably the little round flint building was got ready first, for in *The Gardener's Magazine* of 1842 it says that:

> Nothing is wanting but a collection of shells and minerals, for the sake of those who are fond of these departments of science, and this is about to be formed; a great quantity of shells and some minerals, having been procured for the purpose, though they are not yet arranged.

By 1869 *The Gardener's Chronicle* describes the Shell House with a rich collection of shells and coral from India and New Zealand and heathen gods from Lucknow. There were also shells from the Bahamas, and now the whole fine collection has been cleaned and lit, with local specimens added; few shell houses are so prosperous.

Lord Rolle died in 1842, and his successor planted in the winter of 1843–4 the marvellous avenue of Monkey Puzzles.

Exmouth *A La Ronde*

House, 1798   SY 0184

A La Ronde was built by the Misses Jane and Mary Parminter, an individual and delicate house on an original plan so successful that one wonders for days why round houses are not more common (this one actually has 16 sides). An entrance leads to a central hall from which opens out a series of lovely rooms like segments of a fan. Narrower rooms, fans almost closed, lie between them for storage, with big windows and elegant shelves to keep tidy all the feathers and shells with which the ladies worked. Above is another ring of similar rooms, and at the top a gallery runs round the hall, entirely decorated with shells, a grotto in the air with no feeling of the tomb. There are some portraits of birds made with their own feathers set in the walls, and in the drawing room is a whole frieze of tiny feathers. Here and there all over the open glowing room are the exquisite things the ladies made, much more delicate and perfectly designed than the usual work of accomplishment, but nothing is pernickety or foolish, and one is not made to feel a bull in a china shop. Instead, here is the vanished zenith of feminine elegance, and still, after 150 years, the feeling of delightfully occupied leisure and great content.

The Misses Parminter also built and endowed in 1811 Point-in-View, a tiny chapel with a pyramidal roof set in the midst of four single-storey almshouses for single ladies. Each has four gothick windows—the outside is prettier than A La Ronde.

A la Ronde

The arch at Filleigh

Filleigh *Castle Hill*
Arch and Ruin, eighteenth century   SS 6728
A fine big triumphal arch on the axis from the house; Constantine with a different top. On the other side of the house is a low wall round a large muffle of ivy said to contain a castellated sham ruin. The Menagerie is a Palladian house, and always has been.

Hartland *Lower Valley Farm*
Eyecatcher Arch†   SS 2625
A simple affair, recently destroyed.

Hatherleigh
Obelisk   SS 5404
A simple obelisk of 1860 to commemorate a Lieutenant-Colonel Morris.

Ivybridge *Filham House*
Tower, 1800   SX 6356
A real church, probably of *c.* 1400, of which only the square tower and a small piece of nave remained. In 1800 the owners of Filham added to it a tall stark octagonal prospect tower about twice the height of the mediaeval one; slits and arrow-slits, no castellations. The old tower has now fallen.

Kenton *Oxton House*
Hermitage, 1790*   SX 9383

Kingswear
Tower   SX 8952
An unexciting octagonal tower with big open arches in the bottom storey of the steeply inclined walls.

Mamhead *Mamhead Park*
Sham Castle, 1828–33   SX 9382
Mamhead Castle, by Anthony Salvin, is a sham in red standstone built on the foundations of a real one as stables to the house. It is a very large and impressive folly, built round a courtyard with a tower in the centre of one side and a more elaborate one with round turrets on the corner most visible from the drive. It even has a portcullis to guard the stables, the laundry and the brew house from which beer was piped straight into vats in the cellar under the house. I am told that it is an exact copy of Belsay Castle in Northumberland.

Offwell *Honiton Hill*
Bishop Coppleston's Folly, *c.* 1830   ST 1801
A square, Italianate stone tower, 80 feet high, machicolated, frigged with cast iron and rather dull clumsy detail and an awkward staircase turret. It needs another 200–300 years for the outward aspect to mellow, but its masonry is good already. Bishop Coppleston was Bishop of Llandaff from 1828–49; he built the tower so that he could see Wales, but even 80 feet would not lift him above the hills between him and his diocese.

Bishop Coppleston's Folly

Paignton *Little Oldway*

Tower, *c.* 1890   SX 8961
A water tower standing in the grounds of
Little Oldway, which is behind Oldway, the
municipal pleasure park. The tower is very
plain and square, and subordinated by the
builder, Paris Eugene Singer, to Oldway itself.
This is a vast mansion rightly called 'The
Miniature Versailles', and marks the culmina-
tion architecturally of the Industrial Revolution.

Powderham *Powderham Castle*

Belvedere, 1773   SX 9784
Powderham is similar in almost every way to
Haldon Belvedere, except that the turrets are
hexagonal and there is no attic storey. It is
built of brick and covered with Roman cement,
which has peeled off in great flakes leaving the
brick exposed. The detail of the windows and
the carved stone of the quatrefoils on the
ground floor are standard eighteenth-century
work and in no way extraordinary. At one
time it was used as a cottage, but now it is un-
inhabited and beginning to decay. Although
the tower is dull as architecture when com-
pared with Haldon, it is pleasantly situated
above the estuary of the Exe and the remains
of Brunel's atmospheric railway.

The Cygnet

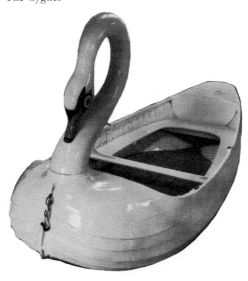

Sidmouth *Knowle Grange*

Grotto, 1805   SY 1387
Sidmouth has more, and better, and better
preserved cottages ornés and sophisticated
rustic charm than any other seaside town.
It was very modish indeed for about ten
years and appeared to be so for another
twenty. Gothick, verandahs, rustic, pretty
windows, flint, stucco, fine trees, conservatories, octagons, and, in the grounds of the
Knowle Grange Hotel, a fine grotto. This
house was built as a seaside cottage for Lord
le Despencer and later belonged to Lord
Bute and Mr Fish (of the furniture). It became
an hotel in 1882 and is now the Council
Offices.

Starcross *Exeter Maritime Museum*

The Cygnet   SX 9782
In 1881 Dixon & Sons, boatbuilders of
Exmouth, built for Captain George Peacock
the vessel SWAN, to seat 16 at dinner, and her
tender CYGNET. The Great Swan of Starcross
was moored in the estuary of the Exe, an
elegant white bird, perhaps a tight fit for
16, but big. A contemporary photograph in
the Museum shows it with wing-sails set, but
moored, and *very* close to shore, with,
presumably, Captain Peacock in a top hat.
In the 1930s it was found to be leaking badly
and the owners decided to use it as a summer-
house. Mr A. G. Cowell remembers how with
great difficulty and the help of local fishermen
he got it on to a farm wagon, manoeuvred it
through a gateway and then on to a platform
in the garden, where he repaired it with sail-
cloth and painted it white again. It was
destroyed in the mid 1960s, but the lovely
little Cygnet is safely preserved.

The impulse to build swan boats like Ludwig II of Bavaria is interesting; in all other
ways Captain Peacock, F.R.G.S., seems to have
been quite unlike him. The Museum tells us
that the Captain was born in 1805 at Starcross, served with the Navy surveying from
1828–40 and then commanded the steamers
of the Pacific Navigation Company. He built
steamers, took them through the Straits of
Magellan, laid buoys, built a lighthouse,
surveyed more harbours, opened a coal mine,

suggested railways, experimented with anti-fouling paints, and was Dock Master of Southampton, retiring in 1858 but going off in 1860 to hunt for nitrates in the Sahara for Napoleon III. He invented a screw propeller, a life jacket, improved railway buffers and cables, and built a steam gondola to prove his invention of the cycloidal propellor. He died in 1883 and is buried at Starcross.

Tavistock *Endsleigh Cottage*
Grotto, early nineteenth century   SX 4874
A cottage orné on a lovely site, above the Tamar instead of above the sea at Sidmouth, designed for the dowager Duchess of Bedford by Wyattville in 1810, with grounds by Repton, who did it proud. A series of winding and criss-crossing rock-lined paths of grass and knucklebones go up the hillside to a short serpentine tunnel that comes out at a still pool and the polygonal shell house, which has a pyramidal slate roof and little gables with simple (alas, not true) cobweb windows. The door is geometrical rustic work of fine branches, with coloured glass, the walls presumably pebble, flint, and rock, under all the ivy. The whole rock interior is lavishly encrusted with shells, including some fine exotics and branch coral to mask the windows. There are low seats and a pebble floor with a little central pool ringed by very special shells.

Across the valley is a 'Swiss Cottage', once thatched, in rustic wood with drain pipes running cleverly down the supporting tree-trunks. They do say that the duchess used to have a fire lit in the cottage so that she could see the ribbon of smoke rising.

Teignmouth
A miniature lighthouse of 1845.*   SX 9473

Torrington
Pyramid   SS 4919
A narrow stone pyramid with blind arches above the Torridge to commemorate Waterloo, inscribed: 'Peace to the Souls of Heroes'.

Westleigh *Tapeley Park*
Grotto   SS 4830
This grotto was presumably built at about the same time as the original Georgian house, but I have not been able to find out anything of its history. Across the grass, it does not look at all like a grotto, rather the bottom of an almost circular stone prospect tower with two pointed doors, four diamond-set square windows and a sharply slanted new round slate roof, high in front. Inside is the grotto; the new doors frame the original tree-trunks. All is shell lined, with some minerals and tufa. There are some fine specimen shells but the infill is not imaginative, so this cannot be classed as a particularly good grotto, but it is very nice that it is so well looked after.

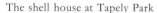
The shell house at Tapely Park

Dorset

Fewer follies than one would expect from such a beautiful and admired county, but the south has a long stretch of chalk downs, and these never lent themselves to improvement; they made a good backdrop but could not be landscaped.

Beaminster *Beaminster Manor*
Grotto, late eighteenth century ST 4802
Beaminster is an attractive town on the edge of the downs, built round a big square. The Manor has a pretty piece of minor grot-work and a good gate moved from Clifton May-bank. Behind the house across the lawn are fine copper beeches, cedars and a mulberry, with a rustic summerhouse. To the left is a stream which crosses a cascade and runs under a low bridge with ragged rock and tufa castellations. Further along a winding walk of box, yew and holly is a little pool surrounded by rock and tufa with an arch in its enclosing wall, and, over the arch, a circular opening with rock fangs. Its date is uncertain; probably late eighteenth century, possibly early nineteenth.

Broadstone *Canford Magna*
Rustic Work, nineteenth century SZ 0295
Fine work by John Hicks, culminating in the Rest and Tea House on Broadstone Golf Course. For details, see the author's *The Unsophisticated Arts,* Architectural Press, 1951.

Horton *Sturt's Folly*
Tower, eighteenth century SU 0407
A massive and very well preserved red brick hexagonal tower on a low hill. On three alternate faces are set circular turrets with low dome-and-ball tops, which rise for two thirds of its 120 feet. Between them, the walls are set a little forward to the same height and end in classical pediments. The tower is seven storeys high, with pointed windows in the bottom part and round-headed ones in the octagon. There is a fireplace half way up but no sign of a staircase—there may have been

a free-standing wooden one. Altogether an impressive puzzle—our date was *c.* 1700, the *Shell Guide* says mid-eighteenth century; so far I haven't been able to find any dates for Humphrey Sturt, who is said to have built it as an observatory.

Sturt's Folly, Horton

Kimmeridge
Tower, late eighteenth century SY 9180
A circular tower three storeys high, with a gothick quatrefoil handrail and machicola-tions, but with a Doric colonnade running round the ground floor, a typical mixture of architecture in a folly—a good tower in a beautiful position on the clifftop.

Milbourne St Andrews
An obelisk crowned with a ball. SY 8196

Milton Abbas *Milton Abbey*
Sham Ruins, *c.* 1790 ST 8202
See page 71.

Morden *Charborough Park*

Tower, 1790   SY 9296

Charborough Park is superbly planted with enormous clumps of trees standing in great sweeps of grass; it is approached up a rhodo-dendron-lined drive, so that one bursts out of the enclosure into the open landscape. The tower was built in 1790 and restored in 1840, after it had been struck by lightning the year before, by John Samuel Sawbridge Erle Drax. It is 120 feet high, octagonal with five storeys. Buttresses go up to the moulding dividing the first and second floors, and terminate in crocketed pinnacles. The path to the tower from the house is most impressive, along a walk bordered with trees, and every 40 yards a massive pair of stone pedestals, to the foot of a flight of 47 steps leading to the tower.

Charborough is often said to be the original of Rings-Hill Speer, which had 'a door of wood, rust-stained', a tablet illegible for lichen, a flat roof with a telescope and lovers called Lady Constantine, or Viviette, and Swithin St Cleeve, all in a novelette by Thomas Hardy. It is still a lovely tower.

Also at Charborough is a grotto where in 1686 'a set of patriotic gentlemen of this neighbourhood concerted in the great plot of the GLORIOUS REVOLUTION'. The grotto is not very elaborate, being a sort of dim cell 20 feet across, 10 feet deep and 25 feet high, lit by a single eye from above. Not very exciting as a folly, but showing that a dark cellary atmosphere was as essential to plotters then as it is now.

In the nineteenth century, John Sawbridge Erle Drax built a big barrel-vaulted mausoleum at Holnest, in which he is said to have held a rehearsal of his funeral, but this was pulled down in 1935.

Moreton *Moreton House*

Obelisk, eighteenth century   SY 8188

See page 120.

Poole Harbour

Simpson's Folly†   SZ 0290

Simpson built a house on the sand, but even after he fled in terror lest he should be engulfed by the sea his house still stood, and was inhabited by undesirable vagrants. So the Poole Corporation blew it up, and now only large blocks of concrete can be seen at low tide.

Portesham *Black Down*

Monument   SY 6085

Sir Thomas Hardy, the friend of Nelson, was born near here and this most hideous monument, exactly described by Edward Hyams as 'a factory chimney with a crinoline', is to his memory. Nelson himself gave Hardy an exquisite clock in the shape of a sunflower; what he would have thought of this is beyond speculation.

Southbourne *On the front*

Shell Garden, contemporary   SZ 1592

See page 255.

Steeple

Bond's Folly, or Grange Arch,   SY 9282
c. 1740

See page 34.

The tower at Charborough Park

Swanage

The Great Globe, etc., nineteenth   SZ 0478
century

Every visitor to Swanage sees the Great Globe and will probably learn that it was given to the town by two quarrymen. Fortunately, in 1971, the very pattern of a local history monograph was published on them (*Curiosities of Swanage* by David Lewer and J. Bernard Calkin, The Friary Press, Dorchester), and the quarrymen disappear, to become John Mowlem, founder of the big firm of London contractors, and his nephew George Burt, later his partner. And the Great Globe is only one of a long series of ornaments that they gave to their native town. John Mowlem did certainly start as a quarry-boy in Swanage but went to London and later set up on his own at Paddington in about 1823. He retired to Swanage in 1844, and set about waking up the town, getting a pier and tramway built to load the stones, giving the town an Institute, a King Alfred Monument (granite column with four anachronistic cannon-balls on top), a tall granite pyramid as tomb for himself and his wife and an obelisk to 'Albert the Good'.

George Burt was now in charge in London, where, as now, things were constantly being demolished, and he gathered up a number of nice stone objects, saved them from destruction and set them up in Swanage. The biggest is the Clocktower, which was first put up in 1854 at the southern end of London Bridge to commemorate the Duke of Wellington in the perpendicular style. It was hopelessly in the way, and Mowlem's took it down without charge and sailed it away by boat to Swanage in 1866–7. Alas, there was an objection to its church-like spire and in 1904 a nasty little cupola was put on top instead. Then there are two cut-down Ionic columns and an Ionic capital; stone, iron columns and balustrades for his own house from the demolition of Billingsgate Market; granite chips to face it from the base of the Albert Memorial; some 'Parthenon' horses; an arch from Hyde Park Corner; three statues from the Royal Exchange, the jawbone of a whale and many other fascinating fragments, far too many to list here, and all safely recorded.

But it is impossible not to quote the inscriptions from a non-Mowlem/Burt memorial, a big stone near Belle Vue Farm near Herston:

BENEATH THIS STONE LIE OUR MULE
SHE WAS A FAITHFUL CREATURE
DRAWING UP THE STONE FROM THIS
QUARRY FOR 32 YEARS. DIED AGED 34 YEARS
ALSO
OUR LITTLE CAT NAMED TOO TOO
WHO FOLLOWED HER MASTER FROM THIS
QUARRY TO HIS HOME AND BACK FOR 20 MNTHS.
R.I.P.

Wimborne St Giles *St Giles House*

Grotto, 1753   SU 0412
See page 165.
At Deer Park Farm there is a good but decaying square red brick pavilion with a finely carved coat of arms and the motto LOVE SERVE. Once there was also a castellated folly with towers, but this has gone.

The Great Globe at Swanage

Durham

Only a few follies, Raby Castle the best.

Barningham
Grouse obelisk, nineteenth century   NZ 0810
When Sir Frederick Milbank moved his shoot from Wemmergill Moor to Barningham he also moved the pink granite obelisk which records his bag of 190 grouse in a 20 minute drive on 20 August 1872. The six guns together got 2,070 in the day, and the season's awful bag for Wemmergill was 17,064.

Bishop Auckland *The Bishop's Palace*
Deer House, 1760   NZ 2129
See page 217.
Near Bishop Auckland at Brussleton there used to be an elegantly proportioned octagon tower built by a member of the Carr family early in the eighteenth century. It had a flight of stairs leading to a large room and its golden stone was nicely blackened by soot, like so many follies in the north, and by a fire in 1935.

Gainford *Gainford Hall*
Column, 1748*   NZ 1817
A big Tuscan column to commemorate the peace of Aachen. It used to be at Stanwick Hall.

Hawthorn *Sailors Hall*
Tower, late eighteenth century   NZ 4446

A tower near the sea, now in a wood so that one cannot tell if it was built for retreat or prospect. It is castellated, with gothick windows.

Raby Castle
Eyecatcher, *c.* 1750   NZ 1322
A folly on a hill behind Raby Castle, built of stone and brick, about 25 feet high, a long castellated façade with pairs of curious tapering stone towers flanking a round-headed stone arch. The space above the arch is filled in with brick on which is painted a gothick window. On each side of the towers are castellated walls of brick with real windows; all this is façade only, but further out again are square brick towers, and one is used as a cottage.

Westerton
Tower, late eighteenth century   NZ 2331
A circular un-crenellated, random-rubble observatory, built by Thomas Wright, 1711–86, astronomer and mathematician, that has only become folly through the passage of time and its position on the tatty green in the middle of a dirty village. The tower is sprinkled with arrow-slits (single and crossed), buttresses and little windows; it has a good door. Most so-called observatories are nothing to do with astronomy at all, merely observation posts for landscapes, but this one was real.

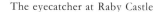

The eyecatcher at Raby Castle

East Sussex

A sharply divided county, with flat rich agricultural weald in the north and chalk downs in the south. Mad Jack Fuller's follies at Brightlington and Dallington are the most endearing nonsenses here.

Brightling *Brightling Park ex Rose Hill*
Group, *c.* 1820   TQ 6821
See page 230.

Saxonbury Tower, Eridge

Eridge
Saxonbury Tower   TQ 5535
A round brick tower which was at one time whitewashed, standing in the middle of thick woods, pine, rhododendron, oak; the summit is in a very dilapidated state, but the climber 66 feet above the ground is rewarded with good views across the country around.

Hastings *Baldslow; Beauport Park Hotel*
Obelisk, *c.* 1790   TQ 8110
For fans of Sir John Soane.

Gannymead
Model Village, 1955   TQ 8110
A model of the Sussex dream; no supermarkets, and even the newspaper office is half timbered.

Heathfield *Heathfield Park*
Gibraltar Tower, 1793   TQ 5821
On the outskirts of Heathfield is a wood full of Nissen huts and broken-down motor cars; about a quarter of a mile from the road, approached up a track, stands this tower. Recently the top floor was burnt out and the fire spread down, but fortunately left remains of the first and ground floors. A note in the *Gentleman's Magazine* for 1793, records the laying of the last stone.

Oct. 26. This day the last stone was laid of the Tower in Heathfield Park and the scaffolding removed.

A little account of this structure intended by the present owner as a memorial of respect to the character of his predecessor, the late Lord Heathfield, and which may be considered as an ornament to our country, may not be unacceptable to our readers.

It was begun on the 2nd March 1792, is built of stone and from the bottom is of octagonal shape to the height of about 15 feet, whence it rises in a circular form to the top of the battlement which is 55 feet from the ground. It is 22 feet in diameter and contains a circular staircase and three apartments which are to be fitted up in a Gothic style, and ornamented with views of Gibraltar and the operation of the Siege.

Over the door on the outside of the tower is a tablet with this inscription 'Calpes defensori', the letters of which are to be formed of the metal of the guns from the Spanish floating batteries and let into the stone.

In each of the two lower rooms are remains of the most exquisite gothick plasterwork, utterly refined and delicate. The walls are white, and round the alcoves and the doors and the windows are thin mouldings, prussian blue and orange. The alcoves are a grey-green and the decoration is painted, orange and prussian blue again. (Visit soon.)

This folly was built by Francis Newbery to commemorate the gallantry of Lord Heathfield at the siege of Gibraltar. Few soldiers have received posthumously such beautiful medals as Gibraltar Tower.

Nearby, in *Cade Street,* is a pillar to mark the assassination of Jack Cade in 1450, when his rebellion failed.

Ringmer *Willingham House*
Grotto, *c.* 1800   TQ 4513
A small and very pretty grotto of the cosiest domestic kind, near the house across the lawn. On top is a wooden octagon gazebo with stairs curving up, and underneath a tiny grotto, heavily overgrown with clematis which chains it to its attendant yew. One side and two halves are open, with Roman Doric pillars and the floor has four circles of knapped flint, centres and infill of pebbles. The walls have 5 feet of flints, shells, ammonites, fossils, minerals—all the correct ingredients, and the roof, which dips in the middle, is all shells. A square slate table is supported on a flint and rock leg.

Stanmer *Stanmer House*
Monument, 1775   TQ 3410
Here is another of those strange Coade stone monuments with three dished sides supported

on tortoises; others at Brocklesbury, Lucan and Mount Edgecumbe. This one was built by a Lady Pelham to the memory of her father. It would be nice to know more about them.

West Firle
Firle Tower, c. 1870   TQ 4607
A castellated round tower, built so that the keeper who lived in it could signal with a telegraph to another keeper in Plashet deer park in Ringmer, seven miles away.

Gibraltar Tower, Heathfield

Essex

A county predominantly flat and farmed, where quite small changes of height give an impression of rolling hills. It has inspired no spectacularly landscaped parks, no wild eyecatchers; the best folly goes underground in Epping Forest.

Alresford *The Quarters*

Chinese Fishing Pavilion, *c.* 1765   TM 0722
A pretty square pavilion decreasing by four pendentives to an octagon roof in two curved tiers, with a curved-roof verandah towards the lake; it was converted into a house in 1951–2. Constable painted it in 1816 when the verandah, with four flat columns and a criss-cross balustrade, stood out over the lake.

Brightlingsea

Bateman's Folly   TM 0917
Bateman is said to have built this tower so that it could be used as a lighthouse, but Trinity House objected, because it was situated in the wrong place. It stands about 25 feet high, and is built of pebbly concrete. Now used by members of the Colne Yacht Club.

Cavendish *Pentlow*

Bull's Tower   TL 8245
A 70-foot-high brick tower, with narrow windows, decorated with crosses and diamonds of dark brick. A tablet above the door bears this inscription: 'Erected to the memory of his honoured parents The Rev. John Bull M.A. and Margaret his wife, on a spot they loved so well by Edward Bull M.A. 1859.'

Colchester *Colchester Castle*   TM 0025

A classical arch, 1747, which is all that remains of a small building, erected by Charles Gray, a local antiquary, who owned the castle. A notebook of Gray's records '1747. Aug. took down ye Rotunda building from ye low place and set it up at the other end of the terrace'. The ruin has built into it a block of Roman masonry.

The Minories, High Street

Summerhouse, 1745   TM 0025
A rendered brick gothick castellated façade, extended on each side with small quatrefoiled walls, in front of an octagon summer house. It looks as though the octagon is the 1745 part, with the façade added at the end of the century when the house was either built or re-faced.

Bateman's Folly, Brightlingsea

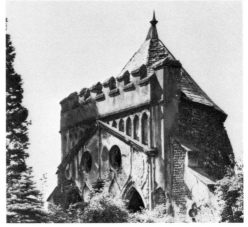

The Minories, Colchester

Colne Engaine *Colne Park*
Column, 1791   TL 8530
Designed by Sir John Soane, and crowned by an urn, but not especially exciting.

Heybridge *The Towers*   TL 8708
Two gothic revival towers in the garden, 1873.*

High Beech *The Catacombs*   TQ 4098
See pages 194 and 197.

Laindon *Arterial Road*
Sham Castle, twentieth century*   TQ 6888
I have been told of a modern sham castle here, built by a previous owner, with two round castellated towers.

Matching Green
Folly Garden, twentieth century   TL 5511
See page viii.
A new folly on the village green, a group of concrete figures set in the rough between two neat gardens. They include a huntsman, an unbribable policeman, Mr. Cliff Michelmore, an Ascot Boy and an Epsom Girl, Miss Douglas Cement, Prince Philip and a gorilla, all made of concrete (with blue glass marbles for eyes) by Mr. H. Smith.

Middleton
Prince of Wales Avenue
The Arch, 1841   TL 8639
A very charming folly indeed. It is not, as the name suggests, in a street in the village, but stands in an avenue of trees across the fields, and can be reached from the church. It is built of knapped flint and brick with large pieces of good mediaeval gothic inset on the front and now probably more ruinous than was intended. Round the arch:

> PLANTED BY OLIVER RAYMOND.
> LLB. RECTOR. OF. THIS. PARISH:
> IX:. NOV: MDCCCXLI: THE . DAY.
> OF. HRH. THE PRINCES BIRTH.

Southend-on-Sea
The Crowstone   TQ 8286
An eighteenth-century obelisk, re-erected here in 1836 which used to mark the eastern boundary of the City of London's jurisdiction over the Thames. I cannot find out if a similar monument marked the western boundary, or even where this one originally stood.

Takeley *Hatfield Forest*
Shell House, 1759   TL 5622
One thousand acres of King Harold's forest, now owned by the National Trust and nothing at all to do with Hatfield, Herts., but lying between Bishops Stortford and Takeley. A very good place for a day out, with magnificent trees and chases, a stream and, by the lake, the Shell House. This was built by the Houblon family, who had the forest from 1729 to 1924, and is a pretty rectangular classical building of knapped flint with unknapped dressing and rustications embellished with shells, vitreous blue glass and spar. On each side wall is a huge white flint star and the keystone of the entrance arch is covered with a displayed bird in white shells, on a flint-chip background. The interior is high with simple shell patterns on a shallow domed ceiling, and white panelled walls with ribbon decoration in a warm pale blue. Once the room was extensively decorated with shell work by Laetitia Houblon and what remains is the finest I have ever seen. There are two panels; one has an architectural frame with free-fall swags, enclosing a picture of seaweed on a rock with four shell butterflies, all most delicately done, as with the heads of pins, in minute shells; some flowers are made with limpets, inside out, perhaps a tenth of an inch across, and there is a passion flower to deceive a gardener. In the other, though the frame is less lovely, the artist has dared successfully to mix real butterflies with the shell ones . . . a stool in sham bamboo chinoiserie must be part of the original furniture. Damp was the enemy; the forest was not drained until the middle of the last century, but anyone interested in shellwork must see the two little panels.

The shell house in Hatfield Forest (see page 323)

Gloucestershire

A large county with a lot of big houses, much landscaping and some very superior follies set in country that varies from the flat green fields along the estuary of the Severn to the windy Cotswolds and drystone walls.

Badminton

Group, eighteenth century ST 8183

The Shorter Oxford English Dictionary gives us '1853. (The Duke of Beaufort's country seat.) 1. A kind of claret cup. 2. A game resembling lawn-tennis, played with shuttlecocks 1874.' Undoubtedly the game was named for the house, which by the 1880s was such a syno-nym for sport that a long series of books on sports and pastimes was edited by the eighth duke and called *The Badminton Library*; but the flying shuttlecocks have in turn imposed their lightness on the follies.

The Hermit's Cell, or Root-house, is described on page 179, but Thomas Wright also designed for the fourth duke the castel-lated farm buildings, the pretty lodges and Ragged Castle.

Batsford *Batsford Park*

Japanese Rest House SP 1934

These are in the famous Japanese gardens

designed by Lord Redesdale when he retired from his post as Ambassador to Japan about a century ago. They are very different in scale and sweep from the usual miniature horrors, but then, he had been there to see. The rest house is set up a slope among very fine trees—this a famous collection—up four rough rock steps with bronze dragon-flies on each side; a third, smaller, one is on the roof. It is a square red brick building with wide eaves of the roof supported on twelve pine trunks round the edge of a red tile platform. On each side of the door is a strip of Japanese characters extolling the virtues of bamboo— there are many clumps of it planted, but none was used in the architecture.

Inside, there is a white board ceiling, red brick walls and more red tiles for floor— perhaps the walls were once covered with silk or paper.

There is a bronze Buddha, two bronze deer and a very nice animal like a veil-tailed Peke stuffed with tennis balls, his paws on a cloisonné ball (see pages 130 and 132).

Berkeley *Berkeley Castle*
Kennels as Eyecatcher,   ST 6999
eighteenth century
See page 218.

Bisley *Nether Lippiatt Manor*
Obelisk*   SO 9106
A stone obelisk on a plinth, with an inscription to the memory of a horse that died in 1721.

Bourton-on-the-Water *The Old New Inn*
Model Village   SP 1621
See page 271.

Chalford *The Grove*
Gazebo   SO 8903
A very steep garden still laid out in the terraces made for drying wool. Right at the top is a lovely gothick gazebo with ogival windows, just one step further towards folly than the average summer-house. Parts of the terraces are held up on arches, and there is a little grot-work, a lion and fragments of stone.

Chipping Camden *Kingcombe*   SP 1539
A very small sham castle with external stairs is being built here. Underneath is a tiny grotto with a kitchen, a secret passage, two hiding places, and sound effects.

Church Icomb
Guy's Folly or Icomb Round House   SP 2123
This nice little folly was built in 1805 in brick and Roman cement. It is high on the top of the Cotswolds and consists of two round towers joined together, one shortish and one taller and thinner, both crenellated, and both stained with moss and wet weather. It is an anti-Napoleonic invasion fort, a look-out for farmer Guy to oversee his workmen when the beech trees grew too tall, or Kitchener used it for watching his troops manoeuvre before the Boer War. *Au choix.* Now scheduled for demolition.

Bourton-on-the-Water

The Grove, Chalford

Cirencester *Cirencester Park*   SP 0102
See page 31. As well as the follies mentioned, there is a hexagon of 1736, Queen Anne's Monument, with her statue on a Doric column, 1741, and a tall obelisk.

Coates *Thames Head*   SO 9801
Father Thames, rather larger than life, with no right hand and no visible river. He reclines with his left elbow on a bale, with another behind him, and a barrel, and a shield with the arms of the City of London. The statue was given by Mr H. Scott Freeman, and the Conservators of the River Thames set it here in 1958 to mark the source of the river. (Now damaged, and removed to safety.)

Fairford *Fairford Park*
Column   SP 1503
Buildings of England refers to a 'column in the fields towards Querrington', and there it is, a beautiful walk from the road and at last not to be reached, distant and romantic in a sea of standing corn, a fine Tuscan column. On the wide square entablature is a drum with a ball on top and a picturesque tuft of weed.

Lower Swell
Cottage, nineteenth century   SP 1726
A cottage with notable details; there is a curious hood over the door and windows in the Indian style. It was made from pieces left over from the building of Sezincote when it was hoped to establish Lower Swell as a spa.

North Nibley
Tyndale Monument, 1866   ST 7496
An unspeakably ugly sleazily tapering stone tower with a pyramidal roof plus cross, with dull blind gothic windows. I have been given two heights for it, 111 feet and 130 feet, but it really doesn't matter. It was designed by S. S. Teulon and is in 'grateful remembrance of William Tyndale, translator of the English Bible who first caused the New Testament to be printed in the mother tongue of his countrymen; born near this spot, he suffered martyrdom at Vilvorde in Flanders on 6th October, 1536.'

Siddington *The Round House*
Tower, eighteenth century   SU 0499
A particularly charming little three-storey

The eyecatcher at Amberley

Rodborough Fort, Stroud

tapering round tower, with castellations and a becoming pine tree. I was told that in spite of appearances it was never a windmill, but was built, with two nearby cottages, by a Dutchman who settled here. It looks rather like a chess-rook.

Stanway *Stanway*
Pyramid, eighteenth century SP 0633
See page 124.

Stinchcombe *Stancombe Park*
Folly Garden, early nineteenth ST 7697
century
See pages 247 and 259.

Stroud *Amberley*
The Gateways, Eyecatcher, SO 8503
eighteenth century
Sir George Onesiphorus Paul built this as an eyecatcher to Rodborough Manor. It is a delightful object, even though when it was converted into a house the big arch was darkly filled in, with a big window at the bottom, and the castellations of the two nice plump round towers were also filled in.

Castellations remain on the curtain wall, and the towers have two-light gothick windows and cross-slits.

Stroud *Rodborough Fort*
Sham Castle, 1761 SO 8504
A large and solid sham castle built by Captain Hawker 'on common land granted by the Lord of the Manor'. It is very conspicuous on a Cotswold hill above Stroud, with round, square, straight, battered, castellated, machicolated towers and walls, but fails lamentably as a picturesque object. It was converted into a house in 1870. The Tower in Woodchester Park is part of an unfinished house for Lord Ducie, partly built in 1846.

Winchcombe *Bleby House*
Grotto, *c.* 1700 SP 0228
A small domed round grotto, about 10 feet across made of rock, tufa and shells with a snaggle-toothed ceiling. Its chief interest is its probably very early date and side windows made of natural holes in two big rocks. Winchcombe was the shrine of St Kenelm, a great centre of pilgrimage, and the grotto is said to stand over the place where his coffin was found.

Greater London

More remains round the outer fringes of Greater London than could be expected; most of the public parks were once private ones and anything large enough may have been kept, though anything small or fragile has usually been pulled down for the sake of upkeep. Scattered here and there are obelisks and columns, perhaps moved in the interests of traffic, but preserved when whole streets are demolished—Victoria, away! Egypt, survive!

Acton *Churchfield Road East*
Obelisk
This is one of the few relics of great houses that remain; a pleasant obelisk to the memory of the Earl of Derwentwater who was executed for taking part in the 1715 rebellion.

Bayswater *Leinster Gardens*
Sham Façade
Two sham façades built to preserve the line of houses broken when the Metropolitan Railway was built in 1863. Behind is nothing but the railway line.

Bethnal Green *Meath Gardens**
A small gothick arch.

Carshalton *Carshalton House*
Grotto and Water House
This was one of the earliest picturesque landscapes—it must have been much larger once—and was probably designed by Bridgeman. The grotto would have been a good one; it is quite complicated and has still some lovely flint niches in the wings, but its lake is now almost always dry (waterworks have changed the levels), and it is a little blunted all over. In the centre are three arches spanned by a curved pediment. On top of the mount is a free rock and tufa grotto arch, now with a holy statue. Inside is a simply vaulted chamber, an ante-room and a third round niched room that may once have been an ice house—a passage runs to it from the other side of the main room.

The Water House is like nothing else; *Buildings of England* suggests Vanbrugh. Whoever the designer was it is superb, a church-tower eyecatcher with pinnacles and lovely colour, red and yellow bricks and stone. It has a five-bay orangery, then a pretty room with an oval ceiling and the pump room behind to take the water up the tower. To balance the orangery is a bath-house with the prettiest imaginable tiles and another room behind. But the outside is the thing.

Carshalton Park
Grotto, probably *c.* 1730   TQ 2761
First Carshalton Park, then Carshalton Place (one never finished, the other demolished), now Park again and public, all landscaping municipally smoothed away. There remains the grotto at the end of a long dry canal. It is plain, with no traces of earlier ornament, but has a certain subtlety. It is under a mount and curves round the head of the canal with its top in another long low curve to end in piers. There is a big round central arch, and two alcoves each side. Inside, there is an anteroom with complicated niches, small and cobby, and then the main room, about 20 feet across under a shallow octagon dome. Once there was a lantern on top.

Chiswick *Chiswick House*
The remnants of the grotto and cascade that can be seen on the many engravings are still here. The rest of the grounds are well preserved and the house has been superbly restored; one of London's best visits.

Croydon
Atmospheric Railway Folly, 1845†
This was a most fascinating folly, now demolished. The Atmospheric Railway was an early experiment in jet propulsion. When it failed (more details in the first edition of this book), the gothic engine-house from the Croydon terminus was bought by the owner of Park

Hill House and put up as a coach house. But there is a fine castellated Norman water-tower set high on an artificial mound in the public park nearby.

East Ham *Byron Avenue*
Marble Halls

Some time before 1953 Edmund Lusignea turned his house into a small palace for his invalid wife, with a baroque parlour superbly beyond the expectations of East Ham, in the best tradition of the London town house, riches concealed. Unfortunately I have not been able to get confirmation of its survival.

Forest Hill *Dartmouth Road*
St Antholin's Spire

The top of the spire of St Antholin's church in the city was taken down in 1874 because it was considered to be unsafe, and was erected here on a circular brick base, around which is another semi-circular wall, and then six columns to make an arbour of twiddly brickwork. The folly now stands in the middle of a housing estate.

St. Antholin's Spire

Gunnersbury *Gunnersbury Park*
Gunnersbury, now a public park, is chiefly associated with the Rothschilds, some of whom lived here from 1835 until 1917, but the folly works, which are borderline, were started between 1763 and 1786 by Princess Amelia, the third daughter of George III.

The tower in Gunnersbury Park

She built a gothick pavilion as bath-house and dairy, with the bath in a flint grotto. It has been much altered, shells and paintings removed, and white tiles put in and arcading added, presumably early in the nineteenth century.

The stables were designed for the Rothschilds by Smirke in about 1836, hidden by a screen with a sham ruin tower about 30 feet high, with the usual pointed windows and crumbling skyline. Another interesting screen, probably later, has niches framed in columns of red clay drain pipes.

On the shore of the Potomac Pond is a good tower built in the 1860s. The ground floor is square, and from this rises an octagon for the next two floors; the first has four pointed windows filled with fine tracery, and the second quatrefoil windows, which are merely decorative, the top room being lit by a lantern concealed by the height of the walls and filled with yellow stained glass, a cunning device for producing a very gothick effect without destroying the line of the castellations. The ground floor is set above a boathouse reached by a staircase inside.

Hampton Court *Hampton Court House*
Grotto*
I have been told of a small but pretty grotto,
richly clotted with ammonites and minerals.

Hendon *Manor Hall Avenue*
Obelisk
When David Garrick lived at Hendon Hall
(which has a most beautiful portico) he put
up on the opposite hill an obelisk to Shakespeare, with statues of Shakespeare and three
muses, all heavily vandalized, round the foot.

Highgate *Kenwood*
Sham bridge, eighteenth century
Here is one of the prettiest pieces of small
landscaping anywhere, with mown grass
descending from the house to two ponds. On
the left of the far one, and apparently crossing
a stream, is a sham wooden bridge, painted
white, exactly where the composition demands. Dr. Johnson's Summer-house is in the
garden, rustic, with a hermitage cross on top,
and from the Heath to the east can be seen
the ruins of an eyecatcher cottage and a neatly
preserved small round nineteenth-century
stone tower in the neighbouring grounds.

Dr. Johnson's summerhouse

Ilford *Claybury Hall*
Grotto†
An account of this, which was destroyed by
fire in 1956, is in a notebook kept by S. Prout
and dated July 1804—possibly Samuel Prout
the painter who was certainly working in
Cambridgeshire and Essex between 1803 and
1805:

'. . . near the house, cloathed in Wood is a
small but curious grotto. Erected by Mr.
H.—The Outside is formed by trunks of
trees.—the inside with shells spars &
minerals laid out with much ingenuity &
taste. On the window is represented Faith
Hope and Charity—on the door the arms
of the family painted by Mrs Holey.—on
the floor around 5 feet in diameter is laid
with horses teeth. . . .'

Kew *Kew Gardens*
Pagoda, 1761; Ruin, 1760, etc.
The present marvellous gardens are those of
Richmond Palace and Kew Palace, joined.
Bridgeman designed the Richmond Lodge
gardens for the Princess of Wales (later Queen
Caroline) and Kent made Merlin's Cave for
her (see page 178). These were the gardens
west of the Holly Walk, and were redesigned
by Brown in the 1760s, while Princess
Augusta's Kew to the east was being designed
by Chambers, with a number of temples and
rotundas and of course the pagoda. If one
goes in by the Victoria Gate and turns left,
the path goes by the incredible flagstaff and
the interesting building designed to take
Marianne North's remarkable paintings and
then goes under the Ruined Arch, built by
Chambers in 1759–60, heavily rusticated with
a tall central arch and smaller ones flanking
it. A cut across past the refreshment pavilion
to the Pagoda Vista will give the best view of
that (see page 113), and to the west is the
Chokushi-Mon, a replica of the Gateway of
the Imperial Messenger made for the Japan–
British Exhibition of 1910 and later presented
to Kew. Chambers also built at least a
Chinese Temple, a Turkish Mosque and a
Moorish Alhambra; alas, all gone, like
Muntz's gothic cathedral and Old Moorish

pavilion. Drawings exist for some of these, and for a hermitage at Richmond. It is tragic that they have gone; much work was done here in the nineteenth century, and taste had changed. Not a folly, but not to be missed, is Queen's Cottage of *c.* 1772 painted by Princess Elizabeth with light decorations of flowers; this is the country cottage we would really like to have.

Kingsbury
Fortified Villa, 1935
One of a quite ordinary row of suburban houses has added to the front two mighty stone towers. They are battlemented and fitted with ordinary casement windows; a flight of steps leads up to one of the rooms on the first floor, while the front door is under them. Nothing could be finer folly than the ordinary house peering above the fortified additions, or a better expression of all the motifs which have led people to make similar buildings the expression of their deepest hopes and fears.

Marylebone *Wimpole Street*
See page 197.

Mitcham 84 *Phipps Bridge Road*
This is one of Mitcham's old roads, almost lost in the general dereliction of outer London. The start is hopeless—we must be in the wrong road, wrong town, wrong England— but there is a charming row of cottages, Everet's Terrace 1824 and then a round tower, lumps of stone with big trimmed pieces for keystones and voussoirs round gothick windows. It is joined to the terrace by a short castellated wall with another window and a matching door, and there is some more at the back. It is said to be about 100 years old, added to the terrace with stone from rebuilding work at the Tower of London which was dumped at Mitcham and prudently used. But one chimney fits on top of the terrace, which seems an unlikely way of building; it looks like that common eighteenth-century pattern of two round towers joined by a wall (and the windows were never made in the 1870s), with one tower pulled down to

Phipp's Bridge Road

make room for another house on the terrace. It would put this *c.* 1790, and the Ordnance Survey map for 1816 suggests that it might have been a lodge gate to Merton Abbey.

Osterley *Osterley Park*
Grotto
A very slight one, in the house and under the staircase as at Chatsworth, but less gloomy.

Penge *Belvedere Road*
A castellated brick tower, now part of a house.

Crystal Palace Gardens
It is heartbreaking to look up *Crystal Palace* in a Baedeker of 1900 and read of the Crystal Fountain, the Alhambra Court, the Tropical Department and the Wurtemburg Collection of Stuffed Animals (about 1500 in number) and the Palace of Illusions, but at least the Geological Department remains. 'It contains full-size models of antediluvian animals,—the Megalosaurus, Ichthyosaurus, Pterodactyl, Palaeatherium, Megatherium, and the Irish Elk (found in the Isle of Man)—together with

The prehistoric animals, Crystal Palace

the contemporaneous geological forma-
tions.—' And there they all are, down at the
bottom of the gardens, best reached from the
Thicket Road entrance, the wild (and highly
educational) animals, grouped round a lake,
predator with victim, a peaceable kingdom
for Penge. The opening of the Geological
Department was correctly celebrated by
dining in the largest dinosaur—the tradition
is preserved in California today; see page 278.

After the disastrous fire of 1937, the park
was closed, and much of it was occupied by
the army during the war, but the monsters
were fenced carefully off and have now been
splendidly re-painted. They are life-size, made
of bronze in 1854 by B. Waterhouse Hawkins,
directed by Professor R. Owen, the whole
inspired by Professor D. A. Anstead. In 1961
a gorilla by David Gwynne was added. There
is a menagerie, boating lake, refreshments
and the animals; a very good expedition.

Ravensbury *Pleasure grounds*
Sham Ruin, eighteenth century
The remains of a small eighteenth-century
sham ruin. The remnant of the tower is the
largest single block of masonry, and although
an uninteresting folly, it is nicely fenced in, so
may survive to be one of the few which will
be seen close to London.

Roehampton *Tibbetts Corner*
Obelisk

. . . On the 22nd November 1776 RESOLVED
that JOHN SAWBRIDGE ESQ the late Lord
Mayor of the City having laid a Foundation
Stone for erecting an Obelisk on Putney
Common to commemorate the invention
of FIRE PLATES to secure buildings from
FIRE by DAVID HARTLEY ESQ, The Committee of City Lands be empowered to erect
and complete the same.

They put up a neat red brick obelisk about
25 feet high with a stone cap and base, but
they did not anticipate the whirl of traffic
that now isolates the obelisk on its patch of
common.
Fine legends have grown up about this
simple object; it is said to commemorate the
first fire-proof house, built with thin iron
plates cased in plaster and set in the floors;
the King and Queen dined in the house with
fires roaring in the room below them.

Shooters Hill
Severndroog Castle, 1784

See page 205.

Soho *Soho Square*
Summer-house Screen
In the middle of the square is a small half-timbered summer-house, very popular with the old ladies who sit there in the afternoons. Besides being a resting place, it also hides a ventilating shaft.

South Kensington *Kensington Gardens*
The Albert Memorial
Many people regard this as a folly.

Stanmore
Obelisk
I have no intention of finding out any more about this one. It is brick, rendered with Roman cement on a rusticated base, like many others. But this is dedicated to Julius Caesar, because Boadicea is said to have poisoned herself in a nearby field. . . .

Streatham *St Michael's Convent*
Tower
St Michael's Convent was once the home of Sir Henry Tate, with huge conservatories and a relatively small landscape garden, complete with ornamental water. At the end of the garden there used to be a small farm, and on the farm road a very pretty two-storey octagon folly, older than the house, brick and rubble stone dressings. The bottom was entered through a gothick door and lit by a gothick window and three slits; it was about 10 feet high, with a shallow vaulted ceiling and was full of grain, ducks and stacked wood. Now the farm has gone, replaced by a big school; but the tower, now blocked up, still stands.

Tottenham *Bruce Castle*
Tower
A good red brick tower about 20 feet high, castellated and deeply machicolated, ringed with blind pointed arches, and pointed windows above.

Twickenham *Cross Deep*
Pope's Grotto
See page 150.

Strawberry Hill
The Chapel in the Wood
A charming chapel built by Walpole to display his collection of stained glass, and a shrine of the thirteenth century which he brought back from Rome. Unfortunately this building is in a very dilapidated condition; the special blue and red tiles have been broken up and the plaster work is down, but the Roman Catholic Teacher's College which now owns Strawberry Hill is going to restore it. A rustic cottage, sham bridge and shell bench have all gone.

York House
Grotto-Fountain
In the gardens of York House, now municipal offices, is a grotto-fountain-group, of bewildering size and content. It arrived, apparently from Italy (and the figures are said to be of Carrara marble), at Whitaker Wright's Witley Court (*q.v.*), in 1904. It seems never to have been unpacked, and at the great sale in 1906 Ratan J. Tata (later knighted) bought it for York House, which he had also just bought, and had it set up as screen to a warehouse, now gone. Mr G. Turner, the borough librarian, tells me that the 'actual subject has always been a matter of controversy, each of the following suggestions having its champions:

a. The pearl fishers
b. A group of Nereides or river nymphs
c. The birth of Venus.'

It might, though, have simply been amassed in the quarries for a megalomaniac client from the large items of unsold watery stock, always on hand for fountains . . .

Wanstead *Wanstead Park*
Grotto, eighteenth century
Here was one of the most famous great houses, by Colin Campbell for Sir Richard Child, and the first big piece of Palladian, 1715. Everyone went there, Hogarth painted a ball in progress; today the grounds are a public park. The canal, now a lake, is still there, with the façade of the grotto, which

Osvald Siren says was designed by Kent. The artificial mount that covered it has gone and some of the base brick structure is exposed—made, I thought, from the bricks of an earlier house. There are the openings to the water in a great pile-up or rocks, minerals, ammonites and hunks of classical architecture, with an arched opening above, set back. Sometimes one can get inside, sometimes not, for the canal is part of the river Roding, and rises, but there is a passage to the water and the boats, with niches and still some decoration of felspar and shells—perhaps the East India Company money was running low by the time the grotto was lined, for some of them are barnacles.

Westminster *Grosvenor Gardens*
Shell-work, twentieth century
Two little square toolsheds with shell work, minimal but better than nothing.

Victoria Embankment
Cleopatra's Needle
At last here is a genuine Egyptian obelisk, one of the most famous relics of the ancient world, 68½ feet high in red granite, weighing 180 tons and flanked by bronze sphinxes, by Mr G. Vulliamy. The Needle, which may have been in the way lying at Alexandria, was given to us by Mohammed Ali, undelivered. Dr Erasmus Wilson gave £10,000 to get it here and up in 1878.

Woolwich *Woolwich Common*
The Rotunda
The museum is inside the gigantic tent erected by John Nash in St James Park to house the banquets for the allied monarchs in 1814. It was much too good to lose, so in 1819 it was put up here on a yellow brick wall matching its segments with some ridiculous columns for trim; but the tent and its great ropes are superb, like the top of a huge pagoda.

Greater Manchester

Industry covers most of the county, but there are a few follies. Obelisks at Atherton, Leigh, Orrell and Rochdale.

Bardsley *Heartshead*
Tower, 1863   SD 9303
A small round one on a hill top to commemorate the marriage of the Prince of Wales.

Manchester *Heaton Park*
Colonnade, early nineteenth century SJ 8893
Part of old Manchester Town Hall which was moved to stand in front of the lake in Heaton Park in 1912. An immense yellow sandstone architrave supported on ionic columns, as usual richly blackened and improved by north country smuts. See page 266.

Ramsbottom
Holcombe Tower, nineteenth   SD 8017
century
A good high black square stone tower standing on a stout arch, to the memory of Sir Robert Peel and confusingly called the Peel Tower.

Nuthall Hall Farm
Gothick Screen   SD 7917
See page 219.

Saddleworth *Pots and Pans Hill*
Obelisk, 1923   SE 0305
A war memorial.

Tottington *Shepherd Street*
Tower Farm   SD 7412
See page 220.

Hampshire

Southampton and its Water, with three tides a day round the Isle of Wight, divide chalk downs in the east from the New Forest in the west. The north of the county is rich and hilly. A big county with a good variety of follies, two fine gothick towers, a lovely arch, a pyramid and a shell garden. There are also a number of columns and obelisks.

Calshot *Eaglehurst*
Luttrell's Tower, *c.* 1780   SU 4701
This beautiful tower was built by Temple Simon Luttrell on the low Hampshire coast opposite Cowes on the Isle of Wight. It is square, with a bow to the north and south, three unequal storeys high; the bow that looks over the sea takes the spiral stair and continues up three more storeys as a tall round tower to a castellated top. It is yellow brick with a great variety of windows, pointed, circular, bay, flat, with varied glazing bars. Below the castellations of tower and turret are bands of pendentive decoration, and there are urns in niches. Inside, there is one big room on each floor, the lowest in the middle, the top one best, with a most beautiful frieze and a fireplace from an earlier building. Luttrell

Luttrell's Tower, Eaglehurst

is said to have engaged in smuggling for the Prince Regent and indeed there are vast cellars under the tower, with a passage to the beach, while there is a conventional descent from the front door in the turret to a double flight of curved steps down the low cliff. When it was first built, he lived in the tower and used canvas buildings for his kitchens and other offices, but later the grounds were embellished with a charming Regency gothic pavilion. Henry James Pye, the booby Poet Laureate, wrote a poem at Eaglehurst on seeing the fleet anchored at Spithead:

> So in each ship's stupendous womb,
> Now gently floating on the deep,
> Peaceful as the silent tomb,
> The Daemons of destruction sleep—
> But wak'd by war's terrific roar,
> Prompt o'er each desolated shore
> Their hell-directed flight to urge,
> And leading slaughter's horrid train,
> With hecatombs of warriors slain,
> To load th'empurpled surge.

Marconi leased the tower during the First World War and used it for wireless experiments transmitting to the Isle of Wight, where there is a monument near the Needles to indicate the other station. Its fine state of preservation is due to continued efforts by Lieutenant-Colonel W. B. V. H. P. Gates in repelling vandals from the beach. It now belongs to the Landmark Trust.

Farley Mount *The Monument*
Pyramid, 1730–40   SU 4129
One of the few follies directly connected with sport, this 30-foot pyramid with four porches commemorates the feats of the horse called Beware Chalk Pit, which was owned by Paulet St John. One day in September 1733 when out hunting Mr St John came suddenly upon a chalk pit, and, too late to avoid it, let his horse jump in; a year later he and the same horse won the Hunter's Plate on Worthy

Down. Over 100 years later in 1847 a Mr Barton Wallop had a similar experience when hunting with the Hursley, but his chalk pit was only 15 feet deep, whereas Mr St John's was 25.

Hambledon *Hopton House*
Tower, nineteenth century   SU 6415
A three-storey square tower of knapped and unknapped flints with brick dressings and castellations, these capped with stone. It once belonged to Folly House, and was probably built *c.* 1840 for a farmer to watch his slacking labourers, it is said. Some of the pretty pointed windows remain and also the stair-rail inside but it has suffered some rough alterations.

There is also a small stone monument in Hambledon to mark the site of the local cricket club between 1760 and 1767 where the game may have been played for the first time; Hambledon took on all England and won.

Highclere *Siddown Hill*
Heaven's Gate   SU 4459
See page 140.

Houghton *Houghton Lodge*
Sham Ruin, *c.* 1801   SU 3432
The lodge gate to a cottage orné, like a little ruin.

Hursley *Cranbury Park*
Ruin, *c.* 1765   SU 4225
Early in the eighteenth century a builder from Southampton called Walter Taylor bought from Sir Bartlet Lucy the ruins of Netley Abbey, which he proceeded to pull down so that he could use the material for housing in Newport and elsewhere. Of course when the keystone from one of the arches fell on his head everyone said he had received his just reward. In 1765 Thomas Drummer bought what was left of the ruins and took part of the north transept to make an elegant ruin in his park. He also tried to buy Winchester Cross for his garden, but when public feeling prevented him doing this he had a plaster cast made instead. Behind the genuine transplanted ruin he built a tower to screen a cottage.

Hurstbourne Priors
Monument and Tower, eighteenth   SU 4447
century
Early in the eighteenth century Thomas Archer is thought to have designed a fine sham castle and a big cascade here—certainly a painting exists which shows it all, plus people, a pavilion, peacocks and turkeys. Two things remain; one is an interesting monument domed and built of random cut flint with niches lined in dark, almost black, bricks. The statue of a Roman emperor stands inside. The other is a massively detailed tower called Andover Lodge built of grey brick with red brick dressings. It has tall arches round the windows of two storeys and circular windows under the castellated parapet. If the probable date of 1712 onwards for the demolished house is correct, then there is also the possibility that Andover Lodge was built at about the same time and so might be earlier than the work at Castle Howard.

Hythe *Forest Lodge*
Chinese pavilion, nineteenth century   SU 4306
The common land here was enclosed by Mr Durrant in the 1840s and Mr Fleuret bought some from him and built a Chinese pavilion on an island with bridges, possibly a summer-house, and an observatory tower demolished in the First World War. The Forest Lodge land has been cut up, and the utterly derelict pavilion is now sinking into a marshy wood on a piece which has become a farm; it is a rectangular wooden building, once painted blue with a small curved roof on a trellis clerestory above the larger roof. Nearby are a few beams of silvery wood in a bog, probably a boat house. It is possible that the pavilion is later than an original pagoda by Mr Fleuret, now gone.

Itchen Stoke
The Arch   SU 5633
A rusticated arch with pediment by the road, probably a gate though possibly an eye-catcher.

The tower at Lee-on-the-Solent

Lee-on-the-Solent

Tower, 1935†   SU 5601

That rare thing this century, a lovely prospect tower, by Yates, Cooke and Derbyshire, scandalously modern in its day and ready for admiration now. It is almost triangular like the towers of two centuries before, but the point to the sea is rounded. Concrete, with incised vertical lines to emphasize its height above a dull series of low buildings at its feet, and a complex vertical-horizontal glass lantern at the top with a rather inelegant viewing platform, possibly heightened from the original design for safety?

Lindford

Pebble House   SU 8137

A house here used to be lavishly decorated, with pebble work, making regimental crests, etc., but only the work on the back and out-buildings still remains.

Lymington *Walhampton Manor*

Grotto, eighteenth century   SZ 3497

This grotto was made by the Boatswain of Admiral Sir Harry Burrard Neal (1768–1840). The bo'sun, the story goes, drowned himself in the Solent when he had finished. Made of broken glass, marble chips and shells stuck on to the walls of a 10-foot square garden house. The use of texture and pattern is extremely clever, the back wall away from the door is decorated with an urn topped with Prince of Wales' feathers, and above this are three elegant arches. All the corners are coved and the surface of the walls is uneven, the decorative motifs making a kind of bas-relief. Vernacular this grotto certainly is, vernacular of the best kind. No other grotto builder uses such a scale-range of objects for his decoration, for there are lions, lizards, mythological serpents, giant starfish, dragon-flies and butterflies. The ceiling is covered with a design of lovely sprays of flowers.

In the house, which is now a school, is a painted map—'Part of the Estate of Sir Henry Burrard, Bart', 1787. At the bottom is a painting of the outside of the grotto made of tufa with a log pediment and arched door, and an iron grille. A mound is also shown, prickly with shrubs like a trifle with almonds, and a little blue pavilion on top. This has now gone, but is probably the site of the plain obelisk to the Admiral.

Since I saw the grotto in very good condition in the late 1940s it had got into bad repair, but has now been carefully restored by Mary Adshead. It has been suggested that some of the motifs—Lion, Dragon, etc.—may symbolize the names of the Admiral's and his bosun's ships.

Walhampton grotto, a lion.

Odiham *Broad Oak*
'King John's Hunting Lodge'   SU 7553
Probably a hunting stand to which a new red brick façade, with three tall Dutch-style gables and ogee-gothick windows, was added to act as an eyecatcher to Dogmersfield Park, where a painting shows it in the park with a castellated octagon belvedere, a tower, lodges and what looks very like another eyecatcher, but all these are gone, and the hunting lodge is now a house, magnificently set in lawns and pleached alder hedges with new octagon pavilions at the sides, so that it has lost all air of folly, but still has a lovely outlook down mown grass with daisies to the Basingstoke Canal.

Portchester
Nelson Monument, Column,
nineteenth century   SU 6107
A 100-foot high square column with a hollow cylinder set across it as a capital and a bust of Nelson in the cylinder; very odd.

Portsdown
Palmerston's Follies, nineteenth   SU 5907–
century   SU 6806
Forts Purbrook, Widley, Southwick, Nelson, Fareham, which were intended for the defence of Portsmouth and were never put to the test. Embattled walls with great red brick barracks behind them, enormous Romanesque arches for entrance; strung along the road.

Portsea
Naval monuments in Victoria Park,   SU 6401
c. 1880*
A Chinese temple, a lion on a column and several others.

Ringwood *Avon Castle*
Pennies*   SU 1403
Two people have told me of a room in Avon Castle with the walls covered with old pennies, more an eccentric wallpaper than a folly, but, if there, compensation for the destruction of the stamp room in Ipswich.

Rowland's Castle
Fitzwycombe's Folly*   SU 7312
A hearsay folly; I cannot find it.

Southampton *Queensway*
The Gas Column, 1829   SU 4313
An iron column (moved from another part of Southampton) to the memory of William Chamberlayne M.P. who put up similar ones to take the City's first gas lamps. All these have now gone.

Southsea
Model Village*   SZ 6498

Sway
Peterson's Folly, late nineteenth   SZ 2897
century
See page 264.

West Meon Hut
The Tetralithon, Druids' Circle,   SU 6324
probably nineteenth century
See page 237.

Rooksbury Tower

Wickham *Rooksbury Park*

Tower, 1826† SU 5812

A big and impressive tower, most beautiful in decay on a hilltop, a prospect tower and eyecatcher to the house, now a school. Fine brickwork shows through Roman cement—it looks like dazzle-camouflage. At the bottom is a castellated octagon, with 10-foot long walls, open on five, big pointed arches and buttressed at the corners. On top, with space all round for a promenade, is a smaller octagon with rectangular arches, tops almost flat under dripstones, and a castellated roof for another view. On one side is a taller circular staircase turret with three storeys and pointed windows. Inside all is ruin, the stairs gone, no ornament left, the shallow dome of the ground floor cracked, but Mr C. H. Tatham's tower remains one of our most spectacular follies. Prospect of survival: nil. (Demolished May 1973.)

And at Woodmancote is 'a rendered brick folly' in a wood, but I have not found it.

Hereford and Worcester

Hereford has every capability of rugged, almost mountainous country and the picturesque Wye, but is also border country, and except for a fine twentieth-century grotto and Shobdon Arches the follies are thin on the ground, moving towards the almost total blank of Wales.

Worcester still has when we say it a warm enclosed rural sound, possibly an echo of 'worsted', though the yarn-village was in Norfolk; and we remember the Malvern Hills, beautiful without drama, and the apple orchards. In fact, the spread from Birmingham is now 30 or 35 miles across with green patches, and there aren't many follies in what is left.

Abberley

Clock Tower, 1883 SO 7568

In the grounds of a preparatory school is a massive square tower which about 40 feet from the ground houses an imposing clock, and continues upwards, bursting into a mass of Scottish gothic pinnacles. The history of the tower is recorded on the foundation stone. 'This stone was laid by John Joseph Jones and his wife Sarah Aemelia (Amy) on May 4th 1883.' This is a sad building, for a peal of bells which was once in the tower had to be sold to keep up the house. If there are any doubts about it being a true folly, size convinces; it is so big, so solid, its stone pinnacles so massive that to exclude it on the grounds that clock towers, monuments and obelisks do not qualify as follies would be impossible.

Abberley Tower

Bredon Hill

Two Towers   SO 9536

One is a small tower, put up at the end of the eighteenth century by Mr Parsons of Kemerton.

The other is a small castellated folly now joined to a house. It was built by Edmund Bell, said to have been the last smuggler hanged in England, in 1841, with the death certified as 'dropsy'.

Broadway

Broadway Tower, 1797 (eyecatcher   SP 1038
to Croome)
See page 67.

Croome Court

Grotto, etc.   SO 8844
See page 65.

Defford *Dunstall Castle*

Sham Castle to Croome   SO 9243
See page 67.

The Panorama, Croome Court

Ewyas Harold

Demolished tower†   SO 3828
This was a disappointment; several people told me about a fine brick tower in Dineter Wood, built by a Scotsman who wanted to go into the Church but failed, and so became a builder, made a fortune and retired here to build a dream rectory and his folly tower, to see from the study. Demolished 'for the bricks'.

Great Witley *Witley Court*

Giant Fountains   SO 7565
Near the ruins of the house are two fountains on a scale so gigantic that we must consider them as candidates for the folly status of the Warmley giant, who must have been part of just such a group as the Perseus and Andromeda here. A third fountain with an enormous shell was moved from Witley to Cliveden.

Hagley *Clent Grove*

Sham ruin, eighteenth century*   SO 9181
A red brick ruin lost in trees, with two round towers and gothick details. The roofs and floors are gone, and nothing remains of any interior decoration.

Hagley Park
Sham castle, 1749
See page 55.

Broadway Tower

The memorial at Lugwardine

Hereford *Castle grounds*

Column, 1806–9   SO 5240

This is an enormous and well placed column; it does impose itself on the memory. It was put up to Nelson, an unfluted stone column with an egg-and-dart capital that climbs on to support an urn. The heavy plinth has a long inscription to the hero's career and glory. A lot of trouble was taken with this; there is a portrait in a trophy and below the capital four anchors hang down the column on loops of rope that echo a rope base.

Hope-under-Dinmore *Dinmore Manor*

Grotto, 1926   SO 4851

See page 272.

Lugwardine *Longworth*   SO 5541

An extremely pretty urn to commemorate a racehorse. Once there was a prospect tower on the hill top two or three miles away but this has gone.

Mortimers Cross *Croft Castle*

Sham Castle Gate, eighteenth   SO 4565
century

For admirers of Sanderson Miller, there is a stylistic possibility that he designed the length of gothick wall in which the gate is set, but T. F. Pritchard of Shrewsbury, who castled the house for Richard Knight, is more likely. In any case the composition of church and house and the superb Spanish chestnut avenues are much better.

Radford

Pillarboxes, *c.* 1890   SP 0254

In the triangle of roads joining Worcester, Alcester and Evesham are the villages of Upton Snodsbury, North Piddle, Flyford Flavell, Naunton Beauchamp, Pinvin, Wyre Piddle, Iron Cross, and the Lenches—Church, Sheriffs, Ab and Rous. Rous Lench and the pedestrian Radford have special pillarboxes, as big as summer-houses, which they resemble, provided for the villagers by the munificent Dr Chaffy, the local parson squire. They are made of half-timbered crazy paving with very steep shingle roofs and the Chaffy coat-of-arms in the eaves. Dr Chaffy also built a 60-foot tower in his garden modelled on an Italian campanile. A visitor to Rous Lench should not miss the school.

One of Dr Chaffy's pillarboxes

Ross-on-Wye

Group, eighteenth and nineteenth   SO 6024
centuries

Ross seems to have had a real outburst of
folly work; the situation on a cliff over the
river and the plentiful red sandstone lent
themselves easily to it once someone started.
This may have been a Mr Kyrle, who died in
1724 aged 88; the work when I saw it looked
later, little gothick pavilions with the remains
of some grot-work and stuffed animals in
cases, a swan in horses' teeth on the floor of
one, and horses' skulls. Most of this has
gone, but the Royal Hotel has a round red
castellated tower and turret and a sham arch.
The Valley Hotel, now a private house, has
a castellated entry and two smaller towers.
The Merton Hotel has a stable yard of amusing gothickry and castellated walks with
turrets, slits, the lot going down into the
valley.

   Across the Wye are the ruins of a castle
near a nineteenth-century house and some
sham pieces added to pep up the real thing.

Shobdon *Shobdon Court*

The Arches, eighteenth century   SO 3963
See page 53.

Spetchley *Spetchley Park*

Root House   SO 8955

A very pretty thatched root house too small
for comparison with Badminton, and a pavilion rather than a hermitage, but in the same
manner. It is about 15 feet high and 10 across
and was presumably made in the eighteenth
century. It stands on eight piers of very
knobby elm, worm eaten but still solid. The
front three bays are open, the rest are walled
in with neat diagonal and diamond patterns in
hazel coppice and a fitted bench to match.
Two of these walls have little ogee windows
that must once have held coloured glass. The
roof, an octagonal pyramid under the blunt
cone of thatch is also worked with twigs,
ribs and centre boss of elm, and there is a
ruinous pebble floor; all the rest has been kept
in good repair.

   The garden is wonderful; the lead statues
are unworthy and the rose lawn is the usual
tragic mistake but Spetchley is a long-estab-
lished garden—Evelyn mentioned one of the
cedars—and has every necessary ingredient
for perfection; love, continuity and a little
neglect. There is an exceptional number of
rare plants growing in great contentment,
with yew hedges and old walls to enclose the
flowers; in late September it is one of the
most beautiful and romantic gardens in
England. See page 193.

Tenbury Wells

Rusty Tin Pagoda   SO 5968
See page 120.

Whitchurch

Memorial Clock, 1867   SO 5417

A square red brick clock tower with engineering brick trim, a pyramidal slate roof and a
weathercock. It is inscribed REDEEM THE
TIME and commemorates John Leech, and his
sisters.

Tenbury Wells

Hertfordshire

Few good follies here at any time, the one big grotto in danger, and London spreading.

Aldenham *Wall Hall*
Sham Ruin, *c.* 1800   TQ 1499
Mr Thellusson owned Wall Hall, a farmhouse with mediaeval associations. In 1802 he added a gothick revival front to the house and called it Aldenham Abbey. He also built the sham ruin, of brick and Roman cement, incised to resemble ashlar. Parts of it are supposed to come from Aldenham church, most probably the window mouldings. The walls enclose three sides of a square, one pierced by a tall and wide pointed arch and the other by a small pointed doorway, standard sham ruin practice, but very nice, ivy-covered and ruinous now in its own right.

Benington *Benington Lordship*
Sham Castle, 1832   TL 3124
A very fine large folly tacked on to a very beautiful late seventeenth-century house. The drive leads through a good gloomy plantation of firs and horse chestnuts to a gatehouse tower complete with sham portcullis. This, like all the rest, is made of flint with stone dressings. On either side of the central arch there are elaborate carvings of knights, head and shoulders only, looking out through rather battered stone visors; one carries a battle axe held across his chest. This gateway leads into a court which is completely enclosed with flint walls. To the left they curve round in a quarter circle stopping at another square tower, with ruined machicolations and castellations against the skyline. The entrance to this is through a very good Norman doorway, above which is a shield, a very eighteenth-century cherub and a runic inscription. Inside is a piece of stone bearing a Greek inscription and below it, in English: 'This part of an ancient monument was discovered on the plain of Troy near Alexandria Troas by the Hon. Captain John Gordon R.N. and given by him to George Proctor of

The sham castle, Benington Lordship

Benington Herts A.D. MDCCCXXXII.' Above these inscriptions is a Norman niche containing a marble statue of Buddha. Beyond this tower is an ivy- and fern-covered lump of masonry through which an arch leads into a narrow, flint-lined walk (past picturesque nooks all very like Banwell), which winds round and out on to the lawn. On the right of the gatehouse from the outside there are some additions to the old house in the same style, amazingly elaborate interlaced Norman arches, and stained glass windows set in the flint walls which end in an irregular skyline.
The whole of this folly is very reminiscent of Banwell: there is the same feeling of the gothick revival as interpreted by Peacock, and the same mixture of fantasy and scholarship, the runic inscriptions and the protective moat running round the outside of the wall, the same mixture of Greek and gothick.

Brookman's Park

Hoddesdon *Woodlands*
Group, *c.* 1800†   TL 3708
This was one of Hertfordshire's prettiest
pieces of improvement, very charming gothick
screens, gates, buttery, pergola, bath house,
orangery and grotto, all put up close together
on a small site by John Warnes, a Quaker
builder, for himself.

Knebworth *Knebworth House*
Lord Lytton Folly, *c.* 1850   TL 2321
A tiny, almost ivy-obscured folly representing
the choir of a church with two very good

gothic revival windows, built by the first
Lord Lytton. A picture postcard has been
published calling it the ruins of Queen Anne's
Chapel.

Little Berkhamsted
Stratton's Observatory, 1789   TL 2908
Admiral Stratton wished to see the ships in
the Thames so he built this round brick
tower, made of the bricks from a house
demolished nearby. First there is an octagonal
base, then four tall blind arcades, a coarse
brick moulding, then eight windows round

the tower for the view, and above that eight castellations, one above each window. Needless to say the Thames cannot be seen from the top, but perhaps the folly story was not true and the Admiral was merely interested in the stars and the view.

Potters Bar *Brookman's Park*
Arch, early eighteenth century   TL 2504
A large round archway set between two square castellated towers, all brick. Windows narrowing to slits in the thickness of the brick go one above the other up the towers, and there are bands of square-section mouldings between them; there is said to be a farthing between each pair of bricks.

The arch was once the southern gate to the estate of Gobions (or Gubbins) and was put up by Sir Jeremy Sambrooke early in the eighteenth century. The designer of the house was probably James Gibbs, so he may have done the arch (it has affinities with Stainborough). The grounds were by Bridgeman. The house was pulled down in 1836 by a new owner who wanted to add the Gobions land to Brookman's Park.

Rickmansworth *Moor Park**   TQ 0595
I have been told of a red brick tower near the golf course which has a peal of bells from Russia, but though a Russian ambassador

Stratton's Observatory

lived at Northwood, I can find out nothing about the tower or the bells.

St Pauls Walden *The Bury*
Pyramid*   TL 1822
A flint pyramid, and possibly a grotto.

Wadesmill
Obelisk, nineteenth century   TL 3517
A small obelisk in a railing by the roadside marks the spot where Thomas Clarkson (1760–1846) determined to devote the rest of his life to the abolition of slavery. There is also a tall gothick Albert-Memorial-style monument to him in Wisbech where he was born, designed by Sir Gilbert Scott, with reliefs of Wilberforce, Sharp and a chained beseeching slave.

Ware *Scott's Road*
Scott's Grotto   TL 3615
See page 169.
The grotto in 1972 is more dilapidated, but fortunately Ware Urban District Council is trying to raise money to preserve it.

Woolmer Green
Folly garden
Carvings, twentieth century,   TL 2618
recently restored

Scott's grotto at Ware

Humberside

A root-house; Carnaby Temple and a beautiful tower at Hornsea; otherwise a sparse area.

Belton *Isle of Axholme**   SE 7806
I have been told of a spectacularly ruined house, with an obelisk to a favourite horse and a hound still standing in the park.

Brough   SE 9426
A Tower to be seen from the A66.

Carnaby *Boynton Hall*
Carnaby Temple, *c.* 1760   TA 1565
An ill-treated folly; it was once a very well-proportioned octagon tower in grey-pink brick with pale slates, built by Sir George Strickland 'on the Model of the Temple of the winds at Athens', but bearing absolutely no resemblance to it. There are three storeys, each with eight round-headed windows, now bricked and shuttered. The elegant roof has a brick lantern, also with eight bricked-in

Hunmanby Gate

arches and a chinoiserie roof with a ball on top. At some time, an outhouse and a chimney were added and the Temple was lived in, but now it is disused and dilapidated. One ceiling was a good one, but has now fallen down. It is isolated and at risk.

Between 1760 and 1770 Sir George embellished his park at Boynton with a garden-house in the form of a castellated tower, a bridge over a road made with stone from a demolished church, rustic bridges, and a gothick dairy.

Hornsea
A very elegant Tower, nineteenth   TA 2147
century
See page 209.

Hunmanby
Hunmanby Gate, 1809   TA 1077
A gateway in the form of a gothic monastic ruin built by Humphrey Osbaldeston in 1809. As squire he felt entitled to take the stone for it from Filey Brig, which is a fine natural breakwater in Filey Bay. An unexpected storm of protest caused the Board of Trade to stop him taking any more, but by then the gate was finished.

It is a very well-detailed arch set in an ivy-covered ruinous wall of most romantically weathered tufa-ish stone, which screens the lodges at the beginning of the drive from the road.

Carnaby Temple

Castle Farm

Sledmere *Castle Farm*

Tatton Sykes Memorial, Wagoners' SE 9365
Memorial, Cross

Castle Farm itself is the true folly, a fortified farm of about 1790. Between two three-sided towers there is a tall gothick arch, with a door into the farm, and above this below the top of the towers some very elaborate castellations, the tall parts made of open gothick arches and the low parts pierced with quatrefoils. On the outside of each tower a wall runs out to hide the rest of the farmhouse.

The Tatton Sykes Memorial is a monument to Sir Tatton Sykes, Baronet, and was built in 1865. It is one of those mid-nineteenth-pieces of architecture which are so encrusted with detail that description is impossible; basically it is a spire rising straight from the ground carrying a staircase inside. About 10 feet from the ground are well-carved stone panels.

The Wagoners' Memorial is a monument to the special service of wagoners raised by Sir Mark Sykes in the First World War, and consists of a drum, like a small Trajan's Column, recording their exploits, splendidly carved by Carlo Magnoni; the best war memorial in England.

The Eleanor Cross was put up in 1900; after 1918 some soldiers were added to the saints under the canopies. And there is a memorial to Sir Christopher Sykes by the entrance to the park.

Isle of Wight

Incredibly little. Certainly the Island did not become fashionable until Queen Victoria built Osborne, but there were some big houses in the eighteenth century, and the chines could have sheltered plenty of conceits. There are obelisks at Appledurcombe and Bembridge, a castellated cowshed at Norris Castle, a Swiss Cottage at Osborne and a tower to Tennyson near Farringford.

Blackgang Chine SZ 4876

This is the only chine to have anything beyond rustic-work; the entertainments include the skeleton of a whale, a gnome village and distorting mirrors. Twenty years ago this was an almost perfectly preserved nineteenth-century pleasure-garden; it has been much altered, but some of the old curiosities remain.

Ryde

Appley Tower, on the sea wall,   SZ 5893
mid-nineteenth century

A pretty round stone prospect tower castellated with a higher turret, and a bay window
to the sea for bad weather. The gardens of
Appley House are now municipal, but when
it was a private house King George and Queen
Mary liked to have tea there.

St Catherine's Down

Pillar, 1811   SZ 4989

Most beautifully situated, an object for a
walk. There is a stone ball on top and the
column is dark with moss. It commemorates
the visit of the Czar to Great Britain; in 1857
another tablet was added to the allied dead of
the Alma, Inkerman and Sebastopol.

Kent

The Isle of Thanet, the north-eastern tip of
Kent, is one of the richest folly patches in
England. It has a good grotto, which has
collected as many theories as the pyramids, an
extremely beautiful tower, a fine mediaeval
gate used as an eyecatcher and a big group of
flint castle-works. The rest of Kent offers
another good grotto and tower and little else;
certainly one would not expect much on
Romney Marshes in the south, but the North
Downs have not even an eyecatcher.

Dane John, Canterbury

Bilsington *Monument Field*

Obelisk, 1835   TR 0434

A nice little obelisk on a pedestal, put up by
'his friends and the reformers of Kent', when
Sir Richard Conway was killed in a coach
accident in London.

Birchington *Quex Park*

Towers, early nineteenth century   TR 3571
See page 207.

Canterbury *Public Park*

Dane John, 1790   TR 1458

Seldom has so small an ornament been so
richly documented. It is set up on a large early
burial mound, a stone column, bottom third
fluted, supporting an urn and standing on a
big square pedestal with a niche in each side.
Above the niches, four inscriptions tell all,
how the field and hill were improved for the
public at the sole expense of Alderman James
Simmons in 1790 and the pillar put in commemoration by public subscription in 1803,
how in 1825 a court of Burchmote thanked
Sir Robert Townsend Farquharson, Bart., for
the valuable iron railing, how the Mayor and
Commons voted £60 a year for upkeep and
at last how they unanimously voted thanks in
1884 for the gift of an iron entry bridge over
Watling Street.

Chatham *Brompton Barracks*

Arches, nineteenth century   TR 7768

There are a number of triumphal arches, set as eyecatchers or just for glory, that are instantly acceptable as follies. Here are two set most beautifully in a big Royal Engineers' barracks which have not yet that quality, but if the barracks were abandoned might well acquire it like the arches at Holdenby. The Crimea Arch, tripartite in stone, was put up in 1860 and the South Africa Arch in 1905, a Constantine in 'Portland stone of specially selected quality'; it has a delightful series of accurate and lively relief carvings by W. S. Frith. They show a blockhouse with barbed wire and telegraph lines, a portable ox-wagon blockhouse, an armoured train diverting round a broken bridge, and a pontoon with seven spans of oxen drawing a wagon while an observation balloon floats over a wood. Behind is Gordon on a camel, unveiled in 1890. There is also Kitchener on a horse, and a tree grown from a slip taken from the weeping willow over Napoleon's tomb.

Chislehurst   TQ 4571

There are said to be two gothick towers in the garden of a house called The Towers, but I have not been able to find them.

Cliffsend *Ebbsfleet*

Viking Ship, twentieth century   TR 3463

'Facsimile of a Viking ship which crossed the North Sea in 1949 to commemorate the Viking raids and Hengist and Horsa'. The Ordnance Survey map, though, says that this is the 'site of the Landing of the Saxons A.D. 499', but there is the ship, looking even more startlingly small than the ships at Oslo. The newspapers in 1949 were full of photographs of the arrival, and of smiling spectacled faces under the fierce helmets.

Dunkirk *Holly Hill*

Tower   TR 0861

A dumpy little hexagonal tower two storeys high, made of flint dressed with stone, and lined with brick; the iron spiral staircase to the roof is down, and it gets steadily less prosperous and harder to find in the thick woods, which have, as well as the tower, a remarkable number of ants.

Gillingham

Jezreel Tower, nineteenth century† TQ 8266

See page 262.

Hadlow

May's Folly; Tower, 1838–40   TQ 6450

In 1830 Walter Barton May built himself a vast gothic revival mansion outside Tonbridge, and about ten years later added the 170-foot tower of brick, rendered with Roman cement, and wisely employed an engineer. The rest of the house has been pulled down, but the tower remains, soaring above the monkey puzzles of the garden, taller than any neighbouring church. It is octagonal and divided into tiers by strong horizontal mouldings, the whole gothick in the extreme, and crowned by a tall and slender turret. There are various reasons given for why it was built. The perennial story of folly builders—that they want to see some distant object—is probably the origin of the story that he wished to see the sea, and forgot the downs. The others are more picturesque; that his wife deserted him to live with a

May's Folly, Hadlow

farmer, and that he built the tower so that whenever she was in Kent she should be reminded of him; or that he wished to thwart a prophecy that the house would go out of his family on his death if he was not buried above ground, and that his coffin was to be deposited on top of the tower. He is in fact still above ground, but in a mausoleum. Whatever reason may have caused him to build his tower, it is one of the largest and most sumptuous follies in the country.

Higham *Telegraph Hill*
Obelisk, 1832   TQ 7172
An obelisk made wayward by the loss of all but the capping stones of the top, so that it is unevenly weathered, standing on rough land and looking most beautiful if approached from Mockbeggar via Hermitage Lane—there is a Tower Hill two miles to the east, so this may be all that remains of a considerably improved estate. The obelisk is of course to Reform, especially to Charles Larkin, auctioneer of Rochester, recording his 'Zealous exertions in promoting the Bill'.

Horsmonden
Tower, 1858†   TQ 7041
This was an odd one, two stark joined towers, one narrower at the bottom like an anti-aircraft shell, pruned of every decoration except their castellations. It was built to honour Sir Walter Scott, and was once elaborately and baronially furnished, but had been derelict for many years.

Knole
Birdhouse, *c.* 1761   TQ 5454
The sad remains of a complex gothick folly to contain a collection of foreign birds, built for Lionel, first Duke of Dorset.

Margate *near Garlinge*
Dent-de-Lion. Screen, pre-1445   TR 3571
Far to the south on the outskirts of Margate is Dent-de-Lion, which is certainly now part of a farm, but as castellations for what viewpoint I have not been able to discover; possibly its solid walls simply made a start

for the barns. It is a fifteenth-century gatehouse, quite real, the remains of the mansion of the Daundelyon family whose arms may still be seen with two remaining gargoyles. There are four beautiful square towers in alternated bands of four rows of narrow red bricks with four rows of knapped flints. It faces south into Kent, but through the tall entrance arch the bungalows of Garlinge are seen instead.

Grotto Hill
Grotto, *c.* 1800   TR 3571
See page 172.

Mereworth *Mereworth Castle*
Shell Room, eighteenth century   TQ 6654
See page 156.
At the end of an off-axis vista from the house on top of a hill at the edge of the woods is a beautiful arch of golden stone on a brick core, well detailed and carved but in poor condition.

Newington *Temple Cottage*
Eyecatcher, eighteenth century   TR 1837
A two-sided, two-storey gothick façade in random stone with dressed stone trimmings. Eleven gothick windows and a door, with a dressy central octagonal lantern on the roof and plenty of picturesque ivy. The stone came from a demolished mediaeval house at Brockhill.

Eyecatcher cottage at Newington

North Foreland *Kingsgate*

Large group   TR 3971

On 2 May 1744, Georgina Caroline Lennox (eldest daughter of that Duke and Duchess of Richmond who built the shell pavilion at Goodwood) ran away with Henry Fox, and their clandestine marriage made a stir which echoes loudly through the diaries and letters of the time. In 1762 she was created Baroness Holland, Henry Fox being at the time Paymaster-General and later Leader of the House of Commons. In 1763 he was made Baron Holland himself, and thereafter strove hard for an earldom, but in 1766 this was directly refused by the King—Lord Holland was considered to be robbing the country on a very grand scale as Paymaster-General of the Forces. He had bought the Kingsgate estate among others some time before from Robert Whitfield; the dates are uncertain, but Caroline Fox wrote to her sister, the Countess of Kildare at Carton, in 1758 about her husband's works at Kingsgate, 'old ruins, towers and gateways', and a gazebo with 'a delightful sofa' in it, so when it was necessary for Lord Holland to retire here in 1766, much was already done. J. L. Nicholl and the amateur architect Sir Thomas Wynne had designed him a fine house with a large Doric portico, inspired by 'Tully's Formian Villa,' and the flint conceits grew up round it. The first was a 'Roman chapel', the Bede-house, with gothick windows and a cross on top. A large part of this went into the sea during a storm, and the

The clock tower, Port Regis

rest of it was incorporated in a pub, now 'The Captain Digby'. Here there is also a little flint tower, right on the edge of the cliff, with a Gothick door facing the sea. Nearby is the flint pedestal that is all that remains of the Harley Tower of 1768, a compliment to one of his few loyal friends. Further along the cliff is a beautiful rough cutting through the chalk towards the sea. At the end, 20 feet of chalk were left uncut and then pierced by a very tall slender arch, an exquisite approach to the shore. Beside it on the cliff top is a large and solid fortification, the Arx Roachim, or Ruolin, 1768 again, about 50 feet square, thick and low, with four squat round towers on the corners whose walls slope back so far that it looks like an inkwell. This was to represent a fort of Henry VIII's time, and once had a tall central tower of white chalk. Near it there was a temple, long since blown down, with a statue of Neptune, possibly Roman, and a dolphin, which was all supposed to replace an arch built by King Vortigern.

Holland House was dismantled long ago, and turned into three small houses. Opposite is Kingsgate Castle, a castellated building so large that it is now a big and comfortable hotel, but designed by Lord Holland for stables and coach houses. It is many times larger than the remains of the house itself, and is built round a court on a strictly mediaeval plan, with five round towers and seven square ones, all superb flint work, dressed with light stone, and intended to resemble one of Edward I's border castles.

In the garden of Holland House is only a castellated flint gardener's cottage and some garden arches, but the grounds used to be much larger than they are now and Lord Holland's boundaries enclosed two further follies. One is a really charming flint clock tower which is called Hackmedown, in the grounds of the convent school at Port Regis, 20 feet high, encircled on the grass by an enlarged version of its own castellated top. The big clock face appears to have been added later, and certainly was never the occasion for the tower, for bones were discovered in the little tumulus on which it stands:

D M
Danorum & Saxonium hic occisorum
Dum de Solo Britannico
(Milites nihil a se alienum Putant)
Britannis Perfide & crudeliter olim expulsis
luter se dimicaverunt
HEN de HOLLAND
Posuit
Qui Duces quaelis hujus Praelii Exilus
Nulla Notat Historia
Annum circiter DCCCL evenit Pugna
Et Pugnam hanc evenisse Fidem faciunt
Ossa quam plurimo
Quae sub hoc & altero Tumulo huic vicino
Sunt sepulta

(Port Regis itself was a 'conventual alms-house' for old retainers, a cloister with five cells, a 'ruined chappel', and a gatehouse.)

The other is a tower 40 feet high, on a square base becoming octagonal, made of flint with stone dressings. Two tablets record its building. 'This beacon was raised for the benefit of navigation by the Corporation of Trinity House A.D. 1818' and 'Permission to raise this beacon was liberally granted to the Corp. of Trinity House by J. P. Powell Esq. of Quex House in this Island on whose estate it stands.' At that time three sets of marks were used to steer round the North Foreland; first, two tumuli; second, Neptune and Harley towers, and third, a red seamark (now gone) and Whitfield Tower (Lord Holland's first tower here, built in appreciation of Robert

Whitfield from whom he bought the land, blew down).

The preservation of all these things, set between Margate and Ramsgate in a very exposed position, is remarkable and they are now very well documented, for both Hugh Honour and Ronald Jessup have done a great deal of research here.[1] Only two things have gone absolutely without trace—Countess Fort, a disguised ice house, and a column to the Countess of Kildare.

Ramsgate *The Harbour*
Obelisk, 1821–2   TR 3964
A dignified obelisk by John Shaw in buff granite, with an almost grovelling inscription to record the departure of George IV from Ramsgate. It is now most curiously set in all the complex sea-side paraphernalia of fun-palaces and soft ice cream; Ramsgate is a particularly attractive resort with fine brick arcades, grot-work and a good cliff lift.

Sevenoaks *Manwood, Uplands Way*
Grotto, twentieth century   TQ 5355
A pretty little 1950s grotto with statues, and stained glass set in the rock work, lush ferns and trickling water. It has a castellated half tower, a square tower with a ball on top and arches at the side.

[1] Hugh Honour in *Country Life,* December 10th, 1953, Ronald Jessup in *Archaeologia Cantiana,* Vol. LXXXI, 1957.

The Ship on Shore, Sheerness

Sheerness

Ship-on-Shore, *c.* 1850   TQ 9475

A ship carrying a cargo of cement ran aground here in a storm. When she broke up it was found that the cement had set in its barrels, and these had broken, leaving nice cylindrical building blocks for anybody who chose to use them. Beside the folly there is a very small public house, which at one time had printed copies of the history of the folly and its builder, but the last copy which was framed in the bar was stolen so that little now is known about the folly, except that it was built by a farmer who owned the land.

Waldershare *Waldershare Park*

Belvedere, 1725–7   TR 2948

A large, double-cube plan, 60-foot belvedere for Sir Robert Furnese with slightly battered walls and Portland stone dressings. Clearly there was once a grand room on the first floor as the round-headed windows show, and smaller rooms above; rectangular windows. At the top is a balustrade. If it once had an open lantern and a cupola on top, it might then have had a little charm. The superb yellow and red brick riding school of 1871, now a barn, is a much better building.

Lancashire

High fells on the east and flat land on the west; both lend themselves mercilessly to towers; Blackpool has the tallest.

Accrington *New High Riley*

Eyecatcher, late eighteenth century   SD 7728

A pretty tower for a start, with very folly gothick architecture, machicolated with hemispheres, which are echoed by semi-circular holes above, possibly for pigeons? It was built as eyecatcher to the manor, which became a farm, and was then moved in about 1800 to the farm itself where it joins fine barns with quatrefoils. The whole story is very confused; certainly the manor, with a watch tower at Old High Riley was pulled down when it was no longer needed for protection and replaced by a new wing, while some of the old stones were used to make the eyecatcher, behind which barns were added later, so that the tower was moved, but the other way round.

Belmont *Holymosside*

Tower, *c.* 1760   SD 6715

A tower, possibly an old one completely done up for the fashion. It is 62 feet high, square, castellated, with some very pretty detail. Stories:

1. An astronomer put it up to see over the murk.

2. Chap had a very big nagging wife, so he built a tower with a stair so narrow she couldn't follow him up.

3. Chap adored his wife, and when she died he built the tower so he could see her grave down in the village.

4. There is a ghost called Henry; a charming young man, or something, moving about.

Blacko

Tower   SD 8642

A beacon tower, on the site of the Malkin Tower which was associated with the witch trials of 1612, or built by a successful grocer so that he could see the sea. In 1954 some art students painted it white, and that is all there is to say of Blacko Tower.

Blackpool

Tower, 1891–4   SD 3137

A good one this time, a little stolid, but delicacy is not wanted on our most lively and raucous seafront. See pages 209 and 211.

Brindle

Tower, *c.* 1840†   SD 6024

A round tower in red sandstone with a ruined arch at one side, built as a memorial to a Mr Heatley:

1. (Old man) *Ah, that is back the way you came, at Hoghton Towers, second left, you'll see it.* No.

2. (House) *Ah, yes, back the way you came, first left.* No.

3. (Ginger boy) *Straight on, next left.* No.

4. (Hoghton Towers at last) *Of course, that's on Bellmore.* No.

5. (Another man) *Lived here all my life, never heard of it.*

6. (The Rector) *Something of the sort on Duxon Hill.* No.

7. (Farmer on Duxon Hill) *Not here, ask Mr Miller, back the way you came, cottage opposite the next farm, Byewayes.*

8. (Mr Miller is the local historian). *Ah, yes, Livesay's Folly on Duxon Hill, that was destroyed about* 1890. *Before my time. . . .*

Broughton *Hampsfield Fell**   SD 5336

Two towers at the Hospice, which was built in 1846.

Clitheroe *Park below Castle*

Turret   SD 7442

Indeed, there is a turret from the Houses of Parliament here, a gift from Captain Sir William Brass M.P., re-erected to commemorate the coronation in 1937, but it is very small, with a castellated lily pond, crazy paving and roses.

Darwen

Jubilee Tower   ST 6923

Rather more splendid than most of the hilltop towers; a tall castellated octagon supported on a wider framework of eight big castellated arches with buttresses. It looks bandy-legged.

Lancaster *Williamson Park*

Ashton Memorial, 1906–9   SD 4761

See page 267.

(Ormskirk)

Folly story   SD 4108

A most persistent folly story ('Have you got the one at Ormskirk?'). Two sisters, endowing a church in the fourteenth century, quarrelled about spire or tower and at last built one of each, but the spire went up in 1430 and the tower in 1550.

Rivington Pike

Replica of Liverpool Cathedral*   SD 6314
& Tower

Alas, I have not been able to see this; Nikolaus Pevsner in *Buildings of England, Lancashire,* mentions as a 'splendid object' this replica of the ruins, which was built by the first Lord Leverhulme. There is also a 20-foot high square stone tower. The doors are blocked up, and the plaque carries only the date, 1735. It has good views of the sunny or sodden countryside.

Silverdale *Tower House*

Gibraltar Tower   SD 4675

A solid square tower with a pretty door, probably built early in the nineteenth century, and associated with Mrs. Gaskell. Also at Silverdale is a pepper-pot tower put up to celebrate one of Queen Victoria's Jubilees.

Jubilee Tower, Darwen

The grotto at Belvoir

Leicestershire

There is some pleasant rolling countryside that would have been quite suitable for ambitious landscaping, but hunting has dominated improvement. Rutland has added two good follies and a piece of vandalism.

Belvoir *Belvoir Castle*
Grotto, early nineteenth century   SK 8235
Only here is there a grotto as well as a hunt. It is quite unlike other grottoes, being near the fantastic castle on open terraces of steep garden instead of down by a lake, and shaped like a tall beehive. It is well made of dry-stone walling with a big double pointed arch for the view and a curved alcove inside. There is a wooden bench round and a tree-section table on a rustic root foot. On top sits an octagonal summer-house entered from the back from a higher path and once also reached by steps. The five sides over the grotto are rustic branch-work; broken windows show traces of red, blue and yellow glass. The other three sides are open to the path, showing an interior painted white with shallow domes, rustic benches and another table.

A photograph, *c.* 1905, shows a smaller rustic building, probably by the same hand, as a background to spring planting.

Burley *Burley-on-the-Hill*
Hermitage†   SK 8910
See page 182.

Old John's Tower, Newtown Linford

Burton-on-the-Wolds *Burton Hall*

Shell room, *c*. 1800   SK 5921

A small square gothick room attached to the house, in a tiny building called The Chapel, an anteroom to an octagonal tiled dairy with a check floor and central fountain. There is a shallow vaulted ceiling with rows of cockle shells lining the groins, but it is all in very poor repair except for the tile-and-pebble floor, and is destined for demolition.

Exton *Exton Park*

Bark Temple and Fort Henry,   SK 9310
eighteenth century
See page 18.

Newtown Linford *Bradgate Park*

Sham ruin, 1786   SK 5310

The imitation of a ruined tower erected to the memory of an old retainer who kept a wind-mill on the hill, and who was killed by the falling of a flagpole which was stood in the middle of a bonfire lit to celebrate the coming of age of the fifth Earl of Stamford's eldest son. That is the tradition, but John Nichols in his *History of the County of Leicester,* 1800, does not mention Old John, only the taste of the noble owner in building his ruined tower, which is quite a pretty one, round, castellated, with a piece of wall and an arch, on high ground.

Scraptoft *Scraptoft Hall*

Grotto, eighteenth century   SK 6506

This has almost ceased to be; the Chinese tea house on top of the grotto mound was demolished long ago, and all the shell lining has gone now.

Sutton Cheney *Bosworth Field*

King Richard's Well   SK 4101

An uneven pyramid with an undressed single stone for cap; a crazy-paving structure to protect a well from which Richard III is said to have drunk.

Thorpe Acre *Garendon Hall*   SK 5120

An 80-foot obelisk, a temple, a triumphal arch and a summer-house. These have several times been mentioned to me as follies, but however derelict they may become, they will I think remain determinedly elegant garden architecture.

Lincolnshire

Not many follies in this large, almost entirely flat county (nor records of many in the past which might have disappeared under the intensive cultivation), but the few are charming ones, mostly on a small scale.

Alvingham *Brackenborough Hall*
Sham Ruin   TF 3691
A small ruinous sham ruin, square and built of stone toppling precariously on a mound in the garden. It was built by Mr Ellis in about 1850, traditionally with stones taken from the old parish church at Fotherby when this was largely rebuilt; certainly the elaborate weathered windows have nothing to do with 1850.

Belton *Bellmount Tower*
Eyecatcher and Sham Ruin,   SK 9339
eighteenth century
The eyecatcher, Bellmount Tower, was designed by W. Eames in 1750. It is not really a tower at all, but a very tall round-headed arch, and above that its own height again of masonry with a blind Venetian window and two *yeux de boeuf*, a roof, and round that a balustrade. On each of the shorter side walls of the tower there are masonry buttresses which go to the height of the building, but their full width does not continue much above the height of the arch, and here half-obelisks are made to run the rest of the distance. In the angle made by the buttress and the tower on either side of the tower facing west are windows to light the spiral staircases, curiously constructed so that the opening is half in the wall of the tower and half in the buttress. The whole arch is stone with red brick quoins, and the outside faces of the buttresses are faced with brick. A very strange building and well worth a visit, for it stands on the top of a hill at the end of a grassy avenue of old trees.

Near the house is a small cascade and a sham ruin; the remains of a fine perpendicular window set in rude rockwork with a wild

Bellmount Tower, Belton

The forge, Belton

arch on each side of the old one.

The village is model in the 1830s style, with Dutch gables, and there is a good smithy with a chestnut tree.

Branston *Stonefield*
Mr Lovely's bizarre gates   TF 0368
I have been here and could find nothing.

Brocklesby *Brocklesby Park*
Hermitage and Grotto, *c.* 1720   TA 1411
See page 180.
As well as the root-house grotto, and pretty
temples, there is a triangular monument in
Coade stone with dished sides like the one at
Lucan and an orangery that once housed the
remains of the collection of sculpture made by
Sir Richard Worsley at Appledurcombe on
the Isle of Wight, which used also to belong
to the family, later Earls of Yarborough. The
park is large and fine, landscaped by Capability
Brown; Newsham Lodge is a particularly
good castellated sham castle, almost on the
Irish scale of gates, with a cottage on the left
then an octagon tower with stair turret, then
wall, half-turret, gate, more wall and a last
square tower. There is the big classical Yarborough Memorial Arch with four pairs of
columns and a pediment, and, towards Great
Limber, a superb 1787–94 mausoleum by
Wyatt.

Denton *Denton Manor*
Grotto, 1823   SK 8733
Near the house is a pretty gate. This was once
the door of a manor of another branch of the
family; it was taken down when the land
reverted and the front door put up here as a
flat object against the trees. It used to be called
the Inigo Jones gate but its date is uncertain
and it looks later. Further from the house, are
ornamental lakes and beside one is St Christopher's, or Sancaster's Well, where an ancient
spring runs in. A painting of *c.* 1800 shows
the well before the grotto with a seventeenth-
century room possibly a fishing house built
over it. Now there is a round grotto under a
mound, about 10 feet across behind a big
toothy rock arch. Inside is rock, marble,
ammonites and minerals with a big shell over
the inscription. The top of this is illegible,
Bright Cynthia and *Soft Philomena's song* alone
emerging. The last four lines invite:

> Approach you then with cautious steps
> To where the streamlet creeps
> Or Ah! too rudely you may wake
> Some guardian nymph that sleeps
>   1823

Then there is another, nacre-side, shell over
the round spring, and delicious water bubbles
slowly up.

Dunston
Dunston Pillar, 1751   TF 0763
Lincoln Heath was wild and dangerous in the
eighteenth century and in 1751 Sir Francis
Dashwood of West Wycombe (*q.v.*) put up
'the only land-lighthouse ever raised', a
92-foot square stone column with a lantern on
top to guide travellers. In 1810, his successor
felt the beacon to be unnecessary and put up
George III instead. In the Second World War,
the column was reduced to 30 feet for the
sake of a bomber base nearby. The statue,
said to be made of a special pre-cast stone of
which the secret is lost and therefore probably
Coade, is in the grounds of the Old Barracks,
Lincoln.

Eagle *Swinethorpe, The Jungle*
Burnt bricks, 1820   SK 8867
See page 187.

Fillingham
Gateway, *c.* 1760†   SK 9685
A minute gothick archway flanked with
little stone towers, cross-slitted right through,
used to stand pitifully by the A15. More and
more of it fell with every frosty winter, and it
has now fallen completely.

Greatford *Major Fitzwilliam's garden* TF 0913
See page 256.

Great Limber
Pelham's Pillar, 1849   TA 1409
A square tower tapering to a lantern with a
window in each face, and an ogival roof. An
inscription says: 'This pillar was erected to
commemorate the planting of these woods by
Charles Anderson Pelham Lord Yarborough
who commenced planting in 1787 and
between that year and 1823 placed on his
property 12,552,700 trees. The foundation of
this pillar was laid in the year 1840 by his son
and the building finished by his grandson in
1849.' There are now over 50 million trees
on the estate.

Merseyside

Very little.

Ince Blundel
Column, *c.* 1750   SD 3203
A Tuscan column with an eagle on the top.

Knowsley *Knowsley Hall*
Eyecatcher, 1755*   SJ 4594
An octagon stone summer-house set as an eyecatcher, and a tower.

Liverpool
Joseph Williamson's Tunnels,   SJ 3890
nineteenth century
See page 195.
Here there are also: '*Liverpool Folly*', a square eight-storey tower near *Christian Street* built by William Gibson of the Theatre Royal in about 1750; a routine obelisk as eyecatcher to *Allerton Hall,* and another obelisk in *Sefton Park.*

Norfolk

A flat county with more magnificent sky-scapes than most flats achieve, broken in the north by the towers of the great wool churches and predictably by some fine columns and towers, but this is not folly country.

Attleborough *On the A11*   TL 0595
A very small monument, a stone double cube 4 feet high: 'THIS PILLAR was erected by the order of the sessions of the peace of Norfolk as a grateful remembrance of the Charity of Sir Edmund Rich Kt. who freely gave ye sume of two hundred povnds towards ye repaire of ye Highway between Wynmondham and Attleborough. AD 1675.'
   On the back of the top cube are carved two intaglio footprints.

Blickling *Blickling Hall*
Pyramid and tower   TG 1829
See page 128.
As well as the pyramid there is a big square castellated two-storey red brick tower, with a single-storey lodge and a tall round stair turret that goes on to climb the height of a third storey on its own to the view. The main tower has an elaborate series of brick ogival niches with one square one on the side opposite the turret.

Brettenham *Shadwell Court*
Grotto   TL 9384
A flint grotto is reported here, with seats in niches, but I was quite unable to find it, and several local people said that it had recently been destroyed, or fallen down.

The pyramid at Blickling Hall

Briningham

Belle Vue Tower   TG 0434
This tower was built in the sixteenth century
as a beacon tower; in the eighteenth century
Sir Jacob Astley possibly restored the tower
and converted it into an observatory. Since
then it has been used in both the recent wars
for signalling. It is a very plain building consisting of four rooms one above the other,
and has been used as a cottage, but the roof
fell in during a gale in February 1971, and it
has not been repaired.

Colney *Colney New Hall*

Grotto-conservatory   TG 1807
This is a typical example of many nineteenth-
century houses or additions which have an
orangery or conservatory with grot-work,
sometimes simple as here, but often very
elaborate with shells, water and statues.

Crimplesham *Crimplesham Hall*

Sham castle, early nineteenth century TF 6604
A very fine large folly, too embowered in
trees to photograph or to draw. It is very
complicated and unusual; the front door leads
into a spiral staircase that leads straight up to
the castellated top of the tall thin tower for
the view. In the middle is a tiled bellcote with
curved roofs and an elaborate classical-
Romanesque frieze. On the right of the
door, a steep outside staircase leads to the
piano nobile, a small first-floor square room
with an unusually fine mosaic of dark pebbles
and horses teeth, the teeth being set on end or
edge as the complicated star pattern demands.

On the left of the door is an open court
with ruined walls into which have been
skilfully worked a number of mediaeval fragments. Three thirteenth-century door arches
were used in the court and a fourth was set
up by itself beyond so that it all makes a very
good ruin indeed.

Denton *Denton House*

Grotto, *c.* 1770   TM 2987
A very pretty little grotto standing in the
garden of the house, made by Stackhouse
Thompson, who is said to have collected all

the shells and coral for it from the Great
Barrier Reef. A front of local flints, with
three arched doors, leads into the grotto itself, which is a small circular room with
domed roof supported on four pillars, the
whole encrusted with shells, fossils and polished stones. There used to be a pagoda here,
too.

Great Yarmouth

Nelson Column, 1817   TG 5306
A great Doric column that imposes itself on
us by sheer size, like the columns at Shrewsbury and Truro. This one was designed by
William Wilkins and is 144 feet high. The
column stands on a particularly fine plinth
with carved wreaths and the well-lettered
names of battles. On top, six mourning ladies
hold out drooping wreaths and help to support an enriched dome, a globe and a gilded
Britannia.

Gunton *Gunton Park*

Tower, *c.* 1840   TG 2435
Going to the tower, the navigator is doubted,
and the driver says
—I think I've seen it, but it's not an Italian
tower, it's a pagoda.
—Golly; keep left.
—There's something through there.
—But that's not a pagoda, that's a temple.
And there it is, all of them in one. How
can it be described? It has three storeys. In
the bottom one, 30 feet high, is a big yellow
brick arch with two rusticated pilasters on
each side, a window between each pair, round
lights over windows, and a pierced brick
balustrade on top; say Roman. First floor,
a smaller rectangle, 25 feet high, with large
arched windows; say Railway. Above, a
glazed rectangular lantern, 15 feet high, three
brick freestanding columns at each corner
(two for the long side), with reeded, faintly
Egyptian capitals; say Crystal Palace. The
roof is green copper, ogee curved with an
oeil de boeuf in each side, and a slender pin-
nacle-flagpole; in the distance, say Chinese.

On each face of the arch is a curved 25 foot
wing on each side, to look equally grand from
both approaches; the gatekeeper lived in
four segments of a circle.

The tower at Gunton Park

The base of the column, Holkham Hall

Heydon *Heydon Hall*
Look-out Tower*   TG 1127
Never heard of locally, never found.

Holkham *Holkham Hall*
Column and Obelisk   TF 8944
There is a beautiful obelisk, 1729, by Kent, south of the house and on the same axis to the north, the column, 120 feet high, to Thomas Coke, first Earl of Leicester of the second creation, who between 1776 and 1816 raised the yield of his land from £2,200 a year to £20,000 and became the father of British agriculture.

It is a super-column, large, mad, imaginative and endearing, well and crisply carved, well preserved, designed Dunthorne R.A.

1845. It is fluted in, let us say, the composite manner, but where volutes are expected, there are cows. On top is a drum and dome; a small Choragic monument crowned by a sheaf of wheat. But the 35-foot wide base is the thing, steps up to a square podium with angle extensions (like those on the Nelson column in Trafalgar Square), but now instead of lions there is a cow (BREEDING IN ALL ITS BRANCHES), a wheeled implement (THE IMPROVEMENT OF AGRICULTURE), a plough (LIVE AND LET LIVE) and a sheep (SMALL IN SIZE BUT GREAT IN VALUE). On the side of the base itself are the inscription and reliefs of gentlemen round a committee table, gentlemen with sheep, and lastly gentlemen with horses and men with spades.

The clock tower at Little Ellingham

The bath house at Melton Constable

Little Ellingham
Clock tower, 1855   TM 0199
One of the most charming and surprising things anywhere. A cruciform building with four two-storey cottages with steep gables, set at right angles to each other. Where they join, a big square clock tower is supported on them, crowned with a lantern-bellchamber and a lead dome. All yellowish-buff brick with red brick dressings and chimneys on the gable peaks in front. The corners of the cross are partly filled by four porches, each a quarter of an octagon pyramid, cut to show one face and two halves. It stands encircled by a path, a clipped hedge and then a grass moat with a bridge over it.

Melton Constable *Melton Hall*
Sham Castle Bath House   TG 0333
Again, one of the most charming follies anywhere; this one is built to look like a church from the house. Inside, there was one very large room for the bath house with the tower as bay window; it runs up another storey with three sham windows, castellations, a sundial and a tiny octagonal slate roof crowned by a large ball and wind vane. Later, a floor was put in and some windows blocked up on the new first floor—the ground floor room is still its original size, with nine pretty gothick windows. All is Roman cement with patches of coral brick, decorated very simply with quoigning. Described, it is not very different from a dozen other pieces of useful gothick, but someone got the proportions just right, and it has some very becoming trees.

Northwold *Didlington Hall*
A large sad estate with late nineteenth- and twentieth-century stables, bellcote, isolated church and graveyard, overgrown heavily in the flat surrounding land. Brick walls enclose the remains of gardens, tennis courts with classical temples for watching, patio, pergola. It must once have been considerably landscaped, for a fine terrace ran above the end of a big lake, complicated with islands; there are water-lilies, a thatched summer-house and ducks but no trace of a promised sham ruin. On the other side of the house, though, beyond the church, lie the ruins of the Thatched Cottage used for 'overflow guests for the cricket matches; they say it was all willowpattern inside'.

Raveningham *Raveningham Hall*
Cast Iron Obelisk, 1831*   TM 3897
Another of the rare obelisks in cast iron; by
J. T. Patience, proclaiming the miles to
London, Norwich, Lowestoft, etc.

South Wootton
Reffley Temple, 1789   TF 6424
A simple brick temple erected 'by a Friendly
Society' and later enlarged. The sphinxes that
flank the door are the nicest thing about it,
though there is a small obelisk of 1756,
Baccho Venerique Sacrum, re-erected. It is a
melancholy place, perhaps a pitiful attempt to
echo the gaieties of West Wycombe without
the landscape or the money.

Westwick
Tower*   TG 2726
A round tower in grey brick.

North Yorkshire

The three counties of Yorkshire have an
astonishing number of follies, far more than
their position would suggest, for follies tend
to decrease in number towards the north and
east. And they are not only many but good;
there is a grade A example of everything
except the grotto.

Aysgarth *Sorrel Sykes Farm*
The Rocket Ship folly   SE 0189
See page 232.

Oldstead Tower, Byland Abbey

Byland Abbey
Oldstead Tower, 1837   SE 5579
A well built and set stone tower, about 10 feet
square with short square corner turrets,
railings between. On the north face a stone
slab tells us that JOHN WORMALD IN THE FIRST
YEAR OF THE REIGN OF QUEEN VICTORIA
CAUSED THIS OBSERVATORY TO BE ERECTED.
J. DODDS BUILDER.

To the south towards the splendid view is a
similar platform, inaccessible, and a door to
the tower with a big lintel:

Here hills and waving groves a scene display,
And part admit and part exclude the day:
See rich industry smiling on the plains,
And peace and plenty tell VICTORIA reigns!
Happy the MAN, who to these shades retires,
Whom NATURE charms, and whom the muse
inspires.
Who wandering thoughtful in this silent wood,
Attends the duties of the wise and good:
To observe a mean, be to himself a friend,
To follow NATURE, and regard his end.

High on each side is an odd fat cruciform
window; unless there is a skylight on the
roof, the stairs must be pitch dark.

A strange tower, pretty a long way off, then
disappointing at the end of a pleasant walk,
then odd and cosy; a pleasant place.

Castellated cowsheds near Gilling West

Castle Howard
Fortified Wall, 1719   SE 7270
See page 26.

Easby   NZ 5809
Column*
A large monument on the hilltop to Captain
Cook who was born at Marton. There is a
statue of him in Whitby.

East Witton
Grotto, 1817*   SE 1586
An arch of rough-hewn stone round a niche
in the hillside, wood-panelled, with table and
seats. There is an A for the Earl of Ailsbury,
the date, and a very battered grotesque head
for the spring, known as Slobbering Sal.

Gilling West *Sedbury Hall*
Folly cowsheds, *c.* 1760   NZ 1805
High on a hillside above the Gilling–Barnard
Castle road is an elaborately castellated wall
with three large blank arches, and tall blank
crossed arrow-slits on either side of them. It
successfully fortifies a range of cow-byres.
There are also some castellated cow-byres
and an arch.

   In a field on an outcrop of rock about 20
feet high, beautifully framed between a clump
of beeches and two ash trees, is a small tower,
c. 1800. The lower storey is arcaded with
gothick arches, and the upper room has tall
pointed windows and is finely roofed with a
stone dome. A battlemented wall with
machicolations runs down on each side of the
tower along the edge of the cliff.

Grewelthorpe *Hackfall Woods*
Group, *c.* 1750   SE 2376
See page 60.

Harrogate
Harlow Hill Tower, 1829   SE 3054
This very plain square stone tower was built
by John Thompson in 1829. In about 1933
the Corporation of Harrogate bought it, and
turned it into a public observation tower,
complete with telescope. The real interest of
the tower is the extraordinary number of sites
and monuments to be seen from its top. They
are catalogued by a local writer as follows.
'It is possible to see seven of the great battle-
fields of England, the scene of 24 minor
skirmishes, 20 market towns, 17 castles, 23
abbeys and monasteries, 70 county houses and
200 churches; and all these with the naked
eye.'

Ilton *Arne Gill*
Tower, 1824   SE 1676
A tiny round tower with a door and three
windows; about 10 feet from the ground the
walls were stopped in a rough line in imitation of a ruin.

Knaresborough
St Robert's Chapel   SE 3557
There is a lot of carved-in-the-living-rock
stuff here, and an old postcard shows the door
and window of the chapel with a giant St
Robert in full armour drawing his sword to
protect the door he looms over. An old man
used to KEEP IT ALL UP, and it was shown, but

he is dead, St Robert is gone and all that remains is a small low cave labelled PISS & FUCK HOLE.

But something new should be done here; Knaresborough is two places; a routine town on top of the cliff worn by the River Nidd and at the bottom a slight folly air along Abbey Road, and the long Crag Top footpath. One keeps expecting something, as there must have been 50 years ago, a visit-place. Now there is only the castellated House in the Rock, *Fort Montague* ('Those who do not wish to pay, do not enter'), a carving of a hare over a door at Mouse Hole, a house called Grimaldi View, and a little wooden windmill.

Leyburn *Thornborough Hall*
Sham Castle   SE 1191
One of the prettiest and most peaceful little sham castles in England, just behind the Rural District Council offices. The usual pattern; two fat round half-towers with a wall between them. In the wall, a big round blind arch with round windows in the spandrels, a pointed door and pointed windows. Another path goes up to the top, flat and grown with grass, so one can sit on a little seat with one's back to a crowning hexagon tower made of smaller stones. Inside is an odd vaulted room with its corners all wrong.

Little Ribston *Ribston Hall*
Two-faced Butler   SE 3854
In the grounds near the edge of a fine pinetum there is a gothick arch in red sandstone, with ivy and every romantic trick, a sad little carved head, stones on the ground and some good flamboyant detail.

The two-faced butler is nearby, a big grotesque head with its tongue out, set over a gate into the walled garden. This face is said to show his expression as he turned from taking an order, and the smiling one on the other side of the gate the face for greeting a guest.

Masham *Swinton Park*   SE 2180
Druids' Circle
See page 242.

Yorke's Folly, Pateley Bridge

Pateley Bridge
Yorke's Folly, eighteenth century   SE 1666
Two piers of stone which stand on the crest of the moors overlooking Nidderdale: they were built by John Yorke of Bewerley, who was born in 1733 and who lived to be 80, to give work to the unemployed at a time of depression in this district of Yorkshire. The men were paid fourpence a day for their labour, and given a loaf of bread when food was exceptionally scarce. Originally there was a third and even larger pier, which collapsed in a gale on the night of 17 November 1893.

The sham castle at Aske Hall

Richmond *Aske Hall*
Sham Castle and Oliver's Ducket,   NZ 1504
eighteenth century
Aske has one of the most beautifully detailed of all sham castles, a complicated building of refined gothick that has been attributed to Chambers, Brown and Kent's young associate David Garrett; I favour Garrett because it is very like a pretty tower designed earlier by Kent for Sir Conyers d'Arcy at Aske but never built.

The castle, which is called The Temple, was made between 1758–67 for the Earl of Holderness. The ground floor is rectangular with half-rounds projecting at the ends, castellated arcading between and variegated balustrades. Above, set well in to make a terrace, is a two-storey octagon with a centre pinnacled door into the lower room and an upper one accessible only by its own staircase at the back, 'for goings-on'. Square castellated side towers are linked by lower walls to the octagon and each of them has a half-circle turret projecting in front, to echo the ground floor.

Oliver's Ducket, for which I can find no date, is an eyecatcher castle on a hill top, made with old stones from Richmond Castle and much more mediaeval in style. The very solid bastion base, with portholes is round, with cruciform projections to a larger circle, angled off. On top stands a round castellated tower with more portholes and trefoiled windows and a door. Nothing seems to be known of Oliver, a ducket is a dovecote which this is surely not, so the name remains obscure.

Temple Lodge
Culloden Tower   NZ 1701
See page 209.

Rievaulx
Duncombe Park, 1730 and 1758   SE 5785
See page 24.

Ripon *Market Square*
Obelisk   SE 3171
A pretty obelisk to commemorate the fact that one of the Aislabies of Studley Royal (*q.v.*) spent 66 years as an M.P.

Robin Hood's Bay *The Cottage, Fyling Hall*
Pigsty*   NZ 9505
A small classical temple, a pediment on four columns, about 9 feet high, with three entrances, 'built by Squire Barry'.

Sawley *Sawley Hall*
Arch, probably *c.* 1848   SE 2567
A bridge, hardly folly, crossing a field road, made with stones from the old Abbey.

Oliver's Ducket

Hazlewood Castle

Routine craggy rock-work with upstanding stones on top.

Scarborough *Peasholme Park*
Pagoda, 1912   TA 0486
See page 132.

Row Brow
Baron Albert's Tower, 1842   TA 0485
A remote and solitary place, with the ruins of a round tower tumbled in a clump of trees. Once it was 20 feet high, built to take a tall pole so that a flag could be flown when the Londesborough family was at Scarborough. The rough sandstone blocks are unusually large, some huge, and have become picturesque, scattered in their ankle-wrenching way on the ground.

Settle
The Folly   SD 8264
A fine late seventeenth-century house; no folly. Probably just bolder and better than its neighbours. There is a small tower nearby, later and duller.

Skipton *Skipton Castle*
Grotto Room, late seventeenth   SD 9952
century
See page 146.

Studley Roger *Studley Royal*   SE 2970
See page 28.

Stutton *Hazlewood Castle*
Tower   SE 4843
A real charmer; a nice squatty little octagon tower of rather random stone, once rendered with Roman cement of which little remains. Two storeys, the top one castellated with round windows that probably once held coloured glass. Once there was a little stair; now it is all blocked in, but for compensation the tower on the grass is surrounded by a wall and a ring of white posts. Some of the stones may have come from a chantry chapel that once stood here; in any case it was built with love.

Tadcaster *Grimston Park*
Tower   SE 5041
See page 209.

Thornton Dale *Scampston Castle*
Deerfold façade   SE 8786
A late eighteenth-century eyecatching façade to an isolated farm cottage, to be seen from Scampston Hall. Of rich red and yellow brick, the centre of the cottage rises in a tiara of castellations, with low castellated wings on each side. A good one.

Northamptonshire

The best of the Midlands counties for follies, lacking only in some eccentricities of the last hundred years. The industrial cities are not very exciting (though the open-cast coalmining can be spectacular) but they occupy little of a most pleasant, cheerful and insufficiently regarded county.

Boughton *Boughton Park*   SP 7566
(These two Boughtons are about 14 miles apart as the crow flies.) The Park has a very good group of lighthearted follies. Unfortunately, when I went there no one mentioned the grotto necessary to any really complete group, but I understand that there is one, north of the house in a small wood. The first thing is the Hawking Tower which must have been the first piece of improvement as it is mentioned, clearly after its transformation, in a letter from Walpole to the owner of Boughton, the second Earl of Strafford, on 28 August 1756, telling how he drove past at night and 'started at the vision of one of my own towers . . . it must have been Boughton'. But it really does not look like Strawberry Hill at all, much more like St Crispin's Cottages at West Wycombe. It is a square stone three-storey tower, and Lord Strafford turned it into an eyecatcher church for the house, adding ogee windows, flatly banded, big quatrefoils, castellations and pinnacles. The outer stair to the top floor is now blocked. The later works of *c.* 1770 include two castellated entrances, and a castellated barn, near the house, a cottage, Newpark Barn which has lost castellations and ornaments, and Bunker's Hill Farm which has kept them—1776, and named after the battle like the farm at Greystoke.

There is a routine obelisk of 1764 and then to the east Holly Lodge, a curious and delightful house with an implement gate and castellations everywhere, on the twin gables and on the outbuildings, all of undressed stone. Behind is a square clock tower with a Chinese-curved roof, and here also are two castellated round towers with an arch between, echoing a similar gate from the east end of the park. Just down Spectacles Lane stand The Spectacles, yet again two castellated round towers with an arch between; indeed, very like a binocular. Unfortunately, The Spectacles have lost their road and simply stand in a hedge. They are very like the earlier eyecatcher at Wroxton—possibly some culture-carrying here—though the lie of the land precludes them from sharing the beautiful placing of Wroxton on its hill.

Boughton House
Chinese Tent, eighteenth century   SP 9082
See page 114.

Brigstock
Lyveden New Building, 1590s   SP 9886
See page 14.

Castle Ashby
Group. See page 190.

As well as Knucklebone Lodge, there is another pretty thatch called Nevitt's Lodge, a fine stout water tower of 1865 in Classigothico, and a dairy with temple façade, a bridge, and an aviary-turned-house which are all by Capability Brown.

Holly Lodge, Boughton Park

Castor *Milton Park*

Kennels   TL 1398

Here is some particularly solid and expensive gothick, including a beautiful lodge, elevated into an Object, a stone octagon of two storeys with buttresses that end in pinnacles. The face to the park is gabled with two elegant arches on the ground floor and a rose window above. The chimneys go into an octagon turret at the back. Chambers has been suggested as the architect, but it looks too finely detailed; I think the possible attribution of the Kennels to him much more likely. These were built in 1767—a mediaeval gate house with a big round tower made of undressed stone with dressed castellations, low lattice windows and two low fat buttresses. The gate is set within a bigger arch in an arrow-slitted wall and then to the right is a lower round tower with a slightly curved conical roof crowned by a hunt weathervane. All newly restored.

Finedon *Exmill Cottage*   SP 9273

The best example I have seen of a frequent conversion, by which the eyecatcher properties of an old tower windmill may be usefully retained; the cabin and sails are scrapped and the top castellated. This was a specially good windmill for the purpose as, instead of having the usual straight tapering sides, it bellies out gracefully at the bottom like a vase. A mill stone set in the side and several stone shields carry various initials, and a stone ribbon, 'EXMILL COTTAGE'.

There was another tower at Finedon—the Volta Tower, a superbly stout round fat bulging tower built in 1863, most elaborately decorated, which looked like the rock of Gibraltar but fell in the early 1950s, killing the owner.

Holdenby *Holdenby House*

The Arches   SP 6968

See page 11.

Horton *Horton Hall*

Eyecatcher and menagerie   SP 8255

See page 139.

Naseby *Naseby Field**   SP 6980

The parents of Edward Fitzgerald put up a memorial at Wray Place in 1823. This was later held to be the wrong site, so in 1936 the county authorities put up another, stating that this was where Cromwell started his charge. I understand that yet a third site has recently been suggested.

Newnham *Newnham Hall*

Sham Ruins, *c.* 1850   SP 5760

Very small and domestic, very near the house on an island, reached by a wooden bridge. One part is about 7 feet by 9, and 12 feet high, possibly with another 3 feet of turret but the ivy is too thick to be sure. A wooden door leads into a minute room lined with white-washed brick. It has four slit windows and 36 nesting holes for pigeons, like the negative gable-ends of houses, each with a projecting brick step. Beside it is an arch in random stone to march, with a low wall; this was probably an ice house.

Even nearer to the house are the prettiest kennels, a little row of three brick-and-half timbered villas with gable windows and ridge-tiles.

Preston Capes *Fawsley Hall*

Eyecatcher   SP 5855

Two cottages in the village were built as an eyecatcher to the hall *c.* 1800 by Lady

The kennels at Milton Park

Knightley. It was intended to take a road through the low arch between them, but this was never done. From the green fields they make a simple and unpretending castle, red brick from a local brickfield, with white geese in front.

Rushton *Tresham's Triangular Lodge*   SP 8482
See page 12.

Stamford *Burghley House*
Bath house*   TF 0506
I am very sorry not to have seen this yet, as it was built by Capability Brown before 1763 in the Jacobean style and so must be one of the first revivals of this style. It doesn't look very exciting in the photographs, but the setting among great cedar trees is good.

Upper Astrop *Astrop Park*   SP 5237
My directions said that here were '2 gothic Rumbold's Well with a replica by the road', carefully copied from the words of a usually reliable informant. Nothing. No well. No Rumbold.

The eyecatcher at Preston Capes

Woodford *The Wellington Tower*   SP 9777
A round house with a double-skirted conical roof, a little square stair-top in a circular railing, a round window and an inscription in a cruciform recess.

PANORAMA WATERLOO VICTORY
June 18 AD 1815.

It is said that Wellington, who certainly often stayed with the Arbuthnots at Woodford House, stood on the top and commented that the surrounding countryside looked very like the battlefield.

Northumberland

Northumberland is such a lovely county, open and wide and free, with the Wall and Holy Island and the castles and the lack of tourist industry that I almost forget that it is thin in follies. . . . It has the atmosphere and geology for them; just there aren't many—obelisks and a column apart, there are more at Alnwick than in all the rest of the county.

Alnwick *Alnwick Castle*
Group of nine   NU 1912
Alnwick must stand high with the lover of the picturesque; the castle is mediaeval, and the barbican superb, with eighteenth-century

guardian warriors on the ramparts, replacing the old figures of lead. Inside, all is Salvin. The great park was magnificently landscaped by Capability Brown in the 1760s and includes the beautifully displayed ruins of Hulne Priory, two important follies by Robert Adam for the first Duke of Northumberland, and a number of lesser nonsenses, mostly connected with lions.

Brizlee Tower was probably designed by Adam in 1781; it is one of the best built and most finely detailed and carved prospect towers in the country, though it does most sadly lack an exquisitely stuccoed room or two. It stands on a hilltop 2 miles from the castle and is circular in four storeys with four projecting bays for slender gothick windows running the whole height, and windows in between. It stands on a wider octagon, with wide arcaded sides below the recessed faces of the tower and narrow niched sides below the advanced ones. There is a castellated openwork balustrade. On top of the tower, following the curves, is an awkward quatrefoil one and then a pretty octagonal top lantern which is crowned by an iron cresset, as this is, of course, a Peel Tower. The inscription reads:

CIRCUMSPICE
EGO OMNIA ISTA SUM DIMENSUS;
MEI SUNT ORDINES,
MEA DESCRIPTIO;
MULTAE ETIAM ISTARUM ARBORUM
MEA MANU SUNT SATAE

It is often said that the Duke designed both Brizlee and the Ratcheugh Observatory him-

Alnwick. Brizlee Tower and two lions

self, but if he did, he was as good as Adam. There is no trace at all of the amateur in either of them. The observatory is a large sham castle even further away from the castle on the other side. Adam is thought to have designed a 'real castle' for this site, but the Duke had asked for a ruin, and got it, so presumably Adam designed that too. The result is a magnificent eyecatcher, crouched on a cliff and extremely convincing. The observatory part is a big square castellated tower with one great room, with three round-headed windows in a bay on each side, filling the walls; one of course is in the door. It is painted cream, with white for the windows and the plaster fan-vaulting cornice. There is a pale stone floor, a pale scrubbed wooden table and three benches; even in the rain it is a room of dazzling light and one of the loveliest ever designed.

On each side of the room is first an arch and then a half-tower. One has a spiral staircase to the ramparts—up, and along to the room— and beyond this is a two-storey cottage hidden in the ruins. On the inside face of the walls are some simple carvings, a grotesque, a fish, a crescent moon, a lion, flags, a sundial.

John Adam designed the Lion Bridge in 1773. It is stone, castellated, with look-outs, a lead lion on one parapet, and a feature which I think is unique; at the end, past the castellations, the stone is carved to imitate wooden pale fencing.

The Monument to William the Lion is stone, *c.* 1860, about 4 feet by 3:

WILLIAM the LION
King of SCOTLAND besieging ALNWICK Castle
was here taken Prisoner
MCLXXIV

The Malcolm Cross, a mediaeval one to commemorate the death of Malcolm, King of Scotland in the earlier Siege of Alnwick in 1093, was restored and put up here in 1774 by the first duchess, who claimed descent from him.

There is a summer-house at Hulne Priory which has the stucco work lacking at Brizlee, and Hulne also once had a menagerie.

Standing in trees on the golf course is the Peace Column, stone with a bell at the top, for the peace of 1814, Nelson, Wellington and Pitt.

Then there are two good pieces in the town. The Pottergate Tower was one of the original town gates, heavily gothicked by the Borough in 1768 with openwork battlements, ogival arches, slits, carved shields, etc., and the angle buttresses running up into turrets. It had a spire, destroyed in 1812.

The Percy Tenantry Column, also called Farmer's Folly, was put up as thanks to the second duke in 1816 for reducing rent during the war years. It rises 85 feet on a neat mown mound with neat flowerbeds, a Doric column with a drum on top inside a railing and on the drum the Percy Lion again with his stretched poker tail. Round the base at the corners, perhaps the inspiration for Trafalgar Square, are four fine lions, all facing in to the column but turning their heads away, all a little different, mouths shut or open. The designer was the Newcastle architect David Stephenson.

Cambo *Wallington Hall*
Sham castles and gargoyles   NZ 0383
W. Hutchinson, in his *View of Northumberland,* published in 1776, describes a visit to the sham castle. The exertions and sweat entailed in visiting remote follies remain unchanged.

We had a view of Rothley Castle at the distance of some miles; the situation appeared rugged and uncommon. On the side which then presented itself, we could discern distinctly no more than the square tower and part of its flankings, placed on a considerable eminence of a rocky and barren aspect. By not taking the proper road, we were led almost round this edifice, which we viewed with no small degree of impatiency. When we came to look upon the northern front, our curiosity was somewhat slackened, but nevertheless we passed down the road about half a mile, and having climbed the fence, ascended the steep to the building. The fatigue was but ill recompensed, for we found this object of our anxious curiosity, no other than an ornamental structure, composed of a square tower, flanked with a curvated wall, embattled, and pierced with loopholes, and each wing terminated with a bastion: the situation romantic, on the verge of a broken precipice. The sides of the hill, to the west and south present a shaken and tremendous rocky steep rent into vast impending columns or massive tables; the stones of the enormous bulk, in many places hang on each other in such loose positions, as if ready to fall into the vale; forming caverns and recesses, and rude heaps of rocks of a most wild and grotesque appearance. To decorate (I presume) this noble scene, the awkward images of a goat and a staring stag, delight the passing children.—On resorting to my book of notes, I find they carry the countenance of peevishness, but as they are just, I will transcribe them. The southern front opens on a small plain, naturally of a circular form, scattered over with huge heads of griffins, broken cornices and ensigns of Calverly (the lamb and flag of Grace) sculptured on white free-stone; in the midst of which stand two preposterous effigies, representative of no known dress, personage or people. And to give the *coup de grace* to this composition, enormous ribs, jaw-bones, and members of a whale, are fastened to the walls for decoration. We entered the tower, in which by way of tables, are three large rude unhewed stones, one in the centre, and one in each recess at the sides, benched with similar stones: pretty enough for the reception of Thomas of Hick-a-thrift or Jack the Giant Killer.

John Hodgson, in his *History of Northumberland* published in 1827, describes what happened after the death of Sir Walter Calverly Blackett, who built the folly, in 1776. Unfortunately it has been the fate of many other follies:

The walls of the whole, though strong, and some degree artificially bedded, are rough, and without a tool mark upon them.

The tower had a gigantic statue at each corner, and a stone roof partly covered with lead. The circular area in front was also set off with images, and with benches and tables of stone for the convenience of parties who visited the place in Sir Walter's time, when Rothley Park was well stocked with deer; and it, and the crags, and the castle, and lake were parts of a whole, which their owner delighted to show to his visitors, several of the images were of Portland stone, and were given to Sir Walter at the taking down of Aldersgate in 1761; where they had formerly stood. Soon after Sir Walter's death, the deer park was wisely turned into a pasture, and the sham castle neglected, but bands of faws, and young clowns of the neighbourhood more rude and mischievous than faws, very needlessly waged war with the giants and griffins in stone, and destroyed them.

Today Rothley Castle is still impressive even in driving rain, two big towers, an arch and some walling. Nearby is Codger's Castle, an angle of wall, still with some castellations and two squat towers with pyramidal roofs, all very random, at the ends. This was built in 1745 'as a defence against the Scots', and designed by Thomas Wright.

Both were for eyecatchers to Wallington Hall, several miles away over the dales, with the Devil's Causeway running south-west to Hadrian's Wall. On the front lawn at Wallington there are four great heads in a row buried up to their necks in the grass. These, the owners told me, were part of old Aldersgate in the City of London; when it was demolished, 'they were bought for £170 and brought up to the Tyne as ballast in an empty cornship. We brought the 4 heads out of the wood in 1929, and set them on the lawn'. This seems to put paid to a *Notes and Queries* story that the four heads were survivors of the Rothley griffins; but of course as Aldersgate was damaged in the Great Fire, it is always possible that *all* the monsters came from it, and were put up at Rothley. Daniel Garrett as designer of Rothley in the 1740s has also been suggested, and there has been mention of a Chinese House by Thomas Wright in 1752, long gone.

Capheaton *Capheaton Hall*
Sham Ruin, early nineteenth century NZ 0481
A small stone chapel, west of the house; two walls at right angles, one a gable with a big arch and a cross on top, the other a low straggle with a square-headed entrance.

About four miles on towards Hexham is a possible eyecatcher to Capheaton, a square low tower of rough stone with dressed stone facing, castellated. There are several pointed windows, some blind, and on top a small tower with square headed doors and windows.

Coldstream *Twizell Castle*
Ruin, *c.* 1770   NT 8440
A foolishness-type folly, so ruinous, so big, so strangely named, that it is irresistibly folly, especially as no one has seen it. Sir Francis Blake began his great house in 1770 and never finished it. Everything is drowned in encroaching, clambering and piled-up green. I think it has round towers.

Haggerston *Haggerston Tower*   NU 0544
A big and ugly tower with a taller turret, left standing when the house was pulled down.

Hartburn
Gothick Façade   NZ 0986
See page 221.

Nelson Village *Plessy*
Tower*   NZ 2478
I have been told by David Glover of 'a round tower in a flat field, similar to the one at Penistone, but shorter. . . . Uninteresting'.

Newcastle-upon-Tyne *The Grey Monument*
Column, 1838   NZ 2464
One hundred and thirty-five feet of Roman Doric, on a big pedestal with Earl Grey on top. The tea is not mentioned, only Liberty and Reform. Column by Benjamin Green,

statue by Bailey. These huge columns that utterly dwarfed everything in sight when they were put up are always exciting; quite different from tower blocks.

Nunwick *Nunwick*
Castellated kennels, 1768   NY 8874
See page 219.

Whitton
Sharpe's Folly   NU 0602
See page 222.

On the B 6305 from Hexham
Obelisk   NY 8561
There are obelisks at Bedlington, Felton, Lanton, Kirkley Hall and Otterburn, but this one is special, on a bleak minor road, about a mile before the junction with the A686, a most beautiful and melancholy obelisk, tall and thin and uncertain, top crumbling, made of rough stone with smooth stone bandings.

The school at Hartburn

Nottinghamshire

It is curious how little there is here; an area once known as the Dukeries might have been full of competing follies, but no. Two good ones, both nineteenth century.

Clipstone *Duke's Folly*

Lodge, 1844*   SK 6065
This, I am told, was built by 'the eccentric fourth Duke of Portland', but the tunnel duke was the fifth duke, and this sounds much less excessive. *Buildings of England* describes it as 'built in imitation of the Gatehouse of Worksop Priory. . . . It has the figures of Richard Coeur-de-Lion, Robin Hood, Friar Tuck, Maid Marion, Little John, Allan-a-Dale, and a schoolroom above the gateway'.

Elston

Middleton's Folly, eighteenth   SK 7648
century?
A trifle. A tiny stone pinnacled building with two doors, one to a chapel and the other to a cellar so that Bobby Middleton, they say, never needed to sit through the sermon without a cosy nip.

Newstead *Newstead Abbey*

Sham forts, mid eighteenth century SK 5253
The fifth Lord Byron was a genuine Bad Baron or Wicked Lord. His reputation was so strong that the sham castle which he built in 1749 was eventually pulled down; it was being used as a school, and even this benign influence was not strong enough to defeat the relish which turned the parties and concerts which he held there into orgies. Another story is that Mother Shipton prophesied that when a boat loaded with ling should cross Sherwood Forest the Byrons would leave Newstead. When a boat was being brought across the forest for use on the lake the local people immediately filled it to the gunwhales with heather, and sure enough the Byrons did leave Newstead. Besides cutting down all the trees on his estate so that his son when he inherited should have no profit from the land, the wicked lord had a 20-gun boat with which he used to conduct mimic naval battles; he had been in the navy as a boy.

The two forts which he built are on either side of the lake, crisp cardboard gothick with round turrets at the corners and square ones in the centre of the walls. Their thin neat detail suggests Sanderson Miller. Horace Walpole saw them in 1760:

> As I returned I saw Newstead and Althorpe: I like both. The former is very abbey. The great east window of the church remains and connects with the house: the hall entire, the refectory entire, the cloisters untouched, with the ancient cistern of the convent and their arms on it, a private chapel quite perfect. The park, which is still charming, has not been so much unprofaned; the present Lord has lost large sums and paid part in old oaks, five thou-

The Fort, Newstead Abbey

sand pounds' worth of which have been cut near the house. In recompense he has built two baby forts, to pay his country in castles for the damage done to the navy.

Near the house is an elaborate classical monument with an urn on top and a long inscription to the sixth Lord Byron's dog BOATSWAIN.

Nottingham *The Rope Walk*
Tunnel, *c.* 1856   SK 5542
See page 195.
And there is a barely Chinese pagoda in the Arboretum, surrounded by cannon.

Welbeck *Welbeck Abbey*
Underground rooms, nineteenth   SK 5775
century
See page 196.

Oxfordshire

Rousham has one of the most famous eye-catchers in England, designed by Kent, but any of us could have done it; perhaps this is why everyone likes it so much. Wroxton has another beauty, Shotover is very early, Crowsley is very sinister, not much else; though there are in fact four good follies near Henley-on-Thames, only one is actually in the county. This is perhaps a place to mention the large number of landscaped and reasonably well follied estates that were established during the eighteenth century along the Thames Valley; it was an obvious place to go, and still is, and still produces a special complacent atmosphere; Pope would not care for it now.

Abingdon *Abbey House*
Sham ruin, *c.* 1860   SU 4998
See page 252.

Blenheim
The Column of Victory and   SP 4416
Triumphal Arch
Some such columns and arches have a folly air; these represent the opposite stolidity.

Buckland *Buckland House*
Ice-house, eighteenth century   SU 3698
See page 37.

A useful folly, a circular brick building with a thatched roof, domed inside with a stone soakaway at the bottom. It has for ornament in front a fine pedimented porch with a slate roof and plain stone dressings on very knobbly tufa. Few ice-houses were given such noble entrances and very few are now more than a hole in the ground, but this one is safely near the house. Moreover, there is a notice telling how it was for the men who filled it one particularly late spring:

THE ICE HOUSE

Mr. Painter remembers filling the ice house on his birthday, 6th April, 1913. I remember clearly because it was my sixteenth birthday. Two men went out in a punt and broke the ring of ice and then got two long poles with iron spikes on the end and pulled the ice into the bank.

Two other men standing on the bank with wooden mallets broke up the ice into small bits and the two who were in the punt had two mesh sieves, wired into a forked stick and they dipped the ice out in the sieves and put it into a wheel barrow. Six men and wheelbarrows, on a chain, wheelbarrowed the ice up the hill and tipped it. Two more in the ice house shoved the ice in, and two more in the ice house levelling it out.

The head gardener, Mr. Gough, heated beer for us and also provided bread and cheese.

The ice house at Buckland House (detail on p. 37)

The ice was wheeled from the ice house to Buckland House every morning and washed before use and the ice lasted practically until the next winter's ice was brought in.

Bobby Kinch, who lived in Mildenhalls, offered me a clay pipe and some twist tobacco. I have smoked a pipe ever since. The other people working with me were

Mr. Dick Clark
Joe Fear
Joe Whiting
Alfred Jordan
Tommy Wells
Billy Wells
Dick Fear, and
Ted Eley, senior

(signed) F. G. Painter

Faringdon *Lord Berner's Folly*
Tower, 1935   SU 2896
See page 272.

Henley-on-Thames *Friar Park*
Grotto, 1890   SU 7683
Friar Park is a huge house in red brick with wonderful art nouveau-gothic frig-work in stone, very reminiscent of *The Blackfriars* pub in London, covered with ornament, peacock tiles, beaten copper doorplates, the bell push in the mouth of a monk and inscriptions everywhere.

The grounds were not large but very elaborate, with a Japanese garden, herbaceous and rock gardens ascending to a model of the Matterhorn, built up with huge blocks of stone. Everything was designed by Sir Frank Crisp and his head gardener Mr P. O. Knowles, and was once wonderfully kept up—'the show-place of the world'; it may now be so once more, but in 1950 most of the illuminations and fantasies in the grottoes, like the crocodiles with electric lamp eyes, were damaged or gone, and I have not been allowed to see it again.

However, another head gardener, Mr W. Arthur Cook, has described it for me as it was in 1937. There were four grottoes; nearest to the house was the water-cave, the Blue Grotto of Capri, with one entrance from the Japanese garden and others by boat from the lakes. It was lit by blue glass skylights and electricity, and in small caves and recesses were model swans, geese, ducks, frogs and toadstools. The main cave had stalactites, fossil trees, white owls, petrified birds' nests, a *Nid d' Amour* full of babies, and rainbow lighting as well as the blue glass.

Further from the house, the Large Cave had a waterfall with coloured lights.

Under the Henley Matterhorn was the Ice Grotto, reproduced from a photograph of the cave in the Glacier du Géant at Chamonix, with stalactites and cavities of blue ice. Water from the glacier entered in a fall and made real icicles (only in winter, or by refrigeration?).

The fourth grotto was a communicating series of caves lined with artificial tufa made with clinker from the glass-house boilers. First, the Vine Cave, with large bunches of glass grapes, and cunningly placed distorting mirrors, one of which reflected the hands of a walled-up monk. Next, the Wishing-Well Cave, where faces of men and women appeared in the water, surrounded by bats, owls, crocodiles, toads and frogs with illuminated eyes. Then the Skeleton Cave with fungus-covered walls, where a skeleton could be made to appear with startling suddenness among smaller skeletons with lamps. Then the Illusion Cave, where a Friar 'passed from life to death in a manner of electrocution', and a tiger changed from ferocity to tameness as one approached. Last, the Gnome Cave, with a large number of model gnomes (perhaps the progenitors of so many later garden glories?), 'portraying various antics, grave and gay'. On the way out was a last distorting mirror that made an echo-dwarf of every visitor.

Nuneham Courtney*
Grotto, eighteenth century　　　　SU 5598
I am told that the remains are still just visible.

Rotherfield Peppard *Crowsley Park*
Grotto　　　　　　　　　　　　SU 7282
A small grotto in a hollow surrounded by trees, a long way down lovely neglected gardens, with a yew alley towards the grotto. There is a simple flint façade, one storey with a heavy double round door and above three triangles with a blind circle in the middle one and shallow niches each side. (The centre one has been yobboed, but will be repaired.) Inside, the little room has narrow arcading all round the walls and a coved ceiling with heads in the corners. There is some simple floral plasterwork. It is very like the much larger flint entrance to the caves at West Wycombe only a dozen miles away and was possibly made in emulation, but nothing is

known of its history at all. In any case it has West Wycombe beaten flat for atmosphere, as sinister a little grotto as you could wish.

Shrivenham *Beckett Park*
Chinoiserie, seventeenth century　　SU 2489
See page 111.

Shotover *Shotover House*　　　　SP 5807
Early gothick sham façade
See page 51.

Steeple Aston *Rousham House*
Eyecatcher, *c.* 1740　　　　　　SP 4725
Kent, when he was working at Rousham for General Dormer, designed this screen standing on a hill some distance from the house. It is perfectly flat, only relieved with supporting buttresses, and is pierced with three arches. Little pinnacles stand along the top like the teeth of a saw-fish. A very plain folly, but a very economical one.

The park is very beautiful—the Cherwell was a great help to Kent and some of his drawings survive, and one sees the changes that occurred during building. The eye-catcher had a steeper gable and its sides were straight and the arches larger; it became muffled.

The Mill Temple, on the other hand, although it has now lost its top, was given more pinnacles and improved thereby. It is a pretty piece of useful gothick on a working mill—it was 'rusticated' by Kent to form an object. Venus Vale was also altered—it looks a little thin in reality; a pond with fountain and three grotto-arches into the bank behind, another grotto-arch further up and statues at the sides.

One of the most satisfactory ornaments—it is no folly in this climate—is the Praeneste, a covered arcade of six beautiful bold arches to stroll in in the rain. And there are some superb urns.

Woolstone
Tower, nineteenth century　　　　SU 2987
A one-room thick, two-storey unfinished Victorian folly in the Vale of the White Horse.

The Temple of the Mill at Rousham

Wroxton *Wroxton Abbey*
See page 3.
Eyecatcher, etc., eighteenth century SP 4142
One of the most beautiful of all eyecatchers,
really superbly placed on a hill-top in front of
beeches, once set across the long drive to
Wroxton from Banbury, but now isolated
from both house and town; there are two
half-round towers in rich warm sandstone
with a big arch between—the approach view
from Banbury was not considered at all.

The grounds were laid out, possibly to his
own design, by Lord North, later Earl of
Guilford, between 1733 and 1748, centred on
two lakes with a cascade and rocaille between
them and a serpentine river, but also using
the gentle hills and the dead ground between
them with exceptional skill. Steps go up
behind the house (we have passed a routine
little octagon tower near the drive), and from
the top can be seen a big yew hedge, a pretty
obelisk and a Roman Doric temple; the eyecatcher was probably once visible from here,
and may still be so in winter. The obelisk,
which was put up to commemorate a visit
from the Prince of Wales for Banbury races
in 1739, immediately draws one, but a formal
lake lies in the way, possibly the remains of a
lay-out by Tilleman Bobart in 1728—the
patte-d'oie abandoned, the lake kept. The
obelisk is seen through a yew arch, but now
the interest is drawn to the left of the lake
where a low bridge with two arches takes the
path irresistibly on to the picturesque landscaping of the lakes, with rushes, swans, yews,
beeches, cedars and a low wall. A temple once
stood on a mound across between the lakes,
possibly Sanderson Miller's 'Gothic open
rotondo', 1750, which had protective curtains
to wind up and down on screws. Its surrounding belt of yews is still there.

A Chinese summer house, bridge and shelter have all gone, but a letter of July 1749
survives: 'if you think we shall escape a wet
day tomorrow, I hope we shall have the
pleasure of your company to cold meat and
Iced cream at the Chinese House'.

The eyecatcher, or Castle, was designed to
be 'a notable object', and so it is, away across
fields now instead of park with a view back to
the obelisk. Any landscaping that connected
the Castle with the lakes and the Chinoiserie
has now gone, but near the house a pets'
graveyard survives, in memory of Busle,
Brazier, Vic, Romon, Flirt, Mocle and Pug.

Salop

Clunton and Clunbury,
Clugunford and Clun
Are the quietest places
Under the sun.

The border country between England and
Wales, once so fierce, and still so splendidly
filled with castles, seems in the last centuries
to have absorbed double quantities of peace
and sun and to radiate them as nowhere else.
Only east of Shrewsbury at Hawkestone and
Tong are there powerful follies; most of the
rest are small, and peaceful.

Acton Burnell
Grotto, *c.* 1750   SJ 5403
See page 169.

The grotto at Acton Burnell

Attingham *Attingham Park*
Eyecatcher, eighteenth century   SJ 5510
Western Lodge is a fine tall piece of gothickry to serve as an ecclesiastical eyecatcher to the house. And see page 22.

Culmington *Callow Hill*
Flounders' Folly, 1838   SO 4983
A most extraordinary tower, 70 or 80 feet high and quite well built, though dull, put up by Mr Flounders of Ludlow, and, with all his trouble and the thousands of examples, castellated with only one merlon on each side of the square. Or would it be fairer to say that the top is plain, with a square block in the middle of each face? It sounds better.

Downton-on-the-Rock *Downton Castle*
The Hermit's Cave   SO 4373
The house is a splendid castled one; Richard Payne Knight's own essay in the picturesque, begun in 1773. We went to look for a bath house and there are remains of what might have been one down by the Terne, below the house, but across the river and to the left the walk becomes walled on the river side and has natural rock on the other. Wall and rocks get higher, and the path runs into an arched grotto which runs out into the light again and has an opening that snails into a round rock room of terrifying earthy darkness. It looks part natural and part man-made. It is 20 or 25 feet high with a light shaft on top for illumination, and the light darkens the faces of a slanting, twisted column that thickens upwards at the end of the spiral.

Hadnall *Hardwick Grange*
Waterloo Windmill, *c.* 1820   SJ 5320
Another work of Lord Hill at Hawkstone (*q.v.*). To commemorate his exploits at Waterloo he built a big red-brick windmill with round-headed, gothick-glazed windows and huge arrow-slits. Now it has been reduced to two storeys and given two chimneys; with the arrow-slits filled in against the wind, it makes a most charming house.

Hawkstone *Hawkstone Park*
Group   SJ 5830
See page 78.

Hodnet *Hodnet Hall*
Classical Ruin, 1970   SJ 6228
See pages 277 and 278

Ironbridge *Tomlin's Garage*
Useful gothick   SJ 6804
See page 262.
An elaborate piece of castle-work designed to ennoble the village smithy and now very reasonably become a garage.

Pitchford
Tree house, *c.* 1760   SJ 5404
This is representative of many similar buildings which are with this exception omitted from this book. These are tree houses. A natural urge to brachiate is sometimes assuaged in man by building these, though they are usually for his children. When the fashion for them started it is hard to say, but certainly *The Swiss Family Robinson* and *Peter Pan* must have given impetus to the movement. The tree house at Pitchford is perched in the branches of a mighty oak, and is reached up a flight of wooden steps very like those which lead down the cliffs at the seaside. The wooden walls of the building are painted to look like stone, so that *trompe l'oeil* makes this folly more attractive than others of the same kind.

Quatford
Tower, 1830   SO 7491
A nice little tower on a rocky outcrop near the church, red brick, castellated, unpretentious. It was built by a builder for himself: John Smalman.

Shrewsbury
Column, Grotto, Tower   SJ 4913
Lord Hill's Column is central and commanding, another huge Doric one with Lord Hill by Marochetti on top of a drum, with a metal

sword and lightning conductor, and four good lions at the corners of the base. The view is said to be magnificent.

Laura's Tower is on a mound in the castle grounds, a small red sandstone octagon tower with a pyramidal slate roof and those odd castellations that have narrower ones at the corners.

The Quarry is a routine city park, except for the Dingle, the lowest part of the converted quarry, fenced and hedged, dogs on lead, no bicycles. Entrance through a rather elegant little gothick gate leads to the lake, and the crown and cream of municipal planting, not so tight as the French broderies, but still impeccable. The path round the lake has several conceits, a nymph with a ribboned shell, an eagle on a gothic fragment and the GATEWAY OF THE SHOEMAKER'S ARBOUR ORIGINALLY ERECTED ON KINGSLAND IN 1679 BY THE SHOEMAKER'S GUILD AND REMOVED TO THE PRESENT SITE IN 1877. THE FIGURES REPRESENT CRISPIN & CRISPIAN, THE PATRON SAINTS OF SHOEMAKERS. A typical piece for its period; a round pediment with coat-of-arms and the figures, a round arch below and fluted pilasters. Behind it is a niche of red sandstone rocks with an oval basin in the middle for a small cast-iron fountain painted new gloss white. There are ferns, hart's tongues and rockery; only Queen Victoria, Garibaldi and the witch-balls are missing for this to be Mole's End.

Also, good rustic summer-house, pretty bandstand and obelisk.

Tong *Tong Castle*
Pyramidal Hen-house 1820–40   SJ 8007
See page 125, and see also **Weston** in Staffordshire.

Westbury
Whitton Folly
A hilltop one, quite derelict*   SJ 3408

Weston Rhyn *The Quinta*
Sham Stonehenge, 1850–60   SJ 2837
See page 245.

Willey *Shirlett High Hall*
Obelisk   SO 6799
In the woods on top, a tall leaning stone obelisk among the larch and spruce, rough stone with dressed corners and a good base, the top much worn, all much braced. There is no inscription now, but they say it is in memory of a retriever that fell down a quarry, or a coal shaft.

Lord Hill's Column, Shrewsbury

The Quinta, Weston Rhyn

The obelisk at Shirlett High Park

Somerset

The most beautiful county in southern England, with Mendip, the Quantocks, the Poldens, flat green-and-black peat bogs, a great variety of landscape and seascape and a great variety of follies in this suitable setting.

Barwick *Barwick Park*
Treacle-eater, *c.* 1775   ST 5614
See pages 227 and 245.

Brympton *Brympton House*
Sham Ruin, 1723*   ST 5215
Much smaller than Alfred's Castle, indeed only a sheltering alcove, but built only three years later, made of fragments for a gate of *c.* 1600; it was very early for work of that date to be thought worth preserving but perhaps the stones were to hand. . . .

The sham castle at Burrow Bridge

Burrow Bridge
Sham Church, 1724   ST 3630
On the road from Taunton to Glastonbury, which goes across the flattest part of Somerset, at the village of Burrow Bridge, a small hill called Burrow Mump sticks out of the plain. On its summit are the remains of a mediaeval chapel with eighteenth-century gothick additions. There is a short tower and a nave. Gaps in the walls are barred with iron railings so that cows cannot shelter inside. Early work again.

In 1946 it was given by Major A. G. Barrett to the National Trust, through the Somerset War Memorial Fund, as a war memorial for the Second World War.

Chew Magna
Chew Tower, *c.* 1770, submerged†
An enchanting little square tower of white stone faced with grey, now under the Chew Valley Lake.

Chilton Polden *Chilton Priory*
Stradling's Folly, *c.* 1840   ST 3840
There is a small tower in the grounds, but the Priory is the Folly to most people. William Stradling was a rich landowner and archaeologist who found the Roman villa at Chedzoy and saved a lot of unlucky ancient bits and built them into his new and very conspicuous house, which he turned into a museum, dispersed after his death. His own 'Description of The Priory of Chilton-super-Polden and its contents' by William Stradling, 1839, describes the house and the larger fragments and describes the 'gigantic panorama which takes in one cathedral, thirty-five churches and chapels, Glastonbury Tor, King Alfred's Tower[1]; two columns, five lighthouses and much else'. He ends: 'I now conclude by saying that, as I believe I have not made use of a word (except as to description of the antiquities) which cannot be understood by the lowest class of my neighbours, that if but one of the old fashioned labourers, the descen-

[1] Stourhead.

dants of Monmouth's hardy scythe-men, will read this book to his family (on what ought to be the "happy Saturday night") instead of spending it at the pestiferous cider-shop, I shall feel amply repaid for my labour.'

Combe Florey

Tower, eighteenth century   ST 1532
Winter's Tower; a two-storey stone sham church, very dull, but possibly once picturesque as an eyecatcher.

Cothelstone *Cothelstone House*

Sham ruin and statue   ST 1832
A beacon tower has been demolished, but on the Quantocks above the house is a very small pink stone sham ruin, gracefully placed in trees, and a strange androgynous statue, rigid, long-haired, with a dog.

Cranmore

Cranmore Tower, 1862   ST 6944
The biting cold and the bleak scenery of the summit of Mendip are not encouraging to the folly builder. This is not the part of Somerset for the flighty sort of folly, and in any case the ones on these hills were all built in the middle of the nineteenth century when Italian models and Arnold's ethics were more highly esteemed than gothick and Chinoiserie. Cranmore, very plain and square, is an example of this change. It was built by Mr Paget. There is a balcony two thirds of the way up and another at the top. It is not in very good condition.

Crowcombe *Crowcombe Court*

Sham Ruins, eighteenth century   ST 1437
See page 48.

Statue at Cothelstone

Curry Rivel

Curry Rivel *Burton Pynsent*

Burton Steeple, 1765   ST 3925
Sir William Pynsent, the last member of the family, bequeathed his estate at Burton to William Pitt, Earl of Chatham, who built this monument in memory of his benefactor. It is a plain column (my notes say Roman Doric, Dorothy Stroud says Doric, *Buildings of England,* Tuscan). It was designed by Capability Brown, and stands on a little hill at the end of a fine ride of oaks and beeches. The spiral staircase comes out on to the capital for the wide flat view without the usual railing. On top of the drum for the stairs is a cupola; a letter from Brown to Pitt says 'The figure I have put on the pedestal is that of Gratitude, conveying to Posterity the name of Pinsant', but alas on top of the cupola is an urn.

In 1948 a cow took a fancy to Burton Steeple and climbed three times up its spiral staircase. Twice it got stuck and was extricated backwards with great difficulty, but the third time it battled its way right to the top, where, smitten with vertigo, it toppled to its death over the edge of the unguarded parapet. The entrance has now been blocked up.

Robin Hood's Temple, Halswell House

Dunster *Dunster Castle*

Conygar Hill Tower, 1770s   SS 9944

This folly is so convincing that many people are surprised and annoyed when told that it is not a beacon tower or outpost to Dunster Castle. Very beautifully situated, it is seen rising above the trees which cover the hill. Henry Fownes Luttrell built it in 1775 as a prospect tower, circular with two upper storeys, four pointed windows at each floor placed evenly round the circle. In Dunster Castle is a painting of the tower with two more, narrower, stages, but as usual this does not mean that they were built.

Elworthy

Willett's Tower, *c.* 1790   ST 0835

To the local stag and foxhunters Willett's Tower is a renowned landmark. It stands on the lower slopes of the Brendon hills, and is now in a state of almost complete desolation. Only the tower still stands, and the remains of a curtain wall pierced with a pointed arch.

Frome *No. 2 Mount Pleasant, Spring Gardens*

Folly Garden   ST 7747

See page 246.

Sometime earlier this century, Mr Hall made a nice little steep garden to match the name of his house. He went round on a bicycle collecting stone from local quarries and 'oolite from an eighteenth-century cloth mill',

and made a complex piled-up village with cottages, churches, cliffs, statues on pedestals, a St Bernard with its barrel under an arch, gnomes, seed-sowers, knights in armour, stained glass, old wash-stand top, shells, minerals, everything suitable that came to hand. The present owners, who have been here since 1964, keep it all up and have added a pool.

Goathurst *Halswell House*

Grotto, Pyramid, etc., eighteenth century   ST 2735

Halswell House in Somerset, like many big houses, has been cut up into flats and segments and houses in the stables and is loved and neglected in parallel patchwork, each tenant apparently in charge of one folly; reception and information are uncertain. It is a beautiful gaunt house halfway up the north face of the Quantocks, a late seventeenth-century façade on an earlier farmhouse. Beside it is a stepped pyramid in Ham stone crowned by a gryphon with a shield.

> This Edifice was created
> In Honour of a pure nymph.

We were stopped from reading the rest of the lines, but told they were by Pope. There is a big pigeon cote with a superb ogival slate roof, burnt and restored by the U.S. army in the Second World War and an ice house under a pretty rotunda. A Druid's Temple seemed lost to all knowledge. There is an elegant sarcophagus to a horse that won a wager, and a big grotto-façade is set in the hill below the rotunda. This is a low gable of random stone. The big central alcove is blind, with an obliterated inscribed tablet; there is a niche each side then rough pilasters, then two more little random arches, filled in. There is a dog's gravestone of 1902; a memorial to a cockerel has been stolen from the façade, but one to a canary has been kept. It is sightless and forlorn; probably the centre arch led into a big room and water flowed from the low arches at the sides.

Then up over pasture land behind the house on a crest of the hills is Robin Hood's Temple, a beautiful, ruinous folly in long and thistled grass, classical, gothick and rustic, probably by Thomas Wright. The central feature is an octagon more than 20 feet across, open in front, ogival arches on slender clustered columns, with a fluted dome inside, and heavy-handed plasterwork of twisted vines. The back wall is semicircular and opens into a room behind, which in turn gives access to the side rooms whose windows are ogival to match the octagon. One was a kitchen. At the back is a surprise, a rustic back door covered in bark and screened by two huge segments of hollow tree-trunk. Bits of elm disease and bark were nailed on all over the back but today are falling like the whole temple. Now, was this built in the eighteenth century to carry on the tradition of the earlier Robin Hood's Temple of the Kemys Tyntes (see page 18) or was that as the old guide books says the same as the Druid's Temple? Halswell needs a lot more research.

Ilchester *Castle Farm*
Bell Tower, *c.* 1800   ST 5324
Across the river from the farm in the middle of the town can be seen a long garden with arcading painted on brick walls. On the final cross-wall is a little two-storey building. The ground floor is open to the river and the garden through big pointed arches. It is lined, like the arch-returns, with neat rustic patterns of thin branches, and has a lacy cast iron verandah on slender columns. In each of the two pointed arches of the first floor, four large mechanical bicycle bells are vertically mounted and there is a large bell-shaped bell between. Every four hours, the eight very sweetly play a tune and then the big bell chimes the hour.

Tower, house and garden were made by Henry Tuson in about 1800; the tower had a sliding glass roof and was used as an observatory. Mr Vaus put in the clock of 1873 and the bells from Gillet and Bland of Croydon for 'the Coronation'.

Kilmersdon *Ammerdown Park*
Column, 1865   ST 7353
Somerset's only story of rival follies is the attempt of Mr Turner to outshine with his 180-foot high tower Lord Hylton's 150-foot high column, which is a replica of the second Eddystone Lighthouse, put up in 1865 as a memorial to the builder of Ammerdown House, Mr Thomas Samuel Jolliffe, by his sons. It was originally surrounded by replicas of antique statues, afterwards moved to the gardens round the house. About 20 years later, John Turner built his own tower in a mediaeval Italian style, only a mile away. His plan was to provide teas, and ascents of the tower, to recoup the cost of building it, but this did not succeed, and the tower was later bought by Lord Hylton. Having become dangerous, the top half was demolished soon after, and the remainder in 1969.

Montacute *St Michael's Hill*
Tower, *c.* 1760   ST 5017
A round prospect tower with a ruined conical roof. It has an internal stair to the base of the cone and thence an external one to a viewing platform 'with three triangular pieces sticking up'.

Street *Windmill Hill*
Column   ST 4836
A big Doric column with too much entasis surmounted by a notable naval crown, to the memory of Admiral Hood.

West Horrington *On the A39*
The Wolf with Romulus and Remus ST 5748
See page 275.

Wrangway *Blackdown Hills*
Wellington Monument   ST 1218
The Great Duke allowed the town of Wellington at the foot of the hills to be named for him, and the town in return put up this magnificent obelisk in 1817–18. It was designed by T. Lee, and was intended, they say, to have a statue of the Duke on top, but the money ran out. I feel quite sure that it was always meant to be just as it is; The National Trust is now restoring it. This is what must have been intended at Moel Fammau (*q.v.*), of which only the podium remains.

South Yorkshire

Locke Park Tower, Barnsley (*left*)
Robin Hood's Well, Burghwallis

This part of Yorkshire includes the two great folly estates of Wentworth Castle and Wentworth Woodhouse.

Askern *Cowling and Sutton*
Obelisk and Tower*   SE 5513
Three-quarters of a mile apart on top of the moors, an obelisk with a spiked cap and a square tower with a short battered base, a deep castellated top and stairs up. Stone, in rough-dressed blocks, and apparently by the same hand.

Barnsley *Locke Park*
Tower   SE 3506
An odd ugly but compelling tower, an Elizabethan theatre sitting on a muddle. A round tower, horizontally banded below eight Corinthian pilasters, surrounded at the bottom by a circle of 16 free-standing Ionic columns with a your-guess entablature. At the top of the tower above the pilasters a band of lions and wreaths and the wooden O, 16 turned columns under a conical copper cap and a weathercock with the initials S.M.C. From Wentworth Castle it looks rather pretty.

(Birdwell) *Boston Castle*
Eyecatcher, eighteenth century†   SE 3502
Near the marker obelisk between the Wentworths there used to be a good stage-scenery tower, built by Lord Effingham to celebrate the Boston Tea-Party, but I find it was demolished to make way for the new road.

Burgh Wallis *Skelbrooke*
Robin Hood's Well, 1711   SE 5113
This minute folly has been carefully moved (undoubtedly because of its attribution to Vanbrugh), so that it is still safely beside the A1 in spite of road works. Who could doubt the attribution? So massive are the stones from which it is made, that it takes only a minute to count the number used in its construction. It is square, with arches in three sides and a niche inside the fourth solid wall. Since it was built the road has risen, and on this side it is buried half-way up the arch, for it is 8 feet high and 6 feet square, yet so just is the proportion that it could be enlarged to Seaton Delaval size and appear in no way thin or mean.

The gazebo at Penistone

Norton
Obelisk   SK 3581
To Sir Francis Chantry, of the Chantry
bequest, inscribed . . . 'from Donkey boy to
Sculptor'.

Penistone
Hartcliffe Tower, *c.* 1851   SE 2503
An extremely plain round stone tower. Mr
Askham built it for Captain Ramsden; nearby
there is a small broken-down gazebo decaying
away.

Sheffield *Longford Road*
Sham castle, late 1930s   SK 3688
A charming little castle, built for himself by
Mr Charles Simmons.

Wentworth Castle *Stainborough Castle, etc.*
                                                           SK 3404
See page 86.

Wentworth Woodhouse
Large group   SK 3798
See page 85.

Staffordshire

A medium-sized county with medium-excit-
ing scenery; not an enormous number of
follies but some very good ones, and a higher-
than-usual level of Chinoiserie.

Alton *Alton Towers*
Group with pagoda, early   SK 0744
nineteenth century
See pages 108, 119 and 235.

Biddulph *Biddulph Grange*
Chinese and Egyptian, early
nineteenth century   SK 8857
See page 119.

Codsall *Chillington Hall*
The Whitehouse, *c.* 1725   SJ 8606
See page 135.

The eyecatcher at Enville

The Chinese pavilion at Enville

Enville *Enville Hall*

Chinese Pavilion, Eyecatcher, etc., SO 8387
eighteenth century

Enville is a mystery to me; when I went there first, this is what I wrote:

There are several little curiosities in the park. The 6-inch ordnance map shows something called "Ralph's Bastion"; down in a wood with a pond, waterfall and birds, is a big yew tree growing on a semicircular bastion with a stone retaining wall. One huge branch is sawn off and

TRAF'S

ASTION

1753

is cut on the end of it.

There is a little Doric summer-house with square rusticated columns, and in the woods, sounding very hopeful, 'Shenstone's Chapel' —locally Samson's Cave. This is a dark cave in the rock, absolutely unlit. A long way down the passage the floor falls a sheer 10 feet to form a round chamber with a crudely domed roof. There is no way down, and though it makes an addition to the not very long list of subterranean follies, it is hardly an exciting one. An ice house perhaps?

'The eyecatcher ending a vista from the house is a good one, a series of three arches separated by castellated walls in the massive gothic style of the mid-eighteenth century. Two of them are walled-in at the back to shelter seats for the view, but the central one is an open arch, with flanking turrets and a pediment, all castellated, and a portcullis.

Sanderson Miller's letters mention a gothic summer-house at Enville for Lord Stamford —probably this is it.'

When Osvald Siren went there, possibly rather earlier, he saw and photographed a most lovely gothick folly, a big span of three ogival arches of the most graceful fantasy with rose and pointed windows, called The Billiard Room, and a little octagonal bark summer-house or hermitage. He says that it was all a wilderness, mentions Shenstone's cascade and the remains of a great fountain with sea-beasts, and says that Healy also refers to a circular temple, a Shepherd's Lodge, a memorial chapel to Shenstone (the Leasows is not far away), a gothick arch and a rustic cottage.

When I went again in 1971 it was far recovered from wilderness, and I saw the good eyecatcher again (let us accept this as the gothick arch), a series of lakes with the great fountain in one near the house (sea-horses round a central triton blowing a shell trumpet), a Chinese pavilion lost in the fine woods which I am sure is what Mr Siren was looking for, though he does not mention it and so can't have found it, and a charming aviary with eight Crystal-Palace wire faces and a central grotto-piece with a little grotto spire. Ralph's Bastion and Samson's Cave could not be found and the new owner had never heard of the Billiard Room. Only one thing stands clearly in all accounts—the gothick eye-catcher. . . .

There is a photograph of the Billiard Room in *China and Gardens of Europe*; I have recorded the Chinese pavilion as well as I could; it is becoming ruinous and is absolutely surrounded by trees on a hill above the top lake. The plan is cruciform, about 60 feet by 20, and 25 feet high, massively made of wood in arched units with much chamfering filled with clear glass and yellow borders. Each unit is a window and a pair makes a door at each end, and above them runs a frieze of quatrefoil windows of frosted glass with painted gothick motifs. Over the crossing is a lantern with more frosted glass, and ogival arches mark the nave and choir; it is really only some outside details and the window tops that are even faintly Chinese but it was once painted red, and the roofs have been replaced, so they may have been curved, and curved on the lantern, and everything may have looked better. Restoration seems unlikely.

Fazeley

Castellated Bridge   SK 1900
This very small follyfied fortified footbridge crosses the Birmingham–Fazeley canal just north of Drayton Basset. A wooden trussed beam spans the canal between two round brick castellated towers about 15 feet high, which have rich fat entases. Inside them are spiral stone staircases to the bridge, which was perhaps so designed to look well from the near-by house. From the path beside the still canal it is entirely charming.

I have not seen this recently, but David Glover tells me that it has been altered and the rather Chinese balustrade taken away; but it was a nice idea.

Forton *The Monument*

Tower   SJ 7621
The Monument is a red sandstone tower with a pyramid roof, built on a hill above the village, 'to commemorate something forgotten'. And several people tell me that there is a fine menagerie here.

Leek *Basford Hall*

Bath house, 1841   SJ 9956
This is the latest bath house I know of; they were thoroughly out of fashion by this time. It is a remarkably large and solidly built castle

with swimming bath, waterwheel, underground passages, dining-room, kitchen and so on, with its own landscaping of canal and lake. The first thing is a fine stout two-storey tower with a taller staircase turret and a flag pole, castellated and machicolated, windows, slits, a battered base. A buttressed wall joins the tower to the bath house, a rectangular building, part three- part four-storey, with Tudor doors and two gables, with monograms. Behind the far gable is a square tower joining an octagonal one, the high crown of all, with a coat of arms of scythe and fleur-de-lys, NEC OPPRIMERE NEC OPRIMI, and the date.

Milford *Shugborough Park*

The Chinese House, arch, cat, etc.,   SJ 9720
eighteenth century
The Chinese House is described on page 112. Once, it stood on an island in a canal with a Chinese Bridge to it, now another channel has been cut for the river Sow and an iron bridge leads to a bigger island and the Cat's Monument, with pussy on top. It presents problems; tradition says that it commemorates a cat which went round the world with Anson on the four-year voyage of the Centurion. But 1767 is the earliest recorded date for the artificial stone it is made of—the cat would have been 27 at least. Or the monument was much later than its death. Or it commemorates a Persian cat seen at Shugborough by Sir Joseph Banks in 1768, '. . . only one is now left, all the rest having died of a distemper'.

On the bank of the river facing the house are the sad remains of the Ruins, some small gothic bits put up *c.* 1750 and said to come from Lichfield, a balustrade and a small statue. There was once more of this unsuccessful jumble, and a row of classical columns on the opposite bank.

The Shepherds' Memorial is another pretty one, though, classical with variations including an odd tortured arch and a relief by Scheemakers after Poussin. Before 1758, and see page 180.

There is yet another Tower of the Winds by Athenian Stuart, *c.* 1765 and so later than Hagley and West Wycombe, and a Doric

Temple and the Lanthorn of Demosthenes 1764–71, also by Stuart (see page 139). His first monument here, though, was probably the Triumphal Arch.

Just outside Stafford the railway to London goes into a tunnel; on the London side it emerges in a moderately deep cutting, and the traveller with his back to the engine sitting on the left-hand end of the seat will see, as he is hurtled down the line, a handsome pitch black arch of impeccable Greek design, standing above the tunnel entrance. Work started late in 1761, but the Admiral died the next year, and the great arch now honours Lord and Lady Anson with busts by Scheemakers, who worked, presumably spasmodically, on it for several years. No other building so illustrates the beauty of soot encrustation as this arch, for it is built of a stone with a special texture which takes the soot in marble-like swirls.

Sandon *Sandon Hall*
Lord Harrowby's Folly, or   SJ 9529
Trentham Folly, *c.* 1910
For sentiment or taste, Lord Harrowby paid £100 for the top of a belvedere tower in the Italian manner when the Duke of Sutherland demolished Sir Charles Barry's Trentham. The stones were numbered, and the belvedere moved piecemeal to a solid brick base at Sandon, among thistles on rising ground. It is square and very large, an open cube of 12 high arches with pilasters and half-columns.

There is also a neat gothic pavilion, wide arch castellations, pinnacles; this seat was erected by Dudley first Earl of Harrowby in memory of his esteemed friend the Rt Hon. Spencer Perceval, Prime Minister of England, who met his death at the hands of an assassin in the lobby of the House of Commons, May 1812.

Lord Harrowby's Folly, Sandon

The Triumphal Arch, Shugborough

Shareshill
Tower, 1741*   SJ 9406
I have been told of a very tall tower here, to commemorate the capture of Porto Bello; it might be visible from the M6.

Stafford
Stafford Castle, c. 1800   SJ 9123
'In 1348 Ralph, Baron Stafford, built a castle,

which was destroyed in 1643. Sir George Jerningham cleared the site, and rebuilding started in about 1800 under the supervision of his son George. The lower storey of the old castle was found tolerably intact buried under the debris of the towers, and was used as the foundation of the new castle, but by 1815 it showed signs of collapsing, so building stopped.

'Two massive octagonal castellated towers, joined by a gateway, stand on a small mound covered with the scrubby desolation of a recently-cleared wood. This building has not been scheduled as an ancient monument, and the cost of adapting part of it so that a care-taker could live there is considered too great to be taken out of the rates. So one more building of greater merit than tatty Eliza-bethan almshouses goes the way of East Cowes Castle and Oatlands Grotto.'

So in 1952. In 1972 the fate of the castle is still undecided, and it is in much worse condition, with the towers falling.

Tutbury *Tutbury Castle*
Sham Castle, mid-eighteenth century SK 2129
This is a most interesting folly, There is a real castle, old walls and towers round the grass, and refreshments all as usual, and on a knoll, which may have been the site of an earlier keep, the Vernons in the eighteenth century built a solid sandstone sham one with round-headed windows and huge buttresses; some mediaeval fragments are incorporated, and there is more sham work, to improve the view from Sudbury, on the south tower. A visitor in 1751 described the demolition of '3 grand rooms' added in 1631–5. The materials from these went into a new house at about the same time as the folly was built, presumably with more of the materials as well as the old windows. It was all there in 1777.

Weston under Lizard
Tower, nineteenth century   SJ 8011
This is a large square red sandstone tower, with three storeys and a taller octagonal staircase turret and flagpole, big but routine. It was a prospect tower to Tong (*q.v.*).

The eyecatcher to Tong

Suffolk

A sparse county again. Obelisks at Ickworth and Helmingham, a column at Butley, and a monument to a horse at Denston.

Bealings *Great Bealings House*   TM 2448
I was told of 'a tall pyramid made with stones from Elephanta' at Woodbridge, and so little remains on the island of Elephanta in the Nile that the pyramid began to loom enormous in the imagination, but I could not find it. Now, too late for another visit, I find that there is a little folly at Bealings put up by Major Moor who bought the house when he retired from India in 1806, for his collection of carvings. So Elephanta, if it has any bearing on the folly at all, must be the island near Bombay.

Coddenham *Shrubland Park*
Group, nineteenth century   TM 1353
Extensive and elaborate early Victorian gardens in the Italianate manner, terraced down one of Suffolk's few relatively steep slopes. There are several pretty trifles; a rustic kiosk with zinc roof, bamboo and pebbles, very carefully designed; an iron seat between iron spear-poles that swing a garland of iron leaves; a Swiss cottage all correctly in wood; a rustic-Chinese shelter with a new roof, rustic sides and ceramic panels as at Dropmore; and a very fine tower in unknapped flint dressed with brick. The plan is one I have never seen before, triangular with one point couped so that the three short sides are about equal; a rectangular staircase turret climbs the centre of the base wall for its three and a half storeys and then goes one higher. The main room on the first floor has been badly divided, but retains a superbly pinnacled wooden gothick door.
Buildings of England mentions a grotto room in the house, by James Paine, and a transparent temple and gloriette by Sir Charles Barry, but I have not been allowed to see them.

Freston
Freston Tower, 1549   TM 1839
See page 11.

Ipswich *Morpeth House*
Stamp Room, 1892†

Nacton *Orwell Park*
Two towers, 1854 and 1859   TM 2241
The house, now a school, has an observatory tower attached and two others, a square brick and stone water-tower and a pretty clock-tower, similar but smaller, with a round stair turret. The initials GT are entwined for George Tilman, and the date, 1859.

Tattingstone *The Tattingstone Wonder*
Sham castle, 1760   TM 1437
The folly at Tattingstone is one of the most famous in the country; whenever follies are talked or written about, the Wonder raises its castellated head. There seems no special reason why; it is for instance, no nearer London and certainly no more attractive than the similar St Crispin's Cottages at West Wycombe in Buckinghamshire, but fame has selected the Wonder and St Crispin languishes.

The Tattingstone Wonder

From Tattingstone Hall and from the road you see a square and simple church tower built of flint and ashlar; from the back, the tower disintegrates into scenery, having only three sides and no roof and the church becomes a screen for three brick cottages. It was built in 1760 for Squire White, who is said to have claimed that as people so often wondered at nothing, he would give them something to wonder at.

Thorpeness

The Fort and other buildings, TM 4759
c. 1920
See page 270.

Wickham Market *Rendlesham Hall*

Lodges, *c.* 1820 TM 3455
Rendlesham Hall has five lodges; three are ordinary, but two are in the most advanced picturesque taste. One is a ruin, with the inhabited part of the lodge concealed in the lower part of a bumbly ivy-grown tower, and an arch going over the drive to an outbuilding. The other is more elaborate, a sham chapter house built of most beautifully worked golden stone blotched with mustard-orange lichen. Most of the detail is as crisp as when it was cut and is of the utmost refinement, exquisite decorated ornament; as usual flawlessly gothick in detail, but utterly of its time in conceited conception.

On plan the building is hexagonal with three wings radiating from it. At the junction of the wings with the central block are six tall pinnacles from which flying buttresses rise to form a huge central chimney. The lodge is behind a low crenellated wall, the piers supporting the gates have gothick niches, and the gates themselves are cast-iron trellis work with spear heads.

Rendlesham lodges *below left*, and *above*

Woolverstone *Woolverstone Park*

The Cat House, 1793 TM 1939
There was an obelisk here too; it was built of freestone and surmounted by a rayed globe, in memory of Charles Berners. A mere 96 feet high, and standing among tall trees, it was yet destroyed during the Second World War as a possible landmark for enemy planes. And very thoroughly it was destroyed too.

The Cat House on the other hand has survived promotion into a landmark. The local story is that the pretty gothick cottage was used to guide smugglers, who knew when they saw a cat in the window that it was safe for them to come in with the contraband. In fact, the huge window facing down the Orwell is a false one, painted on the crenellated wall. At the bottom, looking out through the painted bars used to be a painted pussy cat, grey and white, with an hour-glass painted beside it. Unfortunately, it has been re-done with a cartoon-type cat in front of the bars and no hour-glass.

The eyecatcher Cat House, Woolverstone

Surrey

There were many follies here, many fine parks, some of the earliest and best, south in the sun, handy for town; it has been landscaped over and over; much has gone.

Albury *Albury Park*
Tunnel, etc., 1676   TL 0547
See page 16.

Bisley *Staffordlake, The Caravan*
Folly garden, twentieth century*   SU 9559
I have been told of a good modern garden here, with statues, broken china mosaic, and rock-work.

Busbridge *Busbridge Lakes House*
Group, late eighteenth century   SU 9743
An enchanting romantic garden, with fine trees landscaped along a chain of four lakes, most beautifully overgrown but opened by clear walks and sweeps of mown grass, all bathed in a golden glow of contentment, though at least one folly was surely intended for a shiver.

The grotto at Busbridge Lakes House

Behind the lakes across from the house is a sandstone cliff, bushed and treed, and here is the Hermit's Cave, with suitable yews. The entrance is a round arch of rock-work with a fragment of Roman lettering set into it and under this a pointed arch with a most elegant iron grille gate and a rough round window each side. A besom leans against the gate.

The special trick here is the rock, presumably a variety of ironstone sometimes simple, like crushed macaroni tubes, sometimes complex, like a section through folded pastry. Inside, there is a simple cross-vault of toothy rocks running back about 12 feet to the rock-face, through which the cave proper begins, tunnelled in, dark and winding. After about 30 feet, there is a deep ice house on the right, and the tunnel continues to a big round chamber with a stout central pillar and a suggestion of moulding at the spring of the vault. There are three alcoves to lend confusion and another entry, now part-blocked that once came out not far from the main one. Below is a low *rocaille* bridge, grassed over, with, on a side arch, sensitively carved little bas-reliefs—a child, a satyr's head, probably by the sculptor of a grotesque head on one of the outbuildings.

On from the cave is a charming, very derelict, Roman Doric temple (at least two more have disappeared), and below this is the grotto. The steps lead down past a big beech that has fallen into the water, but still lives. The grotto entrance is made of the same ironstone as the hermit's cave, with a particularly fine lump cut in two and set mirror-image over the door. Above, instead of the usual round window, is a big heart, outlined in end-set slates and once filled in with shells. Inside, the grotto is small but pretty, perhaps the work of two people, for there are two styles; a geometry-based one covers the entrance wall with very carefully chosen shells, native and exotic, ormers, periwinkles, scallops and turrets with shiny chips of dark bottle-glass for emphasis and includes the initials HHT and the date, 1810, in the dark glass. The work on the left-hand wall is in a more random style. The back, which is locally said to have led into a further cave, has been blocked with rock. A spring once flowed from a giant furbelow clam on the floor but now the water finds it own way out.

At the far end of the chain of lakes another, longer, low rocky bridge marks the present end of the grounds. Another temple and a tower used to be on the cliff top hereabouts.

Back towards the house is the pretty Gothick Boat House, in Roman cement and trellis work; it is pedimented, with delicate blind windows, a room with a fireplace and two verandahs.

Near the house is the Ghost Walk, a curved cleft in the lower, 20-foot cliffs of this side, that rise gently to the summit between rocked and grotted walls with niches and alcoves. Once there were many statues, and several natural caves were improved with a shell door or so, but it is now heavily overgrown and much must have gone.

The entrance to the walk, though, through five spectacularly fanged arches, is a notable survival.

Camberley *Messrs Trollope and Colls*
Elephant, 1964   SU 8661
See page 277.

Caterham *Arthur's Seat*
Tower, late eighteenth century   TQ 3555
A rather mournful tower standing in a field on the North Downs behind Caterham. It is built of flint faced with stone, and has brick castellations.

Marden Castle   TQ 3555
The house was built in the nineteenth century in an earlier landscaped park; at the highest point of the land, on the ridge of the North Downs, stands a tiny box of a sham castle, once used as a cottage, but lately abandoned and now vandalized.

Chertsey *St Anne's Court*
Tea House, 1794†   TQ 0565

This was Charles James Fox's St Anne's Hill, with the grounds laid out by Charles Hamilton. The charming grotto-tea house has been almost totally destroyed by hooligans, but I think it worth preserving a description of it as it stood twenty years ago. 'The ground floor of the tea house is entered through two tall ogival gothick arches set close together, and two similar arches open the opposite wall; the side walls are solid. The roof is beautifully decorated in rough symmetry of imitation stalactites, made of little pieces of felspar, the spaces between them are filled in with more spar and interspersed with winding black patterns of tufa. The walls, pilasters and pillars supporting the roof are covered with shells and spar, done with a great feeling for texture. The floor is set with geometric patterns of pebbles, outlined with brick and white bones.

A beautiful free standing wooden staircase with a chinoiserie hand rail sweeps up to a balcony outside the upstairs room where Fox used to take tea.'

Claremont
Belvedere Tower, 1717   TQ 1464
See page 25.

Cobham *Pain's Hill Park*
Group, 1740s   TQ 1161
See page 39.

Epsom *or nearby*
Würlitzer organ house*, twentieth   TQ 2261
century
I have not been able to find this, but have been told several times of a house built round a full-size Würlitzer organ, bought when a cinema was demolished.

Leith Hill
Hull's Tower, 1766   TQ 1443
Richard Hull, a native of Bristol, asked Sir John Evelyn if he might build this tower, and, with permission granted, started to make Leith Hill into a mountain, for the top of the tower is just over a 1,000 feet above sea level. When he died in 1772 he was buried under the

east wall of the tower. Towards the end of that century the tower became a 'harbour for smugglers and gypsies', so the local gentry raised a subscription to make the tower uninhabitable, which they did by filling the inside with rubble and bricking up the doors and windows.

In 1864 an external staircase was added in an octagonal turret, so that the stupendous views from the top could once more be enjoyed by county-counters. The neolithic ditches surrounding the tower were dug at the end of the eighteenth century.

Merstham
Tower, probably *c.* 1840*   TQ 2954
Buildings of England mentions a round folly tower in the trees north of the church.

Gatton Park
Gatton Town Hall, 1765   TQ 2954
What is one to say of this? Gatton was a rotten borough, and in most rotten boroughs the nominations were made without flourish and, as far back as 1765, little question. At Gatton, though, a shrine to democracy was built (I cannot find out by whom), a steeply pedimented little temple on six iron columns, four behind and two before, with a large urn in front:

> *Stat ductis Sortibus Urna*
> *Salus populi Suprema Lex Esto*
> *Comitium Gattoniense MDCCLXV*
> *H M Dolus Malus Abesto.*

When I first saw this as a child, hot from history lessons on Reform, I found it utterly chilling, something to be wiped from the mind; but seeing it again, I have to say, it is pretty.

Mickleham
Box Hill Tower, early nineteenth   TQ 1852
century
A round flint tower with no entrance, standing on a ridge which runs north from Box Hill. It was built by Thomas Broadwood the piano-maker who bought Juniper Hall in the

Box Hill Tower

valley below in 1814 and leased the land on which he put the tower.

To the south, near abortive attempts at fortification, is the grave of Major Peter Labellière of the Marines, who is said to be buried in a hole 100 feet deep. His coffin was lowered in head first, as he believed that at the resurrection the world would be topsy-turvy, and that he would then find himself on his feet.

Nutfield *Wellhouse*   TQ 3157
A very small tower, but loved; it has recently been repointed.

Oatlands *Oatlands Park*
Grotto, 1747†   TQ 0865
See page 159.

Peper Harrow *Oxenford Grange*
Sham ruin, mid-nineteenth century   SU 9444
A beautiful complex of farm buildings; a seventeenth-century house with a splendid Pugin barn and gatehouse; the barn alone establishes him as one of the best architects of his century. Near the farmhouse were the remains of monastic buildings, visible from Chambers' ugly Peper Harrow House, and presumably acceptable in the 1760s when Brown laid out the park, but needing improvement in the 1840s. Pugin built the old walls into an eyecatcher ruin for Lord Middleton, adding a large new Decorated-style window.

The sham church at Peper Harrow

Reigate *Castle grounds*

Sham Ruin, 1777   TQ 2750
The castle is mostly mound, all that remains
of a big eleventh-century motte and bailey.
Some of the remaining stones were built up
into a pointed arch between two round
castellated turrets, arrow-slits and all:

TO

SAVE THE MEMORY

OF

WILLIAM EARL WARREN

WHO IN OLD DAYS DWELT HERE,

AND WAS

A LOYAL CHAMPION OF OUR LIBERTIES

FROM PERISHING

LIKE HIS OWN CASTLE

BY THE RAVAGES OF TIME,

RICHARD BARNES

AT HIS OWN EXPENSE

ERECTED THIS GATEWAY

IN THE YEAR

1777

The inscription, English one side, Latin the
other, is on two pointed stones over the arch.
Between them, a higher level path goes over
through a smaller arch with rustic seats onto
a big lawn with the remains of the keep under
ivy in the centre.

Virginia Water

Sham Classical Ruins and Tower,   SU 9866
c. 1750
For the ruins, see page 142. For the early
triangular tower, see page 204.

The story goes that the plan was chosen to
give views towards Windsor Castle, Saint
Paul's and the ridge of the Hog's Back,
which was then the southern boundary of the
enormous Windsor Park, 18 miles from the
Castle. A square tower would have done this
better; the inspiration must have come from
some other source. It is now called Fort
Belvedere and is a house; Wyattville was
called in to enlarge it into a castellated house
between 1827 and 1829, adding a taller tower
for grandeur and even better views.

West Clandon *Clandon Park*

Grotto, 1770s   TQ 0452
The grotto here is a deep niche cut into the
hillside behind the house, in grounds landscaped by Capability Brown. The entrance is
under a brick and flint pediment, the width
of the grotto, and just inside is a statuary
group of three naked Graces, green with the
genuine grotto damp. The grotto goes
18 feet into the hill and is semicircular on
plan. There is a shallow stone bath sunk into
the floor at the back, and in the walls are
niches holding classical heads and fragments.
The best thing about this place is its construction; the roof is made of redbrick boxes
about 1 foot square filled with rough flints
and copper slag.

There is also a Maori House, brought back
by a Lord Onslow who was Governor of New
Zealand (see *Buildings of England*).

Witley *Witley Park, ex Court*

Grotto, *c.* 1900   SU 9540
See page 199.

The Three Graces in Clandon grotto

Tyne and Wear

Penshaw
Monument   NZ 3253
See page 142.

Rowlands Gill *Gibside*
Column and Mausoleum, mid-   NZ 1859
eighteenth century
George Bowes began the landscaping here in
1729. Today, the house is a tree-filled ruin,
and so are its attendant buildings. The stables
and orangery are no serious loss but the
Banqueting Hall in Gothic has become an
enchanting picturesque ruin and should be
carefully kept as one. James Paine's mausoleum for his father remains, a beautifully free
essay on Palladian themes, now a church, and,
at the end of a vista from it, the Column of
British Liberty. This is a statue 12 feet high,
once gilded, carved here by Christopher
Richardson in 1757. The Tuscan column is
140 feet high.

Whickham
Long John Monument, 1854   NZ 1959
A bust of John English, a stone-mason who
was a famous strongman and wrestler, on a
tall column. It is said to be a self-portrait.

Whitburn *Whitburn House*
Sham Ruin, 1869   NZ 4163
Some re-erected fragments of mediaeval
buildings make excellent follies, like Shobden
or Abingdon Abbey, but this is a dull one, a
big window from St John's church, Newcastle, with other bits.

Warwickshire

A sparse county again: five towers, obelisks
at Farnborough, Radway, Stratford and
Tamworth, and Sanderson Miller's own folly
at Edgehill.

Alcester *Oversley Castle*
Tower, early nineteenth century   SP 0958
A pale castellated tower, now with a 1910
house added to it. Not exciting.

Avon Dassett *Burton Dassett*
Tower   SP 3951
Another unexciting conversion; this time a
tower mill turned into a tower.

Radway *Edgehill*
Radway Tower, 1747   SP 3748
See title page and page 54.
   Sanderson Miller wrote this poem about it,
dated 13 December 1750:

At last I find that I have clear
In Land six hundred pounds a year
Besides a Piece for Wife & Daughters
And something more for Woods & Waters.
My House! tis true, a small & old one
Yet now tis warm, tho' once a cold one.
My Study holds three thousand volumes,
And yet I sigh for Gothic columns,
Such as Sir Roger[1], learned Knight of Taste
At Arbury so well has placed,
Or such as Dacre, Gothic Master
Has introduced instead of Plaister.
With here a large Settee for sleep,
A Window there to take a peep
Of Lawns & Woods and Cows & Sheep,
And Laurel Walk & Strawberry Bank
For which the Paymaster[2] I thank.
The Paymaster well skilled in planting
Pleas'd to assist when cash was wanting
He bid my Laurels grow, they grew

Fast as his Laurels alway do.
The Squire still said, 'Get Ground in Front',
By dint of Parliament I've don't—
But still they say, 'No piece of Water,
No Duckery for Wife and daughter!'
Should that be done they's still cry out
And hourly put me in a pout,
The Place is still not worth a farden,
No Mortal has a Kitchen Garden
So full of Weeds, so void of Cabbage Plants
You can't supply your scullion's wants
No Turnips freshen salted Beef
I know you've apples to our grief,
We're forced to drink to quench our Thirst
of crabbed Cider till we burst.
No pease to eat with Fatten'd pork,
Then haste and set your men to work
With spades and rakes and such like ware
Nor think you're born to sleep in chair.
The soil is good, your garden make,
Then of the produce we'll partake.[3]

[1] Sir Roger Newdigate, founder of Newdigate prize.
[2] Pitt.
[3] The last nine lines are in another hand.

Southam
Monument, 1823   SP 4162
An unlikely commemoration, a monument to 'the first PROVIDENT DISPENSARY'.

Sanderson Miller's Thatched Cottage

Stratford-on-Avon *Clopton House*
Tower*   SP 2055
An octagonal prospect tower with a taller staircase turret.

Warwick *Guy's Cliffe*
Rock rooms*   SP 2966
A series of rock rooms and/or natural caves. *Buildings of England* tells us that in the one in which Guy of Warwick is supposed to have died, one or two letters alone remain of an inscription 'in Saxon characters', translated in Murray's *Handbook* of 1899 as 'Cast out, thou Christ, from thy servant this burthen. Guttie.'

West Midlands

Only three follies around the Birmingham complex, none of them very exciting.

Birmingham *Edgbaston*
Perrott's Folly, 1758   SP 0888
For this folly there are three stories of origin: one for the sporting, one for the sentimental and another for the scientific. All are, however, based on a seven-storeys high tower built by John Perrott, very slender and elegant above the encroaching houses.

The first story is that he was a great hunts-man and more particularly fond of coursing, so when he was too old and stiff to ride he would climb his tower to watch his favourite sport. When his wife died, the sentimentalists maintain, he built his tower to see the grave of his Amy in Belbroughton churchyard 10 miles away. The last explanation is that he was a keen astronomer and built his tower as an observatory, for which purpose it is now used. The sentimental explanation seems the most likely, because how would an old man who could no longer ride, with stiff joints, climb all these stairs, whereas a sentimentalist would like nothing better than the weary trudge up the spiral staircase to hang over the battlements panting for breath, while he stared at the minute grave in Belbroughton.

Halesowen *The Leasowes*
Gothick Ruin, *c.* 1750   SO 9684
Shenstone's charming house and grounds at Halesowen, his pride and joy, the result of so much love and theory, is today almost buried under pebble-dash and a golf course. Here a good window, and there a length of moulding peer out over the striped umbrellas and the rest of the tedious clobber. In a hazel copse near the lake is all that remains of a gothick folly, one standing corner of red sandstone with a little quatrefoil window.

A century-old account of the place explains that the 'beauties and ornamental landscapes exist no longer, a line of canal, close to the place, has interfered with its rural quiet, and brought with it all the disagreeable accompaniments of rude traffic and vexatious depredation'. Now the quiet of the canal is shattered in its turn by the roar of motors on the bypass.

Meriden
Obelisk   SP 2582
Meriden claims that its village green is the absolute centre of England. Other places, doubtless using different methods of measurement, make this claim, but here is something no other centre has, a touching obelisk: 'In Remembrance of those CYCLISTS who Gave Their Lives in World War II 1939–45'.

West Sussex

Like East Sussex, a sharply divided county, again with the flat rich agricultural weald in the north and chalk downs in the south. Neither has produced much in the folly line; there is Goodwood grotto in the front rank, and there are two or three good towers.

Arundel *Arundel Castle*
Hiorn's Tower, late eighteenth   TQ 0207
century
This is one of the last of the triangular towers and is notable for two things; it is called after its architect, Francis Hiorn, and not after the Duke of Norfolk, and it is built in flint and stone checks, very pretty. Otherwise it is dull, not high enough now the park trees are full-grown. Three storeys, three octagonal corner turrets, castellated. Local histories say that it was built so that the duke could see a sample of Hiorn's work before commissioning him to remodel the whole castle. He seems to have got the job, in 1787, but died two years later.

Clayton
Castellated Tunnel Entrance   TQ 3014
See page 261.

Colgate *Beacon Hill*
Holmbush Tower, nineteenth   TQ 2333
century*
A 1916 picture postcard shows an eight-storey square stone tower, castellated, with a corner turret. It looks too solid to have fallen down.

Fisherstreet *Shillinglee Park*
Deer Tower, Eyecatcher   SU 9732
An ugly little squatty tower, a square of two storeys with a plain round tower on each corner and a taller plain round one for the keeper to get higher. Rectangular windows with dripstones and a few slits. No castellations, no arrow-slits, but presumably it made a tolerable eyecatcher across the park. The accepted date is late eighteenth century but Miss Winterton tells me that it was built when the

The Toat memorial

first Earl Winterton added the south front to the eighteenth-century house (burnt, now restoring) in 1885. My guess is late eighteenth century, with ruinous castellations removed and the stucco done in 1885 to brisk it up again.

Goodwood *Goodwood House*
Shell House, 1739   SU 8808
See page 154.

Patching *Michelgrove*   TQ 0706
Here are the remains of a house which was pulled down by the Duke of Norfolk in the last century. There seems no clear opinion if the folly wall is actually part of the old house or was put up as a folly; it is divided into filled-in gothic arches, and there is a tower at one end. Also at Michelgrove is a tower which resembles a clock tower. But the agent of the present duke told me that it was a pigeon cote built to house birds which were to be eaten at the house nearby. These are follies by dereliction, not intent.

Pulborough
Toat Monument, 1827   TQ 0418
This small slender octagonal tower, very plain and stark, takes its name from a nearby

farm. It was built to mark the spot where Samuel Drinkald fell from his horse and died in 1823, though other accounts refer to his death in the Napoleonic Wars. Either way, it's a nice little tower.

Slindon
Nore Folly, late eighteenth century   SU 9708
A true folly, architecturally interesting without any reason or history attached to it, other than it was built by an Earl of Newburgh in the eighteenth century, and that the small room was once used for shooting luncheons. The trees of a wood behind the folly show up the white of the knapped flint and the two parallel walls joined by a semicircular arch and the second arch behind crowned with machicolations, and flanked by a taller square column of flint. The room where the lunches were held is like a small summer-house and is joined to the column.

Despite its eccentricity a nice practical explanation for its odd shape and a reason for its existence has been produced with the usual facility by the local inhabitants, who, however proud they are of their folly wherever it may be, must be able to attribute it to ancient monks, lecherous and drunken squires, or madness; it can never be the simple and often correct reason, of wanting a nice building to look at. In the case of Nore Folly the Earl of

The folly at Slindon

Newburgh happily anticipated the coming of the railways; this is a railway arch or tunnel entrance.

Stanstead *Stanstead Park*
Racton Tower, 1772   SU 7711
See page 204.

Steyning *Wappingthorne*
Water Tower, *c.* 1928   TQ 1811
See page 271.

Tillington *Upperton Monument*
Tower, late eighteenth century   SU 9722
A three-storey plain stone castellated tower, rectangular in plan, with round-headed windows and a taller octagonal staircase turret; probably a prospect tower to Petworth. Now a house. On the other side of the road a small enclosed garden has been made with an octagon trellis gothick summer-house at one end of the lawn and a trellis obelisk to match at the other.

The Vandalian Tower, Uppark

*Pits Hill**
I have been told of a shell house here, but have not yet been able to see it.

Twineham *Hickstead Place*   TQ 2720
Buildings of England gives this as an early seventeenth-century sham castle. That would put it a century before Vanbrugh's work at Claremont and Castle Howard, but to me it has not this air; I think it more likely to be late gothic than early gothick. The owners think that it is part of a monastery known to have been here, and that the oldest part is Tudor like some of the house; certainly in dry weather the outlines of further large buildings are visible under the lawn.

The building is square and brick, very solidly made with small gothic windows and wooden stairs to the first floor. It is too near the house to be a hunting stand; possibly a granary, or a dove-cote? It is decorated with clumsy cross-slit shapes in dark stone; these alone look folly, and might have been added later.

Uppark
The Vandalian Tower, 1774   SU 7817
This was one of the most beautiful follies, an elegant ruin like a Piranesi engraving, with grass and the bent branches of small trees growing on the walls. It was built of dark red brick and Roman cement, standing on a low mound surrounded by a dry ditch. Much of the facing and the top have gone and whole arches are fallen, but a drawing by Henry Keene, who may have been the architect, shows the 'Vandalian Tower' very similar to this one with a tapering pinnacle on each bastion, and the tall windows filled with slender gothick tracery and stained glass. It was built to commemorate a scheme for founding Vandalia, a new colony in America, or the 21st birthday of Sir Harry Featherstonehaugh, who owned Uppark. He was Emma Hamilton's first lover, and a great friend of the Prince Regent; perhaps the stories of Emma dancing on the table might be true.

West Yorkshire

A number of good follies are left between the industrial areas.

Aberford *Parlington Park*
The Triumphant Arch, 1783   SE 4337
See page 141.

Bingley
St David's Ruin, 1796   SE 1139
One of the best situated and most romantically ruined of sham castles; it stands on a steeply-wooded ridge. The woods immediately surrounding the folly were at some time burned and the smoke blackened the stones. Built by Benjamin Ferrand in 1796, it is very similar in plan to Mow Cop, consisting of a tall pointed arch joined to a small tower; a freestanding ivy-clad buttress replaces the wall pierced with *oeil de boeuf* at Mow Cop. (*Buildings of England* suggests that it was built as an eye-catcher to Harden Grange).

Bradford *Apperley Bridge. Woodhouse Grove School*
Elam's Tower, *c.* 1800   SE 1733
A pretty tower on a mound in the trees, square and stone, with huge empty windows. It was built by Robert Elam, who lived at Lower Wortley Manor from 1799–1804, to relieve unemployment—all the stone was carried by hand. Later it held a water tank, but is now a shell.

Bramham *Bramham Park*
Gothick Temple, *c.* 1750   SE 4344
Nothing here is quite folly, but the temple, probably by Paine, is very near it; there is a good obelisk at the cross of five rides, four little obelisks on the lawn, sphinxes, and the gayest of bears on piers in the forecourt.

Halifax *Norland*
Wainhouse Tower, 1871–4   SE 0725
See page 282.

John Edward Wainhouse, who was born in 1817 and died in 1883, owned Washer Lane Dyeworks. He was a pioneer of smoke abatement schemes, and in 1871 started to build a vast chimney on the hills above Halifax; in 1874 building finished, but the chimney was no longer a chimney but a 253-foot high octagonal tower crowned with an elaborate cupola of golden Halifax freestone. Inside there is a shaft 7 feet wide, and 403 steps take the visitors to the fine views of the industrial scene from the top.

Its origin is attributed to a desire on the part of Wainhouse to overlook Pyenest, the neighbouring estate of Sir Henry Edwards. Sir Henry was High Sheriff and the first gentleman in Yorkshire to grow a pineapple in his hot-houses; he also, as Colonel of the West Riding Yeomanry, was reputed to use a saddle cloth costing £200. Wainhouse's

St. David's Ruin, Bingley

Tower cost £10,000. The evidence for this spite is slender, though it is true that Wainhouse built almshouses near Pyenest which he called 'Dyenest'.

Huddersfield

Towers, 1897 and 1902   SE 1517
The dullest kind of monumental Diamond Jubilee lump, the Victoria Tower on Castle Hill, and, four years later, Edgar Wood's lovely clock tower at Lindley. No greater contrast could be imagined.

Ilkley Moor

Cow and Calf Rocks*   SE 1145
Carved with biblical texts.

Leeds *Cardigan Road*

Bear Pit, *c.* 1840   SE 3033
The sixth postal district of Leeds, and especially Cardigan Road, is part of the city's inner ring of suburb, full of the gabled mansions of well-to-do nineteenth-century industrialists. Behind one tall paling lies a black castle instead of a red house. There is a curved retaining wall, and, built into a bank behind it, a very massive sham front made of lumps of soot-black stone. It has three dark entrances barred with rusty iron, which give on three brick tunnels leading into a 20-foot wide brick pit 10 feet deep. One of the turrets has a spiral staircase leading to the top of the bank, so that visitors could see the bear below them, for this really was a bear pit.

   All through the early years of Queen Victoria's reign a Zoological and Botanical Gardens with a lake covered this part of what had been the Earl of Cardigan's estate. In 1858 the site was sold for building, and the lake filled in and Cardigan Road made. Tommy Clapham, the last proprietor, opened another pleasure ground near Woodhouse Moor, a 'Royal Park and Horticultural Gardens', with 'The Largest Dancing Platform in the World'. This was in time built over, and nothing now remains of these two enterprises but the bear pit.

Roundhay Park
Sham Castle, 1821   SE 3437
A beautiful sham castle, built for the Nicholson family, the last private owners of the park. It is square, built of rough stone, with two big round towers with a pointed arch between in front and two half-towers at the back. Over the arch was once a room but this had already been vandalized when Kirby wrote his *Descriptive Guide to Roundhay Park* in 1872....

   ... broken roof, scribbled over with names. The two front towers are more perfect; one of them furnished with a winding or geometrical stone staircase, pierced with ten loop-holes; twenty-seven steps bring us to the room over the archway, and twenty more land us on the roof of the same. These towers are surmounted by battlements to give the building a kind of finish: the design aims at the appearance of antiquity and is partially Gothic.

All castellations now gone, but still a good sham.

Roundhay Castle, Leeds

Rawdon, near Leeds
A small domed retreat   SE 2041

Oakenshaw *Bierley Hall*
Grotto and Druids   SE 1728
Bierley Hall has been demolished. Once
Bradford Corporation intended to make the
grounds into a public park and there are
asphalt paths and the sparse, worn look of
municipality on the banks and some of the
trees, but all is shut up and barred except for
licensed fishermen. A few more years and
romantic decay may quite take over. The
works must once have been, if not splendid,
at least large, for there are the remains of a
series of lakes. A grotto once filled the space
between two of them and the north entrance
can be seen, just visible as thin rock fangs
round a hole, filled in. At the lower end is a
Palazzo del Te tumble of huge boulders and a
thin trickle of water. Over the grotto on the
grass once was a modest Druid's Circle, now
only a few stones stand; the rest are down and
only the eye of faith can see a circle.

The Bramhope Tunnel monument

Otley *All Saints' churchyard*
Bramhope Tunnel Monument   SE 2045
Standing in the churchyard at Otley is this
miniature railway tunnel entrance in the
fortified style, a memorial to the men who
lost their lives while building Bramhope
tunnel on the Leeds and Thirsk Railway
between the years 1845–9. It was erected at
the 'expense of James Bray Esq. the contractor
and of the agents sub-contractors, and
workmen employed thereon'. Also: 'I am a
stranger and a sojourner with you: give me a
possession of a burying-place with you, that
I may bury my dead out of my sight', and
'Or those eighteen, upon whom the tower in
Siloam fell, and slew them, think ye that they
were sinners above all the rest in Jerusalem?
I tell you, Nay; but, except ye repent, ye shall
all likewise perish'—verses from Genesis and
the Gospel of St Luke which indicate the
changing spirit of the railways from the days
when Brunel planted ivy on the tunnel
entrances at Bristol and engines plunged
gaily off the lines every day, as surely as the
pedantic detail of the 15-foot fortified towers
shows the change in ornamental gothic.
   In 1941 this famous monument was rebuilt
as the Caen stone had decayed.
   There is said to be an eighteenth-century
Roman Bath in the grounds of Bramhope
Hall.*

Sharlston *Nostell Priory*
Pyramid Lodge*   SE 4119
This must be large, bigger than the Needle's
Eye at Wentworth Woodhouse, for a whole
pedimented arch with columns cuts through
it.

Silsden *Cringles*
Tower   SE 0446
A curious leaning tower, stone, plain, no
history, no castellations, slightly tapered.

Todmorden *Stoodley Pike*
Obelisk   SD 9424
A colossal obelisk, built for Waterloo, blown
down during the Crimean War, and put up
again after it.

Wakefield *Kettlethorpe Hall*
Boathouse, *c.* 1730   SE 3318
See page 251.

Walton *Walton Hall*
Grotto and Sham Ruin*   SE 3716
I have not been able to see these, and now probably never will, for it would be a shame to destroy the images evoked in *The Squire of Walton Hall*.[1]

Charles Waterton was born in 1782, the 14th of his line to occupy the house, which he inherited at the age of 23. He was an enthusiastic naturalist and travelled far (few men then went up the Orinoco or rode a cayman). He was a skilled taxidermist, made a sham man called The Nondescript from a monkey skin, and had his portrait painted with a cat's head on a book and a bright bird on his forefinger; he walled the house round to make a bird sanctuary, carefully turning out the foxes and badgers, but 38 years later he wrote:

'I once treated a family of Badgers very ill; and yet I feel sorry that I started them from their ancestral settlement. Having finished the park wall in 1826, I sent the foxes and badgers

[1] Philip Gosse (Cassell, 1940).

an order to quit, and seek fresh apartments *outside* of the park; I ought to have retained them.'

Not only did he see far in advance of his time that badgers were useful animals, but he protected the crows and ravens that neighbours shot to preserve their game, and even encouraged picnickers to his island retreat, with its ruin and grotto; 'Cups and fire provided! Mill workers welcomed!' The fires were kept up in the grotto all the year, to keep his cats warm, and for their benefit, too, smoking was forbidden. He was buried here by the lake in 1865.

Yeadon
Rawdon Hermitage*   SE 2238
David Glover has sent me photographs of a neat little domed retreat, probably a gazebo, a solid stone octagon building with three open arches for the view, the round heads rusticated. It seems likely to have perished utterly by now as I could not find it in 1971, and no one seemed even to remember it. There was a rival building on a neighbouring estate and the two were called Spite and Malice.

Wiltshire

A beautiful county with much fine landscaping and follies varying from the almost complete set at Stourhead to the smallest sham henge in the country.

Amesbury *Amesbury Abbey*
Grotto, eighteenth century   SU 1543
Charles Bridgeman laid out the grounds, for the Duke of Queensbury, but they were much worked over, and there are accounts of a grotto called The Diamond where Gay is supposed to have written *The Beggar's Opera*; if so, the grotto was made before 1728; and there are accounts of an elegant Chinese

pavilion and bridge, but these are gone. The Diamond, a grotto façade let into a hillside across from the house, is now inaccessible, the paths being completely overgrown, with unbridged marsh in the middle of them.

Ansty *Wardour Castle*
Grotto, 1792 (?)   ST 9326
See page 163.

Bowood *Bowood House*
Cascade   ST 9770
See page 165.

The wall at Corsham Court

Bradford-on-Avon

Bear Garden, twentieth century   ST 8361
A long narrow garden full of small cement
bears, at school, dancing, sitting, standing
and holding the milk bottle.

Cherhill *Oldbury Camp*   SU 0569

An Obelisk, a White Horse in the chalk and a
fine view.

Corsham *Corsham Court*

Folly wall, mid-nineteenth century   ST 8671
This is a large and most curious folly, a
roughly serpentine wall about 65 feet long
and, with ups and downs, about 30 feet high.
It represents the crumbling front of two round
castle towers with curtain walling; very
roughly built, incorporating some genuine
gothic windows and piers of varying merit,
and one or two strange chimneys on top.
There is a sham coat of arms with the date
1874.

a. It was built to screen the stables from the
approach to the Court.

b. Thomas Broadwood built the tall house
in the street leading to the Court and then
put up the wall so that the grander house was
comfortingly invisible.

c. Thomas Broadwood still built the tall
house, but the owner of the Court put up the
wall so that the interloper's top storeys should
not overlook him.

d. The real pieces came from the nineteenth-
century restoration of Corsham Church.

e. Ditto Chippenham Abbey.

There are no records at Corsham, though
the curator is sure of the nineteenth-century
date, 'probably as late as 1875'.

I can find nothing elsewhere; it remains a
puzzle, England's poor approach to Ireland's
superb Jealous Wall, entirely eighteenth
century in concept, tied to the nineteenth, a
large work, badly carried out.

Fonthill Gifford *Fonthill Abbey*

Fragments, late eighteenth century   ST 9433
The remains of Beckford's house. The Dark
Walk, a grotto walk under the road, can still
be found, and a grotto by Josiah Lane, very
derelict, a tummock that was once a hermitage,
and the ruins of the heavily rock-rusticated
arches of the Boat House. There are two fine
groups of nineteenth-century allegorical statuary and a tiny summer-house near the
stables.

But everything that still exists pales beside
the legends of the Abbey and the great tower,
long gone, but surviving in glowing letters,
engravings and loving popular memory,
the greatest gothick image of them all. For
one thing it was very expensive; half a million,
they said, and for another very convenient;
a ramp spiralling up the tower would take
Beckford's coach and six to the top as easy as
kiss your hand. Crimson silk carpets, a gold
dinner service, a thousand servants. . . .

It began as a humble sham ruin, an escape
from the Palladian family house, and Wyatt
designed it in 1796. The commission was for
the remains of a convent, with chapel, dormi-
tory and fragment of cloister. Beckford
ordered additions, and more additions, and by
1807 wanted it made into a permanent house,
fast. There were hundreds of workmen, huge
bonfires for the work in winter, the builder
put up the tower without a relieving arch in
the foundations, almost 280 feet of it. The
great hall was 120 feet high, the wings 400
feet long. Beckford's huge fortune dwindled,
he went to live quietly outside Bath, building
a meeker tower (page 283), and sold Fonthill.
Later, the clerk of the works, dying, told
Beckford about the gimcrack tower, but the
new owner loved it all, and laughed. On
21 December 1825 the tower slid into a heap
of rubble, only one man saw it fall, and only
the legends remain.

Kingston Deverill
Stonehenge, nineteenth century   ST 8537
This is about 4 feet high, in a field by the Rectory; it is possible that they are ancient stones as they were dragged down from Court Hill, where certainly there are tumuli, by Canon Kingsbury, with the father of Mr Carpenter, who still lives in the village, to help with the cart and horses.

They have been described both as sarsen stones acting as guides towards Stonehenge and as part of King Egbert's dining table, used the night before he beat the Danes at Hindon.

Marlborough *Marlborough College*
Grotto, 1730s   SU 1969
There was a castle here in the twelfth century, but by the time the early Georgian house was built, only the 60-foot mound survived. This was made picturesque by Lady Hertford, daughter-in-law of the sixth duke, with a cascade which has gone and a grotto once 'newer and prettier than Twickenham', which barely survives. I have found no evidence connecting it with Josiah Lane but it is in his district.

Monkton Farleigh
Brown's Folly, 1840   ST 8166
In 1840 Mr Wade Brown bought an estate at Monkton Farleigh and built a square slightly tapering tower with an Italianate top. Before it was finished the Ordnance Survey erected a tent on the roof from which they surveyed the surrounding country. There is a local tradition that it was built to relieve the unemployed in the village of Bathford.

Newton Toney *Wilbury House*
Grotto, *c.* 1710   SU 2341
A very early Palladian house, by Benson, with a grotto which, if contemporary as the owners think, must be one of the very, very first pieces of gothick in the country. It lies under a mound at the edge of a wood; entrance is through a round-headed arch about 8 feet high which leads into a symmetrical square vaulted flint chamber. The crossing of the vault is emphasized with thin slabs of stone set edgewise, and plain red brick arches throw deep shadows into curved niches opposite the entrance and to right and left. Seldom have plain brick and stone, their tone, colour and shadow, been used so effectively to decorate flint. The floor is plain earth.

From the left-hand niche a flint quadrant passage leads into the plantation; once a passage really did lead to the grotto from a secret door in the library but this has been filled in.

A little later a pretty octagon gazebo was built on a mound on the other side of the house, all windows and light, the angles emphasized with attached rusticated columns. There is a pretty umbrella porch, oak under lead with hollow shells and lions' heads as finials to their ribs. Under the mound at the back is a grotto entrance to a boat house; the lake is now dry.

Salisbury *The Council House, Bourne Hill*
Sham Ruin, eighteenth century   SU 1530
The park was laid out late in the eighteenth century for Henry Penruddocke Wyndham, and includes an elaborate little fifteenth-century porch, removed by Wyatt from the cathedral. I think it safe to say that stories of a fine grotto in a garden in the close are not founded on fact.

Savernake Forest
Column, 1789   SU 2365
The Ailesbury Column celebrated, rather prematurely, George III's recovery from madness.

Stourhead
Landscape garden, 1740s   ST 7834
See page 44.

Tollard Royal
The Larmer Gardens, late nineteenth century   ST 9418
See page 256.

Wexcombe
Waterworks Pineapple, nineteenth   SU 2759
century
See page 98.

Whiteparish *Eyre's Folly*
The Pepperbox, 1606   SU 2225
A red brick hexagonal tower with a pyramidal
slate roof, erected by Giles Eyre in 1606, when
he built Brickworth House. It is called The
Pepperbox, which it does exactly resemble,
and has given its name to the hill on which it
stands. What Eyre's intention was is difficult
to determine; utilitarian or decorative,
hunting lodge or belvedere, eyecatcher or
folly? Probably a hunting stand.

Wilton *Wilton House*
Grotto Façade, before 1635   SU 0932
The façade, pedimented and most elaborately
carved, probably by the younger Nicholas
Stone, and remarkably well preserved, has
been re-erected in the woodland garden as a
house front. The vanished grotto, though,
must be deeply regretted; it must have been
England's wettest water toy. It stood at the
end of the Great Walk, three arches under the
pediment, and, up to a raised terrace, stairs
with balustrades of spouting sea monsters.
Aubrey, Hammond and Celia Fiennes all
describe its splendours; black and white
marble pavement, marble tritons to 'weep on
the beholder', and a table in the middle with
a pipe that forced water 'onto the roof curved
like a crown but hollow within . . . a shower
all about the room'. Little rooms opened off
the big square one, worse traps, for the water
ran innocently to make 'the melody of
Nightingerls' until the visitor went in to look,
'but the entrance of each room is a line of
pipes that appear not till moved by a sluice
it washes the spectator for a diversion', and
'Mr. de Caus had here a contrivance by turning of a cock, to shew three rainbowes, the
secret of which he did keep to himself . . . so
upon his death it was lost. The grotto and
pipes did cost ten thousand pounds.'

Eyre's Folly, Whiteparish

Wales

I know of only about three dozen follies in Wales, mostly small, with the best ones in the south.

Paxton's Tower (see page 413)

Clwyd

Denbigh *A543, direction Bodfari*
Castellated farm   SJ 0566
A good castellated wall to hide a farm, not from the house nearby, but from the road.

Harwarden
Sham ruin, nineteenth century*   SJ 3166
The ruin of a real castle, converted in the early nineteenth century into a folly eye-catcher.

Henllan
New Foxhalls   SJ 0468
Old Foxhalls is a tudor farmhouse standing in a beautiful park. Beside it, surrounded by cherry trees, is the ruin of New Foxhalls. This was started in 1592 by Mr Panton, M.P. and Recorder of Denbigh; his neighbour Mr Lloyd, who lived in the old house, prophesied that he would soon be the owner of both houses, and when Panton went bankrupt, having built only one wing of his new mansion, Lloyd bought both the house and land. He removed the oak partitions which divided up the interior and allowed the building to decay. It is now covered with ivy and stands in a field which still shows the lines of formal parterres running through the cherry trees.

Moel Fammau
Jubilee Tower, c. 1810   SJ 1664
Moel Fammau is a high and exposed hill with the sun beating on its shelterless slopes. It is most easily reached from the summit of the shortest (though not the most main) road from Mold to Ruthin. Two miles of path go across the bare open hill to a pile of rubble on the top, which appears and disappears, now above us, now seeming below. On the north-east the land falls to the flat Wirral, to Lancashire and Cheshire, on the west are the mountains going to Snowdon. The enormous distances swim, contract and stretch again; the great wall of China must dip and rise for its 1,500 miles much as this path goes, for this is one of our landscape vistas on the heroic scale.

The pile of rubble, previously dwarfed by the sun and air, becomes suddenly huge. It is the ruined podium of a colossal obelisk in the Egyptian taste, which commemorated the jubilee of King George III. It is about 50 feet square, 30 feet high, and ruinous; the corner bastions have all crumbled and the doors are almost silted up. The fabric is rubble faced with stone, and the walls are 12 feet thick at their thinnest part. Nevertheless, the winter weather here is so fierce that the building collapsed even before it was finished, and it has always been a ruin.

Mostyn
Tower*   SJ 1681
A nice conceit for a crossroads; a square two-storeyed tower standing astride a bridge with another road running underneath. The ground-floor windows are beautifully-made sham ones.

Ruabon *Wynnstay Park*
Sir Watkyn's Tower*   SJ 3044
There is said to be a tower here, built to commemorate Waterloo, but its continued existence is uncertain.

Trefonen *Nercwys Hall*
Sham Castle, 1815*   SJ 2462
A small sham castle by Benjamin Gunmow.

Jubilee Tower, Moel Fammau

Dyfed

Aberystwyth *Pen Dinas*
Column, nineteenth century   SN 5981
A curious column with a flared top, built by
Major Richards of Brynyreithen to look like a
cannon, in memory of the Duke of Wellington, but never finished.

Boncath

Boncath *Cilwendeg*
Shell House, late eighteenth century
A remote and beautiful group of buildings
round a big courtyard. The Accounting Room
has an inscription on slate, 'Builded for
Morgan Jones 1828', and the Dove House, a
small banded Seton Delaval, in 1835. This is
divided into three parts, for chickens to the
left and right and for turkeys in the centre,
with pigeons right across the top. A stone
dove has gone from the roof, but there is still
a big duck pond and a slate fence cut perfectly
to imitate wooden palings. Nearby in the
woods is the shell house, which was probably
built by Morgan Jones' father John in the
1770s or 80s. Again there is cut slate, dressing
an elegant façade. The interior is neglected,
and the dome fell and was replaced by a flat
ceiling early in the nineteenth century, but a
beautiful and rare floor survives, with slate
squares set cornerwise in patterns of the
knuckle bones of sheep and oxen.

Devil's Bridge *Hafod*
Johns' Arch, 1810   SN 7477
This is the survivor of three arches built by
Thomas Johns of Hafod in 1810 to celebrate
the fiftieth year of the reign of George III. It
spans the road from Devil's Bridge to Pentre
Briwnant at the top of the hill, and is made of
small pieces of stone, a gothic arch with a

Derry Ormond Tower

square tapered pier on each side. The whole
of it is covered with minute ferns growing
between the masonry.

Lampeter
Derry Ormond Tower   SN 5747
A high solitary column of stone on a bare
hill near Lampeter. The general effect at a
distance used to be of a routine classical
column. As one walked closer the abacus and
entablature became stone machicolations
supporting a slab of cast-iron like a tea tray
against the dark clouds. All around ran an
iron railing. All this has fallen, but gothick
details remain; arrow-slits to light the staircase
and a pointed door in the base. The column
has very visible entasis and also a certain
amount of twist and fall.

Llanarthney

Paxton's, or Nelson's Tower, *c.* 1805 SN 5420
See page 410.

An impressive and well-sited tower on a hill above the Towy valley, built by Sir William Paxton from designs by Cockerell. It is triangular in plan with turrets at each corner and a central tower rising above them. At one time it was faced with Roman cement. The roofs and all the floors have fallen in and the castellations are falling too, but it will be some time before the tower is completely derelict, as it is very strongly built. Over each of the three doors, in Welsh, English and Latin, is the following inscription. 'To the invincible commander, Viscount Nelson, in commemoration of deeds before the walls of Copenhagen, and on the shores of Spain; of the Empire everywhere maintained by him over the seas; and of the death which in the fulness of his own glory, though ultimately for his own country and for Europe, conquering, he died. This tower was erected by William Paxton.'

Even writing an inscription in Welsh has not deterred the anonymous authors of folly stories; with only one folly in the district to build on, they have produced enough variants on a theme to satisfy several. Needless to say, seven counties can be seen from it, and of the same nature is the story that Paxton had four white horses of which he was so proud that he used to climb his tower to see them being driven out of Tenby thirty miles away; some hills prevent this.

Magistrates and the election of 1802 provide the other stories. Paxton proposed to build a bridge over the Towy, but the magistrates stopped him, so he built his tower. Or, in 1802 he contested Carmarthen with James Williams, squire of Edwinsford, and spent £15,690 4s. 2d. on 11,000 breakfasts, 25,000 gallons of ale, £786 for ribbons, 36,000 dinners, and other items. At one moment he promised that if he was elected he would build a bridge across the Towy; after his defeat people said he was penniless, so he built the tower to prove them wrong. In 1806, however, he was elected to Parliament.

Besides being a successful master of the mint of Calcutta, Sir William was a pioneer of seabathing at Tenby, and was also one of the first directors of the Gas Light and Coke Company. He died in 1824.

1973. The tower was given to the National Trust by Viscount Emlyn in 1965 and has now been restored.

Penally *Tenby*

Tower of the Winds SS 1299

Here there is a cliff-top Greek theatre, most superbly situated looking over Carmarthen Bay, and the most unsophisticated of all such temples, far from the Athenian exemplar, but more exactly placed than the others. Six Norman columns support a dome, with a bell-cage on top and a wind-flag.

The arch at Hafod

Gwent

The Kymin, Monmouth

Kemeys Commander *Kemeys Inferior*

Folly, nineteenth century   SO 3404
A large square sham castle with one corner octagon turret, built of stone. It was heavily restored in 1914 and is now a house. The story is that it was built by a young member of the Kemeys family, who said to his father: 'From my folly you can see seven counties', to which his father answered in the slick folly tradition: 'Yes, and from seven counties they can see your folly'.

During the alterations a massive front door was added with a nice mediaeval porter's grille clamped straight on to the solid wood, so no one can see either way.

Llangattock nigh Usk

Clytha Castle Sham castle, 1790   SO 3509
See page 68.

Monmouth *The Kymin*

Naval Temple and Round House,   SO 5113
1794 and 1800
Outside Monmouth to the east is a very steep and beautifully-wooded hill called the Kymin. At the end of the eighteenth century it became the favourite resort of a dining club which used to meet here on summer evenings. In 1794 the members built a small tower called the Round House, so designed that each window gave a good natural picture of the view. After a great deal of discussion as to what form it should take, they erected the Naval Temple nearby. This consists of a central mass of masonry, with a roof sloping in gentle steps to an arch which rises like an involved chimney, decorated with anchors. About 2 feet below the eaves, another, wooden, roof slopes on downwards supported on rustic oaks trunks painted jet black; this second roof makes a verandah right round the temple. In the space of wall between the two roofs are round white plaques bearing the names of Admirals: Keith Duncan, Boscawen, Hawke, etc. Under the verandah on the east and west sides are niches with seats made of oak planks supported on more rustic tree trunks. Also there is an inscription carved on a piece of stone:

'This Naval Temple was erected August 1st 1800 to perpetuate the names of those Noble Admirals who distinguished themselves by their Glorious Victories for England in the last and present wars and is respectfully dedicated to Her Grace the Duchess of Beaufort daughter of Admiral Boscawen.'

The design of the Naval Temple was taken very seriously; the National Library of Wales has a set of thirteen drawings for it.

In 1804 Nelson visited Monmouth and dined with the members of the club at the Round House. The dining table is now in the Monmouth Nelson Museum, which is the best collection of Nelson relics in the country, and proves him to be as much a master of taste as Wellington was a master of language.

Pontypool *Pontypool Park*
Shell Grotto, 1844   SO 3000
See page 184.

Tredegar *Bedwellty Park*
Grotwork, nineteenth century   SO 1510
A path in the grass begins to pass big isolated water-worn rocks. They get more frequent, and the path turns through a good arch of them into a rock garden with four round rock-drawn beds, one with a fountain, about 20 feet across. The sides, built right up with rocks to shrub crowns, follow round their curves. At the super-rock end to the right is a little raised octagon pavilion with a glass roof. There are also some bits of industrial archaeology: a good park.

Gwynedd

Dolbenmaen *Brynkin Tower**   SH 5143
A nineteenth-century tower on a small wooded hill at the head of the Cwm Pennant valley.

Glynllifon Park *Fort Williamsburg**
Sham Fort, late eighteenth century   SH 4656
One of two built by Lord Newborough to save North Wales from the French. This one is derelict, the other is a house.

Llandrillo
Eyecatcher, *c.* 1870*   SH 0336
Built to look like a chapel.

Llandudno *On the B5117 from Llandudno to Conway*
Folly garden, twentieth century*   SH 7877
In the front garden of Mr J. Evans, coal merchant, and very fine.

Llanfachreth
Arch over road, *c.* 1820   SH 7623
A small clumsy arch built by Sir Robert Vaughan to relieve unemployment. One of those insignificant but memorable follies.

Llanfair-p-g.
Column   SH 5472
Just over the Menai Bridge is the village with a name so incredibly long that before the station was closed people bought platform tickets they didn't need just to get official confirmation that they had been there. There is still a roaring trade in comic postcards.

And on top of Craig-y-Dinas is a 100-foot Doric column with a 12-foot bronze hussar on top, a statue by Matthew Noble of the first Marquis of Anglesey. This is the man who said to Wellington at Waterloo 'By God, sir, I've lost me leg!!' 'By God, sir, so you have!' The leg was buried on the battlefield, and replaced by the first known articulated false one. The Marquis eloped with Wellington's sister-in-law and died aged 83, leaving 18 children and 73 grandchildren.

Maenan *Maenan Hall**
Eyecatcher, *c.* 1790
No further information, but it was recently restored by the Aberconwy family.

Portmeirion
Group, twentieth century   SH 5737
A complex of hotel buildings and ornamental conceits, new and re-erected, most beautifully arranged round a small bay, all done by Clough Williams-Ellis. The bath house from Arnos Castle, Bristol, is here, saved and restored. On his own estate at Penrhyndeudraeth to the north-east the architect has a small folly tower, a wedding present.

The folly at Penrhyndeudraeth

Mid Glamorgan

Glyntaff *near Pontypridd*

Towers.   ST 0888

Dr. William Price of Llantrisant was born on the 4th March, 1800; he was apprenticed to Dr. Edwards of Caerphilly, and in 1820 went to London and a year later qualified as a doctor; he then returned to Wales and started to practise medicine and surgery at Nantgarw, Treforest and Pontypridd. He was a Chartist and at one time escaped to France disguised as a woman to escape arrest. He was one of the pioneers of cremation, and in 1884 he himself cremated the body of his five-months'-old son Iesu Crist, and was tried for this at Cardiff Assizes. He defended himself and was acquitted, the Judge ruling that cremation was not illegal so long as it did not constitute a public nuisance. When he died in 1893 he was himself cremated, this being the first prearranged cremation in Wales.

It was in connection with his activities as a Druid that he built his follies. He used to practise Druidic rites, dressed in a white tunic, scarlet waistcoat and green trousers, wearing a fox's skin on his head and shoulders, which was the emblem of a healer. He considered that Glyntaff was the ancient burial place of the Druids, and illegally he began to build a 'palace' on land which belonged to Lady Llanover, the enthusiast for Welsh national costume and editor of the diaries of Mrs Delany; before he was ejected he succeeded in completing these two fortress-like towers, which were covered with white stucco and which were to serve as flanking turrets to an imposing gateway. His complete Druid outfit and other relics are preserved in the National Museum of Wales, St Fagans.

Powys

Hay *Moor Mansion*

Obelisks and an arch, early   SO 2342
nineteenth century

A gothic arch and two obelisks standing on a bracken-covered hill. They were built by Anna Maria Broadbelt Stallard-Penoyre of the Moor Mansion to relieve unemployment. At the foot of one of the obelisks lie the fragments of a tablet, inscribed B. S. Penoyre, Esq. 1826; as Anna Maria succeeded to the estate in January 1827, these obelisks are presumably a memorial to her father.

Machynlleth

Forge, late nineteenth century   SH 7501

Built by Lord Londonderry; the façade to the forge is a wall of blue engineering brick, rising into three thin turrets at each end and the middle. The door into the smithy is a stone horseshoe complete with the wrong number of nails. There is another horseshoe door to a smithy in Scotland at Dunmore, and a big horseshoe over the door of a forge at Belton.

Trecastle *A40*

Coachman's Cautionary

A squat and very solid stone obelisk which stands by the Llandovery–Brecon road above a sheer cliff deceptively masked by the trees. It carries the following inscription and is only a borderline folly, but very charming:

THIS PILLAR IS CALLED MAIL COACH PILLAR AND ERECTED AS A CAUTION TO MAIL COACH DRIVERS TO KEEP FROM INTOXICA-TION AND IN MEMORY OF THE GLOUCESTER AND CARMARTHEN MAIL COACH WHICH WAS DRIVEN BY EDWARD JENKINS ON THE 19 DAY OF DECEMBER IN THE YEAR 1835, WHO WAS INTOXICATED AT THE TIME AND DROVE THE MAIL ON THE WRONG SIDE OF THE ROAD AND GOING AT A FULL SPEED OR GALLOP MET A CART AND PERMITTED THE LEADER TO TURN SHORT ROUND TO THE RIGHT HAND AND WENT DOWN OVER THE PRECIPICE FOR 121 FEET WHERE AT THE BOTTOM NEAR THE RIVER CAME AGAINST AN ASH TREE WHEN THE COACH WAS DASHED INTO SEVERAL PIECES.

The work of this Pillar was
Executed by JOHN JONES
Marble & Stone Mason Llanddarog
near Carmarthen
Repainted and Restored
by Postal Officials 1930

West Glamorgan

Briton Ferry *Jersey Marine*
Tower, etc.   SS 7494
On the A483 between Swansea and Briton
Ferry. See page 263.

Neath *Ivy Tower*   SS 7598
A circular eighteenth century belvedere,
shooting box and banqueting hall, about
thirty feet in diameter; it has a basement with
a large fireplace for cooking, and above that
is the main room reached by a ramp from the
ground. The chimneys are in the big castellations and it is all built of very random stone
and rubble. A local farmer said that it was a
dance hall in his dad's day, with coloured
glass and all.

Pennard *Kilvrough Manor*   SS 5689
A tiny but charming tower, on one corner of
the little park.

Penrice *Penrice Castle*
Eyecatcher Gates   SS 4988
See page 223.

Reynoldston
Druid's Circle   SS 4890
See page 245.

Ivy Tower, Neath

Scotland

There are few large follies in Scotland, but those few are both superlative, and stranger than anything in the south; most of them are in Perthshire. They are offset by a lot of little dullies; stone cairns, small obelisks and uncouth towers. I have left many of them out.

The tree at Lanrick Castle (see page 98)

Aberdeenshire

Harlaw
Monument, twentieth century   NJ 7525
A rough tapering hexagon with protruding stones and a pyramid roof, put up in 1911 to commemorate the Battle of Harlaw in 1411.

New Deer
Monument, nineteenth century   NJ 8846
Two storeys square, then octagonal, then an octagonal spire.

Tarves *Prop of Ythsie*
Tower, nineteenth century   NJ 8732
A square bare stone tower with battered base and the penultimately minimum number of castellations—one gap each side. Machicolations. Slits.

Angus

Arbroath *Hospitalfields*
Mortuary, nineteenth century   NO 6441
A massive nonsense with every possible Scottish Baronial feature; towers and turrets of all shapes with and without pyramid roofs, spires, crosses, twisted columns, all are there.

Dundee
Triumphal Arch, 1848   NO 4030
In 1844, a temporary arch was put up to welcome Queen Victoria, and four years later this permanent and elaborate arch with octagon turrets was designed by J. T. Rochdale, who did the monument at Stirling.

Monikie
Panmure Monument, 1852   NO 5036
Large and elaborate again, this time a column with rusticated bands, on a hill to the south, commemorating the first Lord Panmure.

Argyll

McCaig's Folly at Oban

Dulmally
Monument, nineteenth century*   NN 5132
A large stone monument to the bard Duncan Ban MacIntyre, on the old road to Inverary. Four columns stand at the corners of a square base supporting a drum.

Oban
McCaig's Folly, 1900   NM 8630
See pages 267 and 268.

Ayrshire

Alloway
Burns Monument, 1820–30*   NS 3418
Thomas Hamilton of Edinburgh put this up on the north bank of the Doon, near a lot of Burnserie. It is the Choragic Monument of Lysicrates on a triangular Egyptian base, each side dedicated to one of the three divisions of Ayr. In the Greek bit, each of the nine columns stands for a muse.

Failford
Burns 'Parting from Highland Mary'* NS 4626
A square stone pillar commemorates 14 May
1786. There is a globe on top with a ring
aslant round it.

Kilmarnock
Burns Monument   NS 4338
More Burnserie, but too big to omit. A huge
temple like a vast Albert Memorial in red
standstone on a big platform crowned with
an 80-foot tower. A statue of Burns by W. G.
Stevenson is under the canopy and inside the
platform is a Burns Museum.

Tarbolton
Tower, nineteenth century   NS 4427
A large castellated and machicolated stone
tower with pinnacles, to celebrate William
Wallace burning the Barns of Ayr.

Berwick

Westruther
Castellated Cottages*   TN 6350
An eyecatcher to Spottiswood House. A
trifle, but a change from commemoratives.

Caithness

Thurso *Thurso Castle*
Harold's Tower, nineteenth century ND 1268
A sham castle put up by Sir John Sinclair over
the grave of Harald Earl of Caithness, killed
here in 1196.

Dumfriesshire

Moffat
A Ram on a Cairn, nineteenth   NT 0905
century
Minute but charming, a tribute to the importance of sheep farming, opposite the old
baths—Moffat was once a sulphur spa.

Thornhill
Column, 1714   NX 8796
A massive affair, bottom-heavy, with the
winged horse of the Queensbury family on
the top.

Dumbarton

Helensburgh
Henry Bell and the *Comet*   NS 2983
Henry Bell designed the *Comet,* and launched
it in 1812—the first practicable passenger
steamer in Europe, 3 horse-power, five years
after Fulton started the *Clermont* on the Hud-
son. A large obelisk in polished granite
stands to his memory here, and there is
another at Bowling where the *Comet* was
launched. In Hermitage Park is Bell's original
flywheel and anvil, a carpet-bedding replica
of the ship, and a £10,000 real one made in
1962.

East Lothian

Haddington *Garleton Hills*   NT 5076
The Hopetown Monument, a tall brick
monument that looks like a factory chimney.

Fife

Colinsburgh *Balcarres Crag*
Folly Tower and Arch   NO 4803
This is a very good one indeed, a trim eyecatcher to Balcarres, probably built very
early in the nineteenth century by Robert
Lindsay, brother of the Earl. It is most
beautifully situated, built of rough grey stone,
a round tower with two lower ruined walls
in good repair, set at right angles. The
pointed arches in the walls and the door,
window, cross-slit, *oeil,* and castellated top
of the tower are all boldly trimmed with
chic white dressed stone.

Kinglassie *Redwells Hill*
Blythe's Folly, 1820   NT 2399
Another good one, a most elegant square tower in random stone; four lightly tapering storeys banded apart, and complicated castellations, on a high windy hill.

Leven
Shell Garden, nineteenth century   NO 3801
See page 254.

The shell garden at Leven

Invernesshire

Glenfinnan
Tower, 1815*   NN 5958
A neat round tower with a statue of Prince Charles Edward on top, put up to commemorate his attempt to recover the throne, by Alexander MacDonald of Glenaladale, who then died, aged 28. Another inscription tells us that 'This pillar is now alas! also become the monument of its amiable and accomplished founder.'

Loch Oich
Well of Seven Heads, 1812   NH 3404
A bloody one. Seven brothers murdered the two sons of a seventeenth-century Clan Kappoch chief. They were caught and killed and their heads washed here in the waters of the spring and laid at the feet of the Noble Chief in Glengarry Castle. The obelisk commemorates in Gaelic, French, English and Latin the 'ample and summary vengeance which . . . overtook the perpetrators of the foul murder . . .', and is topped by the seven couped heads round the Hand of Retribution holding a dagger.

Kirkcudbrightshire

Borness *Kirkandrews*
Castellated Farm, early twentieth   NX 6245
century*
A farm and laundry behind a castellated screen, unusually late, built by James Brown from Manchester.

Lanarkshire

Carluke *Miltonhead*
Memorial   NS 8551
A nice little nothing, a deserved tribute; a triangulation-type stone to Major-General William Roy, 1726–90, 'Father of the Ordnance Survey', who started his life's work with a military map of Scotland between 1747–55.

Crawford
Obelisk, late nineteenth century   NS 9621
A pretty one, with a square stone ringing the top, to stand for the tombs of the Crawfords that never got built because of a family quarrel.

Glasgow   NS 5965
A tall Nelson obelisk on Glasgow Green and an elaborate nineteenth-century column to the Battle of Langside, in Queen's Park.

Hamilton *Chatelherault*
Classical Screen   NS 7155
See pages 135 and 136.
(The enormous echoing alarm of the Hamilton Mausoleum, very well looked after and on view, should on no account be missed.)

Midlothian

Bilston
Dryden Tower, mid-nineteenth century NT 2764
A square stone tower standing in the fields south of Edinburgh. About 60 feet high, with a semicircular bastion and tall blind arches. It is castellated and machicolated and three of its four very tall pinnacles remain.

The Binns *Midhope Tower*
Tam Dyell's Folly, *c.* 1830   NT 0578
A round stone tower about 60 feet high, built on an avenue vista from Hopetown House.

Corstorphine *Corstorphine Hill*
Clermiston Tower, 1871–2   NT 1973
A square stone tower five storeys high with a round turret, castellated, built for the centenary of the birth of Sir Walter Scott. It stands on a thickly wooded hill and can be climbed by a creaking wooden stair.

Edinburgh
Fountain, Huge Temple, Whale's   NT 2574
Jaws
See page 134.
Near Greyfriars Church in Candlemakers Row is a fountain with the statue of a hairy dog, Greyfriars Bobby, a terrier who watched over his master's grave from 1858 until 1872.
    There was a crossed arch of two whale's jaws in the Meadows, south of the Old Town, but I can get no recent confirmation of this.
    Edinburgh's most astonishing construction was Sir James Gowan's *Rockville* in Napier Road, indeed one of the most incredible houses ever built, but this has been demolished.
    Edinburgh's largest folly is on Calton Hill,

the National Monument begun in 1822 to honour the Scottish dead of the Napoleonic Wars. It was to be a model of the Parthenon and a splendid half-temple remains, left when the funds ran out, split length-ways, 12 Doric columns and their architrave.

Penicuik *Hurley*
Tower and Grotto, mid-eighteenth   NT 2461
century
I have not been able to find any trace of the grotto here, nor any information about it, but the tower has an engaging story. It is called Arthur's O'on. There seems to have been an original Arthur's O'on at Stenhousemuir near Falkirk, a Roman tower whose owner demolished it. This vandalism so enraged the owner of Penicuik that he built a copy. The stables are likewise classical and there is Ramsay's monument.

Moray

Crook of Alves
York Tower, late eighteenth/early   NJ 1463
nineteenth century*
Beside the River Knock, off the A96, is an octagon tower three storeys high, castellated and shuttered, to mark the spot where Macbeth met the witches.
    Also off the A96 is a similar tower on Cluny Hill to Nelson.*

Peebles

Blyth Bridge *Netherurd House*   NT 1345
Whale Arch
Arches made of the jawbones of stranded whales have of course always been more common in the north of Ireland and Scotland than in southern England, but they were a favourite form of vernacular decoration wherever they turned up in the nineteenth century. There are several in Scotland; at Latheron in Caithness one has survived from 1869.
    This one has no known date or history, but

is a particularly pretty one, the jaws set into stocky square random stone piers with odd little rectangle-semicircle-pyramid terminals on top.

The whale arch, Blyth Bridge

Traquair
Folly Gates   NT 3336
The gates were never to be opened after the '45 until a Stuart sat on the throne of Scotland again, and this oath has been kept. This would be dull in a dull place, but here there are mossy bears upright on the piers and the drive is overgrown with grass.

Perthshire

Blair Atholl *Blair Castle*
The Whim, 1762   NN 8865
See page 98.

Dunkeld *Dunkeld House*
Hermitage, 1758   NO 0143
Ossian's Hall on the rocks over the falls sounds interesting, and the walk to it is lovely, through beech trees, but this hermitage has never been more than an eighteenth-century tea house in a very picturesque setting. It has been thoroughly and carefully restored by the National Trust for Scotland, but could

never have had the romantic air its name demanded, which is reserved for some good toothy grot-work on the east side going down to river level.

The building is a rectangle of stone with a slate roof and semicircular ends. The land end is a half-drum of reeded stone; inside, the reeds lead into a circular anteroom with niches and then into an oval room with straight sides, the far end an open balcony over the falls. There is pleasant routine decoration, but the paintings of the life of Ossian are gone.

Lanrick *Lanrick Castle*   NN 6903
See pages 98 and 418.

Perth *Kinnoul Hill*
Tower   NO 1323
This is an unusually elaborate eyecatcher for Scotland, a round tower with pieces of wall and an arch, set on a crag high above the Tay, to be seen and to see from, 'built in imitation of a Rhineland castle'.

Pitlochry
Cluny Memorial Arch   NN 9558
See page 275.

Taymouth Castle
Superb rustic work, nineteenth   NN 7947
century
See page 188.

Ross & Cromarty

Evanton *Fyrish Hill*
The Gates of Nagapatam,   NH 6166
eighteenth century
Not pineapple or family tree class, but one of Scotland's few Grotesque Architecture follies, with the Rousham–Creech Arch crazy air and a wonderful setting to match, on the 1,500-foot summit of Fyrish Hill. It was built by

The Gates of Nagapatam

General Sir Hector Munro of Novar, presumably towards the end of the eighteenth
century, to help local unemployment by
reproducing the gates of the city of Nagapatam where he won a famous victory. He
also suppressed a mutiny at Patna, and captured Pondichery as well as Nagapatam. What
he built, though, is a boldly castellated wall,
rising in the centre over a big pointed arch
which is flanked by two smaller ones. There
is a stone something else beside it, defying
analysis.

Roxburghshire

Dryburgh
Wallace on the Hill   NT 5932
See page 215.

Fairnington *Fairnington House*
Baron's Folly   NT 6528
No details for this; nineteenth century, I
should think. A small octagon gazebo in
random stone with dressed stone trim to the
corners and the five pointed windows and the
door. It has a pyramidal slate roof and a cast-
iron curlicue on top.

Nearby at Penilheugh is a round stone
column on a round stone base and a gallery
and lantern on top. Built after Waterloo.

Teviothead *Harwick*
Cone, nineteenth century   NT 4105
A nice tall white cone on a hilltop to the
memory of Henry Scott Riddell of Scorbie,
songwriter, 1798–1870. It is banded into
three sections, has a good heavy entrance, a
few slits and an urn on top.

Stirlingshire

Dunmore *Dunmore Castle*
Pineapple, 1761   NS 8989
See page 96.

Stirling
The Wallace Monument, 1869   NS 8095
See page 215.

Sutherland

Dunrobin *Dunrobin Castle*
The Hunting House, 1732   NC 8501
A large summer-house, looking purely
seventeenth century, absolutely filled with
the trophies of nineteenth-century travel and
big-game hunting, become, I think, a folly
by quantity. In the castle, an overwhelming
display of tiger skins and the Sutherland
Wild Cat of Cat-land crest become fire-cat
to uphold the shovel and tongs.

West Lothian

Linlithgow
Tower*   NT 0078
I much regret not having seen this tower,
which sounds like a taller rocket-ship folly.
It is 60 or 70 feet high with a very tall conical
roof and an incurved waist, standing on a
golf course.

The cone at Teviothead

Ireland

Lovely follies, from the spectacular and well-preserved to those lost and abandoned on the fields of vanished demesnes; even these are better preserved than they would be in England, for follies are kindly regarded here, and few heave a brick at them.

Most and best are in the east, centre, south; Dublin and the Newtonards peninsula are particularly rich. Some of them, especially folly gates, are almost as big as their houses; at Ballysaggartmore the gates were so splendid that no house got built at all.

The references here are to the half-inch edition of the Ordnance Survey maps, but it is wise to take the advice given in *Ireland Observed* and have also Bartholomew's new quarter-inch maps, which have too open a grid for initial search, but helpfully continue to show the demesnes with areas of small dots even where the house has gone.

The main gates at Markree

Armagh

Lurgan

A Mechanical Man   J 0758
On 26 April 1762 John Wesley visited James Logan to see his famous mechanical man. . . .

> It was the figure of an old man standing in a case with a curtain drawn before him, over against a clock which stood on the other side of the room. Every time the clock struck he opened the door with one hand, drew back the curtain with the other, turned his head as if looking round the company, and then said, with a clear, loud, articulate voice: 'Past one, two three', and so on. But so many came to see this (the like of which was not to be seen in Europe) that Mr. Logan was in danger of being ruined, not having time to attend to his own business; so, as none offered to purchase it or to reward him for his pains, he took the whole machine to pieces; nor has he any thought of ever making anything of the kind again.

On 4 June 1773, Wesley went again and Logan said that he now intended to make not one man but two, not only to speak 'but sing hymns alternately with an articulate voice'. 'How amazing', wrote Wesley, 'that no man of fortune enables him to give all his time to the the work'. There is another account of the old man adding clichés to the clock, 'Past twelve! Oh, how time runs on!' One cannot be sure quite what was made, or what Wesley saw, but not a cogwheel remains.

Cavan

Cavan

Fleming's Folly*   H 4104
There is said to be a folly on a hilltop here, far inland, which Mr Fleming built so that he could watch the ships at sea, but I have not been able to find out any more.

Clare

Birchfield *Birchfield House*

O'Brien's Tower, early nineteenth   R 0489
century*
The Cliffs of Moher are high and wild, and Cornelius O'Brien built a castellated house here, now in ruins. He also built a stout stone castellated tower with a smaller plain one attached, to improve the natural beauty of the place, and this has survived better. At Derreen he put up in 1835 a huge Ionic column by public subscription taken from his tenants, to bear witness to his efforts to publicize the improved cliffs.

Dromoland *Dromoland Castle*

Temple, early eighteenth century,   R 3970
and Grotto
The grotto or hermit's cave is an odd igloo-shaped one with a fireplace, almost totally dark and of uncertain date, possibly earlier than the early eighteenth-century Temple of Mercury, which is a good Doric rotunda built over the grave of Sir Edward O'Brien's favourite racehorse. The story is that he wagered the whole of Dromoland on the horse and it won; certainly he built an expensive temple. He also made a gazebo on a nearby hill so that he could watch his horses training.

Cork

Blarney *Blarney Castle*

Druid's Circle and Tower,   W 6075
nineteenth century
This is where the stone is. There is also a plump round nineteenth-century castellated tower put up by Father Matthew Horgan, and a small but most beautifully placed sham circle, or rather group of stones, called The Rock Close. One feels that such works, because of Stonehenge, should be set on open

moorland or at least as far from the house as possible, but here the stones are under fine trees with the castle as background and make a lovely picturesque composition, more Chinese than Druidical.

Foaty Island *Fota House*

The Turret, *c.* 1820   W 7971

Rather a stylish tower, an eyecatcher to Fota House, by John Hargrave of Cork for Sir Richard Morrison. Stoutly built but sprightly, in rough-hewn stone with the dressings paler and smoother. It is two storeys high and square with a big central portecochère the same height. On one corner at the back is a bold round staircase turret. All is richly castellated, machicolated and drip-stoned, and the cross-slits are enormous.

Glanmire *On the coast*

Father Matthew's Tower, 1843–5   W 7374

An eyecatcher to Blackrock Castle across the estuary of the Lee, not far from Fota and rather like it, but designed by George Richard Pain. A three-storey round stone tower with light stone trim and elaborate windows, square-headed at the bottom, then Decorated, then Tudor. It has a little pointed arch, stone wall round, and, in front, Father Matthew leaning on a column with a pleading right hand outstretched; a charming monument.

Kilcrohane *Sheep's Head Peninsula*

Tower*   V 8238

I have been told of a castellated tower here, built by Lord Brandon.

Luskin's Bridge *On the River Dripsey*

Leader's Folly, *c.* 1860*   W 4476

Five great pieces remain of an aqueduct built by Mr Leader to get water for a new house but the channel and more piers collapsed when the water was first turned into it.

Donegal

Bundoran *On the coast at Bundrowers*

Tower*   G 8258

A small roofless square tower of engaging simplicity and squareness, enlivened with toothy castellations of jagged lumps of rock.

Down

Banbridge

Crozier Monument   J 1346

Long inscriptions commemorate Captain Crozier who left England with Franklin in 1845 in command of the *Terror,* to look for the North-West Passage. The whole expedition was lost.

'He was born at Banbridge September 1796 But the place of his death No man knoweth to this day.' There are charming little relief carvings of the ship among the icebergs and the ugly hexagonal pillared dome on which Crozier stands is supported by four flying buttresses down which cringe four wavy-coated polar bears.

The Crozier monument

Clandeboye

Helen's Tower, 1867   J 4979

This is a famous tower, marked in its own right on quite small maps for no reason that I can see, for it is distinguished only by a smug air of piety and privilege. It was built by the fifth Earl of Dufferin and Ava (Ambassador to Russia and Turkey, Viceroy of India) to the memory of his mother. Inside, top storey, are inscribed in letters of gold her poem for his 21st birthday and poems for her by Tennyson, Robert Browning and Kipling.

Lord Dufferin also built at Helen's Bay a fantastic viceregal railway station with coroneted cushions in the private waiting room.

Donaghadee

Folly Castle, 1818   J 5980

See page 74.

Grey Abbey *Grey Abbey House*

Gothick Eyecatcher, late eighteenth century   J 5868

This is best seen from the road, as it is now a house, and has been restored and rendered over, losing corbels from the pinnacles and other details, but, pale and rightly grey, it is very pretty indeed from a distance. There is a steep crow-stepped gable between pinnacles, a central quatrefoil, two big cross-slits with a pointed arch between, once open, surely, but now filled in with a three-light window. The most cutout-cardboard façade of all.

The eyecatcher, Grey Abbey

Mount Stewart House

The Dodo Terrace, etc., 1920s   J 5569

See pages 257 and 258.

Newtownards

Scrabo Tower, 1858   J 4974

Another famous tower, but a much gayer one, mysteriously designed in the Scottish Baronial style, built of pink sandstone capped with black basalt by the tenants of the third Marquis of Londonderry to their good landlord; but one is told that 'Scrabo means sod of the cow'. It is square, with small corner turrets at the top of the tower and conical roofs to all.

Portaferry

Whalebone Arch, nineteenth century*   J 5951

Not very large, I think, and not in the Blythe Bridge class, but these arches are said to be rarer in Ireland.

Quintin *Quintin Castle*

Tower, early nineteenth century   J 6350

This is one of the smallest possible folly towers, charming and unforgettable. Quintin is a splendid castle house with a heavy square tower in the centre and four smaller ones at the corners, all with stepped castellations, and walls to match, set on jagged rocks above the sea. The gates are like stage-settings too, with stout wood portcullises painted white between a tall square tower and a shorter one.

Then the drama ends, and to the south, parallel to the sea run three quiet terraces,

The tower at Quintin

hanging gardens on castellated walls, and at the end of them is the little octagon tower.

Rubane *Rubane House*
The Pebble House, *c.* 1740   J 6160
See page 95.

Scarva
King Billy in Hawthorn, 1883   J 0644
A neat white house, once the railway station. It had a splendid stout figure with white metal eyes, sitting in a top hat on top of the wall, trained and trimmed for 85 years, and given an orange sash once a year to recall the passing of the King through the village on his way to the Battle of the Boyne. Alas, the present owner's wife says that he wants a PLAIN GARDEN, and will soon demolish also the box knots and the big red hearts and stars and blue diamonds from the concrete paths.

Tollymore Park
Group, late eighteenth century   J 3432
See page 91.

Dublin

Ballymount   O 1534
See page 15.

Ballymount

Blackrock *Maretimo*
Tunnel Face, nineteenth century*   O 2229
A tunnel in the rare Egyptian style.

Dalkey *Norano Road*
Roman Cement Man, early   O 2727
nineteenth century
On a rocky outcrop, very like the back of a whale, stands a man in Roman cement, a bearded sailor with what might be the remains of a harpoon in his hand. He wears white trousers, a blue coat and black hat, and has an anchor and a capstan behind him.

Dalkey Island
Tower, 1840*   O 2428
A small round tower built for famine relief, just feeding people being immoral.

Donabate *Turvey House*
Shell house, eighteenth century*   O 2151
I heard of this too late for a visit, and with no details; a shell house and a shell tunnel. It might be an igloo like Dromoland or a great work like Carton. . . .

Dublin
Obelisk and Sham Ruin, nineteenth   O 1534
century
Smirke's obelisk in Phoenix Park to the memory of the Duke of Wellington is 205 feet high, 1817, and a particularly splendid one. They say that after the unveiling a party was given in the huge battered base and when the guests were gone the last slab was put in place with a drunken footman negligently left inside and still there. It is Egyptian monuments that rightly collect these entombing legends, like Mad Jack Fuller in his pyramid at Brightling.

The sham ruin is a trifle in the grounds at the back of Gandon's fine Custom House, made from fragments saved after the fire that gutted it in 1921; two linked columns, a piece of another and two statues.

Finglas†   O 1438
This is where Dr and Mrs Delany had Delville, their small estate (see page 31). Nothing remains, but Finglas is often mentioned by Mrs Delany, and it is nice to know where it was.

Glasnevin *Farmleigh*
Water Tower, late nineteenth century O 1628
An astonishing and costly water-tower, built for Lord Iveagh in granite in a bastardized Romanesque style with a battered base, clock, machicolations, and pyramidal green copper roof.

Killiney *Mount Mapas*
Cone, 1792 O 2624
See page 233.

Lucan
Lucan House O 0335
See page 221.

Luttrellstown *Luttrellstown Castle*
Gothick Ruin* O 0437
A finely landscaped park with temple, bath-house, a demolished wood house, a cascade and a gothick ruin, a huge sham arch of tufa, one of the most romantic and beautiful anywhere, I believe.

Montpelier *Montpelier Hill*
Hell-Fire Hunting Lodge* O 0921
Only ruins. It was built as a hunting lodge by Speaker Conolly of Castletown in 1720, and turned by the painter James Worsdale and the first Earl of Rosse into a Hell-Fire Club cosy in 1785; rather late and unfashionable, one feels, but presided over by a huge black cat.

Rathfarnham *Rathfarnham Castle*
The Bottle Barn O 1428
See page 220.

Stillorgan *Hospice of the Order of St John of God*
Obelisk, *c.* 1730 O 2127
See page 123.

Fermanagh

Castle Coole
Cottages *Ornés** H 2643
These are said to be very pretty ones, a heather cottage and a Rustic Lodge with thatch supported on tree-trunks.

Crom Castle
Tower on Island* H 3524
A small castellated tower on an island near the ruins of the castle.

Florence Court
Chinese House, Grotto*, etc. H 1734

Marble Arch *The Glen*
Grotto* H 1435
A series of fine natural caverns, with a big natural rock arch, and a real (or artificial) grotto on the hill behind.

Galway

Lawrencetown *Belview*
The Follies, late eighteenth century M 8620
See page 93.

The Volunteer Arch, Lawrencetown

Portumna *Portumna Castle*
Tablet, 1797 M 8504
The ruins of the early seventeenth-century castle, which was burnt out in 1826, are splendid and dramatic. Among them is a tablet to a dog:

> Dying about April
> 20 1797 aged 11 year was
> Interred near this Place.
> Alas, poor Fury. She was a dog.
> Take her for All in All
> Eye shall not look upon her like again.

Kerry

Ardfert *Ardfert House*
Gothick Arch, eighteenth century*   Q 7821
The house is a ruin, but there are the remains of a formal garden and a very elegant gothick folly.

Ballybeggan Castle
Grotto, 1756*   Q 8615
A grotto by Dr Delany, now ruinous, a large façade-type grotto made of local minerals.

Kildare

Allan *Hill of Allan*
Tower, 1859   N 7621
A tower built by Sir Gerald Aylmer with the masons' names carved round the base.

Belan *Belan House*
Obelisks, eighteenth century   S 7790
See page 124. The house has gone, but as well as the obelisks there are two pillars to Lord Adleborough's favourite hunters.

Brannockstown *Harristown House*
Chinese House, eighteenth century   N 8910
See page 116.

Carton
Shell Cottage, eighteenth and   N 9538
nineteenth centuries
See page 155. There are also umbrellos supported on more of the cast-iron tree-trunks and a most beautiful double dairy, a toy with a marble churn and blue-and-white tiles in front of the working one. And an obelisk.

Celbridge *Castletown*
Conolly's Folly and the Wonderful   N 9733
Barn
See pages 121 and 220.

The Curragh
Donnelly's Hollow, and His Arm,   N 7812
nineteenth century
Dan Donnelly was a boxer, champion of Ireland, born in Dublin in 1788. He was a carpenter first, and is claimed to have started his career in the ring with a flourish by beating Tom Hall in the Curragh in 1814. In December 1815, though, he won immortal fame by beating George Cooper here, the champion of England. The crowd of 20,000 people followed the hero out of the Hollow, stepping carefully in his footsteps, and there 59 footsteps still go, curving up through the grass, lovingly retrodden by all, and exhaustingly deep.

The monument is a squat obelisk 8 feet

The Shell Cottage, Carton

The Wonderful Barn, Celbridge

high, but in The Hideout at Kilcurran is a painting of him, and a ballad, and details; his arms were the longest in the history of pugilism and he could button his knee breeches without stooping. In the glass case is his long black arm, mummified to tendons, complete with shoulder blade and an elegant pointing hand.

Kildare *Kilnagorna*
Shell House, nineteenth century   N 7212
A thatched cottage on the main road to Cork, just south of the town, with a slate-roofed wing. The front and the walls of the little yard are shelled all over with cockles, now bleached white, and inlaid with representational items in fantastic scale and bright colour. Mirror-glass is used for an over-window and a crown, there are red roses, a shamrock and harp. There is a good village scene and an interesting almost-abstraction of church-with-spire, tower and windmill.

Naas*   N 8919
A column at *Furness House,* brought from Dangan Castle.
A tower and pavilion at *Oldtown.*
A shell house, no clue to size or quality, at *Newlands House.*

Kilkenny

Belline *Belline House*
Rustic Temple*, *c.* 1790   S 4523
This is a Doric temple with tree-trunk columns, and sounds like the one at Dropmore.

Piltown
Tower*   S 4623
Three storeys of a huge and ambitious tower are said to have been started here to a member of the Ponsonby family killed in the Peninsular War, who then returned safely, so the tower was abandoned.

The shell cottage, Kildare

Leix

Abbeyleix *Heywood House*
Gothick Ruin*   S 4384
This, I have been told, is quite an elaborate though unexciting one made from pieces of the old Abbey.

Emo *Emo Park*
Tower, *c.* 1790*   N 5406
The house was begun by James Gandon and finished by Richard Morrison; probably the tower was designed by Gandon. It was not in very promising condition when the only photograph of it I have seen was taken in 1948; it is a cube pierced by a big round-headed arch, with an octagon tower on top, first-storey windows alternating round-head with rectangle, circular ones above all and flat-band moulding. One conjectures a tall pyramid roof, but nothing is left to prove it.

Limerick

Castle Oliver
Tower, *c.* 1850*   R 6619
A photograph of the house shows a clotted pile of Scottish nonsense and the description I have been given of the folly tower on a nearby hill, with double turrets on the telescope theme, sounds as if the tower is of the same date.

Glin *Glin Castle*

A Tower and Lodges*   R 1247

Photographs show several extremely pretty eyecatcher lodges, miniature castles in the style of the house, which the owner calls 'pasteboard Gothick', *c.* 1790–1812, and very nice too. The lodges have low round towers and curtain walls, painted white, with dark trim on the castellations. Hamilton's Tower, 1830, is on the hill opposite.

Cong *Ballymacgibbon*

Tower*   M 1455

Probably not very exciting. Built for Sir William Wilde, father of the poet.

Killala

Tower on Hilltop*   G 2030

A gothick lodge, Glin Castle

Mayo

The Neale

Step Pyramid and Temple   M 1959

The house has long gone and the demesne lies derelict, but there is a good stepped pyramid left, wide and shallow, like the one at Mount Mapas, but taller, eight steps and cube top, in random stone. It was designed by the Earl of Charlemont for his sister, to use up the stones

in a rough field, they say, but not very thoroughly. When I saw it the temple was a Roman Doric open hexagon with a dome, but now the top is open too, and it is like a small West Wycombe.

Meath

Castlerickard *Churchyard*

Pyramid to Swift   N 7349

See page 124.

Tobertynan House

Ruined Tower   N 7349

A sorrowful ruin, disregarded in the fields among tree stumps with new houses near. What Tower? That one. There isn't a tower here at all! Yes, there. Well, now you mention it, so there is! Thought it was part of the trees! Someone comes with a story for it, one of the old lords built it to watch his horses race from . . . there was a fine room up there. . . .

And so there may have been, for there are the rich springs of four windows in the two remaining walls, and a lower storey beneath; one corner has gone completely.

Coole *Larch Hill House*

The Fox's Earth   N 8545

See pages 231 and 232.

The tower at Castlerickard

One of the obelisks, Dangan

Dangan *Dangan Castle*

Obelisks   N 825 I

The castle is a ruin, and most of the embellishments of the demesne have gone. Two obelisks remain in the fields, on arches in the
Irish manner, but not at its grandest. One of
them has only a stump above the arches, the
other is almost complete and a little more
elaborate, with a base to the obelisk itself.

Four Knocks *The Naul*

Eyecatcher, eighteenth century   O 1162

The house has gone but across the fields is a
hexagon, beautifully detailed, with a good
balustrade, on a steep mound, not really very
well composed.

Kells *Caenannus Mor*

Lloyd's Tower, 1791   N 7375

A notable tower, 100 feet high, round, undressed stone and beautifully proportioned,
belted inconspicuously into halves. It has
two lines of windows going up; pointed,
rectangular inscriptions, pointed, rectangular
and round. The top is a remarkable one for
its date, a massive torus supported on corbels
with a railing round an octagonal lantern with
a cage for the view and a lid on top. Only the
lantern suggests the eighteenth century at all;
from a distance one says 1850. But there is
no doubt; it was built by a pupil of Gandon
and we are told all:

Lloyd's Tower

THIS TOWER WAS DESIGNED BY
HENRY BAKER ESQR ARCHITECT
WAS EXECUTED BY
MR JOSEPH BECK STONE CUTTER
MR OWEN MCCABE HEAD MASON
MR BARTLE REILLY OVERSEER
ANNO 1791

They deserve every word of it. On the
other side of the tower is a crisply cut coat of
arms and

THIS PILLAR WAS ERECTED BY
EARL BECTIVE IN MEMORY OF HIS FATHER
THE RIGHT HONOURABLE SIR THOS TAYLOR BART
ANNO 1791

Nearby on the hill top is a grave yard,
tumpy grass graves almost returned to field.
A large Celtic cross explains that it was

ERECTED TO THE MEMORY OF THE POOR
INTERRED HERE DURING THE OPERATION OF
THE ENGLISH POOR LAW SYSTEM 1838–1921.

Some of the graves have small lumps of
stone like slaves' graveyards in the Southern
states of the U.S.A.; one is carefully carved

THOMAS BRADY
DIED JANUARY
AGE 14 1881 AD
R I P

Monaghan

Rossmore Castle
A folly*   H 6731

Offally

Charleville *Charleville Castle*
Grotto, eighteenth century   N 3123

The Pearce Arch, Gloster

Gloster
Eyecatcher, 1730s   S 0894
This is a very nice folly indeed, a friendly and
charming object with careful square mouldings, about 20 feet high. It was designed by
Sir Edward Lovett Pearce as a vista-closer
at the end of a *clair-voyée* from the house, but
this is now overgrown, the house invisible,
and the obelisks which flank the arch overgrown with ivy. They are thickset ones with
niches in the bases, and are clear enough,
but the exact original form of the arch is less
obvious. The piers were extended upwards,
but are now stumps, and how they ended and
what finial stood over the arch and the round
window over it no one seems to know.
Perhaps a heraldic animal.

Roscommon

Ballyfarnan *Kilronan Castle*
Root-House-Grotto Lodge   G 8614
The ugly house is quietly falling into un-
distinguished ruin, but it has a remarkable
lodge. The rough stone gates are overgrown
with ivy, and the drive passes what must have
been a lodge but also surely did duty as a
hermitage. It has two chambers, one curved
with a fireplace and three oval windows in the
walls of rock tufa and trees. The next room is
rectangular and smaller with another fireplace
and traces of plaster, set back behind 8-foot
piers of incredibly water-worn rock, magnificent specimens. Trees and ivy go above and
around; it is almost impossible to see and
will soon be gone, but it remains for the
moment a fine hermitage.

Root-House-Grotto, Kilronan

Rockingham
Two Sham Castles, etc., early   G 8403
nineteenth century
See page 72.

Sligo

Hazlewood House
Grotto*   G 7134

Markree *Markree Castle* G 6925
See pages 225 and 426.
The house was made castle in 1803 by Francis Johnston and given a charming scenery-castle lodge with exceptionally delicate lattice windows. In 1832 Francis Goodman designed a more ambitious entrance for the other end of the main drive. It is beginning to sag a little here and there but some well-placed ivy compensates while it destroys.

Well back from the road, the whole 100 yards of it lie in a great castle arc facing the sun. In the centre is a big arch between a round tower and a larger tower with a tall turret on top. To the left of this is the lodge, and then a square tower with double castellations and beside the low tower, two more, plainer. The walls then curve without interruption to two stout final castles, gates between round towers, about 15 feet across, each large enough to take a carriage arch but here allotted merely gates.

Sligo
Harbour G 6936
Another metal man, on a plinth in the middle of the entrance to the harbour; this is the one Jack Yates painted. See Tramore, page 439.

Woodcock Cardan's Tower

Tipperary

Clogheen *Knockmealdowns*
Grubb's Grave S 0013
A famous trifle; a white beehive on quartz boulders with a slate plaque to mark the grave of a Quaker, Samuel Richard Grubb of Castle Grace, born March 1855, died September 1921. He is already said to be buried standing up, which isn't bad for 50 years.

Knocklofty *Knocklofty House*
The Googy S 1421
A small castellated octagon tower on a hill opposite the house, brick and a little stone, faced with falling rough-cast. It has a tall octagon dome, five blind windows, two empty ones and a door. A little utilitarian tower, but in its day it must have been pleasant for a picnic.

Templemore
Woodcock Cardan's Tower S 1071
A stout round tower in random stone about 75 feet high, with machicolations intact, castellations mostly gone, and a piece of curtain wall to the east. It had three floors with a spiral staircase, but the whole interior is now ruinous.

Templetouhy *Killoran House*
Tower S 1971
Nothing could be more elegant than this little tower; it almost answers any description of Woodcock Cardan's but this is a work of art, very plain in pale grey stone relieved with pretty lichen. The top projects a little and is castellated, with two bands of small square holes below for decoration. Pointed door, round-headed then pointed windows up the three storeys, and a small sham-ruinous curtain wall to a little finial turret.

Exterior of grotto at Curraghmore

Tyrone

Caledon *Caledon House*

The Bone House   H 7543

This must have been one of the largest and most ambitious works ever executed in this medium, which was usually reserved for floors and relieved with pebbles. Here there was an arch with pillars made with ox bones instead of the usual sheep but the top has gone and who will restore it? The quantity of bones is surprising; they say the oxen were eaten by Owen Row O'Neil's army but the Orrery Papers for 24 June 1747 explain: 'we came to a resolution of building a bonery, to strike the Caledonians with wonder and amazement by fixing an Ivory Palace before their view. We have already gathered a great number of bones, and our friends the butchers and tanners have promised to increase their number.' Just as age has mellowed the stone of the raw eighteenth century and brought the trees to their full splendour, so it has destroyed some of the less important media; 'Ivory' tells us what this must have looked like new.

Clogher

Brackenbridge's Tower   H 5351

An undated and dateless folly. One's guess swings from 1740 to 1900; there is no other tower like it for comparison. How does one date three crisp storeys of square stone tower decreasing in stages with featureless rooms inside, plain round and square windows for it and the plainest possible iron balustrade? (Mr Brackenbridge is upside down because at the resurrection the world will turn upside down.) A guess for the date: 1840.

Waterford

Cappoquin *Dromana House*

Indian Gate, *c.* 1835   X 1099

Not on the grand scale of the best Irish gates, but a rarity in style, a small Brighton Pavilion-gate with lodge, dome and minarets, which gains fantasy by standing on a bridge.

Curraghmore

Shell House, 1754   S 4315

See page 166. There is also a tower put up by the first Lord Waterford to his son, and a very odd and haunting figure, like a pyramid with a head, in the fields.

Lismore *Ballysaggartmore*

The Gates, nineteenth century   X 0498

See page 225.

Brackenbridge's Tower

Tramore

The Metal Man, nineteenth century   S 5802
On the cliffs, above fine wild rocks with sea-birds thick on the stacks, are three tall plain cylindrical stone columns with plain round flat caps and square flat pedestals on top. The innermost one is crowned by a giant metal man coloured like life, in blue coat, red waist-coat, gold buttons, white trousers and black hair; he looks rather like Lord Byron, and points loftily down and out to sea, presumably too it was at least intended that there should be three, for the bases are there on the other two, and presumably they were day-marks. (More men at Dalkey and Sligo.)

The metal man, Tramore

West Meath

Athlone *Waterston*

Pyramid Eyecatcher   N 0442
A fine large piece; a magnificently propor-tioned rectangular block, banded with dressed stone. A big round-headed arch reaches the whole height, blind but for a rectangular door. On this stands an octagon with simple blind windows, lightly curved at the top, and then on this is a tall stark octagon pyramid.

There is said to be a hermitage here too, but no trace could be found. It may exist only on a drawing.

Belvedere *Belvedere House*

The Jealous Wall, 1760   N 4147
See page 222.

Devlin *Rosmead House*

Gates, late eighteenth century*   N 6063
Engravings show the gates designed by Samuel Woolley, as Mr Smyth first put them up in lovely elegance at Glananea. The house was much less elaborate and Mr Smyth was called Gates Smyth, or sometimes Smyth-with-the-Gates and he hated this so much (and indeed others had built bigger and uglier ones) that he took them down, but became Smyth-without-the-gates. A loser.

The central arch is neglected and beautiful,

but much has gone, or was left behind, including a unicorn sitting with arched neck on the top.

Glassan

The Pinnacle, 1769   N 0947
A tall round untapered column of random stone with the date on a tablet and a semi-spherical, or weather-blunted cap. I was told about this as being 'an obelisk marking the geographical centre of Ireland', but it is not an obelisk and certainly does not look at all like an eighteenth-century work; perhaps the obelisk fell down and the tablet was saved with the idea.

Killua *Killua Castle*

Obelisk   N 6668
A forlorn and lovely ruined house made castle in about 1830 with lodges to match, and an obelisk to commemorate the planting of the first potato. It is odd that this vegetable should inspire such homage; the author has been given a silver potato in a blue velvet box, presented on the occasion of the opening of the first potato works on 8 August 1918, by the Union Agency, Bombay, in India, and probably there are other tributes.

Tullynally *Tullynally Castle*

Grotto, eighteenth century   N 4470
A pretty little grotto in rough rock, about 10 feet across inside with an octagon domed roof. The walls round five sides are brick with every fifth course set back and seats of water-worn rock; perhaps the brick once supported some more elegant decoration, for a pebble floor survives with an asterisk pattern in light on dark. The other three sides are open, a

door and two windows with rock, tufa, ferns and ivy. The approach is pretty too, from great open terraces across the ha-ha south of the house and then into the woods to the grotto facing west.

View from the grotto, Tullynally

Wexford

Great Saltee Island*
The owner, Prince Michael the First, made a limestone throne here with an obelisk and a plaque, and also had a set of crown jewels and full regalia.

Wicklow

Enniskerry *St Kevin's Reformatory*
Grotto, eighteenth century*   O 2317
Another grotto heard of too late for a visit. The grounds of the old demesne run down to the river where there is a grotto under the trees.

Powerscourt
Tower, Ruins and Grot-work   O 2116
eighteenth and twentieth century
A grand house by Richard Castle with a formal garden laid out in 1745. The design of terraces going down to a great lake is of course unusually late, but the steep site with its superb view over the Wicklow mountains

justified this daringly old-fashioned plan. Work went on for more than 200 years, with some unfortunate additions in the middle of the nineteenth century (there are far too many statues), and then in about 1875 the top terrace and ramps were most beautifully pebbled over, light and dark, with geometrical patterns.

The good picturesque ruin was made when the eighth Viscountess Powerscourt became a Roman Catholic and part-pulled down the Protestant church. With the rest of the stones Lord Powerscourt and two gardeners built the tower in 1910–12, carefully copying a silver pepper-pot from the dinner table. It is round, neat, castellated, splay-footed. Steps curve down to a massive door and the tower is protected by a bastion embellished with guns from the Armada and the Battle of the Boyne, cressets, a large mortar, decapitation irons and a stone phallus.

Two years earlier, in 1908, a boggy patch was drained to make a garden in the Bypass Japanese style. To follow the great terraces, winged horses and Tritons, nothing more comical could have been conceived; there is a red wooden bridge 7 feet long, a pale turquoise 'pagoda' 10 feet high, a 2-foot china elephant, and dozens of small stone mushrooms. This almost blinds the eye to the eighteenth-century grotto still standing behind it, which has delicately pretty cascades with ferns, moss and tufa falling beside an openwork grotto built of petrified sphagnum moss. There are two entrances, arches leading to a free-standing column in the centre, and a walk up through another arch to a view of the house, and then one can walk up the terraces and admire the pebblework again.

Japanese garden at Powerscourt

Les Vauxbelets, Guernsey

Islands

A small island, all owned by one person, would seem the perfect folly setting, but so far as I know only two owners have improved their islands in this way, though there are a few memorial towers and obelisks on the larger ones, and a good Grotto Chapel. Perhaps the recluse-mentality of island buyers conflicts too much with the basic exhibitionism of all building beyond the stage of shelter.

Most of the towers in the Channel Islands* are fortifications but the massive defence works put up by the Germans during their occupation of the Islands during the Second World War will surely be follies in the future.

Guernsey*

Here a Japanese House, or Pagoda, was built at Saumarez Park by the third Lord Saumarez (d. 1938) after he was Ambassador to Japan. This, the Delancey Obelisk and the Doyle Column were all demolished by the Germans, though the Column has been rebuilt.

St Peter Port
Victoria Tower, 1848
To commemorate a visit by Victoria and Albert in 1846. This is a square castellated tower 100 feet high in red granite, with a battered base and a central smaller octagon turret on top in the middle.

Les Vauxbelets
La Grotte, or the Little Chapel, 1923 on
A world-famous piece of shell-and-china work in the vernacular style, most elaborately and lovingly made and continually embellished. It was built by Brother Déodat, who wanted to make a grotto like the one at Lourdes, and started in March 1914. Someone unkindly said that at 9 feet by 4½ feet it was ridiculously small, so he promptly pulled it down and built another, 18 inches wider. In 1923 he pulled this down too and began the present one which is about twice the size and took two years to make before he even started to decorate it with the free materials of pebbles

and broken china. Publicity began, and gifts of china and shells flowed in, and still do. Brother Déodat died in 1951.

It is a complicated design, with four semi-circular side-chapels, a three-storey spire, pinnacles and a grotto underneath. The most enterprising part of the decoration is the roof ridge, lined with ormer shells and teapots.

Jersey*

St Helier
Obelisk to the memory of Peter le Sueur, five times Constable. A later Constable has had a public lavatory put up behind it.

St Martin's
At La Chasse crossroads stands a small granite building with 1626 carved over the door. It was built in 1900 by Constable Messervy.

Isle of Man*

Bradda Head
Milner's Tower, 1871   SC 1770
This is said to be in the shape of the key or lock of Milner's first safe, but it looks to the unknowing eye like a square tower with tapering round angle buttresses and a taller round staircase turret. On the walls of its two storeys are the tallest arrow-slits ever. The inscription is over the door:

ERECTED BY PUBLIC SUBSCRIPTION TO WILLIAM MILNER IN GRATEFUL ACKNOWLEDGEMENT OF HIS MANY CHARITIES TO THE POOR OF PORT ERIN AND HIS NEVER FAILING EFFORTS ON BEHALF OF THE MANX FISHERMEN A.D. 1871.

Peel *Peel Castle*
Fenella's Tower   SC 2484
A nothing. Scenes in Scott's Peveril of the
Peak were set in Peel Castle, where this tower
is part of a gun emplacement; Fenella jumped
from it into a small boat to join her lover.

Corrin's Tower   SC 2484
Quite real and very interesting. This was
built in 1806 by Thomas Edward Corrin, 'a
sturdy Nonconformist' who was determined
on burial in unconsecrated ground, and put it
up as a mausoleum for his wife, two children
and himself, above his house at Knockaloe
Beg. It is square, solid, slightly tapering, 50
feet high made of stone from a nearby quarry
with limestone for the tomb and coping
stones and the trapdoor frames on each floor.
Right up the centre, filling most of it, runs a
big square pillar which comes out at the top
of the tower round, with a semispherical cap.
I am told that this pillar supports all the
floors, only one of which touches a wall;
Corrin must have had ideas on building as
well as on burial.

There are four storeys. All the big windows
seem to have been almost immediately
blocked, on the ground and first floors by
tombstones. On the first floor the inscriptions
are to his parents and grandparents as well as
to his wife 'whose Body became the Coffin of
her unborn Infant', another daughter and a
Jane Corrin who died in Ohio in 1831—'All
flesh is grass'. On the ground floor are two
more inscriptions to his wife.

Outside the tower is a neat grass plot where
he and his wife and children are buried. On
each side is a pillar; to the east, *Corrin's Pillar,
1839,* with an inscription to his wife and to
the west *Corrin's Pillar,* 1840. A slab is lettered
F.C. and carved with a cross, anchor and heart.

By 1836 the solid tower was mysteriously in
bad repair and Corrin wanted to demolish it,
but it had become a sea mark and Trinity
House bought it.

Ramsay
Albert Tower   SC 4695
A square machicolated tower with almost
invisible castellations and slits, and 'Tudor'
windows in the top storey on Lhergy Frissell
Hill, to commemorate a visit by Victoria and
Albert by yacht in 1847. The Prince landed
and a local barber took him up to the hilltop.

Orkneys*

Birsay
There is a memorial tower to Kitchener on
Orkney. A postcard shows a large square
stone tower, battered for about 30 feet, then
straightened for a little with a nicely detailed
tough castellated top.

Scilly Islands*

Tresco *The Abbey Gardens*
Valhalla, *c.* 1840
Augustus Smith from Hertfordshire leased
the Scilly Islands in 1834 and ruled as Lord
Proprietor until he died in 1872. Clearly he put
all his energy and life into the welfare of the
desperately poor islanders. He reorganized
the land into reasonable farms, changed the
system of tenure so that they stayed so, made
roads, stopped smuggling, enforced school-
ing 30 years before any other authority,
improved agriculture, built a church and
quays and extended a pier. He designed himself a house near the ruins of St Nicholas
Priory, and started the fine sub-tropical gardens on Tresco, where there was not so much
as a bush.

In the gardens in about 1840 he built a long
stone grotto where he set up a collection of
figureheads, carvings, cannon and other relics
from the ships that had been driven on to the
islands and wrecked (often the islanders' only
source of wood). He went on collecting them
as they came, and so did his descendants; the
earliest date in the catalogue is seventeenth
century, the latest 1925. Today it is easy, we
all admire a good figurehead, but Augustus
Smith made his Valhalla of things that were
both contemporary and vernacular, a very
personal taste indeed. The carvings have now
been beautifully restored and regilded (there
is a notable eagle), and Valhalla is now safely
a museum.

A Short Bibliography

Information on many follies comes from contemporary paintings, estate maps and prints, or from the many district, house and county books to be found in local collections, and I have listed neither these nor all the many general works on garden and landscape architecture and design that I have consulted.

ANONYMOUS, *Decoration for Parks and Gardens* (1800, J. Taylor)

ATTIRET, J. D., *An Account of the Emperor of China's Gardens at Pekin* (1752)

AUBREY, JOHN, *Brief Lives* (various editions)

BANCE, B. (ed.), *Maisons de Campagne, Châteaux, Fermes, Habitations Rurales, etc.* (Paris, undated)

BROWNE, SIR THOMAS, *The Garden of Cyrus* (various editions)

CHAMBERS, SIR WILLIAM, *Designs of Chinese Buildings, Furniture, Dresses, Machines and Utensils* (1757)

— *Dissertation on Oriental Gardening* (1772)

CLARK, KENNETH (LORD CLARK), *The Gothic Revival* (1950)

— *Landscape into Art* (1949)

CLIFFORD, DEREK, *A History of Garden Design* (1962 & 1966)

COLVIN, BRENDA, *Land and Landscape* (1948)

COLVIN, HOWARD and HARRIS, JOHN, *The English Country Seat* (1970)

CRAIG, MAURICE and THE KNIGHT OF GLIN, *Ireland Observed* (1970)

DAVIS, TERENCE, *The Architecture of John Nash* (1960)

DELANY, MRS, *Letters, edited by Lady Llanover*

EASTLAKE, CHARLES, *A History of the Gothic Revival* (Reprinted with an introduction by J. Mordaunt Crook, 1970)

ERDBERG, ELEANOR VON, *Chinese Influence on European Garden Structures* (1936)

ERNOUF, BARON, *L'Art des Jardins* (1890)

FLEMING, JOHN, *Adam Gothick* (The Connoisseur, October 1968)

FRANKL, PAUL, *The Gothic* (1960)

GILPIN, WILLIAM, *On Picturesque Beauty* (1792)

HALFPENNY, WILLIAM, and JOHN, *New Designs for Chinese Temples, etc.* (1750-2)

— *Rural Designs in the Gothick Taste* (1752)

— *Rural Architecture in the Chinese Taste* (1757)

HEELEY, JOSEPH, *Letters on the Beauties of Hagley, Envil and The Leasowes* (1777)

HUSSEY, CHRISTOPHER, *The Picturesque* (1927)

JENKINS, FRANK I., *Some Nineteenth Century Towers* (R.I.B.A. Journal, February 1958)

JOURDAIN, MARGARET, *The Work of William Kent* (1948)

KIRCHER, ATHANASIUS, *China Monumentis qua sacris qua profanis, illustrata* (1672)

KNIGHT, PAYNE, *The Landscape, a Didactic Poem* (1795)

LANG, S. and PEVSNER, N., *Sir William Temple and Sharawadgi* (Architectural Review, December 1949)

LANGLEY, BATTY and THOMAS, *New Principles of Gardening* (1728)

LE ROUGE, *Jardins Anglo-Chinois* (1776-88)

LIGHTOLER, T., *Gentlemen's and Farmer's Architect (Façades to place before disagreeable Objects)* (1774)

LYLE PUBLICATIONS, *Monumental Follies* (1972)

MACAULAY, ROSE, *Pleasure of Ruins* (1953)

MANWARING, ELIZABETH, *Italian Landscape in Eighteenth Century England* (1965)

MIDDLETON, CHARLES, *Decorations in Parks and Gardens* (no date)

NEUHOFF, JOHAN, *Illustrated Report* (1669)

NEVE, *The Complete Builder's Guide* (1736)

NUNNEZ, *Architectural Hints* (1806)

OVER, CHARLES, *Ornamental Architecture in the Gothic Chinese and Modern Taste, being above fifty intire new designs . . .* (1758)

OVERTON, THOMAS COLLINS, *Original Designs of Temples* (1746)

— *Rural Residences . . . Observations on Landscape Gardening* (1818)

PAPWORTH, J. B., *Hints on Ornamental Gardening* (1823)

PRICE, SIR UVEDALE, *An Essay on the Picturesque* (1794, enlarged 1797–8)

— *A Letter to H. Repton* (1795)

— *A Dialogue on the distinct Characters of the Picturesque and the Beautiful* (1807)

REPTON, HUMPHREY, *A Letter to Uvedale Price, Esqr. on Landscape Gardening* (1794)

— *Sketches and Hints of Landscape Gardening* (1795)

— *Observations on the Theory and Practice of Landscape Gardening* (1803)

— *An Enquiry into the Changes of Taste in Landscape Gardening* (1806)

— *Fragments in the Theory and Practice of Landscape Gardening* (1817)

ROWAN, ALISTAIR, *Garden Buildings* (1968)

SIRÉN, ŎSVALD, *Gardens of China* (1949)

— *China and Gardens of Europe* (1950)

STEEGMAN, J., *The Rule of Taste from George I–George IV* (1936)

STROUD, DOROTHY, *Capability Brown* (1957)

— *Humphrey Repton* (1963)

SWITZER, STEPHEN, *Icholographica Rustica* (1718)

TEMPLE, SIR WILLIAM, *The Garden of Epicurus* (1685)

WALPOLE, HORACE, *On Modern Gardening* (1770, published 1785) and the *Letters*

WARE, ISAAC, *A Complete Body of Architecture* (1756)

WHATELEY, SIR THOMAS, *Observations* (1770)

WOODBRIDGE, KENNETH, *Landscape and Antiquity* (1970)

WRIGHT, THOMAS, *Universal Architecture* (1755)

WRIGHTE, WILLIAM, *Grotesque Architecture* (1767)

The volumes of *The Architect's Journal, The Architectural Review, Buildings of England, Country Life, The Gardener's Magazine, The Journal of the Royal Horticultural Society, The Royal Commission on Historical Monuments* and *The Victoria County History.*

Index